CW01660730

The
One *King Lear*

M. William Shak-ſpeare:

HIS

True Chronicle Hiſtorie of the life and
death of King Lear and his three
Daughters.

With the vnfortunate life of Edgar, *ſonne*
and heire to the Earle of Gloſter, and his
ſullen and aſſumed humor of
Tom of Bedlam:

As it was played before the Kings Maieſtie at Whitehall vpon
S. Stephans *night in Chriſtmas Hollidayes.*

By his Maieſties ſeruants playing vſually at the Gloabe
on the Bancke-ſide.

LONDON,
Printed for *Nathaniel Butter*, and are to be ſold at his ſhop in *Pauls*
Church-yard at the ſigne of the Pide Bull neere
St. *Auſtins* Gate. 1608.

The
One *King Lear*

SIR BRIAN VICKERS

Harvard University Press

Cambridge, Massachusetts

London, England 2016

Copyright © 2016 by Sir Brian Vickers
All rights reserved
Printed in the United States of America

First printing

Library of Congress Cataloging-in-Publication Data

Names: Vickers, Brian, author.
Title: The one King Lear / Sir Brian Vickers.
Description: Cambridge, Massachusetts : Harvard University Press, 2016. |
Includes bibliographical references and index.
Identifiers: LCCN 2015038987 | ISBN 9780674504844 (alk. paper)
Subjects: LCSH: Shakespeare, William, 1564–1616. King Lear—
Criticism, Textual. | Shakespeare, William, 1564–1616. King Lear. |
Transmission of texts—England—History—17th century. | Shakespeare,
William, 1564–1616—Bibliography—Folios. 1623. | Shakespeare,
William, 1564–1616—Bibliography—Quartos. | Okes, Nicholas.
Classification: LCC PR2819 .V53 2016 | DDC 822.3/3—dc23
LC record available at http://lccn.loc.gov/2015038987

For my son Philip
musicus et medicus

Contents

Preface

Ever since I was first attracted by Shakespeare, *King Lear* has for me been his greatest play, a unique fusion of cruelty and compassion. It offers a painful challenge to the characters in the action—as to the spectators—of how to make sense of previously unrepresented extremes of evil and suffering, and how to respond with moral outrage and compassionate help. I know that many other readers and theatergoers share this view, and I take it that all of us will be concerned to know which text best represents Shakespeare's conception of the play.

The two authoritative texts are the single-volume Quarto edition (1608), printed by Nicholas Okes for Nathaniel Butter, and the First Folio (1623), printed by Isaac Jaggard for a consortium of publishers, which collects thirty-six plays. The two texts differ in their makeup: the Quarto lacks 102 lines (also many smaller phrases and single words) not found in the Folio, whereas the Folio lacks 285 lines (and some phrases and words) not found in the Quarto. Fortunately, the missing sections are different and complementary. If you were to complete either version by adding the passages preserved by the other, you would have, in terms of characters and events, two identical plays. The texts would still differ in many textual variants, due to the execrable printing of the Quarto and officious editorial interventions in the Folio, but they would contain the same play. The remarkable truth is that while other Shakespeare plays have texts that differ between the Quarto and Folio (*Hamlet*, *Othello*), only *Lear* has two interdependent versions that interlock perfectly.

Shakespeare's plays began to be properly edited in the eighteenth century, and since then editors have restored the two texts of *Lear*—each of which derives from Shakespeare's manuscript—to their original unity. For nearly four hundred years this version gave us "the bitter-sweet of this Shakespearian fruit," as Keats described it in his sonnet "On Sitting Down to Read *King Lear* Once Again."[1] But in the late 1970s a revisionist movement began, arguing that it had been wrong to "conflate" two substantially different texts (a claim that already begs the question by assuming what it intended to prove) and that the Folio version represented Shakespeare's own revision of the Quarto, made in about 1609–1611. The manifesto of this movement was a collection of essays edited by Gary Taylor and Michael Warren, *The Division of the Kingdoms: Shakespeare's Two Versions of "King Lear"* (Oxford, 1983), with a preface by Stanley Wells. Since Taylor and Wells were also the chief editors of the *Oxford Shakespeare* (1986) they had the great good fortune—or misfortune—of being able to give this theory material existence by printing two separate texts of the play: *The History of King Lear*, "based on the Quarto," as they put it, and *The Tragedy of King Lear*, "based on the Folio." Regrettably, their claim to be printing two independent versions was nullified by their emending each text in the light of the other, producing just such a "conflated" text as they had scorned.[2] In 1997 W. W. Norton published the *Norton Shakespeare*, a new college text but based on the *Oxford Shakespeare*. It reprinted the Wells and Taylor "Two Versions" of *King Lear*, but hedged its bets by also including a third version, the traditional unified text. Thanks to its adoption by these publishers, the revisionist theory has since become the new orthodoxy. Third editions of both the Oxford and the Norton *Complete Works of Shakespeare* are underway as I write, both in print and in electronic versions.

My book challenges this orthodoxy for having fundamentally misinterpreted the evidence. The revisionists claim that the passages missing in the Quarto but found in the Folio were subsequently added by Shakespeare. I argue that they were, in fact, omitted by the printer, Nicholas Okes, because he had underestimated the amount of paper that he would need. (Paper was the second most expensive item on a printer's account book, and printers went to great lengths to avoid waste.) To prepare readers for my detailed evaluation of the Quarto and Folio texts, in the opening Chapter I give a brief account of how books were printed in the hand-press period. My aim is to describe the basic processes and how they could affect the transformation of a handwritten text into print. In addition to introducing the mechanics of printing in a nontechnical manner I also describe what I call the "dynamics" of typesetting: the moment-by-moment adjustments that the compositor makes in fitting text space, the amount of authorial copy that he has been given, into print space, the amount of paper that the printer and publisher have provided. With the advent of electronic word processing such adjustments are made automatically, but in hand-set books each letter and each punctuation mark are created by three-dimensional objects that need to be correctly aligned, and even the white spaces are created by blank pieces of type. Every line of text—prose or verse—has to fit within the space provided, and while this becomes second nature to an experienced compositor, his work depends on a prior calculation of the exact length of a text. Compositors used various space-saving devices to accommodate a text when space was tight, but in the worst scenario they simply had to omit words or whole lines.

In Chapter 2, I show how the printers of several Shakespeare Quartos, like those of the 1623 Folio, used the whole repertoire of space-saving devices to adjust text space to print space, but still had to leave out passages that would not fit. I then apply this analysis to the *King Lear* Quarto. Chapter 3 shows how Nicholas Okes desperately compressed the text, deploying the standard space-saving techniques, although to a far greater extent than any other Jacobean printer setting a Shakespeare Quarto. In addition to these mechanical devices, he made considerable use of two typographical ways of saving space: setting many passages of verse as prose and running lines of verse together. I illustrate the resulting overcrowded and confusingly printed pages in Appendix 2. In Chapter 4 I analyze the cuts made by Okes and his compositors as printing progressed, revealing a sustained and not unintelligent attempt to shorten expansive and descriptive passages, and to omit words and lines that were not essential to a scene. Appendix 2 provides a page-by-page analysis of the space saved, both by adjusting and cutting the text, which amounts to more than 400 lines. Had the text been printed in the normal way, Okes would have needed twelve full sheets, not the ten-and-a-half that he had estimated.

In the second part of this book I move on to the Folio. Chapter 5 brings together the work of several scholars who have identified Shakespeare's characteristic spellings, as documented by the sole manuscript in his handwriting, the two additions he made to the unpublished collaborative play *Sir Thomas More*, and the Quartos printed from his manuscripts during his lifetime. These spellings are found throughout the *King Lear* Quarto, confirming that it was set from the manuscript that he provided for the King's Men in 1605. Many of these Shakespearian spellings recur in the Folio text of the play, which was evidently set in part from his original manuscript, as it had been copied for the company's "Booke" or reference manuscript used in rehearsals and performance and from which the actors' parts had been copied. The revisionists made much sport with the traditional unified version, alleging that those who accepted it were guilty of imagining some "lost" or "mythical archetype."[3] Printers regularly destroyed manuscripts once they had printed a book, so that of *King Lear* is indeed lost; but it was never "mythical," for two authentic witnesses to it survive, the Quarto and the Folio, both deriving from Shakespeare's handwritten copy.

The 1623 Folio is popularly supposed to incarnate all thirty-six plays in an authoritative form, and it has recently acquired additional status after the Oxford Shakespeare editors described it as the "most theatrical" version of his work, since half of the total plays it contains had not appeared as Quartos and were set in type from the theater companies' Booke of those plays. A contrary argument would hold that the Quartos in fact deserve this title, since they represent the texts as Shakespeare originally delivered them to the company, and that the Folio is in fact an edited text. Many studies have shown that Isaac Jaggard, like most of his fellow printers, regarded the spelling and punctuation in a manuscript as being in his domain, but his interventions into Shakespeare's text extended much further. In Chapter 6 I build on the work of other scholars to show that Jaggard's editors "modernized" Shakespeare's spelling and standardized his grammar in line with the changes in English usage that had been especially marked after 1600. These changes affect Shakespeare's wording and word order in many places of *King Lear*, but the Folio editors also took it on themselves to regularize Shakespeare's prosody, changing about 125 lines in order to create regular iambic pentameters and often damaging his verse in the process. In the light of these interventions, it seems right to describe this play, like all the others in the Folio, as a "post-theatrical" text. In addition, as I show, the Folio also standardizes Shakespeare's stage directions, as found in the Quarto, omitting many of his vividly imagined theatrical effects. The Quarto is undoubtedly closer to the play as he conceived it.

In Chapter 7 I discuss the cuts made by the King's Men and preserved in the Folio. Despite the printers' discarding of play manuscripts, about twenty of them have survived until this day, still containing the markings used for theatrical performance. These include many passages marked for deletion by the "book-holder" or "bookkeeper" as he was known (the term "prompter" is anachronistic). One contemporary play text performed by Shakespeare's company makes omissions just as theater companies do today, in the middle of a speech (preserving the cue lines at start and finish) and often in the middle of a scene. Whoever shortened *King Lear*, however, cut the end of speeches and of scenes, most damagingly throughout Lear's deranged trial scene (3.6). In addition, a whole scene (4.3) was omitted that fulfills three essential functions at this point in the play. There are numerous other cuts that destroy important narrative and ethical sequences, showing none of the care for continuity evinced in the Quarto omissions. Of all Shakespeare's mature tragedies, *King Lear* is the most complex and carefully designed. He consulted an unusual number of sources for the main plot, added a subplot, and intertwined the two into an almost seamless whole (there are a few loose ends, as critics have pointed out, but none of any importance), and he brought them both to a tragic climax of his own making. It is inconceivable that he would then have damaged his own design by making the crude cuts found in the Folio: it would have been an act of self-mutilation.

I realize that these chapters will make a great demand on readers unused to looking at texts so closely, but this is the only way in which we can properly understand the role played by compositors, editors, and theater personnel in the transmission of Shakespeare's play. If *Lear* is important to you, every significant detail is important.

The final part of this book considers the "Two Versions" theory and its aftermath. In Chapter 8 I make my own evaluation of that theory, joining forces with a dozen independent scholars, whose expertise ranges from textual criticism to professional experience in the theater. The revisionists' case rests entirely on their claim that Shakespeare himself made the Folio cuts, but while we might hope to identify an addition by him, how can we identify a Shakespearian cut? The revisionists' further claims—that Shakespeare made cuts in order to speed up the action; that he omitted passages from the Quarto that he subsequently found "redundant" or "disposable"; that he omitted other passages in order to change the characterization of Albany and Edgar—equally lack any evidence. Moreover, as several scholars objected, they are post facto rationalizations, made after the event by a process of speculation and guesswork as to the abridger's possible motives. It is true that cuts to any play will "speed up the action"—indeed, how could shortening a play not speed it up? But although the Folio's cuts might have reduced performance time by a few minutes, that hardly compensates for the damage done to the play's structure and ethics. It is also true that cuts will affect some roles more than others, but the Two Versions theorists illicitly infer intention from effect. No evidence exists that Shakespeare intended to change the roles of Albany and Edgar, and several experienced scholars have argued that had he meant to do so he would not have been satisfied with cuts alone, but would have added new material, as he did in the few cases where we have positive evidence of him revising a play. As for the revisionists' claim that the cuts were made in the interest of "theatricality," the scholars cited here object that the small cuts often leave the actors no time to prepare for their next appearance, which can involve changes or adaptations of costume. Of the larger omissions the drastic curtailment of Lear's mad trial scene has received universal criticism, the most telling point being that several recent productions by major theater companies in England that had intended to follow the Folio text found in rehearsal that the cuts diminished the scene's intensity and meaning and reverted to the Quarto. The consensus of these independent scholars, whose work appeared in scattered journals over a period of several years and is brought together here for the first time, was that the Two Versions theorists had failed to justify any of their claims.

Readers who are unacquainted with the course of Shakespeare studies over the last forty years may wonder how the revisionist theory gained acceptance if it lacked any supporting evidence. I try to answer that question in the Conclusion, where I show that proponents of the Two Versions thesis did not wait for a scholarly consensus to emerge, but in effect created one of their own by the enthusiastic praise that they lavished on each other's work both within their collective volume and elsewhere, untested by counterarguments. When critical reviews began to appear, the revisionists ignored their substance and abused their critics, describing them as "reactionary": they themselves, needless to say, were "revolutionary." They claimed to have brought about a "Copernican revolution" in Shakespeare scholarship, and asserted that all future editions of his work would endorse their belief that he regularly revised his plays. Their self-promotion succeeded in drawing attention to their claims and influenced two major publishers to rupture this masterpiece of world literature into two supposedly independent texts. I hope that this book may bring about a new consensus and restore *King Lear* to its original unity.

My scholarly interest in *King Lear* dates back to my time as an undergraduate at Trinity College, Cambridge, beginning almost by accident (the English faculty in that period paid little attention either to bibliography or to textual criticism). In 1960, while preparing to sit for the Charles Oldham Shakespeare scholarship, I bought a secondhand copy of G. I. Duthie's "Critical Edition" of the play. It begins with a 200-page introduction discussing the nature of the manuscript that lay behind the Folio and Quarto versions, considered on a case-by-case basis. Duthie's old-spelling text has been the only one (until we have the much-anticipated New Variorum edition by Richard Knowles) to list at the foot of each page every variant between the two Quarto and Folio texts, together with significant emendations by later editors. Duthie completed his wonderfully helpful edition with an additional sixty pages of notes discussing individual readings. Although his edition is outstanding in its presentation of all the relevant bibliographical evidence, I now know that it was seriously misguided in its interpretation of the origin of the 1608 Quarto. Like everyone else at that time, Duthie followed W. W. Greg in theorizing that the play was a "reported text," put together by actors who had seen or performed in it. In accepting the dominant theory, I was unaware that in 1931 a young American scholar, Madeleine Doran, had suggested the correct explanation for many of the evident faults in the 1608 Quarto—that it had been directly set from Shakespeare's manuscript, as he had delivered it to the King's Men in 1605.[4] Unfortunately, Greg, the leading authority on Shakespeare textual studies between the 1920s and the 1960s, dismissed Doran's theory, and her work remained largely unknown. It was not until the 1980s that the "reported text" narrative finally died out and scholars began to accept that the Quarto had been set from Shakespeare's manuscript.

That explanation received independent endorsement from the second most important event in twentieth-century textual studies of the play, Peter Blayney's magisterial study of the 1608 Quarto.[5] Blayney explicitly limited himself to the bibliographical reconstruction and analysis of Okes's output in the period 1607–1609, amassing an astonishing amount of detail about typesetting, printing practices, business activities, and much else. The most important finding for the evaluation of the *Lear* Quarto was that it was the first play that Okes had printed, his inexperience resulting in many typographical errors. Blayney also demonstrated that due to his working directly from Shakespeare's "messy" manuscript rather than from a clean scribal copy, Okes had to change his normal way of printing. He usually set the text "by formes," a process in which the printer carefully calculates in advance where each page begins and ends and can be confident that he will be able to accommodate the text within the allotted number of pages. Blayney showed that, probably due to the difficulty of estimating the length of Shakespeare's manuscript, which also contained several features of a play book that would have been unfamiliar to him (such as the intermingling of prose and verse, and the treatment of stage directions), Okes set the play "seriatim," in the normal reading sequence. This choice made life easier in the short term, since he could get by with a rough estimate of the amount of text needed for each page, but it created other difficulties during printing.[6] Blayney emphasized that his book was strictly about the play's printing and that he had avoided literary analysis.

I had admired Blayney's book when it appeared, but had not properly realized the significance of these two facts. That I did so came about by another happy accident, when in 2008 I was invited by Professor Simon Eliot to teach two classes on Shakespeare bibliography and textual criticism in the annual MA course on the History of the Book that he directed at the Institute of English Studies, University of London. I chose to teach the Quarto and Folio texts of *King Lear*, and for several years in succession I worked with students in recreating the physical processes by which Okes and Jaggard, respectively, discharged their task. Using photocopies I reconstructed some of the sheets as Okes's compositors produced them, which we compared with the Folio versions. As I looked at these afresh each year, it dawned on me that all the visible peculiarities of the Quarto—its crowded pages, with verse set as prose; its verse lineation (largely correct in the Folio) being adjusted so as to take up less room; and the use of common space-saving devices such as turning lines over, abbreviating words, using ampersands, and omitting spaces after commas—could all be explained by a very simple theory: that Okes had miscalculated the amount of paper that would be needed to print such a long play. In this book I work out the consequences of that insight.

In writing this study I have been indebted to several colleagues who are acknowledged authorities in bibliography and textual criticism. Professor William Proctor Williams of Akron University, Ohio, kindly read most chapters in draft form and offered many valuable suggestions. We also engaged in several animated discussion in the British Library tea room, and it would have been interesting to ask other users to guess from our gestures what our "line" was. Professor David McKitterick, Fellow and Librarian of Trinity College, Cambridge, read the chapter on printing practices, much to its benefit, and we shared a stimulating telephone conversation during which we used a ruler to measure the various widths of the page columns in the 1608 Quarto. Anyone monitoring the call would have been puzzled by the recurring figures cited, "80 to 81" or "94 to 95" (millimeters). Peter Blayney made some helpful comments on a late draft. My greatest debt is to my old friend Professor Henry Woudhuysen, Rector of Lincoln College, Oxford, who read an early draft with a keen eye for error and followed that up by reading almost all of the final version and offering corrections and criticisms that made me rethink and, I hope, improve several chapters. None of these colleagues is responsible for any errors or misconceptions of my own.

I am grateful to the master and fellows of Trinity College, Cambridge, for allowing me to reproduce images from the Library's copy of the 1608 Quarto that Edward Capell bequeathed to the college, the copy I had used as an undergraduate.

In preparing this book I have been particularly indebted to Professor Warwick Gould, FRSL, FRSA, until recently Director of the Institute of English Studies, University of London, for much encouragement and practical help. I am also grateful to Professor Roger Kain, CBE, FBA, Dean of the School of Advanced Study, for allowing me to benefit from the editorial skills of Valerie Hall one day a week, who with patience and good humor transformed my many messy drafts and corrections into a more coherent shape. In November 2013 I had the privilege of giving the final Keith Walker Memorial Lecture at University College London, where I first presented my case that the cuts in the 1608 Quarto were made by the printer. For the invitation and for hospitality on that occasion I should like to thank Professor Helen Hackett, Professor Rene Weis, FSA, and Professor Peter Swaab. I owe especial thanks to that book lover and literary agent Peter Strauss, who was coincidentally in the first class I taught on the text of *Lear*, for putting me in touch with John Kulka, executive editor-at-large at Harvard University Press. John has been the ideal editor, supportive, encouraging, and patient. At HUP I have been well looked after by Joy Deng, and at Westchester Publishing Services I thank Melody Negron, Senior Production Editor, and my copyeditor Gail Naron Chalew.

I have been indebted to the work of many scholars and have tried to acknowledge my debts scrupulously. Two of them, however, demand special notice. Madeleine Doran's keen intelligence and observational powers called in question many received ideas concerning *Lear* and stimulated me to follow her spirit of inquiry. Her younger colleague at the University of Wisconsin, Richard Knowles, has been preparing the New Variorum edition of this play for many years, during which time he has published the most acute critiques of the Two Versions theory, models of informed scholarship and civil disagreement, and generously shared some of his research findings with me. I salute them, from a distance in space and time:

Friends of my soule, you twaine,
Rule in this realme, and the gor'd state sustaine.

A Note on References

I QUOTE THE 1608 Quarto from the facsimile edition by W. W. Greg, *King Lear 1608 (Pied Bull Quarto)* (London: Sidgwick and Jackson, 1939; Oxford: Oxford University Press, 1964). Because the pages are unnumbered I quote the signature followed by the line number: thus "G3v27" refers to the third page, verso, of sheet G, line 27. I have through-numbered the lines in the Illustrations (Appendix 1); readers who wish to locate the quoted passages in the facsimile may construct a ruler by tracing the line numbers given there onto a separate piece of paper.

I quote the 1623 Folio from *The Norton Facsimile: The First Folio of Shakespeare. Based on the Folios in the Folger Shakespeare Library Collection. Prepared by Charlton Hinman. Second edition. With a new introduction by Peter Blayney* (New York: Norton, 1996). This volume uses the most legible pages from a number of copies in the Folger. I cite passages by reference to the "through line numbering" (TLN) system established by Hinman, which numbers "every *typographical* line" (xxiii).

Throughout, all act, scene, and line numbers are to *The Riverside Shakespeare*, second edition, ed. G. Blakemore Evans, with the assistance of J. J. M. Tobin (Boston: Houghton Mifflin, 1997).

I have attempted to reproduce the exact layout of the early texts, since that provides the main evidence of irregularities in the printing. All texts are in old spelling, but I have copied neither the long "ſ" nor ligatures.

The One *King Lear*

PART 1

The Quarto, 1608

1

King Lear at the Printer

In this chapter I aim to give a brief description of the standard printing procedures in the age of hand-press books and how they affected the text of *King Lear*. It describes the mechanics of printing and the routines with which books were printed in this period, and is based on the standard scholarship, which I synthesize as clearly as I can.[1] In the next chapter I discuss what I call the "dynamics of typesetting," the human choices by which the compositor adjusted *text space*, the extent and makeup of the author's text, to *print space*, as defined by each page within the total amount of pages estimated. At the risk of boring those familiar with bibliography and textual criticism, I need to be sure that readers understand the terms and technical processes that feature in subsequent discussions.

The Manuscript

In the sixteenth and seventeenth centuries dramatists would sell their work to a theater company, which then effectively owned the play. In order to be performed legally the text would have to be approved by the Master of the Revels. For the printing of plays and of most other texts as well, the authorization for printing between 1586 and 1606 was done by sixteen disparate men employed by either the Archbishop of Canterbury or the Bishop of London for this task. However, in 1607 the Master of the Revels won the right to exclusively authorize the texts of plays for printing.[2] Although some unauthorized transactions took place, the vast majority of play books were legitimately sold by a theater company to a stationer (a term that then combined, in varying proportions, the roles of printer, bookseller, and publisher). Having bought a play, stationers could protect their right to print it by entering it in the Register of Copies kept by the Stationers' Company, their guild organization. This step was not essential, but approximately two-thirds of all books in the period from 1557 to 1642 were formally registered.

Shakespeare had written *King Lear* for his theater company, the King's Men, which, according to the conventions of early modern publishing, thus owned the right in the copy. Companies often released plays for publication about two years after their performance for the small but loyal reading public that bought play texts and, in some cases, to promote a revival.[3] The first recorded performance of *King Lear* was on December 26, 1606, as is shown by its entry in the Stationers' Register on November 26, 1607, on behalf of Nathaniel Butter (the main partner) and John Busby, with Sir George Buc as the licenser:

> *a booke called Mr. William Shakespeare his historye of Kynge Lear, as yt was played before the Kinges majestie at Whitehall uppon St. Stephans night at Christmas last, by his Majesties servantes playing usually at the Globe on the Banksyde.*[4]

This has all the signs of a legal entry, given that Buc was Master of the Revels, but for an absurdly long period scholars doubted its authenticity and that of the play. In their Preface to the First Folio, John Heminge and Henry Condell, actors who had been colleagues of Shakespeare since 1594, described themselves as friends who had taken on themselves the "care, and paine, to have collected & publish'd" his writings. Whereas readers previously had been "abus'd [deceived] with diverse stolne, and surreptitious copies, maimed, and deformed by the frauds and stealthes of injurious impostors," his works "are now offer'd to your view cur'd, and perfect of their limbes; and all the rest, absolute in their numbers, as he conceived them."[5] We know much more about the provenance of Shakespeare's plays than his fellow actors did, who may have been unaware that several of the plays in the Folio were co-authored.[6] With the phrase "stolne, and surreptitious copies" Heminge and Condell were referring to a small group of unauthorized publications, such as the spurious First Quartos of *Romeo and Juliet* (1597) and *Hamlet* (1603), for which Shakespeare's theater company released authorized texts in 1599 and 1604–1605, respectively. Unfortunately, some eighteenth-century editors misunderstood their diatribe as referring to the whole class of Shakespeare Quartos, most of which were perfectly authentic. It is much to A. W. Pollard's credit that he realized that the phrase referred only to this small group of what he called "Bad Quartos," comprising *Romeo and Juliet*, *Hamlet*, *Henry V* (1600), *The Merry Wives of Windsor* (1602), and *Pericles* (1609), although the narrative of piracy by which he accounted for their appearance is no longer accepted.[7]

The 1608 Quarto of *King Lear* was not among Pollard's group of "Bad Quartos," but the poor quality of its printing led some scholars to tar it with that brush. Pollard had speculated that these unauthorized texts were put together by memory by actors who had taken part in or witnessed performances, a theory that Tycho Mommsen had proposed in 1857. In 1879 another German scholar, Alexander Schmidt, theorized that the 1608 Quarto of *Lear* was taken down by shorthand during performance.[8] As Henry Furness summarized Schmidt's essay, with his usual deference to German scholarship (largely justified at that time), "1. The Quartos make no distinction between verse and prose; not even when the lines rhyme at the end of a scene. 2. Many errors of the Quartos are mistakes of the ear, not of the eye. Capriciousness of the actors' diction is noticeable in the use of expletives, like 'come', 'do', 'go to', 'how', 'sir', &c. In common life Englishmen are fond of beginning their sentences with such little words, which, like tuning-forks, give the key in which they intend to speak." These and other reasons, Schmidt concluded, "prove that the Quarto-text of *King Lear* lacks authority, and that its various readings are to be expunged from our editions."[9] There's the rub, for such a verdict sets the text in a no-man's-land of indeterminable authenticity.

Unfortunately, two scholars who enjoyed unqualified respect during the twentieth century endorsed Schmidt's explanation. E. K. Chambers, writing in 1930, suggested that shorthand might have been used for the 1608 Quarto, which has "long continuous passages of verse printed as prose" that are "almost entirely punctuated by commas. They look to me like the result of shorthand notes well taken, but not properly worked upon at the stage of transcription."[10] W. W. Greg lent it his support in a series of essays and books from the 1930s on, culminating in his study of the Folio in 1955, where he repeated the same supposed signs of reported texts, including "grotesque mishearings," printing verse as prose, mis-lining verse, and "helpless punctuation."[11] The stigma of the label "reported text" clung persistently to the *Lear* Quarto, although the feasibility of any report using the systems of Elizabethan shorthand to take down such a complex play during performance had been thoroughly disproved.[12] Reputable scholars came up with varying theories to explain the mistakes in the Quarto: G. I. Duthie (1949) suggested that the Quarto had been put together as a collective act of memory by the whole company; Alice Walker (1953) thought that the boy actors playing Goneril and Regan had been responsible; and W. W. Greg (1955) partly endorsed both theories.[13] As late as 1968, in his Introduction to the *Norton Facsimile* of the First Folio, Charlton Hinman classified *King Lear* among "Plays first published in 'doubtful' quartos,'" along with *Richard III* (1597) and *Othello* (1622), and declared that in all three cases the Folio and Quarto "are not independent witnesses to the true text: readings in which they both agree, far from being doubly authenticated, may both be wrong."[14] In 1980, a century after Schmidt, P. W. K. Stone suggested that reporters could have taken the text down in repeated visits to the theater.[15] The collective impact of these theories was to sow doubt and uncertainty concerning the authenticity of the 1608 Quarto. In the chapters that follow I return to all these supposed signs of a reported text (mishearings, confusion of verse and prose, actors' expletives) and offer better explanations for their occurrence in Q1 *Lear*. For the moment, though, it is worth underlining the fact that in the austere world of bibliographical scholarship, like any other, mistaken theories and assumptions can persist for an improbably long time.

Their persistence beyond 1931 was already unjustified, because in that year a young American scholar, Madeleine Doran, had published a pioneering study that largely vindicated the 1608 Quarto from these mistaken assumptions.[16] Taking issue with Chambers, she refuted Schmidt's theory of a text "taken down by stenographers in the theatre" by describing some general features of the unauthorized or "Bad Quartos" put together by actors from memories of performances fleshed out with one or more actor's "parts." Such texts (the 1603 *Hamlet* is a good example)

> are considerably shorter than the authentic texts; they contain lines repeated in different parts of the play, sometimes even anticipating lines not occurring until later in the text as composed by the author; some of them have whole scenes transposed; they exhibit a good deal not merely of erroneously printed but of actually corrupt verse; and they contain many errors of mishearing and much nonsense. The first quarto of *King Lear*, on the other hand, despite its misprints, misreadings, omissions, and faulty printing of verse, is substantially the same play, line for line, as the folio.[17]

Furthermore, in a reported text, one or two parts are generally more accurate than others, depending on which roles the reporters had acted, but that is not the case in the 1608 Quarto, where the errors are evenly distributed.[18]

Doran challenged other elements in Schmidt's case, including his claim that Q1 observes no distinction between verse and prose:

> It is true that a great deal of the verse is printed as prose; but it is also true that much of it, even most of it, is printed as verse. Much of this, in turn, is incorrectly aligned, but, for all that, large portions of the text are correctly printed. If we had to do with a stenographer who was unable to divide verse correctly into lines we should not have all the good verse that we do, for there is not often any difference, so far as the ease with which it can be divided is concerned, between that which is correctly and that which is incorrectly printed.

Doran added a further consideration that would reduce the likelihood of a reporter working by ear: "If anything can contribute to the correct division of lines, it should be rime," whereas several passages of rhyme are printed as prose. Nevertheless, Doran observed, despite these irregularities more than half of the thirteen scenes are correctly printed.[19]

Doran's vindication of the 1608 Quarto from the stigma of a reported text was accompanied by a truly original argument for its authenticity, namely that it contained unusual spellings known to occur in other authentic Shakespeare texts, together with types of misprints that could be explained as misreadings of Shakespeare's idiosyncratic handwriting. The significance of this argument is that it would establish the 1608 Quarto as having been printed directly from Shakespeare's manuscript, and not from reporters' memories. I return to these matters in Chapter 5, where I review the parallel evidence that the Folio also contains evidence of having been set in part from a Shakespearian manuscript, independently of either the First or the Second Quarto (1619).

In the Printing House

When a stationer had acquired the right to publish a book he could either print it himself, if he had a large enough business, or hire a printer with whom he would settle the book's format, that is, "the number of type-pages printed on one side of a sheet, which is folded one or more times." (The hand press could only print one side of a sheet at a time.) The two formats that concern us are the folio and quarto. Each side of a folio contains two type pages. "When the sheet is folded in half, left to right, on the short axis, two leaves and four pages result." For a quarto "the sheet is folded twice, and contains four type-pages on each side, for a total of eight per sheet."[20] The publisher and printer also had to agree on the size of the edition, usually about five hundred for play books. "The choice of edition size and format directly influenced the cost of the paper, a major expenditure in the production balance sheet. As a rule, a job-lot of paper was ordered from a paper merchant specifically for a given book," and the printer was "invariably paid by the publisher," either for the paper alone or "for both paper and printing."[21] The publisher and printer would also agree on the type to be used. "The standard play-quarto format with a black-letter text setting had given way to pica roman type in the 1580s. The format was a specialty niche in the market" and "almost invariably the text face in plays." The standardized format meant that "the only areas of variation left to the individual printer were the title page, preliminaries, and the first page of the text."[22]

The printing process consisted of five stages: composition, imposition, printing, correction, and the distribution of the type back into its cases so that the cycle could begin again. Most of the two dozen printing offices in early seventeenth-century London had two or more presses, but smaller enterprises, like that of Nicholas Okes, who printed the 1608 Quarto of *King Lear*, were only allowed one (although a second, often older press might be used for producing proof sheets).[23] The main workmen were the master printer; the compositors, who set the type; and the pressmen, who printed off the sheets. As Peter Blayney showed in his groundbreaking study, Okes probably began work on the *Lear* Quarto in the second week of December 1607 with three workmen: "Compositor B set the type, one pressman printed the sheets at half-press, and a third party (quite probably Okes himself) proofed at least some of the formes." Okes is known to have employed two apprentices and would have hired journeymen when needed. In January 1608 a second compositor began to share the task of typesetting: "C seems to have worked more slowly, and perhaps less competently than B." This tends to suggest that he was less experienced, and Blayney thinks it "quite likely that he *was* an apprentice. If the same were true of B, then we could probably equate relative competence with experience" and identify B as Thomas Corneforth, bound to Okes's predecessor in September 1605, and C with John Reynolds, bound to Okes in March 1607. Their collective efforts resulted in the Quarto of *King Lear*, which Blayney places among "Okes's half-dozen worst-printed books of 1607–9."[24]

The best description of standard printing procedures was given by Joseph Moxon (1627–1691) in the first treatise on printing, published in the 1680s but generally accepted as an accurate account of hand-press printing in the earlier period.[25] The compositor stands before a frame supporting, at an incline, two cases of type—the upper containing majuscules (capital letters), numerals, and common symbols and the lower case containing minuscules—arranged in larger or smaller boxes according to the frequency with which they are used in English.[26] (A separate case contained italic type.) The compositor holds in his left hand the composing stick, a tray that holds pieces of type and blank spaces sufficient to set about eight lines of text.[27] In Moxon's account, the compositor

> first reads so much of his Copy as he thinks he can retain in his memory till he have Composed it, as commonly is five or six words, or sometimes a longer Sentence. And having read, he falls a Spelling in his mind; yet so, that his Thoughts run no faster than his Fingers: For as he spells 'A', he takes up A out of the A Box, as he names 'n' in his thoughts, he takes up n out of the n Box, as he names 'd' in his thoughts he takes up d out of the d Box; which three Letters set together make a Word, viz. 'And'; so that after the d he sets a Space.[28]

As Moxon describes it, the basic composing process involves a double mental activity: the compositor retains five or six words "in his memory," names the letters "in his thoughts," and for each word "falls a Spelling in his mind." The mental process is also, inevitably, an auditory one, and knowing this fact helps us to realize that some printing errors were caused by the compositor's phonetic memory, not from the text having been taken down by shorthand during an actual performance or dictated to a scribe from memory.

The prime example of "mishearings" alleged by Schmidt, Chambers, Greg, and others to prove that the 1608 *Lear* Quarto derived from reporters comes from one of Lear's mad scenes. Shakespeare gives him a heightened vision of arbitrary authority within society with this question and answer, addressed to blind Gloucester: "thou hast seene a farmers dogge barke at a begger . . . And the creature runne from the cur, there thou mightst behold the great image of authoritie, *a dogge, so bade* in office" (I4r23). That is how the Quarto compositor interpreted Shakespeare's manuscript; the Folio text preserves what must have been the true wording: "*a Dogg's obey'd* in Office" (4.6.158–9). Another example of the compositor memorizing his text and then setting it phonetically is Cordelia's disclaimer of any military intent in returning to England, where the Quarto reads, "No blowne ambition doth our armes *in sight*" (I1v23); the Folio preserves the correct spelling "*incite*" (4.3.27). In the Quarto, Lear's anguished final question reads, "why should a dog, a horse, a rat *of* life" (L4r17), where the Folio correctly reads "*haue*" (5.3.307)—"of" for "have" is a common solecism in colloquial English to this day. These auditory errors used to be mistaken as evidence that the 1608 Quarto was a corrupt text, taken down by dictation. Now we can see that such errors occur naturally when a compositor "falls a Spelling in mind." This phenomenon was familiar to historians of printing, such as William Blades: "Every compositor when at work reads over a few words of his copy, and retains them in his mind until his fingers have picked up the various types belonging to them. While the memory is thus repeating to itself a phrase, it is by no means . . . uncommon, for some word or words to become unwittingly supplanted in the mind by others which are similar in sound."[29]

The compositor sets each word as he has memorized it and separates the words with a space, together with punctuation, until he has nearly filled the line. As Philip Gaskell described this process, "he changed the spaces between the words one by one until the line was a tight sliding fit in the stick, picking out rejected spaces and choosing additions or replacements from his central box of mixed spaces. This process, which gave a straight right-hand margin on the printed page, was called justification. Short lines were justified with spaces and quads so that they would lock up tight in the forme with the rest."[30] It was necessary to achieve a tight fit to prevent the types, in Weiss's words, "from falling out of the type-page during the various transfers it would receive before ending up on the bed of the press. The compositor had spacing materials in a variety of widths for use in justification. The reference standard for type-body width was based upon the letter 'm', the widest letter. Blanks in this width were termed em-quadrats, em-quads, or simply ems." Today we are used to electronic word processing, by which we can insert a space by merely depressing a key and can align a page automatically, and we may forget that in hand-press printing every space has to be created by inserting appropriately sized blanks; this process is especially important in setting poetry or verse drama. As Adrian Weiss commented, "Readers are usually unaware of the fact that, to a compositor's eye, the white space between the end of a shorter verse line and the right hand margin is not simply empty white space, but is an area packed with faceless pieces of lead."[31]

The compositor continues setting and justifying until he has composed four or five lines of type firmly justified; then he transfers them to the galley, a wooden tray not much larger than the page he was setting. When he completes a page the compositor adds the catchword: as Moxon described it, "the first word of the next Page, or if the Word be very long and the line very short, two syllables, or sometimes but one of that word." Modern readers are familiar with catchwords in early printed books, but may not always realize their function in ordering the pages. The catchword helps the printer in imposing pages in the forme (see the later discussion) and the binder in assembling gatherings in the correct order. The compositor adds a signature, usually starting with an "A" (either upper or lower case) on the first page of the first sheet and proceeding through the alphabet as far as the last sheet. He only needs to add signatures on the first three odd-numbered pages of a quarto to give sufficient instructions to the binder. As Moxon explained the process, on page 3 the compositor sets A2, the figure 2 being "no part of the Signature, but . . . only adjunct to shew the *Book-binder* the Second Leaf of that Sheet, that he may the surer Fold the Sheet right," and on page 5 he sets A3. "The Rule is, that all Odd Pages should have a signature if they stand on the *Out-Side* of the Sheet; and the reason for the Rule is, that the *Gatherer*, *Collater* and Bookbinder may the readier lay Sheets right, if they be turned wrong."[32]

The next stage in the printing process is known as "imposition." Once the printer completed the requisite number of pages, he would " 'impose' them on a flat table or stone in such a manner that when an impression was taken from them on a flat sheet and the pages afterwards folded to form part of a book, the pages would be in the proper order." The compositor would arrange the pages of type in their correct position and then "place round them a bottomless frame called a 'chase' . . . and proceed to fill up the intervening spaces between the pages and between them and the chase with pieces of wood or metal below type-height called 'furniture,' " while the pages "thus arranged in the chase are called a 'forme.'"[33] As we have seen, a single folio sheet, folded and printed on both sides, would contain four pages, with pages 1 and 4 on the outside or "outer forme," and 2 and 3 on the inside or "inner forme." As R. B. McKerrow explained, "to avoid the enormous amount of sewing that would be involved in binding a book in this fashion, and also the thickening of the back which would result from it, three or four sheets were frequently placed together in one gathering, and sewn through at the same time." In the early modern period three sheets per folio gathering, or "a folio in sixes," was the most usual configuration, in which the outermost sheet contained pages 1 and 12 on the outside, 2 and 11 on the inside, and so on.[34] In a quarto book "in fours" the gathering consists of a single sheet that is folded and cut to present eight consecutive pages. The outer forme "contains the pages which, when the sheet is first folded, will be on the outside of the fold," namely pages 1, 4, 5, and 8. The inner forme contains the pages that in a folded sheet are within the fold, namely pages 2, 3, 6, and 7.

The standard Elizabethan printing house had a limited supply of type, in various fonts; these limited resources affected the number of formes that could be set at once. The sheet was printed on two separate occasions, beginning with either the inner or outer forme. Once printed, the damp sheets would be hung along the center crease for drying, until the reverse side could be printed, the sheet then being "perfected" or completed. When the desired number of copies of each sheet had been printed, fulfilling the given print run, the forme would be removed from the press, and the type would be washed in lye water to remove the ink, rinsed, and left to dry. Then the compositor would break up the pages and "distribute" the type a line at a time, returning each letter to its proper box, while retaining the headline and other recurring items (rules, ornaments, signatures) as the "skeleton" to be used on the remaining sheets.

Proof Correction

To return to the printing sequence, once the compositor completed a forme, two workmen could begin the printing process: the beater inks the type and the pressman winds the forme in under the platen and pulls the handle to make the impression. At this point the correction process can begin. In modern times the whole text is set up in type, and a few sets of the complete work are printed off for independent proof checking, usually by three agents: the printer, the publisher, and the author. Once the work has been checked by the responsible agents, a corrected set will be printed. If the work concerned has special difficulties or complexities, further stages of proofing may be required, each separately numbered and superseded by the one following, until a satisfactory text is achieved. In books of the sixteenth and seventeenth centuries, however, the shortage of type, the expense of paper, and the need to keep the presses running made it impossible to produce a complete set of proofs. It used to be thought that early modern books were proofread only after the final stage of printing, but a number of recent studies have shown that "at least two proofs were necessary to achieve the printed condition of most texts."[35] Peter Blayney has produced convincing evidence that, out of the twenty formes making up the *Lear* Quarto, thirteen "were proofed against copy before presswork."[36]

Proof correcting went through an ideal sequence of four stages, described by Moxon in great detail.[37] In the first, the compositor would place the forme on the correcting stone for the pressman to print a single sheet or "pull" from the freshly set type. (It appears that most printers kept a spare, old press for this purpose, so that the main press(es) need not be displaced.)[38] On this "foul proof," major printing errors, such as stickfulls of type printed upside down or duplicated paragraphs, would be corrected; that sheet would then be discarded. Those corrections made, a second "pull" would be taken, and the pressman would start printing. Whoever was employed as proofreader, either a professional corrector or one of the printing house staff, such as the master printer or a compositor between stints, would receive "the Proof and his Copy to Correct it by" (in theory at least: in all too many instances the corrector did not consult copy) and would mark up a whole forme.

The correction process, so simple in an age of electronic word processing, was much more difficult in the hand-press era. "Once on the press, any further corrections were performed without removing the forme from the press, which is what stop-press corrections means."[39] If there are only a few faults, Moxon writes, the compositor unlocks the forme on the stone just enough to loosen the quoins or wedges, finds the fault needing correcting "in the metal," and "Sticks the point of his Bodkin into the Neck of the Letter, viz. between the Beard and the Face, and lifts it with the point of his Bodkin so high up above the face of the other Letters, that he can lay hold of it," remove it, and replace it with the correct letter.[40] If the two letters are of equal thickness, he has no problem in justifying the line after the fault is corrected, but if they are not he has to insert or "take out a space where he finds most convenient," and "if there be a long word or more left out" the compositor has to make adjustments that can cause knock-on effects forward or backward within the forme.[41] Every such operation was liable to introduce errors, some small, such as a letter "hanging"—not being "square and upright"—so that it received the ink unequally, and others large, such as incorrect word divisions, lost words, or jumbled text.

While the corrector was marking up a forme, printing continued, at a rate that may seem uncomfortably fast to us. The hourly unit of presswork for printing one side of a sheet was a "token" of 250 sheets, and the standard work rate was 1,250 sheets perfected per day at full press: thus we must visualize the pressman "cranking out four sheets per minute." (As for the compositor, he was expected to set two formes per day, alongside his other duties.[42]) The corrector could not take too long over the task, because the press might have printed a hundred or more sheets by the time that he had completed his work. As Peter Blayney observed, "press-correction was always hasty, for the longer it took, the fewer copies of the forme could be printed in the corrected state."[43] In 1617 Samuel Purchas complained that although he had "perused and corrected" at home almost every sheet of his book as the printers had delivered them, "sometimes through their slow negligence in sending them, or over-hastie diligence in printing many off before they could be corrected, many faults have passed in many Copies."[44] David Gants has noted that, in the 1616 edition of Ben Jonson's *Workes*, a 1,028-page folio, "many places . . . show an unusually high proportion of unfinished proofing, including eight instances where over one-third of the copies of a page exist in uncorrected form. Assuming a production run of 750 copies," that proportion "indicates that on occasion between 200 and 300 sheets were printed between the initial and final stages of correction."[45]

To avoid wasting paper, printers did not always discard the sheets or "revises" carrying corrections, but retained them alongside the corrected ones, all of which were collated and sent as assembled, but unbound books, to the publisher. As a result of this printers' economy many surviving copies of the same printed book differ in one or more formes. Charlton Hinman's epoch-making collation of fifty-five of the seventy-nine copies of the First Folio in the Folger Shakespeare Library discovered that five sheets containing marginal proof corrections had not been discarded, but were bound up in surviving copies.[46] His study of the surviving Folio corrections revealed the extent to which the goal of proofreading in the early modern period also differed from our own. In modern times the primary concern of proofreading is to ensure the accuracy of the text, and each of the three agents involved checks the printed text against the authorial copy. The modern printer may be as concerned as his predecessors were about the overall look of the printed page, but with modern technology that should not be affected by proof correction. Hinman showed that the Folio proofreader (whom he identified as Isaac Jaggard) "appears to have been perfectly content to trust the compositors to reproduce the essential substance of the copy they used. For there can be no escaping the conclusion that the ultimate objective of the proof-reading that was done for the Folio was rather to eliminate the superficial blemishes than, by regular checking of proof against copy, to ensure substantive textual accuracy."[47] Given that the Folio is a volume of more than 900 double-column pages, a conservative estimate might expect a frequency of 5 errors per page or 4,500 in total. Hinman showed that the proofreaders in 1622–1623 left only about five hundred visible changes, but Blayney has reminded us that proofing went through two stages and that "whatever was usually done to formes before presswork, it was done rather more carefully to the Folio forms."[48] Of the surviving corrections, Hinman found that only a half-dozen were made by reference to copy, and in three times as many cases "the proof-correction process for one reason or another resulted in corruption rather than correction." In several instances "the later of the two Folio states is more seriously corrupt than the earlier one." It is chastening to read Hinman's conclusion that "very few *substantive* errors . . . were noticed at all" and that the proofing of the First Folio "achieved little indeed except in the way of obviating a fair number of superficial faults."[49] Many of the Folio corrections were made in the stints set by a workman, probably an apprentice, whom Hinman named "Compositor E," who joined Jaggard's shop in 1623, just in time to set a portion of the Tragedies, including *King Lear.* The printing staff, alert to his inexperience and liability to error, proofread his stints with more care, but not well enough.[50] By contrast, Jonson "oversaw the printing of his *Workes,*" and David Gants has located "some sort of intervention to correct a forme or formes" in more than 75 percent of the eighty-five gatherings, authorial interventions that went far beyond "the changes usually made by the corrector," resulting in "over 2,500 changes." Although Jonson's attention dropped off across the whole volume, with a "general decline in frequency and scope of press corrections as printing proceeded," one could wish that Jaggard had devoted a fraction of that attention to the Shakespeare Folio.[51]

Hinman's vast undertaking—comparing fifty-five copies of the Folio line by line—was only possible thanks to his invention of an optical collating machine.[52] Up until that point—and indeed, for many tasks since—bibliographers had always collated manuscripts and books manually, choosing one exemplar as a reference point and comparing the others with it, one word at a time. As we have seen, early modern printers did not discard sheets already printed, once errors had been found and corrected. The presence of both corrected and uncorrected sheets in Shakespeare quartos was noticed in the first *Cambridge Shakespeare,* edited by W. G. Clark, W. Aldis Wright, and John Oliver (1863–1866). That the 1608 *Lear* Quarto contained sheets in both states was noted in the first modern study of the play's textual problems, made in 1875 by the great German scholar Nikolaus Delius, who collated several copies.[53] The task of collating was pursued more systematically by P. A. Daniel in 1885 and definitively by Sir Walter Greg in 1940.[54] Greg collated the twelve surviving copies of the Quarto, which contains ten sheets, and identified a total of 167 variant readings, which he divided into two groups.

He classified 148 as substantive—that is, alterations "made for their own sake"—and 19 as consequential, or "consequent upon others." As he explained, "When for the sake of correction one word was substituted for another, it often of course occupied a different amount of space in the line, and some adjustment had to be made elsewhere in order to fit it in. In the case of verse this might be done by altering the quads at the end of the line; but if the line happened to be full, and generally in the case of prose, more complicated methods had to be adopted."[55] Comparing the uncorrected sheets, which he labeled "Qa," with the corrected ones ("Qb"), Greg found that the proofreader made many unnecessary changes to the spelling, but that two-thirds of his corrections were right.

Greg's assessment was based on the Folio reading, which he took to be authoritative. He also noted instances where the Folio reproduced readings found in the uncorrected Quarto sheets, which showed that the copy or copies used by Jaggard's compositors must have contained a mixture of corrected and uncorrected sheets.[56] A telling example of their reliance on an unreliable source is Edmund's deceitful explanation for having had Lear and Cordelia sent to prison. In the corrected state it appears in this cramped form[57]:

> *Bast.* Sir I thought it fit,
> To send the old and miserable King to some retention, *and ap-*
> Whose age has charmes in it, whose title more, *(pointed guard,*
> To pluck the common bossome of his side (K4v21–24)

The three italicized words ending the second line and partly turned down into the line following are found neither in the uncorrected sheet nor in the Folio, even though, as Greg put it, "They are necessary to the verse, and it seems impossible to doubt their authenticity."[58] The Folio compositor was evidently using a defective copy of the Quarto. Another example of a correction made by Okes's proofreader but not picked up by the Folio is Albany's denunciation of Goneril: "proper deformity shewes not in the fiend, so horrid as in woman" (H4r17–18), where the Folio follows "seemes," the reading found in the uncorrected sheets, giving a weaker sense. Similarly with Albany's satisfied discovery of a theodicy at work in the fact that a servant killed Cornwall after he had blinded Gloucester, the 1608 Quarto reads, "This shewes you are above you Iustisers" (H4r37–38). The uncorrected state read "Iustices," as does the Folio.[59] In these, as in many other instances, the Folio is not the authoritative text.

Although successful in reading the manuscript copy in these instances, there are many more instances where the corrector of the 1608 Quarto changed readings from the proof without authority, evidently because he had not consulted the copy, was relying on guesswork, or else was convinced that he could make better sense. One of Regan's false claims concerning Lear's "riotous knights" is that they encouraged Edgar to kill his father:

> Tis they haue put him on the old mans death,
> To haue the wast and spoyle of his reuenues: (D4v11–12)

This corrector's version of a passage in Shakespeare's manuscript puzzled Compositor B, who originally set "To haue these——and wast. . . ." As Greg commented, "The compositor was evidently unable to read his copy, since he inserted hyphens in place of illegible letters, but these are a guarantee of his care and honesty." The printer evidently had access to an independent source descending from Shakespeare's authentic manuscript, probably the theater company's Booke prepared by the theater scribe as the reference text for rehearsal and performance. It reads "th'expence and wast," which, Greg added, "proves the corrector's order to be wrong, and the object of the inversion . . . quite obscure."[60] When Regan explains why she and Cornwall have suddenly arrived "out of season" at Gloucester's house, she claims that it is due to "Ocasions noble *Gloster* of some poyse" (D4v31; 2.1.120). The uncorrected Quarto reads "prise," the Folio "prize," both derived from Shakespeare's manuscript and giving perfectly acceptable sense; editors who prefer "poyse" have doubtful authority. When Lear also arrives at Gloucester's house and is frustrated not to be welcomed by Regan, he is first angry, then pleading. The uncorrected sheet reads "the deare fate, | Would with the daughter speake, come and tends seruise" (E4v4–5). Okes's corrector changed the noun to "father" (as Greg noted, Shakespeare probably wrote *fat^r*), and changed the pronoun to read "his daughter"—"nothing but a facile guess," Greg objected. It is not unlikely that an angry Lear would be capable of presenting himself as "the father" and Regan as "the daughter," the third-person pronoun reducing them both to their roles, so affirming his hierarchy over her. Okes's proofreader then solved the problem to his satisfaction by reading "commands her seruice." The Folio gives "commands, tends, seruice," evidently correctly, because "*tend* is a recognized aphetic form of *attend* and was used from 1600 on in the sense of await or expect." As Greg observed, "Lear's mood in this speech alternates between peremptory haste and considerate moderation,"[61] and it seems to me that the Folio reading captures the unpredictable speed at which he oscillates between the two, as if he were trying to adjust to his new role as a considerate guest. He even tries to excuse Cornwall's failure to welcome him—"may be he is not well"—adding another five apologetic lines on the psychosomatic effects of "Infirmitie," only to break off in anger as he again notices Kent in the stocks: "Death on my state, wherfore should he sit here?" (E4v13; 2.4.105–113).

The proofreader made several errors in correcting the revises. When Cornwall's Steward greets Kent, the uncorrected sheet reads "Good deuen to thee friend" (E1r3; 2.2.1). The corrector changed it to "Good euen," which is obviously incorrect because Regan has just referred to "dark-ey'd night." The Folio made better sense of Shakespeare's manuscript, as preserved in the company's Booke, reading "Good dawning." The stream of insults that Kent delivers includes, in the uncorrected sheet, the incomprehensible term "three snyted." This is probably a simple case of a turned letter, "n" for "u," letters that were in contiguous sort boxes and often confused.[62] Okes's proofreader, however, changed the term to "three shewted" (E1r13), whatever that might mean, and it was left to the Folio compositor to give the true reading, "three suited" (2.2.16). After Kent attacked the Steward, Cornwall orders the stocks to be brought out for this "stubburne ausrent knaue," as the compositor interpreted Shakespeare's handwriting. The proofreader substituted "miscreant" (E2v2), reasonably enough but incorrectly, as the Folio shows, reading it as "ancient" (2.2.126). Left alone in the stocks, Kent sums up his humiliated condition, as the compositor deciphered it: "nothing almost sees my rackles ꜝ But miserie." An easy correction for the proofreader was to change it to "my wracke" (E3r4–5), but this was wrong: the Folio compositor read the manuscript correctly, as "miracles" (2.3.165). When Lear goes out on the heath Okes's compositor made him describe "this crulentious storme," generating another apparently easy correction, "tempestious storme" (G1r30)—but this was a pure guess, resulting in a tautology. The Folio compositor could make better sense of the handwriting in his copy, giving the distinctive epithet, "contentious Storme" (3.4.6). As the storm rages and Lear descends into madness, Gloucester risks his life to get him to safety, urging Kent to "take vp thy master" and repeating the injunction a few moments later, in the original version: "Take vp to keepe." Guesswork led Okes's compositor to read "Take vp the King" (E4v13), but the Folio compositor either had a more legible manuscript to work from or else was a better reader of handwriting, and so gave the true text: "Take vp, take vp" (3.6.95).

Modern readers have absorbed the Folio readings, as chosen by generations of editors, and may not realize how fortunate we are that the King's Men had preserved the Booke so carefully. We all know Gloucester's evocation of the tumult in the elements from the Folio:

> The Sea, with such a storme as his bare head,
> In Hell-blacke-night indur'd, would haue buoy'd vp
> And quench'd the Stelled fires (3.7.59–61; TLN 2131–2133)

Okes's compositor first set "storme of his lou'd head" as "layd vp" and "steeled fires"—four errors. The corrector substituted "storme on his lowd head," "bod vp," and "stelled" (H1v16–18)—getting one right out of four.

Greg's study of the variants in the 1608 *Lear* Quarto was a major contribution to our understanding of the contingencies affecting the transmission of Shakespeare's text, but his brief was to analyze the corrections, good and bad, not to chart the errors that remain uncorrected. Okes's commitment to proofreading did not extend very far. As the corrector put right the errors that he had noticed, he introduced new ones.[63] In many cases he found nonsense and left it unamended, as in the following selection, where I follow the Quarto reading either with Q2 or the Folio: "thourt disuetur'd" (D2r29) for "thwart disnatur'd"; "fitkering" (E2r22) for "flicking"; "flechuent" (E2r36) for "fleshment"; "caterickes, & Hircanios" (F4r4) for "Cataracts, and Hyrricano's"; "starre-blusting" (G1v38) for "Starre-blasting"; "tralmadam" (G3v36) for "trial madam" (Q2); "festuant" (H1r5) for "festinate" (F2); "bitt" (H2v28) for "kill"; "vent" (I1r37) for "vext"; "argue-proofe" (I3v23) for "Agu-proofe"; "cheuore" (K1r16) for "che vor'ye"; "thequesse" (K3v17) for "the guesse"; "Conspicuate" (L1v34) for "conspirant"; and "foredoome" (L4r4) for "foredone." Unsurprisingly, scholars have expressed universal disappointment with the Quarto as an artifact. Delius noted that the printer was fortunate to possess a complete copy of the play, as recently performed, but judged that "this copy must have been very careless and unreadable, for otherwise the innumerable mistakes, faulty versification, and omissions of the printers, are almost inexplicable. The mistakes arose for the most part from the compositor substituting, for any word which he could not read, the word which looked most like it in *Ductus Literarum*, without paying much respect to any meaning at all, much less to Shakespeare's meaning."[64] Greg described it as "badly printed" by "an inferior printer" and concluded that "the quarto text is a very bad one, both in comparison with that of the folio and with any of the more reputable quartos of other Shakespearian plays."[65] Alice Walker judged that "[n]o play in the canon, whatever its transmission, contains quite such arresting nonsense as this quarto."[66]

These and other judgments on this "very bad" text were qualified by Peter Blayney's groundbreaking study of the career of Nicholas Okes (1574–1645). When Nathaniel Butter and John Busby, the two stationers sharing the edition (Butter being the main agent) chose Okes in the winter of 1607, he was relatively inexperienced. He had only been admitted as a master printer in January of that year and had acquired his own printing house as recently as April: *King Lear* was the first play he printed, a fact that explains many of the difficulties he experienced.[67] In his preface Blayney pointed out that there had been several studies of the Quarto as a material object, notably Greg's "masterly" study that "drew attention to many of the typographical peculiarities of the book in addition to analysing the significance of the variants." Despite Greg's work, however, "few of the physical features of the book have been adduced in support of textual arguments. The reason is not that their evidence is textually irrelevant, but that no context has been established in which their significance can be evaluated." To provide the relevant context Blayney set out to establish this printer's "norms" by studying his complete output between 1607 and 1609.[68] At the end of that analysis Blayney judged that the *Lear* Quarto was among his "half-dozen worst-printed books."[69]

Okes's problems began with the copy, Shakespeare's manuscript, as it had been submitted to the King's Men in 1605–1606. Evidence suggests that, for a work written in English, printers expected to receive a fair copy transcribed from the authorial manuscript by a scribe hired by the printer. This was an additional expense, but had obvious advantages. "Although a compositor could set type from virtually any rough draft, the quality of a printer's copy directly affected the accuracy of typesetting." Such a copy would probably be more legible, but "more importantly, a printer would require a transcript that was consistent throughout in terms of the size and spacing of the script, a factor that is not significant in manuscripts intended for a reader, but critical to a compositor in the process of casting-off copy," a procedure yet to be discussed.[70] It has been estimated that a scribal copy would only cost two to three shillings.[71] Blayney criticized Okes for his "penny-pinching use of cheap labour" and the "cheap-minded expediency" with which he treated the problem of setting print from Shakespeare's messy manuscript, "without spending the necessary money to cope with it."[72] If Okes had spent a few shillings on a transcript of Shakespeare's manuscript, his task and that of textual students four centuries later would have been much easier.

Imposing: By Formes or Seriatim?

To complete this primer of early modern printing we need to consider the choices available at the imposition stage. As we have seen, in a single Folio sheet, folded so as to make four pages, those that lie on the inside of the sheet constitute the inner forme, namely pages 2 and 3, and those that lie on the outside make up the outer forme, containing pages 1 and 4. The printer can set the formes in whichever sequence he likes, and it might seem simplest for him to set the pages in the normal reading order (or *seriatim*), but this practice had several disadvantages. In a "folio in twos" the compositor would have to set page 1 as half of the outer forme, and put it aside. Then he would be able to set and "impose" pages 2 and 3 as constituting the inner forme. He could send that forme to be printed and then return to page 4, but meanwhile page 1 has been lying idle, tying up that much type. Given these disadvantages we can understand why early modern printers devised a more efficient system: "setting by forms." This process depended on the master printer or compositor accurately "casting off" or calculating the extent of his copy. The term "casting off" was also used for the preliminary estimate of the amount of paper that would be needed, but for setting by formes a more exact calculation had to be made. Joseph Moxon gave a full account of the "*Counting* or *Casting off Copy* (for both Phrases are indifferently us'd)" and outlined an arithmetical method suitable for "Counting off either *Printed* or *Written Copy*"—the latter being "more difficult, because subject to being "irregularly Writ."[73] Casting off involved counting the number of pages in the written copy and then multiplying it by the number of lines in a page and by the number of letters in each line; this gives "Total A." Having decided on the format and the font, the printer calculates the number of letters that the font will take up in a line, including spaces, multiplied by the number of lines per page, giving "Total B." In Moxon's worked example the first total was "191,135, the number of Letters in the whole Written Copy," and the second was 1,551. Thus, A divided by B "gives 123, that is, 123 Pages in Quarto, which divided by 8, the number of Pages in one Sheet, gives 15 Sheets and 3 Pages."[74] That seems quite straightforward, but many complications could occur.

The printer needed to consider several other points before he has "exactly counted off." First, he must take account of "the Breaks that come in the Copy," such as "Chapters, Sections or Paragraphs," allowing "room enough to set them and their Titles [headings] gracefully in."[75] Some play texts—the majority of those in the Shakespeare First Folio—are divided into acts and scenes, such breaks often being set off within a "box" enclosed by the ruled lines created by brass rules, usually with blank lines above and below. Play books normally record, with varying efficiency, characters' entrances, usually set on a separate line, and exits, sometimes set on a separate line, but often set in the text. All play books identify speakers, a speech prefix being included in the opening line of every speech, even those of only one line, each prefix being indented two spaces. The master printer or compositor casting off copy needs to allow for all these characteristics of a play book, and if he is setting text from a manuscript he must also consider its density on the page and estimate accordingly. As Moxon pointed out, "scarce any Copy is so regularly Written . . . but that some places are Wider, and other places Closer Written than the generality of the Copy."[76] Moxon had probably never seen the theater manuscripts surviving from the early seventeenth century, or else he would have had to allow for other factors, such as crossings out and corrections written between the lines, in the margin, or even as additional slips pinned to the pages—all further hazards for the printer trying to estimate the amount of paper to be ordered and the total print space needed to produce an economically viable book.

Once he has estimated exactly how many pages will be needed for the whole work, the compositor marks the exact point where each page will end and underlines the last word, which becomes the catchword.[77] Once he knows the exact contents of each page, the printer can set either the outer forme or the inner first, as he wishes; also, the copy can be divided between two or more compositors, working separately. This method was particularly useful in setting large books, such as the First Folio, which runs to more than 900 pages, each page consisting of two columns of type, sixty-six lines long. The 1623 volume is a "folio in sixes," a sequence of groups of three sheets, folded or quired one inside the other. Thus the twelve pages constituting a quire need six formes, containing twelve pages. Had a quire been set seriatim it would have needed enough type to set seven pages, a quantity of type far greater than most London printers owned. In 1955 Charlton Hinman published a ground-breaking essay in which he demonstrated that, contrary to previous thinking, the Shakespeare First Folio "was set throughout, not by successive pages, but *by formes.*"[78] Hinman showed that most of the Folio pages had been set in pairs by two compositors working simultaneously, each from a different type case.

Once the printer had estimated how much text would fit in the first five pages, the compositors would begin with the inner forme of the inner sheet and work through to the outer forme of the outer sheet. As Peter Blayney has described the process,

> Pages 6 and 7 were the first to be set, sometimes by two men working simultaneously, but more usually by a single compositor. When those two pages (the first forme) had been made ready and given to the press, pages 5 and 8 (the next forme) were set. Those two pages were far enough apart for the copy to be physically divided between two compositors, so they were usually set by two men working simultaneously. While the press printed pages 5 and 8, the compositors distributed pages 6 and 7, and then set pages 4 and 9. After another distribution they set pages 3 and 10, then pages 2 and 11, and finally pages 1 and 12. So although the last seven pages of each quire were set in numerical order, the first five pages were set in *reverse* order.[79]

In the essay that first drew attention to this important issue Hinman emphasized the difficulties involved in this process: the compositors had to know exactly where each page began and ended, which meant that "the setting of cast-off copy had to be effected with considerable precision, and that such precision would be difficult to achieve unless the casting off were itself at least reasonably accurate."[80] Hinman observed that estimating the page divisions from a dramatist's manuscript would be difficult; even harder to estimate would be "copy very untidily made up from various sources, interlined, supplied with marginal additions partly in verse and partly in prose, and so on." Some of the problems that faced Elizabethan compositors may seem strange to our eyes. In modern times a copyeditor will mark up the copy for a printer by adding handwritten or typed instructions on a typed text, a process that makes it easier to set copy in type while observing a publisher's house style. But in the sixteenth and seventeenth centuries such editing consisted of handwritten annotation on a printed or handwritten copy, which added another level of potential confusion. Where the Folio compositors worked from copy that had been "copy-edited" in this way, Hinman found, "miscalculations . . . and gross inaccuracy would be more likely to occur . . . than with unedited copy, since the counting of lines and words would be more difficult."[81]

The advantages of setting by formes also applied to play quartos, many of which were set in this manner.[82] The disadvantages of setting a quarto seriatim are clear: where pages 2–3–6–7 constitute the inner forme, and 1–4–5–8 the outer forme, the printer would have to set seven pages before he could send the inner forme to be imposed and printed. The necessity of setting seven pages placed a great strain on the printer's stock not only of type but also of the "quadrats" (or "quads"), blank pieces of type of varying thickness needed for spacing.[83] Nicholas Okes experienced both problems in printing *King Lear.* In his marvelously detailed analysis of the 1608 Quarto Peter Blayney analyzed the wear and tear on the printing type, caused by the physical damage it received when put under pressure each time a forme was used to print five hundred or more sheets.[84] Blayney was able to reconstruct the sequence in which the type was "distributed" or returned to the compositors' cases after use. This analysis established that most of the 1608 *Lear* Quarto was set seriatim, in numerical sequence. Blayney noted that Okes set by formes elsewhere, but suggests that he failed to do so in this instance due to the messy state of Shakespeare's manuscript: "*Lear* was set seriatim (quite probably because the manuscript was difficult to cast off for the more customary setting by formes)."[85] This decision had other, evidently unforeseen consequences for Okes, because seriatim work requires more type. Blayney showed that Okes's chosen font of pica roman was not really adequate to the task, resulting in a "shortage of type . . . which affected the work—and consequently the text."[86] By examining virtually every letter in Okes's pica fount Blayney discovered that "[o]ne sort on which *Lear* placed an unusually heavy strain was italic *E.*"[87] The compositors must have been disconcerted by the need for *E* caused by the frequent recurrence of the stage directions *Enter* and *Exit*, compounded by the recurrence in dialogue of the names *Edgar* and *Edmund*, necessarily printed in italics, according to current typographic conventions, and that of "*Edg.*" as a speech prefix. Unable to meet the demand for the italic *E*, Okes's compositors had to substitute the roman E and even the swash E. The capital italic *A* was also in short supply, and Blayney accounts for the sudden change in referring to Albany at 4.2.29 (K4v14), where he is suddenly "*Duke*" in the stage direction (previously "*Alb.*")—a change that some literary critics might theorize as a change of attitude to this character on Shakespeare's part—as "nothing more than a simple expedient adopted because the *A* box was empty."[88] These are no doubt trivial matters, but the short supply of a particular letter also caused the compositors to change the spelling of words, choosing a variant ending in *-y* rather than *-ie*, for instance, when they were short of the letter *i*.[89] In modern textual criticism scholars have taken the use of variant or alternate choices as evidence of compositors' spelling preferences, and hence the relative stints of their work and the specific kinds of influence they might have had on the text. In both areas of study, such theories need to be checked against the material conditions of the printing shop, and one authority has expressed doubts as to the validity of such analyses.[90]

The single most important fact concerning the 1608 Quarto that Blayney established was that "Okes had not printed a play before, and none of the pica in the house is known to have been used for one by his predecessors. This fact put an unprecedented strain on the supplies of numerous sorts. . . . And what *Lear* used in the quantities most unprecedented in the pica books of 1605–07 was space-metal."[91] Not being able to set the requisite amount of space after punctuation marks or between words, the compositors left all too many instances of type packed together. In his study of the variants in the *Lear* Quarto, Greg compiled a long list of its "literal errors and other typographical abnormalities," which includes twenty-two instances of words being run together for lack of space.[92] These include "ofnothing" (C4v26), "learneto" (D1r25), "fatherscurse" (D2v5), "beenewise" (D3r33), "thenlet" (F4r20), "placemy" (G1r25), "mydispleasure" (H1r1), "foolsdo" (H4r11), "beaydant" (I1v14), "Idoe" (K2v18), and "Andfire" (K4r34).

Blayney painstakingly reconstructed the printing of each sheet, finding several indications that the text was set seriatim.[93] In the short term this choice gave Okes more flexibility, because if a sheet "was not set by formes it is unlikely that the text was cast off accurately into pages."[94] With each sheet he printed Okes kept his options open until "the time of imposition, when eight galleyfulls of type (each containing a number of stickfulls of type rather than a necessarily-exact number of lines) were arranged as eight 38-line pages."[95] Adrian Weiss has argued that seriatim setting "presented no problems," in that, for instance, an "overflow" of text "could easily be resolved during imposition simply by . . . shifting an equivalent number of lines forward in the remaining pages. Conversely, a line or partial line could be pulled back to the bottom of the previous page to solve a setting problem."[96] But this presupposes that the compositor has enough space to absorb the unexpected material. The most serious consequence of Okes having chosen to set *Lear* seriatim, I argue in chapter 3, was the compositors' constant uncertainty concerning the space available as they set each page.

From a reader's first view, the 1608 *Lear* Quarto stands out as a disconcertingly irregular text, starting from its page width. Many Jacobean plays, whatever the accuracy of their text, present a tidy impression on the page. Passages of verse occupy the same amount of text from start to finish, prose passages seem to have been designed for the space they occupy, and the more important stage directions are centered. In the *Lear* Quarto, however, barely two pages look the same. Of its seventy-nine pages containing print, twelve were set in a narrow spacing (as for verse), at about 80–81 mm, thirty-five were set in a wide spacing (as for prose), at about 93–94 mm, and thirty-three pages use both the narrow and the wide setting. This unpredictable mixture produced a series of ragged-looking pages (see Plates 2, 3), but it points to more fundamental problems. The inexperienced Okes was faced with a play text written in both prose and verse, in which the alternation between these two media was unpredictable, being determined by changes in the characters on stage and depending on Elizabethan conventions (see Chapter 3). Although Okes did not set by formes, he necessarily had to estimate the amount of space he would need. Blayney suggested that "the whole text must have been cast off, in that the number of sheets it was to fill had been predetermined."[97] However, Blayney is rather evasive on this important issue, to which we must return.

We need to bear in mind how difficult it must have been for an inexperienced craftsman printing a play for the first time. If the "copy" was already divided into a fixed number of lines, such as in an already printed book or the manuscript of a poem, it could—at least in theory—be "cast off with such accuracy that the exact contents of each type page could be predicted." However, it was much more difficult to estimate the length of a prose manuscript.[98] In casting off prose, as Blayney has reconstructed the process, the printer "would have had to adjust a composing stick to the required measure and set one or more sample lines in order to ascertain the ratio between manuscript and printed lines. But as long as he made proper allowance for variations in the size of the handwriting, and for paragraph breaks, chapter headings, and the like, an experienced printer could usually cast off prose without undue difficulty." However, when estimating the length of a play containing both verse and prose, Blayney added,

> the printer will have to keep switching from one method to the other. In verse passages, and in prose dialogue consisting mostly of very short speeches, he can simply count the lines, but each longer prose speech will have to be measured. He may also have to make decisions about stage directions written beside the text rather than in it: should any of them be centered, and should there be space above or below? Can an exit share a line with the end of a speech, or should it have a line to itself? And in prose passages he will have to remember that speech prefixes, although written to the left of the text, will be indented in the printed page, and must therefore be allowed for in the first line of each speech.[99]

Some of these considerations were evidently foreign to Okes's printing shop. The 1608 Quarto usually centers stage directions (with some significant exceptions, to which we return). But at 1.2.145 what should have been the direction [*Enter*] *Edgar*, during a speech by his bastard brother, was printed outside the text in the left-hand margin (C2v9), evidently a last-minute addition. Oddly enough, the compositor made the same error a few scenes later, in another speech by Edmund, where the direction *Enter Edgar* again appears in the left-hand margin, freely floating (2.1.18; D3v9). He did so again with the instruction "*Enter Glo*" in the right-hand margin (2.4.295; F3r13), also detached from the text and lacking the necessary full stop. Because the cheapest and quickest way to set the left-hand margin was with a "reglet," a piece of wood "a Quadrat high, of several Thicknesses" as Joseph Moxon described it, running the length of the page, the compositor must have either had to cut the reglet or change the furniture as an afterthought.[100]

There are other visible indications of a compositor's oversight. Greg drew attention to one at a page break—the point where Cornwall, Regan, and Goneril vow vengeance on "the vilaine *Gloster*" (3.7.1–6). This sequence occupies the end of one sheet and the beginning of the next. The Quarto reads (misprinting the catchword "*Corn.*"):

> *Regan.* Hang him instantly.
> *Gon.* Plucke out his eyes. (company.
> *Cern.*
>
> ---
>
> *Corn.* Leaue him to mydispleasure, *Edmūd* keep you our sister
> (company.
> (G4v37–38; H1r1–2)

In Greg's words, this error "shows . . . that the compositor, when nearing the end of the page, set up in his stick more lines than were needed to complete it. He happened to turn up the end of one line. When he divided the page immediately before this line he remembered to set up the turned- over word again *below*, but forgot to take out the original setting *above*."[101] (In practical terms, this may not have been the compositor's mistake alone; responsibility for it depends on who is doing the imposition as well as the composing.) Blayney spotted a similar error on another page ending a sheet. At the end of Act 2, scene 1 Regan is delivering an admonishment to Gloucester, but the page ends suddenly, leaving a speech prefix suspended:

> bestow your needful councell
> To our business,which craues the instant vse. (*Exeunt.*
> *Glost.*
> (D4v37–38)

The next page begins like this:

> *Glost.* I serue you Madam, | your Graces are right welcome.
> *Enter Kent, and Steward.* (E1v1–2)

As Blayney accounts for this confusion, "the compositor set the last line of the scene before transferring his stickful of type to the galley. The final line," spoken by Gloucester, "does not quite reach the margin, but there is not enough room for the closing '*Exeunt.*' The compositor therefore turned this word up into the previous line rather than down into the line containing the opening stage direction" for the next scene. "When the type was transferred to the galley, the turned-over word was left in what became D4v38, while the line to which it belongs became E1r1."[102] The result of this accident is that Gloucester's line is isolated on the page and—for the reader—in the mind's eye, on the stage, immediately before the stage direction for the next scene, as if the two characters enter while he is still present.

The 1608 *Lear* contains other traces of the compositors' combination of inexperience and inattention that are potentially more serious. The Quarto's standard page contains thirty-eight lines, with two anomalous pages of thirty-nine lines. The first of these longer pages (F2^{r}) continues from the preceding page (F1^{v}) Lear's speech rejecting Regan's suggestion that he return to Goneril: "Returne to her,and fiftie men dismist . . ." (2.4.210–215). Assigning letters to the lines will help us focus on the lack of coherence between them:

A No rather I abiure all roofes, and chuse
B To wage against the enmitie of the Ayre,
C To be a Comrade with the Woolfe and owle, (F1v36–38)

D Necessities sharpe pinch, returne with her, (F2r1)

Lewis Theobald restored sense to this incoherent utterance by transposing the second and third lines, so that "Necessitie's sharpe pinch" links up with "the enmitie of the Ayre."[103] He successfully corrected the error, without being able to explain how it occurred. Blayney points out that because "the transposed lines both begin with 'To' . . . it would have been extremely easy for the compositor to omit one of them by eyeskip." If he had omitted line C, and the omission had been noticed during proofing, restoring it to its proper place would have resulted in this page having an extra line, with the necessity of altering the catchword. The compositor belatedly set line C and inserted into his text, but "forgot . . . that line B belonged *between* the two new lines that he transferred straight from his composing stick into that gap." He then overcame the oversight by inserting an additional line in the next page (F2^{r}).[104] As for the other page containing an extra line (G2^{r}), Blayney noted "signs of something having disturbed the type," but could find no "evidence to suggest what may have been omitted and restored." This page contains a long and incoherent speech by Poor Tom, and it may be that the compositor had underestimated its volume, and he had to add an extra line to accommodate the full text before ending (ironically) with the catchword "vnaccom-//odated" (G2r39). Blayney pointed out that the two thirty-nine-line pages "occur in inner formes which were printed after the corresponding outer forme" and regarded it as a coincidence that each of these "is the third page of a sheet." In both cases "the discovery of an omitted line in the first half of an inner forme" resulted in the decision to lengthen a recto rather than a verso."[105] Readers who study these accounts may be left wondering how many other words or lines in the 1608 Quarto might have been omitted accidentally. In Chapter 4 I argue that many were omitted deliberately.

As we have seen, in attempting to correct the compositors' errors Okes produced the 167 variant readings that Greg discussed. Peter Blayney praised Greg's work and added a few "minor additions" before studying the *Lear* variants in the context of seventeen other Quartos that Okes printed in 1607–1608.[106] From several illuminating commentaries I select two. In his madness Lear recognizes that the naked beggar Poor Tom represents basic humanity, as the uncorrected sheet reads: "no more but such a poore bare forked Animall as thou art, off off you leadings,come on bee true" (G2v1–2; 3.4.108–109). Okes's proofreader deleted the last two words, so that the speech ends "come on," with no closing punctuation, although plenty of space remains. The Folio gives the undoubtedly correct reading, from Shakespeare's manuscript: "Off, off you Lendings: Come, vnbutton heere" (TLN 1888–1889). Because the deletion achieved nothing, Blayney suggested that "the proof-reader was as baffled as the compositor."[107] On another occasion, he argued, the corrector was guilty of an "overzealous deletion" in Gloucester's speech protesting that Cornwall's "purpost low correction" of Kent by putting him in the stocks is one usually given to "basest and temnest wretches for pilfrings" (E2v19–20). The compositor's original attempt to decipher Shakespeare's handwriting was incomprehensible, reading "belest and contained." Greg commented that "basest" was "Certainly correct" and suggested that the proofreader "must have crossed out or underlined 'taned' and written 'temnest' in the margin, meaning the compositor to alter the word to 'contemnest' "; but the compositor misunderstood and "substituted the marginal correction for the whole word in the text, thereby making nonsense."[108] Blayney endorsed Greg's "analysis of what happened," but objected that "Shakespearean usage does not *require* a second superlative, nor does uncorrected Q give any reason for supposing that the word in [the] copy ended with 'st.' " Rather, he argued, the original reading "is more consistent with 'basest and contemned,' " citing analogous constructions in Shakespeare.[109] This would be an acceptable reading, although there would be no necessary reason for adopting it. But Blayney drew on his remarkable knowledge of early modern printing in support, pointing out that "a quarto proofsheet has two pairs of pages arranged head-to-head on the printed side," each pair consisting of "a verso on the left and a recto on the right." In this case E2v (the page containing "temnest") is on the left and E3r is on the right, which contains, at much the same eye level, Edgar's resolve "To take the basest and most poorest shape." Blayney commented, "That line, I believe, is probably where the idea of changing 'contemned' to 'contemnest' originated."[110] That seems to me a brilliant application of bibliography to textual criticism, and I hope that future editors of *King Lear* will take note.

Thanks to the work of Greg and Blayney we can see that inexperience and inattention during the mechanical printing process account for many deficiencies in Okes's *Lear* Quarto. A large shift in modern bibliography has insisted that a book is not merely a vehicle for information and entertainment but a material artifact, subject to the same social and economic conditions as other artifacts. This is a welcome change of attitude, but it follows that a book is equally subject to human choices and human errors.

2

Adjusting Text Space to Print Space in the Shakespeare Folio and Quartos

In all types of publication the amount of text that the author supplies must be accommodated to a given amount of space in the printed artifact, whether it be a book, an essay, or a newspaper article. In our age, electronic word processing gives authors a constant record of the length of their text. In some forms of communication today authors can write as much as they wish, the text being infinitely expandable, limited only by the capacity of the computer and the patience of the reader. In cases where a length limit applies they can shorten their script retrospectively, working back from the end and cutting wherever they wish. In the age of hand-press books, by contrast, writers and printers were subject to constraints. As we have seen, the process of estimating length was crucial to determining the quantity of paper that the printer would order. When the estimate had been correctly made, printing could be carried out smoothly, but any error could create serious problems. Because paper amounted to nearly a third of printing costs, careful calculation was essential so as to avoid waste by using only part of a sheet. As Philip Gaskell observed, "enough paper would normally be ordered at once for the whole edition (which was one reason why casting-off was an early necessity), and as far as possible it would be supplied as a single lot, of even size and quality." Many books in the hand-press period were printed on a single batch of paper throughout, but others used two or more lots of paper, sometimes due to the stationer or printer having miscalculated the book's length.[1]

From these considerations of establishing the necessary balance between what I call "print space" and "text space," which will determine the quantity of paper needed for the whole book, we can return to the compositor setting type, who was often (if not always) concerned to make the most economical use of the space available and also to produce a pleasant visual appearance.[2] As we saw in the previous chapter, the compositor had to "justify" each line of type, so that it fit the "measure" or width of the agreed page dimension (narrow for poetry, wide for prose). If "the last word would not fill his measure precisely," Moxon noted, the compositor "either drove the line out (if he had too much room) or got it in (if he had too little) by altering the amount of space between some or all of the words in the line" to "fill up the Measure." This altering of space was the compositor's fundamental action, repeated an incalculable number of times, but it could be executed well or badly.

Normally the compositor put one space after each word, but if "necessity compells him to put more Spaces between the Words," that will have the unfortunate effect of producing wide "*Whites*," or blank spaces, which "are by Compositors (in way of Scandal) call'd *Pidgeon-holes*, and are by none accounted good Worksmanship, unless in cases of necessity." By "necessity" Moxon meant situations where the ratio between the number of words in the copy and the space on the page fell into debit, so to speak. The ideal state is one of balance, because the consequences of excess to one side or the other are potentially serious:

> A good Compositor takes care not to Set too Close, or too Wide; for if he Set too Close, and should happen to leave out a Word or two, it will give him a great deal of trouble to get those Words in; Nay perhaps when he comes to a Break he drives out a Line, for which Line perchance he may be forc'd to Over-run all the

> Pages that are Set forwards upon that Matter. And if he Sets too Wide, and he chance to Set a Word or two twice over, he may be forc'd to make *Pidgeon-holes* e're he come to a Break, and then perhaps his Break is got in too, and his Page a Line too short, and he forc'd to Over-run several Pages e're he can drive that Line out.[3]

Moxon's account of the secondary effects of under- or overestimating the ratio between written or printed copy and of the immediate context helps us to understand some of the deficiencies often noticeable in the printing of Elizabethan plays. We must realize that, for the compositor, each line is a finite unit, as is each cast-off page, and he had to strive to accommodate the text within those limits. Moxon mentions some devices by which a compositor, having received the proof corrections, recuperates errors he has made in setting his text. He will face a series of difficulties in correcting a large omission:

> If there be a long word or more left out, he cannot expect to Get that in into that Line, wherefore he must now Over-run; that is, he must put so much of the fore-part of the Line into the Line above it, or so much of the hinder part of the Line into the next Line under it, as will make room for what is Left out: Therefore he considers how Wide he has Set, that so by Over-running the fewer Lines backwards or forwards, or both, (as he finds his help) he may take out so many Spaces, or other Whites as will amount to the Thickness of what he has Left out.[4]

Depending on the place within the forme at which the error occurs, the compositor can flexibly move a prose text backward or forward; in setting verse he can "over-run" by turning the final word(s) of a line either up into the line above or down into the one below.

Moxon illustrates the consequences of the converse error of duplication, where the compositor has "set a word or small sentence twice" or "set a Line or Lines twice," before describing what for him was evidently the last resort: "If the Compositor is not firmly resolv'd to keep himself strictly to the Rules of good Workmanship, he is now tempted to make *Botches;* viz. *Pidgeon-holes, Thin-Spaces,* no *Space* before a *Capital, Short* &s, *Abbreviations* or *Titled Letters, Abbreviate Words,* &c. And if Botching is any Case excusable, it is in this; for with too great *Spacing-out* or too *Close Setting,* he many times may save himself a great deal of Labour, besides the vexation of mind, and other accidental mischiefs that attend Over-running."[5] Having earlier berated compositors for leaving no space before a capital letter, Moxon here lists other—in his eyes—disreputable devices to save space, such as replacing "and" with an ampersand (&), abbreviating words by omitting a letter such as a terminal *e*, or replacing a double with a single vowel (*ou* to just *o* or *u*). Another way to save a space uses a convention surviving from the abbreviations used in medieval manuscripts, substituting "*Titled Letters*"; that is, as his modern editors define them, "Letters with the tilde or contraction-sign over them, ã ẽ ĩ õ ũ . . . , to indicate an omission, generally the suppression of m or n." As these editors observe, "it is surprising that Moxon can contemplate their use, even as a reprehensible shift, at such a late date."[6] As we shall see, the early modern printers of Shakespeare used every one of these devices.

Adjusting Space in the 1623 Folio

Charlton Hinman's discovery that the Shakespeare First Folio was set by formes established for the first time the crucial significance of casting off copy. In addition to the basic difficulties of estimating the length of texts written in a mixture of prose and verse, he emphasized the added complication of setting from copy that had been annotated—suggesting that

> some of the textual peculiarities in plays that were set from much-edited copy may sometimes stem neither from the text that actually stood in the copy nor from the wholly thoughtless mistakes of a compositor but from his deliberate efforts to compensate for inaccurate casting off and to accommodate, as it were, the copy to its allotted space. For there are many indications that the Folio compositors were quite accustomed to expand or compress their type-pages in response to space requirements established by casting off; and there are also indications that

> the adjustments which they effected sometimes involved altering thc tcxt of the copy.[7]

This was a truly epoch-making but also disturbing discovery, because in cases where only one text of a play survives, how can we tell where text has been deleted and where added?

In a brief survey Hinman identified a few of the devices used by the Folio compositors both to compress and expand text, as required. Some adjustments "could be made by purely typographical means. Long lines of verse could either be set as two lines of the type-page or as one line with a 'turn-over' up or down. Short speeches, normally always given separate lines, could be otherwise dealt with if space were short." For example, a cursory glance indicates that the Folio text of *The Tempest* is often notably crowded. On page 4 (sig. A2v) the compositor had to cram two short speeches into one line and resort to a turn-over, whereas page 7 (sig. A4r) not only has two turn-overs but also "five times . . . prints two speeches in one line." By contrast, the facing page 6 (sig. A3v) is very " 'open' . . . no turn-overs; a new line for each of many short speeches."[8] Hinman showed how the compositors used a range of purely typographical space adjustments, such as varying the size of the lined boxes that enclose act and scene headings and inserting more quads to fill vacant space or fewer when space was tight. As he found, "the commonest of all the devices employed by the Folio compositors for space adjustment" was the "white" or "blank line" between scenes or above and below a stage direction. Where prose passages occur in uncrowded pages, "words are fully spelled out and openly spaced. When compression was necessary prose was set more closely and various abbreviations and contractions were occasionally used as well." But the same abbreviations "could also appreciably shorten a long line of verse, and the Folio is accordingly sprinkled, both in verse and in prose passages, with ampersands and with such substitutes as 'w^{c}' for 'which', 'y^{t}' for 'that', 'M^{r}' for 'Master', 'cā' for 'can', 'L.' for 'Lord', and so on—though these are not common in open pages."[9]

Although Moxon stigmatized such adjustments as "botches," Hinman judged them to be "harmless enough," because "they do not meddle with the text proper."[10] Other devices for gaining or—

especially—saving space, however, could be harmful. If expansion were needed, by setting one line of verse as two "a compositor could, quite literally, make ends meet. And conversely, when compression rather than padding out was needed, he could print two lines as one." Hinman cited a revealing instance from the Folio text of *Hamlet* "in a close-set page that contains no white lines at all and shows two turn-overs" of verse lines. The crucial point is the last line of the second column, where the compositor had to achieve his goal of fitting the text into the page and reaching the catchword "But." Then, yielding to "necessity," as Moxon would say, he condensed a line-and-a-half into one:

> To those of mine. But Vertue,as it neuer wil be moued,
> Though Lewdnesse court it in a shape of Heauen:
> So Lust, though to a radiant Angell link'd,
> Will sate it selfe in a Celestiallbed,& prey on Garbage.[11]

Hinman observed that, by replacing "and" with an ampersand "it was just possible to get the extra half-line into this full page without resorting to more drastic measures: the resetting of a little verse as prose, perhaps—or simply leaving something out." All who care about Shakespeare will be horrified at the thought of printers, having miscalculated how much text they could set within the cast-off copy, simply leaving something out. Hinman's comments are hardly reassuring: "there is abundant evidence that the amount of text that could be got comfortably into a page was frequently misjudged; and it would hardly be surprising if, in an already crowded page, something not considered essential were left out."[12]

Where only the Folio text survives, identifying omissions is speculative, as I have observed. The survival of a separate Quarto edition allows us to see that the Folio printers did indeed make omissions. In the opening scene of *Othello*, when Iago is recounting to Roderigo the reasons why he hates Othello (1.1.8–17), the Folio text "lacks after its fifteenth line, to the prejudice of both sense and grammar, the part-line 'And in conclusion' that appears in Q1."[13] The same miscalculation, Hinman added, might explain why "some of the verse that is printed as prose in the Folio also represents, not difficult marginal scribblings in the copy, but only another way of dealing with a space problem—of 'justifying', as it were, a page rather than a line."[14] We will find abundant instances of verse being set as prose, together with many other forms of space saving, in a number of Shakespeare play quartos, including *Lear*.

Hinman's subsequent study of the printing and proofreading of the Shakespeare First Folio was a landmark in bibliography and textual criticism. Where previous scholars had studied "the nature of the copy used by the printer," Hinman concentrated on the related but less discussed problem: "the kinds and amount of modification to which this copy was subject during the printing process itself."[15] His reconstruction of this process drew attention to some anomalies resulting from errors made in the printing office, such as the Folio treatment of *Much Ado about Nothing*, set from the 1600 Quarto. Hinman briefly noted the signs of severe space shortage on the final page of the play, where the need to accommodate the text into the last fifteen lines resulted in the severe compression of some prose passages.[16] All other Folio plays end with a decent-sized font setting the word "*FINIS*," sometimes accompanied by a type ornament, when space allowed. On this page, in painful contrast, "*FINIS*" is printed in smaller type than usual and crammed into the sixty-seventh line of the right-hand column, on the direction line with the signature.

Scholars have been slow to apply Hinman's findings, but one who did so was Eleanor Prosser, in a pioneering and little-known study. Having provided readers with a reproduction of this Folio page in reduced format, she analyzed the adjustments that the compositors had to make to rectify "a serious error in judgment" in casting off copy.[17] The left-hand column and part of the right consist of verse (5.3.33, 5.4.1–90), but already here Compositor C had to compress the text as best he could. At 5.4.33 (TLN 2587) he simply "deleted a line ('Heere comes the Prince and Claudio'); at 2633–34 [5.4.78–9] he turned verse that would have needed three lines of print space (one for an overrun) into two lines of prose." At 2639–41 (5.4.80–2), "to hold each long verse-line to one type-line . . . he deleted a word in each of three consecutive lines (*that*, *that*, and *such*)."[18] Compositor C also introduced several abbreviations, restricting Claudio's final speech (112–116) to four lines of prose by twice substituting superscript forms ("y^{u}" and "y^{t}"), once using a tilde ("questiō"), and including an entry not on a separate line but in the text, and in the briefest possible form: "*Enter. Mes.*" In addition to these "purposeful adjustments," as Prosser termed them, Compositor C added an ampersand to a speech by Beatrice (5.4.95; TLN 2655), although the gap in the last line shows that there would have been plenty of room for him to set "and." This is a phenomenon we shall meet elsewhere. I suggest that when setting a column or page of type a compositor had readied himself, so to speak, either for compression or expansion, adopting a mindset that he maintained throughout, at the risk of a few superfluous adjustments. This is an instance of a compositor having adopted what I would call the "compression mode" and carrying it through to the end, even though it was no longer needed.

Last-Minute Adjustments: *Romeo and Juliet* (1599) and *A Midsummer Night's Dream* (1600)

Two other Shakespeare Quartos show how printers accommodated within a given print space more text than had originally been expected by using expedients also found in the 1608 *Lear* Quarto. In the inauthentic 1597 Quarto of *Romeo and Juliet*, Mercutio's speech beginning "Ah then I see Queene Mab hath bin with you" is set in verse and runs to thirty-five lines (1.4.53–95).[19] In the authentic 1599 Quarto, "Newly corrected, augmented, and amended," as the title page claims, issued by Shakespeare's company, the Lord Chamberlain's Men, it runs to forty-three lines. It begins in verse, but at once lapses into densely set prose for thirty-seven lines, of which I quote the first six, adding vertical lines to mark the verse lineation[20]:

Mer. O then I see Queene Mab hath bin with you: |
She is the Fairies midwife,and she comes in | shape no bigger thē
an Agot stone, on the forefinger of an Alderman, | drawne with
a teeme of little ottamie,[21] | over mans noses as they lie asleep: | her
waggō spokes made of lōg spinners legs: | the couer,of the wings
of Grashoppers,her traces of the smallest spider web,her collors

The use of three tildes in the first few lines, an ampersand later on, and the general crowding of the typesetting show the constraints that the compositor experienced as he tried to cram the text into the space available. The rest of the page (C2r) continues to set verse as prose, but the continuation over the page reverts to verse:

> This is the hag,when maides lie on their backs,
> That presses them and learnes them first to beare,
> Making them of good carriage (C2v)

Mercutio's speech is not only wrongly set but it also has a confusing sequence of lines printed in the wrong order, as P. A. Daniel argued in 1875. In the first excerpt Mercutio describes the constituent parts of Mab's chariot—its wagon spokes, cover, traces (straps), collars, whips, lash, down to "her waggoner, a small grey coated Gnat"—without referring to the chariot itself. It subsequently makes its appearance, in three lines not found in the unauthorized 1597 Quarto, compressed into two lines of prose:

> A man.|Her Charriot is an emptie Hasel nut,|Made by the Ioyner
> Squirrel or old Grub,|time out amind,the Fairies Coatchmakers:|

The misplacing of these lines, together with other textual variants, suggests that the 1599 Quarto was printed directly from the manuscript, "with intermittent consultation of Q1 by the two Q2 compositors at certain points where Shakespeare's manuscript was damaged or illegible."[22] As Gwynne Evans argued, there are two possible explanations for this last-minute adjustment. Mercutio's speech begins on C2r, which occurs in the inner forme, along with C1v, C3v, and C4r. If the Quarto was being set seriatim (with the pages in reading order), then "the outer forme was already in type . . . and it would be time-consuming and expensive" to reset the whole of sheet C. Alternatively, if the compositor had "decided to set sheet C by formes," he may have begun

> with the outer forme, setting C1r, C2v, C3r and C4v.When he came to set the inner forme, he discovered that, in casting off

his copy for the outer forme, he had either miscounted or had failed to allow for marginal additions in the MS. in Mercutio's speech. Since, by the time he recognised his error, the outer forme (containing the last three-and-a-half verse lines of the speech at the top of C2v) was already printed off, or being printed off, he had either to cut the speech down to the 27 lines remaining to him on C2r or to set the 38 verse lines as prose. To his credit, he chose the second alternative.[23]

As several examples have shown, when space was short compositors could set verse as prose. Another expedient, which we have not yet encountered, was to adjust the verse lineation, running ten-syllable lines together so that they would take up less room. In the 1600 Quarto of *A Midsummer Night's Dream*, as John Dover Wilson first pointed out, there is a sequence of hypermetric verse lines at the beginning of Act 5 (5.1.1–22). In his transcript Wilson italicized the disarranged verse and inserted vertical strokes "to show where the lines should rightly end"[24]:

Enter Theseus, Hyppolita, *and* Philostrate.
Hip. Tis strange,my *Theseus*, that these louers speake of.
The. More straunge then true. I neuer may beleeue
These antique fables,nor these Fairy toyes.
Louers, and mad men haue such seething braines,
Such shaping phantasies, that apprehend | more,
Then coole reason euer comprehends.|The lunatick,
The louer, and the Poet | are of imagination all compact.|
One sees more diuels, then vast hell can holde:
That is the mad man. The louer, all as frantick,
Sees *Helens* beauty in a brow of *Ægypt.*
The Poets eye, in a fine frenzy, rolling,|doth glance
From heauen to earth, from earth to heauen. |And as
Imagination bodies forth|the formes of things
Vnknowne: the Poets penne | turnes them to shapes,
And giues to ayery nothing,|a locall habitation,
And a name.|Such trickes hath strong imagination,
That if it would but apprehend some ioy,

It comprehends some bringer of that ioy.
Or in the night, imagining some feare,
How easie is a bush suppos'd a Beare?

In the first draft it would seem that Shakespeare began with two examples of overactive fantasy, "Lovers" and "mad men," but subsequently added a third, "the Poet." He linked the three in the first sequence of italicized lines and invented the famous description of the poet's activity in the following sequence of six lines, reduced here to five-and-a-half. Dover Wilson pointed to six other mis-lined passages in Theseus's speech,[25] of which I select one, where Theseus reads over the titles of the entertainments offered by his master of the revels, Philostrate:

A tedious briefe Scene of young *Pyramus*
And his loue *Thisby;* very tragicall mirth?
Merry, and tragicall? Tedious, and briefe? | *That is hot Ise,*
And wōdrous strange snow.|*How shall we find the cōcord*
Of this discord? (5.1.56–60)

There the presence of two tildes in one verse line betrays the compositor's effort to accommodate text space to inadequate print space.

Dover Wilson noted that when the eight passages of "disarranged verse," amounting to twenty-nine lines, are "dissected out," then we are left with "fifty-five lines of regularly divided verse, which are complete in themselves both in sense and metre, and must clearly, at some stage in the history of the text, have stood by themselves and run continuously." These lines, "being written on the margin of the MS, in such space as could be found, they presented a problem in line-arrangement which the compositor was quite unable to solve," and thus he crammed them into the available space, in the process destroying the true lineation. Wilson believed that the inserted lines were "mature Shakespearian verse" and thus added at a later point than the first version of the play in the mid-1590s.[26] Although few scholars have accepted this theory, his explanation of the mis-lineation has been universally approved. W. W. Greg, the leading authority on textual matters for many years, hailed Wilson's explanation as "one of the most convincing inferences made by that brilliant critic," because once the "passages falsely divided, in which the lines of type bear no relation to those required by the verse" are omitted, "the remainder of the speech runs on consecutively and makes perfectly good sense." It follows that this "remainder" is "the speech as originally composed, and that the anomalous passages represent additions crowded into the margin of the manuscript without regard to metrical division. This is a bibliographical argument, and the conclusion may be accepted as tolerably certain."[27] Greg would not pronounce on Wilson's suggested dating because it fell outside the realm of bibliography, the study of observed characteristics of a printed book.

To Save a Half-Sheet: The Quartos of *1 Henry IV* (1598)

Where the printers of these two Shakespeare Quartos were able to accommodate text overlooked or added late, when printing the First Quarto editions of *1 Henry IV* (1598), Andrew Wise encountered the same overall length problem that Okes faced with *King* Lear. I refer to "editions" in the plural, because in the 1880s J. O. Halliwell discovered a hitherto unrecorded fragment of an earlier edition of the First Quarto "in the binding of a copy of Thomas's *Rules of the Italian Grammar*, 4to, 1567."[28] The fragment, now known as "Q0," consisting of four leaves of sig. C (corresponding to 1.3.201–2.2.111), was set in the same printing office responsible for Q1, and the adjustments that Wise made provide invaluable evidence of the lengths to which an Elizabethan printer could go to save paper.[29] As S. B. Hemingway summarized the evidence,

> Q0 was earlier than Q1. The typesetter of Q1 evidently had orders to save space when possible, in order to avoid the necessity of running into a new Signature. Q1 finishes, neatly, on K4, verso. Q0 must have, or would have, run into Sig. L. The typesetter of Q1 adds one line to each page-length. Further, he once runs two speeches into a single line (1.3.249–250), an instance of what W. W. Greg described as "continuous printing,"[30] thus saving a line; once, at the beginning of 2.1, he omits the "spacing before the initial stage-direction, thus saving another

> line; and twice (2.1.91–3; 2.2.29–31) he compresses three prose lines into two, thus saving two lines more. Altogether, in the portion of the play covered by this fragment, twelve lines are saved.[31]

To want to save 12 lines out of a total of 311 shows the solution of a printer in dealing with a "necessity," as Moxon would term it, one that we shall see again in the 1608 Quarto of *Lear.*

Wise's treatment of the text of *1 Henry IV* in his Q1 deployed a whole range of space-saving devices to save the half-sheet that he would otherwise have had to include, no light matter financially, considering the 500 or 750 copies he had contracted to print. As we have seen from Moxon's account of "the rules of good Workmanship," in the hand-press period compositors were expected to leave a space after each word and after each punctuation mark (our electronic age observes the same convention). Even a cursory glance at the original Quarto or its facsimile shows that Wise could not afford to observe these conventions. On every page the compositor squeezed lines together and omitted spacing after punctuation marks, in some cases as many as thirty-nine times on one page (sig. G3r), thirty-eight times on another (E3[r]), with further high scores of thirty such spaces omitted per page (G2v), 29 (I3r, K1v), 27 (E2v). By my count—which does not claim absolute accuracy—on the 78 pages of this Quarto, 1,200 necessary spaces were omitted, an average of more than 15 per page. To give an idea of the uncomfortable results of such compression, I quote a few examples, first from Hotspur:

> Of guns,and drums,and wounds,God save the mark: (B2v)
> drinke,but I tell you(my Lord foole)out of this nettle
> danger,we (C4v)
> And constant:a good plot,good friends,and ful of
> expectation:an (C4v)
> Away,away you trifler,loue,I loue thee not, (D1v)

Shakespeare's stylistic characterization of Hotspur, with his impatient, emphatic utterance, gave this compositor considerable trouble. Not having enough print space for the needed text space, the compositor was also typographically challenged by Hal's linguistic inventiveness ("Thou hast the most unsavoury similes,"[32] as Falstaff complains) and had to run together many of his abusive comparisons: "this . . . cristall button,not-pated,agat ring,puke stocking,Caddice garter,Smothe tongue," (D2v); "that reverent vice,that gray iniquity,that father ruffian,that vanity in years,wherein . . ." (E3r). Falstaff's wit also posed problems to a compositor trying to justify each line as economically as possible: "you tailers yard,you sheath,you bowcase,you vile standing tuck" (D4v). Unfortunately for Wise, his compositor's attempts to compress the text into the available print space sometimes resulted in an incoherent running together of words—"Balktintheir own bloud" (A3r), "ofswift Severns" (B3r), "sir:skore a" (D2r), "Marry myLo.there" (E1r), "offiery" (E4v), and "Thisinfant" (G1v)—desperate and ugly solutions that make one wonder whether the master printer checked his work. We will see the same feature in Okes's *Lear* Quarto, and no doubt many other printers faced this problem.

In early modern printing some space-saving adjustments, such as replacing "and" with an ampersand, were needed more often in prose. Because prose filled a wider measure, overrunning a line could have serious consequences for the rest of the page. Wise's compositor resorted to this device nine times in prose, in one instance twice in a line at the beginning of a new page: "worde,outfac't you from your prize& have it, yea&can shew" (sig. E1r).[33] He also used an ampersand in three cases where it may not have been needed, because the last line of each speech has plenty of space (E3v, G3v, K3v). These may be signs of him wanting to justify a line without dividing a word, but they may also be instances of the compression mode—a compositor's mindset that determines in advance his goal of saving space on all possible occasions. In setting verse each line had to be justified in a narrower column width, and in order to avoid turning a line over Wise's compositor again introduced ampersands, ungainly though they appear in verse:

> Three times they breathd & three times did
> they drinke (B3r)
> What? drunk with choler, stay, & pause a while (B3v)[34]
> Do so, & those musitions that shall play to you (F3r)[35]

These are all lengthy verse lines: in the Folio the last quoted is set as a line-and-a-half. At least by using this symbol the compositor avoided turn-overs, as he did on all but two occasions (K1v), the second of these being due to his having crammed one-and-a-half lines of verse into a single line of text. Another simple device, found only in the play's prose scenes, was to eliminate an *n* or *m* by placing a tilde over a vowel: "vpō" (B1v), "hāgman" (C2v), "proficiēt" (D3r), and "thē" (I3v). On one occasion—again, the beginning of a new page—this device occurs twice in one line: "the life of a mā:but to coūterfet dying" (sig. K3v). The compositor was evidently anxious to save space from the outset, even tolerating this ugly fusion of letters and punctuation marks. In the event, when he came to the end of Falstaff's speech, nine lines later, he had a half-line empty, but he could not have known that when he started the page.

A related space saver—printing numbers as digits, not letters—occurs mainly in prose: Mistress Quickly's "holland of viii.s. an ell" and a loan of "xxiiii pound" (G3r) and Falstaff's "this xxiii. Years" (C3r), his wish for "a fine thiefe of the age of xxii. or thereabouts" (G4v), and his gloating at having defrauded "the Kinges presse . . . I have got in exchange of 150. Soldiours 300. and odd poundes" (H2v). But the compositor also used this device in verse:

> *King.* Which 1400. years ago were naild (A2v)
>
> *Sher.* I will my Lord: there are two gentlemen
> Haue in this robbery lost 300. markes (E4r)

In both instances spelling the number in full would have meant a turn-over. In less crowded places the compositor could relax, setting "three hundred Markes" (C2v) and "three score and ten myles" (C3v) in prose passages, "ten thousand" (A3r) and "A hundred thousand" (G2v) in verse.

As mentioned earlier, the most effective space-saving device available to Wise and to other printers of play texts was to set verse as prose. In a scene written predominantly in verse, where the rebels quarrel over the division of the kingdom, the compositor prosified this exchange between Hotspur and Glendower, reducing ten lines of verse to eight of prose:

> *Hot.* Lord Mortimer,and coosen Glendower will you sit down? and Vncle Worcester,a plague vpon it I haue forgot the map.
> *Glendow.* No here it is;sit Coosen Percy, sitgood Coosen Hotspur,for by that nameas oft as Lancaster doth speakeof you, his cheekelookes pale,and with a rising sigh hee wisheth you in heauen.
> *Hot.* And you in hell, as oft as he heares Owen Glendower spoke of. (E4v1–8; 3.1.3–12)

This passage bears many of the marks of space saving that we will witness in the 1608 Quarto of *King Lear.* On five occasions the compositor omitted spacing after a comma or semi-colon. In Glendower's speech several words are run together without spacing, allowing the compositor to squeeze thirteen words into lines 4 and 5 of that excerpt. The fact that two lines are virtually empty shows that the desire to save space is a mindset that, once in place, can ignore local conditions. There would have been enough room to set these speeches with normal spacing. Pursuing the need to save space, the compositor reduced a speech by Mortimer (F1v; 106–110) from four lines of verse (Folio) to three lines of prose, and shrank one by Hotspur to the same amount (F3v; 247–50). By means of these cuts the compositor managed to save five lines in this scene—a trivial sum, no doubt, but in context they can be seen as essential to keeping each page within its allotted limits.

The arrangement of verse lines was a fruitful resource for compressing the text. Two half-lines could be set in one line, as in these instances:

> *North.* At Barkly castle. *Hot.* You say true (C1r)
> *Doug.* Yea or to night. *Ver.* Content. (H3v)

This was a useful device, also applicable in prose.[36] But in some cases the compositor's juggling with half-lines created confusion, as in this exchange between the king and Westmoreland, concerning Hotspur's defeat of Douglas:

> [*King.*] And is not this an honorable spoile?
> A gallant prize?Ha coosen,is it not? In faith it is.
> *West.* A conquest for a Prince to boast of. (A3r; 1.1.74–7)

There Westmoreland's response ("In faith it is") should have begun a fresh line, avoiding the apparent silliness of Henry both asking a question and answering it. Another instance of awkward space saving occurs in the great reconciliation scene between Hal and his father:

> *Prin.* I shall thereafter my thrice gratious Lord,
> Be more my selfe. *King.* For all the world,
> As thou art to this houre was Richard then . . . (G1r; 3.2.92–4)

It is somewhat undignified for any character, let alone a king, to start a thirty-six-line speech in the rear part of a verse.

In well-planned Elizabethan printing, stage directions were given a separate space to themselves, taking up one or more lines, with entries centered on the page and exits placed on the right-hand side. But in Wise's predicament—trying to fit a play text into no more than ten leaves—such a spacious treatment was a luxury he could not afford: stage directions had to rub shoulders with the text, whether prose or verse.[37] The visual effect, however, is often unpleasantly cramped, because the stage directions are squeezed in at the end of a line.[38] This is perhaps less objectionable in the case of exits, which are often dispatched to the extremity of the page, but there is something undignified in the compression of this line:

> *King.* Make vp to Clifton,ile to S.NicholasGawsey. *Exit Ki:*
> (K2v; 5.4.58)

Having been the speaker of the line, the king seems to be brusquely hurried off the stage. By Elizabethan printing conventions it was especially unpleasing to have entrances crammed into a line ending, an expedient that appears more frequently in the Quarto's later sheets.[39] At times the compositor placed the entrance out of sequence, as when Falstaff addresses Quickly before she is on stage:

> How now dame Partlet the hen,haue you enquird *Enter host.*
> yet who pickt my pocket? (G3r; 3.5.52–53)

Or in this even more awkward placement in verse:

> [*Wor.*] Therefore good coosen,let not Harry know
> In any case the offer ofthe King. *Enter Percy.*
> *Ver.* Deliuer what you will,ile say tis so.Here coms your coosen.
> *Hot.* My vncle is returnd (I4r; 5.224–27)

By compression, Wise's compositor succeeded in reducing Vernon's speech from two lines to one. He also occasionally managed to set two stage directions in the same line, if somewhat awkwardly:

> *Enter Chamberlaine.* *Exeunt.*
> *Gad.* What ho: Chamberlaine. (C2v; 2.1.47)

He did this again in the scene with Francis the Drawer (1042–1043), and for a crucial switch from high seriousness to Falstaff's witticism about his girth, he had to cram both directions in the margin:

> [*King.*] And God befriend vs as our cause is ivst. *Exeunt:manent*
> *Falst.* Hal,if thou see me downe in the Battel *Prince,Falst.*
> And bestride me,so,tis a poynt offriendship. (I3r; 5.1.120–122)

At least Wise achieved his goal of fitting *1 Henry IV* into ten leaves and saving himself some money. In setting his 1608 Quarto of *King Lear* Nicholas Okes found himself in the same predicament and used the same expedients to deal with it.

Desperate Measures: The Folio Text of *2 Henry IV*

The typographical adjustments that we saw in the Folio text of *Much Ado* dealt with a limited problem, fitting a surplus of text space over print space in the play's final page. Those needed for the Folio *2 Henry IV* were in response to a major estimating error, which landed Jaggard in the same kind of difficulty that Okes would face in 1608. As with *Lear*, a Quarto edition (1600) of *2 Henry IV* had preceded the Folio; in both cases Jaggard seems to have worked from a manuscript transcript of the theater company's Booke. In the chronological order chosen by Heminge and Condell, *2 Henry IV* follows *Richard II* and *1 Henry IV*. In examining the signatures of this section of the Histories Charlton Hinman uncovered evidence of some last-minute alterations.[40] Each of the three genres represented in the Folio is separately signed. The signature "A" is given to Comedy, "a" to History, and "aa" to Tragedy: each signature is separately foliated and each genre section consecutively paginated, but there are many irregularities.[41] Within the Histories sequence *2 Henry IV* begins at the verso of f6 (74) and continues regularly to the verso of g6 (86). But at this point the printer intercalated an additional quire (signed "gg"), comprising eight leaves as opposed to the normal six, and paginated confusingly ("87–88, 91–92, 91–100"). This anomalous quire, however, turned out to be a shade too long to accommodate the rest of this play, resulting in the text of *2 Henry IV* ending on the verso of leaf 7. To fill the last unnumbered page Jaggard set in large type on the recto (gg8r) an Epilogue, not found in the 1600 Quarto but evidently still present in the company's Booke, and on the verso (gg8v) he added a list of characters.[42] Hinman judged this expedient to be "both atypical and wholly unnecessary," but it successfully filled the eighth leaf "with additional matter, lest it present the reader with nothing but two blank pages."[43] The next Folio play, *Henry V*, restores the sequence, occupying signatures h1r–k2r, but is also untidily paginated ("69–95"). Hinman suggested that "there were almost certainly copyright difficulties over *Richard II* and the two parts of *Henry IV*" and that printing had proceeded "while these difficulties were being ironed out." But in the process Jaggard and his staff made a serious miscalculation, underestimating "the number of leaves that would eventually be needed between already-printed quires c and h," for it turned out that something more than one ordinary quire would be needed for what remained of *2 Henry IV*; hence the anomaly of "an eight-leaf quire."[44] Hinman's tentative reconstruction of the printing of this abnormal quire revealed several unusual features in the workmanship, including the presence of three compositors. The casting off was made more difficult by the high proportion of prose in *2 Henry IV*, as in the other Falstaff plays. The printer's miscalculation led to his use of what Hinman judged (somewhat austerely) to be "such merely ornamental matter as an epilogue and a table of 'The Actors Names.'"[45]

Eleanor Prosser was the first literary critic to draw on Hinman's work in her important and underrated study of the Folio's treatment of *2 Henry IV*, which includes many illuminating insights into the relation between text space and print space. When Jaggard and his compositors set *The Tempest*, the first play in the volume, Prosser observed, they "had not yet settled on certain conventions that were later to require allotting additional lines for certain kinds of stage directions and speeches." In consequence, "[t]he text of *The Tempest* is mercilessly cramped. Only four of the thirty internal entrances are spaced; in plays set thereafter, they are usually allotted one or two blank lines. Two speakers are placed on one line eight times and ten entrances are crammed to the right of the dialogue; thereafter, these appear to be largely emergency measures. None of the songs is set off with blank space; thereafter they usually are." In plays set after *The Tempest* occasional "tight" settings reflect local problems caused by mistakes in calculating the number of lines needed for a page, but "page-by-page miscalculation cannot . . . account for the extreme pressure under which B was working in the first half of quire g in *2 Henry IV*."[46] Prosser identified the four pages where Compositor B had to "accommodate far more copy than normal" (sigs. g1v, g2r, g2v, g3r) and estimated that on g3r the casting-off process "allotted a minimum of thirteen lines more than customary."[47] Even a cursory glance at the Folio text in the first half of the quire shows densely packed type, scene headings reduced to a minimum, and the six columns of prose dialogue filling virtually every line to the margin. By contrast, setting in the second half of the quire is "open," with a generous amount of space for the scene headings and stage directions, while the dialogue seems to breathe more easily.

Having established the effects of space shortages on typesetting elsewhere in the Folio, Prosser analyzed in considerable detail the effect on *2 Henry IV* of the disturbances in the printing sequence that Hinman had documented. She suggested that the initial error, necessitating the insertion of an additional quire, was due to someone having "momentarily forgotten that nine pages of *Richard II* remained to be completed." In addition, Jaggard and his staff, not having realized that *2 Henry IV* is a "very long play," had used space liberally on the preceding play, the shorter *1 Henry IV* and "even seem to have wasted it," perhaps knowing that an extra quire had already been allocated.[48] It may also be that their initial calculations of the length of *Part 2* had been based on the 1600 Quarto, from which 157 lines had been cut for political reasons, censoring Shakespeare's presentation of the rebels' grievances from their point of view.[49] Such cuts would not have been deleted from the playhouse Booke, a transcript of which may have become available later, serving as copy for the Folio text. Whatever the cause of the error, the result was that Compositor B had to deploy a whole range of devices to compress the text. I only summarize here those findings that will prove relevant to the 1608 Quarto of *Lear*, but Prosser's keen eye for what I have called the dynamics of typesetting—the moment-by-moment interaction between the compositor and the text that he must fit into a given space—makes her book necessary reading for everyone concerned with what became of Shakespeare's plays at the printers.[50]

Having cast off copy, the two compositors setting the Folio *2 Henry IV* would have started work in the middle of the additional quire. As Peter Blayney observed, either workman may have set the sixth page (g3v), but thereafter B set the fifth page (g3r) and worked backward to the first (g1r), while A set the seventh page (g4r) and worked forward to the twelfth and last (g6v). Prosser chose to consider the pages in reading order, the order in which they were cast off, and noted "the first signs of pressure" on g1v, where the scene heading is compressed, as are the stage directions, but where there is otherwise "no place where B could have held his type-lines to fewer than normal."[51] But she failed to notice that, after Northumberland's nihilistic desire for chaos—"Let Order die," with its magnificent peroration, "And darknesse be the burier of the dead"—a one-line speech was omitted: "This strained passion doth you wrong my lord" (1.2.161). This may have been an accidental omission, but Compositor B might have felt that this little speech would not be missed. If so, that was an easy remedy compared to what awaited him on g2r, where he had to resort to "extraordinary measures" to compress the text, beginning with the battle of wits between Falstaff and the Lord Chief Justice (1.2.75–230; TLN 348–479). Prosser observed that, "when adjusting to compensate for local miscalculation, compositors usually concentrated their efforts at or near the end of the right column, when the excessive amount of copy became apparent." On this page, however, "B's consistent compression throughout both columns indicates his awareness from the beginning that he must be alert to every opportunity."[52] (The same awareness from the outset of the urgent need to save space is seen in Okes's *Lear* Quarto.) B could save some space "by legitimate means," as in this piece of repartee:

> *Fal.* My Lord? (Wolfe.
> *Iust.* But since all is wel,keep it so: wake not a sleeping 416
> *Fal.* To wake a Wolfe, is as bad as to smell a Fox.
> *Iu.* What?you are as a candle,the better part burnt out 418
> *Fal.* A Wassell-Candle, my Lord;all Tallow : if I did
> say of wax, my growth would approue the truth.
>
> (1.2.152–158; TLN 415–420)

As Prosser pointed out, "At 416 Compositor B held to one line by tightening spacing and using a turn-up. At 418 he held to one line by using a shortened prefix and omitting the spaces that would normally follow the prefix and the question mark. (Here, as elsewhere, even the period had to be sacrificed.) In a normal setting he would have run the word *out* onto a second line."[53]

Compositor B used other standard typographical devices, all of which recur frequently in the Folio, to save space on this page. He replaced *and* by "the ampersand—which he uses almost solely when he is compressing or justifying a long line."[54] Whatever his norm, B used the ampersand eleven times between g2r and g4r, perhaps the most frequent usage in the Folio.[55] On g3r, instead of the standard practice of setting entrances on a separate line, on three occasions "he set all of the entrances to the right of short lines (at 648, 665, and 729). In addition, he twice set two brief speeches on one line (661 and 675). All three of these measures had been reserved almost exclusively for emergencies since the setting of *The Tempest*," but now Moxon's "necessity" called for them.[56] Like other compositors, B saved space by shortening a word's spelling from that found in the Quarto, simply removing one letter: "biterness(e)," "gal(l)s," "wil(l)," "cal(l)," or reducing "Lord" to "L." He abridged other words by omitting a consonant and setting a tilde over the preceding vowel: "cānot" (404), "remēbred" (723). He frequently omitted spaces after question marks, after commas, and between words. He abbreviated speech prefixes, reducing "*Snare*" to "*Sna.*" Compositor B also reduced "pray you" to "pra'ye" and "familiarity" to "familiar"—ruining one of Mistress Quickly's malapropisms—and three times substituted "y^{u}" for "you" (695, 698, 703). Even Prince Hal had a "thou" reduced to "y^{u}" (g3^{v}; TLN 806), in a speech where the compositor felt obliged to leave out several lines. In the following passage the Folio omits everything in italics:

> the rest of [thy] Low Countries haue [made a shift to] eate vp thy Holland; *and God knows whether those that bal out the ruines of thy linnen shal inherite his kingdom: but the Midwiues say, the children are not in the fault wherevpon the world increases, and kinreds are mightily strengthened.* (C4r; 2.2.22–27)[57]

Those cuts may not damage the play as a whole, but it is nonetheless disturbing that a compositor felt authorized to make such an omission. Compositor B twice saved space by using numerals: "A 100. Marke" (642), and "30.s" (703). These space-saving devices are clustered in the first half of quire g and occur seldom thereafter.[58] Such small omissions would, of course, be pointless if their purpose had been to reduce a play's performance time, but they are easily understandable in terms of the compositor's perennial problem: how to fit a text into the space available, exacerbated by a major error in casting off. These may seem trivial adjustments to the text in the cause of saving space, but, as Francis Bacon observed of household economics, "thc provcrb is true that 'light gains make heavy purses.'"[59] In the printing trade, many small omissions allowed the compositor to fit the text into the available space and perhaps alleviated the need for a few larger cuts.

But in the case of 2 *Henry IV* these devices did not suffice, and compositor B was forced to frequently tamper with Shakespeare's text. Prosser pointed out that, on g2r, "only twenty lines into the left column, we find evidence that, under exceptional pressure, B would even revise his copy or make deletions. None of the changes we shall note is characteristic of the scribe; none is an improvement, reflecting authorial revision": each represents an intervention by the compositor.[60] In the battle of wits between Falstaff and the Lord Chief Justice, Compositor B omitted words and whole phrases to save space, of which I give a selection, italicizing the omissions:

Q your lordship, though not clean past your youth,haue yet
some smack of *an ague*in you,some relish of the saltnes of time
in you,and (B2v; 1.2.96–9)

F Your Lordship (though not clean past
your youth) hath yet some smack of *age* in you: some rel-
lish of the saltnesse of Time, and (TLN 368–70)

The Folio compositor succeeded in limiting that speech to seven lines by deleting Falstaff's teasing repetition of "*in you*" and by revising his mischievous diagnosis of his opponent's imputed illness (an ague implying unseemly twitching) to the anodyne "age."

Q Well, God mend him. I pray *you* let me speak with
you. (B2v; 1.2.109–110)

(you.
F Well, heauen mend him. I pray let me speak with
(TLN 380)

Having dutifully replaced "God" with "heauen," B omitted the first "you" but was forced to turn up its repetition into the line above, an unusual resort in prose, but one that we will frequently find in the Quarto of *King Lear.* Prosser commented on this device: "Given the compositors' reluctance to use a two-word turn-up (they are very rare in the Folio) and the evidence of pressure throughout the page, it is highly probable that the deletion of *you* was a conscious device to hold the speech to one line."[61]

In the following examples, by removing Falstaff's impudent mock courtesy and a repetition, Compositor B avoided the overrun of the speech to a third line:

> Q This appoplexi as I take it?is a kind of lethergie,*and't please your lordship,a kind of* sleeping in the bloud, a horson tingling.
>
> (B2v; 1.2.110–113)
>
> F This Apoplexie is(as I take it)a kind of Lethar-
> gie, a sleeping in the bloud, a horson Tingling.
>
> (TLN 381–382)

The space constraints are clearly visible in the next examples. Despite reducing "*doe become*" to "*be*" and substituting an ampersand, the Folio compositor had no room for a full stop after "Physitian":

> Q and I care not if I *doe become* your phisitian.
>
> (B3r; 1.2.145–146)
>
> F & I care not if I be your Physitian (TLN 393)

While the Quarto reproduces the Lord Chief Justice's word-play on "double" and "single," the Folio compositor lacked space for it, and also cut the intensive form "yet," meaning "still":

> Q is not your voice broken, your winde short, *your chinne double*, your wit single . . . And will you *yet* call yourselfe yong?
>
> (B3v; 1.2.182–185)
>
> F Is not your voice broken? your winde short?your wit single? . . . and wil you cal your selfe yong?
>
> (TLN 442–444)

In all these instances Prosser painstakingly reconstructed the physical context on the Folio page to show how the compositor's adjustments, even of just one word, prevented him from overrunning. But the "excessive amount of copy" that the cast-off process had "consciously allotted" to g2r—"a minimum of eleven excess lines and perhaps, if pressures of space were responsible for the long cut, as many as seventeen or eighteen"—forced B into taking what Hinman called drastic measures.[62] For example, as the Chief Justice denounces him as a pretender to youth who is in fact "blasted with antiquitie," Shakespeare gives Falstaff this immortal *apologia pro vita sua:*

> Q My Lorde, I was borne *about three of the clocke in the afternoone*, with a white head, and something a round bellie
> (B3v; 1.2.187–189)
>
> F My Lord, I was borne with a white head & som-
> thing a round belly. (TLN 445–446)

The loss of that wonderfully irrelevant detail makes us grateful that the Quarto of 2 *Henry IV* has survived. But worse is to come. In Prosser's words, "at this point, B was into the final half of the right-hand column [of g2r] and apparently getting desperate," with Falstaff in full flow. So Jaggard's compositor abruptly silenced Sir John, as he embarked on another priceless claim to virtuous heroism. The Folio omitted all the words in italics:

> there is not a dangerous action can peepe out his head but I am thrust vpon it. Wel, I cannot last euer, *but it was alway yet the tricke of our English nation, if they haue a good thing, to make it too common. If yee will needs say I am an olde man, you should giue me rest: I would to God my name were not so terrible to the enemy as it is, I were better to be eaten to death with a rust,than to be scoured to nothing with perpetuall motion.*
> (B4r; 1.2.214–220; TLN 468–469)

As Prosser pointed out, "The cut occurs only ten lines from the bottom of g2r, and in the last ten lines there is no good opportunity to compress. B may simply have thrown up his hands."[63] Modern readers may do the same, in shock and horror at his omission.

Compositor B removed another distinctive piece of Shakespearian wit in their next encounter, where the Chief Justice gives judgment in the cause of Quickly vs. Falstaff:

> Q you *haue as it appeares to me* practisde vpon the
> easie yielding spirite of this woman, *and made her serue your*
> *vses both in purse and in person.* (C2v; 2.1.114–116)
>
> F I know you ha' pra-
> ctis'd vpon the easie-yeelding spirit of this woman.
> (TLN 714–715)

B saved space by reducing *haue* to *ha'* (although a leading legal figure would hardly use such a colloquialism) and left out two phrases, amounting to seventeen words, thereby depriving the Lord Chief Justice of another spritely piece of word play. But at this point on g3r, "B was approaching the end of the page. Both deletions enabled him to avoid using two lines."[64] But of course B was probably not acting alone. As Hinman observed, "Shakespeare's text may sometimes have been tampered with by other persons than compositors."[65] The crisis resulting from this miscalculation in the Histories demanded solutions far beyond Compositor B's responsibility. The approval of Jaggard, and perhaps of others in the stationers' syndicate, would have been needed to authorize inserting a quire of eight leaves, a considerable expense in a print run of 700 to 800 copies.[66] In general, when faced with such miscalculations, Jaggard or a subordinate would probably have been on hand to supervise the necessary adjustments.

Eleanor Prosser's penetrating account of the shifts to which a compositor could be reduced by an error in casting off copy should be required reading for all who care about "the integrity of Shakespeare's text."[67] One aspect of her discussion is particularly relevant to how Okes treated *Lear* in 1607–1608, namely the Folio's attitude toward verbal repetition. We have seen how Compositor B dealt with Falstaff's ingratiating repetitions: unfortunately for him and his fellow compositor ("A," as he is known), the second part of *Henry IV* includes two other notably garrulous characters, Mistress Quickly and Justice Shallow. When "Our Hostesse of the Tauerne," as the Quarto calls her, tries to bring Falstaff to a long overdue reckoning, her flow of words contained one repetition too many for Compositor B:

> Q I haue borne,and borne,and borne,and haue bin fubd off, and fubd off, *and fubd off*, from this day to that day
> (C1v; 2.1.33–35; TLN 643–645)

In this passage B could simply omit one of Quickly's iterations without great loss, but subsequently we find him putting some uncharacteristic wording into her mouth, as she responds to Falstaff's rude dismissal, "throw the queane in the channell":

> Q Throw me in the channell? Ile throw thee *in the channel*,
> (C2r; 2.1.48–49)
> F Throw me in the channell? Ile throw thee there.
> (TLN 656)

As Prosser noted, "by the substitution of a logical *there* for the second *in the channel* . . . B prevented the Hostess's speech from running to six lines."[68] But when was Quickly ever logical?

Readers who know 2 *Henry IV* from the standard editions, which—like most versions since the eighteenth century—are based on the fuller text preserved in the 1600 Quarto, will be surprised and perhaps shocked by the liberties taken by the Folio and may well wonder who was ultimately responsible. Prosser divided her path-breaking analysis into two parts: "Textual Changes by the Folio Compositors" and "Textual Changes by the Scribe."[69] For the former, no one can doubt that she has brilliantly reconstructed the dynamics of typesetting, as the compositors strove to compress too much copy into the available space.[70] For the latter, however, some scholars might feel that to credit "the scribe" with such a wide range of responsibility for textual changes is to give him a far greater role than we normally associate with a penman. The changes were certainly made with a pen before typesetting began, but their extent suggests that the person who made them should rather be called an editor, having the functions sometimes exercised by modern editors, not only making the text conform to a printer's habitual practices but also making alterations to the author's style (as Maxwell Perkins did for Hemingway). Someone other than the compositor, probably Isaac Jaggard, must have taken responsibility for the major decisions needed to compensate for the gross miscalculation of the number of pages needed for the two parts of *Henry IV.* I imagine that the compositor alone would hardly have omitted so many lines, both of prose and verse, without other authority or approval.

The editor's role emerges more clearly in the later part of the play. Once the two compositors (B now having been joined by A) could begin setting type on the additional, intercalated quire gg, their need to save space vanished. But, ironically enough, they now faced the opposite problem, for the eight-leaf quire offered more space than they needed, and Prosser itemized in admirable detail the devices they used to expand copy at every opportunity.[71] These included inserting more blank space in scene headings and stage directions, using longer spelling, expanding speech prefixes, enlarging "M" to "Maister," adding punctuation, and substituting "a reasonably comparable but longer synonym (*had'st* for *wert*)." Compositor B also "expanded verse copy by the simple expedient of dividing one line into two" and showed considerable skill in dividing up lines of prose "at every possible opportunity" or even setting them as "pseudo-verse." Altogether, by these methods "B stretched his copy so that it takes fifteen type-lines more than it would normally require." Finally, Prosser argued, it was Compositor B who "resorted to one last desperate measure: adding words." Prosser suggested that Compositor B "inserted words or brief phrases merely to expand the given sentences of the Folio copy," but when operating "under extreme pressure . . . he occasionally resorted to adding longer phrases and even lines entirely of his own invention." The instances she cited have not convinced all textual scholars, but her evidence seems to me to rule out authorial revision.[72] I would instead argue that it was "the scribe" or editor who made these changes, but the modern reader needs to register the rather chastening implications of the attitudes that Jaggard and other printers took to Shakespeare's text. For us it is a precious substance of which we would not lose an iota, but in the early modern printing office the text of Shakespeare, or of any other writer, was a flcxiblc or plastic commodity, which the compositor and editor could expand or compress as need arose, so that it was liable to suffer omissions and even insertions by a foreign hand.

Given the complete change of direction with the intercalated quire, from the "compression" to the "expansion" mode, it is strange to find in printing the remaining parts of the text that substantial deletions continued to be made. Here we can see enough evidence of an editorial hand to enable us to question his reasons for cutting Shakespeare's text. In the second tavern scene, one motive was apparently to remove impropriety, for the Folio deprives Doll Tearsheet of her abusive reply to Falstaff's jest about bent pikes, sieges, and "charged chambers," omitting "*Hang your selfe, you muddie Cunger, hang your selfe*" (D3r; 2.4.53–54). Despite having allowed Falstaff's earlier wordplay, the Folio editor cut off his extension of it: "*No more Pistol, I would not haue you go off here, discharge your selfe of our company, Pistoll*" (D4r; 136–137). As for Doll's memorable comment on current semantic usage, the Folio removed all hint of innuendo:

> Q a captaine?Gods light these villaines will make the word *as* odious *as the word occupy, which was an excellent good worde before it was il sorted*
>
> (D4v; 2.4.147–50)
>
> F A Captaine? These Villaines will make the word Captaine odious
>
> (TLN 1171–1172)

That demure version destroys the whole point of her joke. Evidently someone in the house of Jaggard decided that such impropriety was unsuitable for a reading edition of Shakespeare.

A similar consideration may have applied to Shakespeare's use of verbal repetition to characterize Mistress Quickly and Justice Shallow. Here impropriety was not the issue; rather, I suggest, it was a question of the degree to which readers would put up with repetition on the printed page. Although verbal repetition is frequent in other Folio plays, Jaggard's editor of 2 *Henry IV* may have thought that this degree of "linguistic surplus," however acceptable on stage and however accurately it represented the way people speak in everyday life, was just too much for the reading public for whom this expensive volume was produced. His omissions in quire g eliminated one memorably vivid detail:

> O runne Doll, runne runne good Doll, *come, she comes blubberd, yea!will you come Doll?* (E3v; 2.4.389–391; TLN 1418)

Although more than enough space was available in quire gg, where the compositors were struggling to fill the page, the Folio edited the 1600 Quarto, set from Shakespeare's manuscript, so as to abbreviate the equally wordy (if senile, rather than garrulous) Justice Shallow. His doddering repetitions suffered the same fate, losing all the italicized words:

> giue me your *good* hand, giue me your worshippes good hand (E6v; 3.2.82–3; TLN 1617–18)
>
> Let me see, let me see, so,so,so,so,*so (so,so)* yea marry sir (E4v; 97–8; TLN 1632–1633)
>
> That we haue, that we haue, *that we haue*, in faith sir Iohn we haue (F2r; 216–217; TLN 1751–1752)
>
> Dauy, Dauy, Dauy, Dauy, let me see Dauy, let me see, *yea mary*[73] (I3r; 5.1.9–10; TLN 2796)
>
> come, come, *come*, off with your boots (I3v; 54; TLN 2844)

Allowing these repetitions to stand would have eased the compositors' task of dealing with an unexpected surplus of space, but the editor—or "scribe, in Prosser's terminology, must have felt that Shallow's repetitions were "excessive—an offense against decorum."[74] Alas, his sense of linguistic decorum was not Shakespeare's, a sad fact that must often be acknowledged as we examine the Folio editors' treatment of his text. Here, as a further distortion, the editor was cutting while B was trying to expand the text. As Prosser remarked in connection with their varying treatment of lineation, "the scribe and the compositor were working at cross purposes.”[75] Some readers may feel that not much is lost by reducing the garrulity of Quickly or Shallow—other, that is, than thc printcr’s notional goal of faithfully reproducing an author’s words.[76]

All the alterations made by Compositor B that we have reviewed so far have been purposeful, designed either to prevent a speech running over into an additional line or to fill as much space as possible. Some of his adjustments, however, seem to accomplish nothing. Eleanor Prosser itemized the devices he used in “stretching his copy” in the later pages of quire gg. In one instance he expanded the normal speech prefix “*Falst.*” to “*Falstaffe*” and added the Christian name “Robert” in the text to the Quarto’s “Shallow,” making a double change where, in fact, the former would have sufficed to fill the space. Prosser commented that this “may be one of several added words we find in B’s settings that do not facilitate using extra lines,” without reflecting on its cause.[77] It seems to me that this is another instance of the “compression mode” being carried through after it was no longer needed. On signature g3r of 2 *Henry IV*, for instance, where Compositor B needed to save space in Mistress Quickly’s long speech recalling the exact place and time when Falstaff “didst sweare . . . to marry me,” he three times replaced “thou” with the superscript form “y^{u}” (TLN 695, 698, 703). On the verso of that page, in Hal’s self-critical speech deploring his friendship with Poins, at line 806 Compositor B resorted to the superscript form “y^{u}” even though he had in fact plenty of space, since the final words of that speech fill less than half the line (813). Similarly, while Compositor B purposefully used the ampersand on g3r to enable him to complete a speech without overrunning into the next line (688, 719), in one of Falstaff’s impudent speeches to the Lord Chief Justice, Compositor B twice used the ampersand (TLN 706, 707) when there would have been no need, as he himself may have realized when he set the final words, with almost a half-line unfilled. We will see the same phenomenon—space-saving adjustments being made that turn out not to have been needed—when we examine the 1608 Quarto of *Lear*.

Different Author, Same Problems

Lest readers think that Shakespeare was singled out for special treatment by his printers, I add a few examples from another dramatist whose texts suffered the same fate. Ben Jonson's literary output was considerable, spanning a career longer than Shakespeare's and involving many more printers, with whom he had a closer relationship. Recent research has confirmed the traditional picture of Jonson intervening in the printing house to read proof and make corrections, but many decisions were those of the printer alone. In 1600 the stationer William Holme published *The Comicall Satyre of Every Man out of His Humor*, a quarto consisting of seventeen sheets, far longer than the average play text. Its popularity allowed Holme to reissue it by the end of 1600, printed by Peter Short, who reduced it to sixteen sheets, as W. W. Greg first showed.[78] Two compositors were used, dividing the original text in the middle of sheet (I2 / I3), which meant that "each then had to save two leaves, or four pages, in resetting." Compositor A had the easier task, since Q1 had a blank leaf at the beginning, on which he could set the title, and he managed to compress the next four pages of the original into three. He then "adopted a page of 37 lines in place of the original, with the result that by the end of his sheet E . . . he had saved exactly 36 lines, or one page of the original, and had come into agreement with his copy. He now quietly dropped his extra line, reducing his page to 36, and followed the original page for page to the end of his section."[79] Compositor B had to save "three pages of text on a total of 67," but "did not lengthen his page as A had done." Greg pointed out that the two pages forming the first opening of his section, I3v and I4r, were already 37 lines long" and suspected that the compositor "failed to notice that they were exceptional: 38 lines would probably have made the page inconveniently long."[80] As we shall see, Nicholas Okes used that page length for *Lear*, perhaps already looking to save space, and twice expanded it to thirty-nine lines. (So far as I know, no comparative study of quarto line lengths has been made.)

A brief comparison of the two editions of *The Comicall Satyre of Every Man out of His Humor* confirms the methods widely used to save space. Throughout his section Compositor B "set close," as Moxon would call it, removing the white space above and below act and scene headings and stage directions. He reduced spacing between words and after punctuation marks, often saving a line in the process. He systematically relined prose speeches, but in some cases failed to save space.[81] He reset stage directions into the text (see, e.g., I3v, L3r, M1r) and regularly turned the last word of a line up or down. He retained ampersands and words abbreviated with a tilde and occasionally resorted to the same contractions.[82] He used shorter spellings, "he" for "hee" and "bear" for "beare" (K4r), but did so inconsistently, preferring "dogge" for "dog" and "bee" for "be" and adding an "e" to "trauails" (L2r). In the same speech he reduced "beene" to "ben," used a tilde, but also expanded "mary" to "marry" and "be" to "bee" (L4v). None of these changes is as drastic as those made by Okes, but Peter Short had a much simpler task, for his compositors had set from printed copy, generously spaced, and produced an "astonishingly exact" reprint. Greg, having noted that "Compositor A began working with minute accuracy, but grew slightly less careful as he proceeded; B is on the whole even more faithful," expressed his "complete surprise . . . to find Elizabethan compositors working with such fidelity as this."[83] Would that Nicholas Okes had had such good workmen.

Scholarly work on Jonson's text received an enormous boost with the publication of the new Cambridge edition, both as a seven-volume print edition and in more extensive online form, which contains textual essays to the plays and poems.[84] *Eastward Hoe!* (1605) also enjoyed instant popularity, for George Eld printed three quartos between September 1605 and March 1606. Here again a Jacobean printer took the opportunity to reduce expense, reducing the first quarto from nine sheets to eight "through various devices of compression and by increasing the length of the page."[85] This Quarto contains some unusual features, caused by censorship rather than the need to save space. In the first issue of Q1 four pages (E3r–E4v) had to be canceled and replaced with a half-sheet insert, probably "a hurried and inadequate attempt to eliminate dangerous material in the course of printing." The printer also reset three pages, leaving notable blank spaces, and in one speech "prose lines are set as 'verse' to fill space," an expedient seen in the First Folio and elsewhere. The page length is 39 lines, but in two cases, where "the central topic is the affairs of the court," it is reduced to 37 and 35 lines, a sign of other cuts. According to Suzanne Gossett, the most unusual feature is that Q1 *Eastward Hoe!* seems not to have been printed from cast-off copy: "even if necessary estimates were made, the play was set seriatim," for "formes and gatherings end in mid phrase and mid word. Signature A ends 'steele in-' and Signature B begins 'strument'; Signature B ends 'ope the' and Signature C begins 'dores'; Signature E ends 'I'll be' and Signature F begins 'sworne,'" and so on. She comments, "No printer would cast off to the middle of a word or the middle of a phrase, so poor casting off alone cannot explain what happened to Signatures A and C. In fact, because A4v is one of the pages with a lot of white space but still ends with a divided word, it seems almost certain that something was removed after the pages were laid out."[86] As Peter Blayney showed, for Okes the advantage of seriatim setting was that he could keep his options open until "the time of imposition, when eight galleyfulls of type (each containing a number of stickfulls of type rather than a necessarily-exact number of lines) were arranged as eight 38-line pages."[87] Perhaps Eld similarly opted for the open-ended nature of seriatim setting because he expected some trouble from the authorities and could make deletions as required without ruining his whole layout. But, curiously enough, the same phenomenon recurred with *Bartholomew Fair*, performed in 1614 but not printed until 1631, as John Creaser has observed.[88]

Many of these last-minute alterations are only visible to scholars collating copies of the original editions, but one instance—the use of smaller type—is instantly noticeable. The Quarto of *Sejanus* (1605) was printed by George Eld, who did a heroic job in applying to a vernacular composition the apparatus of a humanist Latin edition, replete with "detailed and copious marginalia (there are just over three hundred Latin notes), and passages within the main text that set out to reproduce Roman inscriptional style." (Tom Cain noted that this was the first, and last, time that an English play was treated in this manner.[89]) Jonson prefixed to the play an *Argument* summarizing the action, ending with a pungent account of how Tiberius manipulates Sejanus into complacent enjoyment of his rise to power until, by means of "a long doubtful letter, in one day hath him suspected, accused, condemned, and torn in pieces by the rage of the people." In something of an anticlimax to that devastating conclusion, Jonson, a known Catholic, added a paragraph about the heavens' inescapable punishment of "all traitors and treasons," apparently to anticipate accusations of disloyalty in the aftermath of the Gunpowder Plot. The addition brought Eld into difficulty. The *Argument* occurs on A4, confirming Cain's suggestion that "[a] inner was one of the last formes to be printed," which meant that Eld "had not only already cast off copy, but was probably well on with a printing sequence that had begun with the following page, B1. Thus, the late addition of this paragraph forced Eld to the drastic step of setting the original text of the *Argument* in much smaller, long primer type, as opposed to the Roman pica used for most of Sejanus."[90]

In another Jonson quarto, *The Masque of Queenes* (1609), printed by Nicholas Okes, smaller type had been anticipated for the side notes in which Jonson listed his sources and explained philological significances. Unfortunately, as Mark Bland has shown, "a wrong assumption had been made about the size of the side notes, with the result that they occupied much less room than was expected." On three pages (B2r, B3v, B4r) there are large expanses of empty space, "pigeon holes" as Moxon called them, a glaring error. But their presence allowed Bland to deduce that the masque must have been set by formes and that the compositor must have set and corrected the outer forme of sheet B before he began work on the inner. "It was only when the compositor began to set the sidenotes for B that the error would have become obvious, and for the same reason: the text had to be spaced generously for B3v and B4r as well. These blocks of space had to be put in place and they were the only way in which the compositor could have corrected his error."[91] Again we see that in the hand-press period, in order to produce empty space, three-dimensional material objects were needed.

This chapter has shown how early modern printers reacted to a discrepancy between text space and print space by adjusting the former. Miscalculations or late additions turned the print space into a Procrustean bed on which the plays had to be trimmed down to fit. This phenomenon has been sporadically noticed by individual scholars, but by bringing these examples together I hope to have established that the remedies taken by Nicholas Okes, when he found himself in difficulties, were all regularly used by Elizabethan and Jacobean printers, if not in the quantity he employed.

3

Nicholas Okes Compresses the Play

THE EVIDENCE THAT we have seen of space problems experienced by the printers of six Shakespeare Quartos, together with the Folio, concerned texts that had already been prepared for printing. The exception was Q1 of *1 Henry IV*, which had been preceded by the sheet "Q0," in which Andrew Wise thought it worthwhile to make hundreds of corrections in order to reduce the paper consumed from ten and a half sheets to ten. The relation between labor costs and materials in early modern printing was clearly significant, and it was a major issue that Nicholas Okes faced in producing the 1608 Quarto of *King Lear*.

The basic problem involved the amount of paper to be ordered, either by the printer or the stationer. Blayney's analysis of the paper on which *Lear* was printed showed that most of the sheets in the surviving copies display three pairs of watermarks, one of which does not occur in any book printed by Okes before *Lear*. Further, having investigated more than 200 quartos printed between 1606 and 1608, Blayney established that the only books containing these watermarks were printed for Nathaniel Butter: thus, "there can be little doubt that Butter provided the paper for *Lear*." Blayney judged that "the proportions of the paper in *Lear* suggest precalculated delivery before work began" and that "the size of *Lear* was estimated and contracted for in advance."[1] In preparing the 1608 Quarto Nicholas Okes left the first leaf (A1) blank on both recto and verso and printed the title page on A2 recto, with the verso blank (signature A is only a half-sheet). Then follow nine signatures, B–K, each of eight pages, regularly set, concluding with sheet L, of which the final, eighth page ($L4^v$) is blank. As Blayney showed, Okes differed from other printers by leaving the outer pages of his printed books blank, "to protect the print when folded or stitched copies were stored without wrappers."[2] Thus, the total number of sheets that Okes allowed for printing *Lear* was a half-sheet for the preliminaries and ten for the text, with the final page blank, a total of seventy-nine pages containing printed matter. These ten-and-a-half sheets supplied by Butter already exceeded Okes's norm. Blayney showed that whereas his predecessor had printed substantial volumes, needing up to thirty-six sheets, the average size of the books Okes printed in 1607 was seven-and-a-half sheets, and by 1609 "the average size of his 68 books was still below 9 sheets."[3] Okes's inexperience in this genre, *Lear* being the first play he printed, was responsible for what I believe to have been a serious underestimate.

As Blayney summarized the printing history of the *Lear* Quarto, work "probably began the second week of December 1607," less than a fortnight after the play had been entered, "by which time Nathaniel Butter had delivered the copy, received an estimate, and delivered the paper."[4] The question naturally arises: if Okes found the paper quantity inadequate, why did he not go back to Butter and ask for a supplement? No definite answer can be given. Modern bibliographers suggest "that astute publishers 'shopped around' for the best deal" and when it came to play books usually chose printers of less than the highest quality.[5] Perhaps Butter had struck a hard bargain; or perhaps Okes was so eager to do this job for Butter that, with the paper having been estimated and contracted for in advance, he did not feel comfortable about going back and asking for more; or perhaps he felt that he could cope with the purchased amount.[6] In extenuation of both stationer and printer, W. P. Williams has pointed out that "if one looks at W. W. Greg's *Bibliography of English Printed Drama* at plays printed around this time one sees that most ran to 8 or 9 sheets."[7] Blayney calculated that between 1604 and 1609 Okes printed thirty-seven quartos in 305 sheets, an average of 8.2 sheets.[8]

Ten sheets, with an extra half for the prelims, may have seemed to Okes a reasonable quantity for a cheaper play quarto, but it was to prove inadequate.

The key decision lay in the choice to set the text seriatim, not by formes. Blayney suggested that Okes probably chose to set the pages in their numerical sequence, rather than casting off copy and making an exact estimate of the extent of the text space, because Shakespeare's manuscript was difficult to read. As we have seen, the major disadvantage of this casting-off method was that it made a great demand on the printer's stock of type, including spacing quads. But a greater disadvantage, I argue, had to do with the expectations of the compositors as they set each sheet. Despite the fact that Okes hired a second compositor in January 1608, who shared in the printing of sheets H–L, Blayney concluded,

> At no point in the work (after C3v, that is) is there reason to suspect that any part of the copy was cast off in the usual sense. The division of labour during the later sheets did not lead to the early completion of any particular forme, and at no time was the setting constricted by the fact that a subsequent part of the text had already been printed. But in another sense the whole text must have been cast off, in that the number of sheets it was to fill had been predetermined. There is some evidence that the sheets were not set between rigidly-fixed reference marks, for on two occasions compositor B turned a word up into a line which he had not yet realized was the last line of a sheet. But it can be assumed that there was an ever-present awareness of the need to fit about a tenth of the text into each sheet, and this may have affected the setting from time to time. From the somewhat "crammed" appearance of the last three pages it would appear that the final (but not necessarily the only) adjustments were left rather late.[9]

This is a crucial issue, and Blayney's account is not entirely satisfactory. To say that "in another sense the whole text must have been cast off" is not quite the same as saying that Okes "had estimated the amount of space he would need." The questions are, how accurately did he do so, and what happened when his calculations proved inadequate? It is also not clear why Blayney should single out page C3v as the point at which seriatim setting certainly began, for in an earlier discussion he suggested that sheet C was "almost certainly" set seriatim.[10]

The open-ended nature of seriatim setting allows changes and adjustments to be made in any of the pages as yet unimposed, a fact that helps account for the impression readers may have when studying the unpredictable printing patterns in the 1608 Quarto, as if—to use a phrase normally applied to an uncoordinated storytelling—Okes's compositors were "making it up as they went along." If there were really no reference marks on their copy, that would mean that they were involved in an unplanned typesetting process stretching over ten sheets and nearly eighty pages. Had the book been set by formes, the compositors would have had twenty predetermined points to keep to (each sheet being set from two formes), and within each sheet the security of eight catchwords marking their scheduled progress. It is true, as Blayney says, that Okes's compositors needed "to fit about a tenth of the text into each sheet," but if Shakespeare's manuscript was indeed messy and if the copy had not been cast off, they would have been hard pressed to estimate what a tenth of *King Lear* would amount to. Other scholars have noted the crowded appearance of the last three pages,[11] but in fact Okes and his compositors had realized the need to save space long before then.

Whatever the combination of causes, the effects of inaccurate estimating can be seen on every page of the 1608 Quarto. Nor are these merely technical or aesthetic features, such as unpleasantly cramped or crowded printing (see Plates 1, 2, 6). As I argue in the next chapter, the inaccurate page estimate also caused Okes's compositors to take the most drastic measure of all: omitting more than a hundred of Shakespeare's lines. Fortunately, the 1623 Folio preserves an independent text, set from a copy of substantially the same manuscript as the Quarto, the Booke originally prepared by the King's Men in 1606 for use in the theater, perhaps in a subsequent scribal transcript. It preserves the passages cut in Okes's printing shop, but omits 285 lines found in the Quarto, most probably due to performance cuts, as I shall argue in Chapter 7. Without the Folio as an independent witness we should never have known about the omissions Okes made to accommodate his printing of *King Lear* within the amount of paper he and Butter had allotted to it.

Having allowed for the running titles and catchwords, the Quarto of *King Lear* was printed with thirty-eight lines of text per page, with two pages (F2v, G2r) containing an extra line. On the first page Okes gave great prominence to the head title, "*M. William Shak-speare* | *His* | *Historie, of King Lear*," which takes up fifteen lines of text, and on the last page, despite being evidently short of space, he gave the equivalent of six lines to his *FINIS*. Modern readers might wish that he had given the text greater priority.

Space Saving

The visible evidence of the space-saving devices that Okes and his compositors were forced to use takes several forms. Rather than the standard explanations that the many peculiarities of the 1608 Quarto were due simply to the compositors' negligence or to the state of Shakespeare's manuscript, I argue that they were a deliberate attempt to compress the text into a smaller printing space than was available. To make a reliable estimate of the relation between what I have called "text space" and "print space," I base my calculations on Jay L. Halio's edition of the 1608 Quarto in modern spelling.[12] Halio presents the text with the correct distinction between verse and prose, as found in the Folio. (His page setting for prose is about 10 percent wider than that of the 1608 Quarto, but more suitable than the narrow columns in the *Riverside* edition.) Halio gives the correct verse lineation; he regularizes entrances, exits, and other stage directions. In effect, he prints the text as if Nicholas Okes had achieved consistency and accuracy throughout. Purist scholars may wonder to what extent the result, with all its faults removed, can still be called "the first quarto of *King Lear*," but it does enable more exact comparison with the Folio.[13]

The text of the play runs to 2,973 lines. The table in Appendix 2 is divided into three sections. Section I gives the basic details of the Quarto text as printed by Okes, identifying the forme, outer or inner (column A), and page (column B). Column C records the extent of Shakespeare's text contained on each page by reference to Halio's edition, whereas column D gives the total number of lines as actually printed in the 1608 Quarto. Column E records the number of lines taken up by stage directions fully displayed—that is, set as separate lines—although Okes did not accord them the luxury of blank lines above and below, as other printers did. Column P distinguishes three types of stage directions not fully displayed: omitted <SD>, placed in text line [SD], and placed in margin of text {SD}.

In Section II of the table, columns G–L, I list the common typographical devices used by Elizabeth printers to save space on a small scale, as when justifying a line of type. These include the use of tildes, ampersands, turned lines, numerals for numbers, and so on. Although these were standard devices, Okes differs from his peers in the very great frequency with which he used them, as my subsequent discussion, "Space Saving in Contemporary Shakespeare Quartos," will show (see below).

The third section of the table, columns M–R, is the most important for my argument, because it shows the methods that Okes used that affect the substance of the text: reducing verse to prose, running parts of verse lines together so as to occupy less space, the omission of stage directions, and cuts in the text.

Typographical Adjustments

Section II of the table documents six types of mechanical adjustments made in printing the Quarto, of the kind that textual scholars refer to as nonliterary, typographical features. As my examination will show, none of these adjustments could have been motivated by aesthetic or any consideration other than the printer's desire to save space. On their own, they cannot affect the total number of lines saved, but some can do so in conjunction with other methods.

Contracted Words

Okes's compositors could always shorten a line of text by abridging words. We know that compositors had their own regular spellings, one preferring *heere*, another *here*, and in this area of free choice it is usually impossible to know whether or not a shorter spelling has been adopted in order to save space. By comparing the 1600 Quarto of 2

Henry IV with the Folio text, mostly set by Compositor B, Eleanor Prosser showed that on several occasions he saved space by choosing an abbreviated spelling, omitting a terminal "e" or "l." The survival of uncorrected and corrected states of the 1608 Quarto of *King Lear* allowed Greg to include among his main list of all the variants between the two states those occasions where Okes's compositors were forced to abbreviate a word to accommodate a correction.[14] Greg did not discuss the matter of other contracted spellings: I will discuss it later in connection with the practice of "indenting the stick."

It is important to distinguish between words abbreviated by "necessity" and Shakespeare's occasional use of contractions to define a colloquial register and register a character's norms and deviations. Contracted forms flourish below the formality of blank verse, as in the Fool's repertoire of homely proverbs and sayings aimed at exposing Lear's foolish error, or in the vigorous abuse that Kent heaps on Oswald. In Shakespeare's normal register for kings and rulers, colloquial contractions would be an offense against decorum, but he gives them to Lear when he is in two phases of unkingly behavior: in his madness and also in his short-lived fantasy of living with Cordelia "like birds it'h cage" (K4r19; 5.2.8–25). We can be fairly sure that Shakespeare gave the king these familiar contracted forms—"The good shall deuoure em . . . wele see vm starue first, come" (35–36)—not Okes.

The Tilde

An unmistakable compositorial device to save space was to use "titled letters," as Moxon called them, adding the tilde (a line placed above a vowel) to indicate that an "m" or "n" had been omitted. Prosser gave several instances of this device used by other compositors pressed for space in the Folio texts of *2 Henry IV* and *Much Ado about Nothing*.[15] As I have shown, in *1 Henry IV* (1598) Andrew Wise used the tilde three times to save space in prose scenes. Those usages are few in number compared to those forced on the compositors of the 1608 *Lear*. As column L shows, they used tildes on forty-four occasions, "necessity" producing some awkward and unsightly expedients, such as in the following two passages:

> *Seruant.* My Lord, I know not what the matter is, but to my iudgmēt,your highnes is not ētertained with that ceremonious affection as you were wont (C4r8–9; 1.4.57–59)

> *Edg.* Be thy mouth, or blacke, or white,|tooth that poysons if it bite,|
> Mastife,grayhoūd,mungril,grim-|hoūd or spaniel,brach or {Lym,}|[16]
> Bobtaile tike,or trūdle taile,|*Tom* will make them weepe & waile, | (G4r29–31; 3.6.67–70)

In the second instance Okes's compositors reduced Tom's speech, containing eleven lines of verse (as preserved in the Folio), to seven of prose, but retaining the initial capitals for the first five lines. More drastically, on three occasions the compositors were forced to abbreviate a character's name or title within the text, as if it were a mere speech prefix:

> *Cord.* Then poore *Cord.*|& yet not so, since I am sure
> My loues|more richer then my tongue. (B2r8–9; 1.1.77–79)

> *Lear.* My L. of *Burgūdie,*|we first addres towards you. (B3v8; 1.1.189–190)

> *Duke.* Shut vp your doores my Lord,tis a wild night,
> My *Reg* counsails well,come out at'h storme. *Exeūt* (F3r36–37; 2.4.308–309)

In each of those cases abbreviating the name was combined with other space-saving devices, the ampersand and the tilde, evidence of a local typographical crisis. In the third instance, although there is some blank space between its last line and the stage direction, the compositor made three local adjustments: reducing the name to "*Reg*" (with not even a full stop to mark it as an abbreviation), reducing "of the [storme]" to "at'h . . . ," and omitting the "*n*" in "*Exeūt.*" This was perhaps another instance of "automatic shortening" procedures. An even more desperate attempt to cram the words into the measure of the line was to omit two consonants at one go, as here, and turn up the last word:

Bast. This curtesie forbid thee,shal the Duke | instāly
And of that letter to,|this seems a faire deseruing (know
(G1r20–21; 3.3.21–23)

The standard interpretation of this phenomenon goes back to Greg's paper of 1936, pointing to the presence of two settings throughout Q1: a narrow one for verse, which would be justified at a given point inside the right margin, and a wider one for prose. Richard Knowles recently invoked Greg's account in commenting on how Okes's compositors used "a short measure on about half the pages of Q1, where a preponderance of verse lines would invite the use of many space leads for the justification at the ends of lines of type."[17] As column L shows, this observation is certainly correct regarding the use of the tilde in justified lines of verse (twenty-two times). However, many of these instances are due to the compositor having compressed more verse lines than the measure could accommodate, generating this secondary effect. Furthermore, the text contains almost as many instances of the tilde used in prose set in the wide measure (nineteen times, as well as in one stage direction). Thus it must be seen as a typographical space-saving device for the compositors, whichever stylistic medium Shakespeare had chosen at that point.

The Ampersand

A by now familiar way of saving space was to replace the word "and" with an ampersand (&). Charlton Hinman noted that "the Folio is . . . sprinkled, both in verse and in prose passages, with ampersands," used to make the text fit into a given line and avoid turn-overs. Eleanor Prosser observed that in Wise's Quarto of *1 Henry IV* Compositor B normally used the ampersand to justify a long verse line, but as I have shown, he also used it nine times in prose. Okes's compositors far exceeded these frequencies. Greg's examination of the variant states of the *Lear* Quarto revealed that the compositors used it twice in the uncorrected state, as a consequence of other corrections. In their finished work, as column M shows, they resorted to the ampersand to compress the typesetting on an additional thirty-five occasions, often without a space preceding or following: "&the"(B1r37), "age,&"(C1v36), "honour,&"(C2r10), "pretence&"(C4r18), "out,&" (D2v7), and "gon,&" (D2v27). On one occasion they used ampersands no less than five times, starting with this speech:

> *Lear.* Blow wind & cracke your cheekes, rage, blow
> You caterickes, & Hircanios spout | til you haue drencht,
> The steeples drown'd the cockes, (F4r3–4; 3.2.1–3)

and continuing down the page (see Plate 2). These are all signs that the available print space was not large enough for the text space.

Numbers as Numerals

Another device that compositors used out of "necessity" (in Moxon's euphemism) was to set numbers as numerals. Compositor B did so six times in compressing the Folio text of 2 *Henry IV* to fit it into reduced space. This is the only space-saving device that Okes used less frequently than the other compositors I have taken for comparison. As shown in column M, his workmen used this device on five occasions, as in these instances: "some twelue or 14. moonshines lag of a brother" (C1r18; 1.2.5) and "here do you keepe a 100. Knights and Squires" (D1v37; 1.4.241). As the first of those examples shows, where more space was available, part of the number could be spelled out in full: "But this heart shall breake, in a 100. thousand {flaws}[18] | Or ere ile weepe' (F3r3–4; 2.4.285–286).

Turned Lines

The easiest of the purely typographical adjustments, or the one demanding least forethought, is one often used when justifying the line of type; if a line proves to be too long, the compositor can fit it into the available space by turning the last word(s) up to the line above or down to the line below. Hinman noted this use of turn-overs in some crowded pages in the Folio texts of *The Tempest* and *Hamlet*, while Prosser identified several instances in the Folio 2 *Henry IV*. In his 1598 Quarto of *1 Henry IV*, Andrew Wise only needed to use the turn-over twice. In the 1608 *Lear* Quarto, in stark contrast, as column O records, Okes used a turn-over on sixty-five occasions.

An additional factor in the *Lear* Quarto affecting the use of turn-overs was the compositors' relineation of verse to save space, which made it harder to fit a long verse, whether Shakespeare's original or one of their own conflations, into one line. At all events, the displacing of the final word(s) obviated the need to take up a second line. There are many instances where the compositor had to combine a turn-over with another space-saving device, such as the tilde. (In quoting verse lines that the Quarto compositors have run together, I indicate the Folio line division with a vertical line.)

> *Fran.* Is it no more but this, a tardines in nature,|
> That often leaues the historie vnspoke|that it intends to
> My Lord of *Burgundie*,|what say you to the Lady? (do,
> Loue is not loue | when it is mingled with respects that
> Aloofe from the intire point|wil you haue her? (stāds
>
> (B4r19–23; 1.1.235–240)

Eleanor Prosser noted that the Folio compositors regularly used turn-unders to compress copy, but that the turn-unders rarely exceeded one word. Okes's workmen were often obliged to turn two words up or down (here represented by two vertical lines), sometimes even incorporating a tilde or an ampersand as well: "the Dragon & || his wrath" (B2v12–13), "thy Gods || in vaine" (B3r17–18), "what || you are" (B4v13–14), "Duke || & her" (E4v14–15), "begin || to vnsettle" (G3r8–9), "from || my chin"(H1r33–34), "bid || you hold" (H1v31–32), "seruices || are dew" (H3v22–23), "the || rude wind" (H3v26–27), "of || the deepe"(H4r7–8), "demonstratiō || of griefe" (H4v26–27), "match || thy goodness" (K1v18–19), "familiar || with her" (K3r17–18), "ap- || pointed guard" (K4v21–22), and "arraine || me for't" (L2r16–17). On one desperate occasion the compositor had to turn up three words: "done || to cure it" (I2v30–31).

But Okes's chronic lack of space made him take the unusual step of using a turn-over in prose that had already been set in the wider measure. He did so five times, also in combination with other space savers, as when Cornwall considerately excuses Edmund from witnessing Gloucester's blinding:

> *Corn.* Leaue him to my displeasure,*Edmūd* keep you our sister
> (company.
> The {reuenges}[19] we are bound to take vpon your trayterous father,
> Are not fit for your beholding , aduise the Duke where you are
> (going
> To a most{festinate}[20]preparatiō we are bound to the like,
> Our post shall be swift and {intelligent}[21] betwixt vs
> (H1r1–6; 3.7.6–12)

The capital letters beginning each line there suggest that the Quarto compositor thought he was setting verse, but the lines are unmetrical and the Folio confirms that Shakespeare wrote them as prose.

Medial Spacing

The last typographical adjustment in Okes's *Lear* that I consider concerns the spacing of type. In a normally printed hand-press book, compositors left a space between each word and after every punctuation mark (comma, semi-colon, colon, full stop, question mark, exclamation mark, and parenthesis). As we have seen, Moxon recognized that, in cases of "necessity," a compositor pressed for room could omit such medial spacing, thus creating "botches" and failing the principles of "good workmanship." But Elizabethan and Jacobean printers of play texts were prepared to ignore such principles when short of space, Okes among them. Many pages of his *Lear* cram the words together, producing an unpleasantly crowded impression. In his study of the Quarto variants Greg noted that, where adjustments had been made in the correcting process "by altering the spaces between words," this was often "roughly and carelessly done, sometimes by the complete removal of a space where one was normally required (as after a comma) or by the insertion of one where none should be (as before a comma)."[22] Greg judged that the irregularities of spacing between words were "far too frequent and too variable to record" in his list of "Misprints in the Original," although he did include twenty-two instances of words run together.[23] Such compositorial failures were not as glaring in Okes's *Lear* as those in Wise's 1598 Quarto of *1 Henry IV*, but they still included such "botches" as "ofnothing" (C4^{v}), "learneto" (D1^{r}), "beit" (D1^{v}), "pitionmore" (G3^{v}), "tralmadam" (G3^{v}), and "beaydant" (I1^{v}). Having noted that "in early printing it is common to find the space that should *follow* a comma omitted," Greg announced that he had taken no notice of "this irregularity" and evidently did not connect it with the printer's thorough-going attempt to save space in every possible way.[24]

Nor did Peter Blayney in his discussion of "the spacing of medial commas in unjustified lines," in which he recorded the difficulties in establishing any meaningful data. For one thing, "commas from at least four founts were used, and the 'normal' centring of the character on the type may have differed from fount to fount." For another, Blayney found it problematic to establish the normal practice of the two compositors: B, who worked on the *Lear* Quarto throughout the period of printing, from the second week of December, 1607 to the second week of January 1608, and C, who joined him in the New Year. Blayney's analysis found that, while

> C's average differed from that of B, B's own practice was so wildly erratic that tabulations and averages are practically meaningless. C set approximately 20% of his unjustified commas without a space. B's overall average was considerably higher, but there is little or no sign of consistency. Several patches of exceptionally frequent close spacing can probably be explained as the result of space-shortage—the difference between K3^{v} (spaced 16: unspaced 3) and K4^{r} (spaced 4: unspaced 22) can be explained in this way, and provides a good example of the range of variation—but it is also probable that B was simply inconsistent.[25]

That passage is, I believe, the single reference to a "space shortage" in the only published volume of *The Texts of* King Lear *and Their Origins*, Otherwise, Blayney did not comment on the compositors' many devices to save paper; perhaps the second volume would have discussed this issue. My own computations can be seen in columns

P and Q of the table (Appendix 2). At the simple level of space saving, I estimate that Okes's *Lear* contains approximately 875 medial commas without spacing, which for a text of seventy-nine pages gives an average of 11 unspaced commas per page.[26] This is not as extreme as Wise's *1 Henry IV*, which has approximately 12,000 unspaced commas in seventy-eight pages, or 15 per page, but it does confirm any reader's initial impression that Okes made a consistent attempt to compress the text and avoid as far as possible overrunning the line, in either verse or prose, and so wasting precious space.[27]

The effect of these economies was to squeeze words together with an unremitting density, as can be seen from a few examples taken from Lear's role (see also Plates 1, 2, and 6):

> doth Lear walke thus ? Speake thus? . . . either his no-
> tion,weaknes,or his discerning'are lethergie, sleeping
> (D1v25–27; 1.4.227–229)
>
> Rumble thy belly full,spit fire,spout raine,
> Nor raine,wind,thunder,fire,are my daughters,
> (F4r16–17; 3.2.14–15)
>
> Make no noise,make no noise,draw the curtains,so,so,so,
> Weele go to supper it'h morning,so, so,so, (G4v3–4; 3.6.83–84)
>
> when I haue stole
> vpon these sonne in lawes, then kill,kill,kill,kill, kill,kill.
> (I4v1–2; 4.6.185–187)
>
> Howle,howle,howle,howle. O you are men of stones
> (L3v8; 5.3.258)
>
> O thou wilt
> come no more, neuer,neuer,neuer, pray you vndo this button
> (L4r17–18; 5.3.308–309)

While the need to save space—as in Wise's *1 Henry IV*—was the main reason for the "botching" of commas, a contributory cause was the fact that, due to his having chosen to set seriatim, Okes was short not only of some individual types but also of quads, the blank pieces of type used for inserting spaces. Blayney's comparative study of Okes's entire output in the years surrounding the 1608 Quarto, the single play text that he printed, established that "what *Lear* used in the quantities most unprecedented in the pica books of 1605–7 was space-metal."[28] A shortage of quads explains many instances of spacing being omitted, but the overriding reason was the pressure on the compositors to prevent a particular line of prose or verse from running over and disturbing the whole page.

It may be worth repeating the point that none of these typographical expedients can have had any function other than compressing a text into a smaller space. With its 44 tildes, 37 ampersands, 5 uses of numerals for numbers, 65 turn-overs, and 875 unspaced medial commas, the 1608 *Lear* can claim to have used more space-saving devices than any other Shakespeare quarto.

Textual Adjustments

Section III of the table in Appendix 2 shows the methods Okes used to save space by altering the display of the text on the printed page. Each of these methods destroyed Shakespeare's conscious use of a dramatic convention.

Verse Set as Prose

The expedient by which Okes saved most space was by setting verse as prose (the details are set out in column F). This adjustment may seem purely typographical, but some modern scholars have failed to realize that the distinction between prose and verse had a real meaning in Elizabethan drama. R. B. McKerrow, for example, setting out the principles on which he proposed to edit Shakespeare, delivered this categorical statement: "The truth is no doubt that, at least in dramatic writing, there was no clear and consistent distinction between verse and prose" and that it "was in any case slight and of little importance."[29] McKerrow could hardly have been more mistaken. Elizabethan dramatists carefully differentiated between prose and verse, each with its own range of applications; indeed, the distinction was clear from the outset in the way their manuscripts were arranged. Extant play texts used in the theater are written on folio-size paper, separately folded sheets forming units of four pages. As W. W. Greg found, in some of the manuscripts he had consulted, "A common practice, before starting to write, was to fold the leaf down the middle, and then fold the folded leaf yet again, so that when flattened out each page was divided into four equal columns some two inches wide. In the left of these were written the speakers' names. The text was begun at the first fold, and if verse would fill approximately the two middle columns, leaving the right-hand column for stage-directions; if the text was prose it was written across all three columns."[30] Greg emphasized that this practice of folding was "not invariable," but the prose-verse distinction, which carried significant information about the characters' social status, mood, nationality, or even state of mind, was carefully observed in printed texts.[31] There is good evidence that Elizabethan actors must have spoken verse with a greater emphasis on meter and rhythm than we are accustomed to and used a more naturalistic delivery for prose. The shift from one medium to the other must have been audible in the theater, for several plays comment on it. In most situations blank verse is the norm; it is the dominant medium of tragedies and history plays, of rulers and counselors, with prose used for contrastive effect, representing a lower status level, that of servants and clowns. Normality is defined not only in social but also in linguistic and psychological terms, for those not having full control over their language—foreigners, dialect speakers, drunkards, those who have gone mad—are relegated to prose. In these instances the distinction between verse and prose is external, representing norms and exceptions.

But there is also an internal distinction, where the difference between prose and verse expresses a contrast internal to the play as an aesthetic system or represents the deliberate act of a character who is not bound to speak prose by the mimetic representation of everyday life. One such internal contrast between the two media can be described as Shakespeare setting nature against art. Where prose is the established norm in a scene, verse can be made to look affected. When Rosalind, Jaques, and Celia are speaking prose, Orlando enters with just one line of verse:

> Good day, and happinesse, deere Rosalind.

At this Jaques (sticking to prose) leaves in disgust: "Nay then, God buy you, and you talke in blanke verse" (*As You Like It*, 4.1.30–32). A similar contrast involves the lover trying to turn his natural feelings into poetry, for "the art of numbers" (the rules of prosody) requires discipline and detachment. When Longavile, one of the courtiers who have vowed a three-year abstention from the company of women, breaks his vow and writes poetry, he is dissatisfied with the result:

> I feare these stubborn lines lack power to moue.
> O sweet Maria, Empresse of my Loue,
> These numbers will I teare, and write in prose.
> (*Love's Labour's Lost*, 4.3.53–55)

In his love letter to Ophelia Hamlet documents his inability to sustain the artifice, abandoning his attempts at verse and reverting to prose as an index of a feeling that cannot be bound in formal constraints:

> Doubte thou, the Starres are fire,
> Doubt, that the Sunne doth moue,
> Doubt Truth to be a Liar;
> But neuer Doubt, I loue.
> O deere Ophelia, I am ill at these Numbers: I haue not Art to reckon my grones; but that I loue thee best, oh most Best, beleeue it. (2.2.118–122)

There, real suffering and real sincerity could be expressed only in prose. In other dramatic contexts, the shift from one medium to another conveyed dissimulation. This convention was not unique to Shakespeare. In Marston's *The Malcontent*, Malevole speaks verse in his own character and prose in his disguised persona, the move between the two being recorded in the stage direction: "*Bilioso entering, Malevole shifteth his speech.*"[32] Those who disguise or dissimulate in Shakespeare often change to the lower medium.

In *King Lear* Shakespeare limits some characters to one medium: Cordelia only ever speaks verse, with the possible exception of

"Nothing" in the Folio text (1.1.89; TLN 95), although that occurs in a verse scene. The servants speak prose, except for Goneril's Steward Oswald, when allowed into his mistress's confidence. The Fool's natural media are prose and rhyme, not blank verse. When characters move between verse and prose it is never random; the move is always motivated by Shakespeare, either out of individual choice or for local effect. The opening scene, in the anteroom of power, begins in prose with a relaxed conversation between courtiers before the public gift-giving ceremony. That contrast is reversed at the scene's ending, as Goneril and Regan put away pretense and reveal their true selves. Some characters from the upper medium descend to prose in a domestic setting (Gloucester and Edmund, Edmund and Edgar, Lear and the Fool). Others move up from prose to verse for specific reasons, as Kent does in his quarrel with Oswald and Cornwall. He begins in prose, in his assumed role as a servant of Lear, but as his anger grows he rises to the more resonant medium of verse to denounce "such smiling rogues as these," remaining at that level for the rest of the scene (2.2.72–173). Edmund's shifts between the two media are motivated not by anger but by calculation, most markedly when he closes a conversation with his father or brother in prose and switches to verse to communicate to us the success of his plotting, ending, "All with me's meete, that I can fashion fit" (C3r5–10; 1.3.171–176) and "[The][33] yonger rises, when the old doth fall." (G1r20–23; 3.3.20–24). The first of these transitions is correctly observed in the Quarto, the second not.

Shakespeare makes the most innovative use of the two media for Lear's madness. In Elizabethan drama people who go mad usually descend to prose, as if they can no longer get their thoughts in order. Shakespeare, having shown Lear's mental disorder by reducing him to prose, makes Lear alternate between the two media, reverting to the "sane" sphere of verse when he so powerfully denounces injustice in speeches that would make less effect in prose. These changes are rarely indicated in the Quarto, but always in the Folio. In the extraordinary scene in the hovel, when Poor Tom appears, Lear at once identifies with him, speaking prose—"Did'st thou give all to thy Daughters? And art thou come to this?"—and again: "Ha's his Daughters brought him to this passe? Could'st thou save nothing?"

But when Kent corrects him—"He hath no Daughters Sir"—Lear's anger at being contradicted brings him back to verse: "Death Traitor, nothing could have subdu'd Nature | To such a lownesse, but his vnkind Daughters" (3.4.49–75; TLN 1830–1852). This change of medium goes unmarked in the modern theater, but to an audience attuned to the significance of the contrast between verse and prose, that must have been a surprising break with convention. If so, audience members would have been startled by Lear's reaction when the blinded Gloucester recognizes his voice (Folio text):

Lear. Go too, they are not men o'their words; they told me, I was euery thing: 'Tis a lye, I am not Agu-proofe.
Gloucester. The tricke of that voyce, I do well remember:
Is't not the King?
Lear. I, euery inch a King.
When I do stare, see how the Subject quakes.
I pardon that mans life. What was thy cause?
Adultery? thou shalt not dye: dye for Adultery?
(I3v22–28; 4.6.103–111; TLN 2550–2557)

In the Folio (but not in the Quarto) Lear's remaining speeches in this scene are all in verse, as Shakespeare allows him to intermittently regain vestiges of sense and authority. But in his final speech he relapses into the medium within which dramatic convention would have constrained him:

Lear. I will die brauely like a bridegroom, what? | I will be Iouiall, come, come, I am a King | my maisters, know you that.
Gent. You are a royall one, and we obey you.
Lear. Then theres life int, nay, and you get it, you shall get it with running: *Exit King running.*
(I4v13–16; 4.6. 199–203; TLN 2642–2645)

The Folio introduces verse lineation for the first four lines, but not entirely convincingly, failing to recognize a complete pentameter in "I am a King, my maisters, know you that?," and mistakenly sets Lear's last sentence as verse. It also substitutes the anodyne "*Exit.*"

for the Quarto's truly shocking stage direction, set from Shakespeare's manuscript.

I have made this little excursus into Shakespeare's use of prose to make what should be an obvious point: the textual criticism of a literary work cannot afford to be a purely technical matter concerning the marks of printing type on paper. To edit or communicate a play by Shakespeare correctly requires some knowledge of the dramatic conventions governing language and form as Shakespeare and others observed them. Early modern printers presumably understood the rationale for the use of prose and verse according to character and situation, for they mostly observed the distinction correctly.[34] There were exceptions, as we have seen, due to the need to compress a text to fit a lesser space. This was the case in the Folio *Much Ado* and *Othello*, as well as in Q1 of *1 Henry IV*, where Wise's compositors frequently reduced verse speeches to prose, saving one or two lines on each occasion.

Nicholas Okes and his compositors setting the Pied Bull Quarto may have understood this convention, but were forced to ignore it by severe space constraints. No other Shakespeare quarto evinces such a large-scale confusion of the two media. (A full realization of the extent to which Okes muddled the two was hindered for many years by the fact that some modern Shakespearians were unaware of these artistic conventions.) As column F records, Okes and his employees used this most visible form of text adjustment to save space on thirty-two occasions, turning 485 lines of verse into prose and in the process saving 151 lines of print space. For instance, this speech by Goneril is set in the Quarto as one block of prose. However, it is clearly in verse, as the inserted line divisions from the Folio show:

> *Gon.* Not onely sir this,your all-licenc'd foole,|but other of your insolent retinue|do hourely carpe and quarrell, breaking forth|in ranke & (not to be indured riots,) Sir|I had thought by making this well knowne vnto you,|to haue found a safe redres, but now grow fearefull|by what your selfe too late haue spoke and done,|that you protect this course, and put {it}[35] on|by your allowance, which if you should,the fault | would not scape censure, nor the redresse, sleepe,|which in the tender of a wholsome

> weale,|might in their working doe you that offence, | that else were shame, that then necessitie|must call discreet proceedings.
> (D1v5–14; 1.4.201–214)

In this instance Okes reduced fourteen lines of verse to ten lines of prose. In nearly all cases the change is unmotivated, having no connection with the character's mood or mental state. Commentators on *King Lear* have previously regarded the compositors' rendering of verse as prose as simply a sign of their clumsiness[36] or as the result of authorial revisions and additions.[37] But since playhouse manuscripts often distinguished prose as the medium that extends across the folio sheet, such mistaking of verse for prose was hardly accidental. Nor is it likely that Shakespeare would have suddenly abandoned his customary observation of the distinction between prose and verse, which he had practiced in nearly thirty plays.

Relined Verse

Commentators on the 1608 Quarto of *King Lear* generally describe the phenomenon of relining verse as "mis-lineation," leading to unsupported speculations that Shakespeare might have written out his verse without properly dividing it.[38] It was not until George Steevens did so in 1793 that editors observed the convention by which a half-line closing one speech and a half-line beginning another were treated as forming a single decasyllabic line, with the second hemistich being set just below the first. When Okes's compositors were confronted with a half-line beginning a speech they set it full left, but to save space they then picked up the following verse, redivided it to fill out the first line, and so on, as in this passage (Folio line divisions are indicated):

> *Fra.* This is most strange,|that she,that euen but now
> Was your best obiect, | the argument of your praise,
> Balme of your age,|most best,most deerest,
> Should in this trice of time | commit a thing,
> So monstrous to dismantell | so many foulds of fauour,
> Sure her offence | must be of such vnnaturall degree,

That monsters it, or {your}[39] for voucht affections
Falne into taint, (B3v34–B4r3; 1.1.215–223)

In 1930 E. K. Chambers noted that "mislineation is a constant feature in Q. The verse is often put wrong by an initial error, and runs from central pause to central pause, until another error or the end of a speech recovers it. Occasionally it is entirely unmetrical."[40] It was not an "error" on the compositor's part but a deliberate device to save space, in which meter had to be ignored—if, indeed, Okes was at all aware of prosody. We need to remember that "printers were by and large coarse, uneducated tradesmen who laboured hard and long for their keep" and could not be expected to have had a "refined taste."[41]

Okes's compositors also ran verse lines together, sometimes cramming two lines into one, or three into two, as here:

Glost. Good friend I prithy take him in thy armes,
I haue or'e heard a plot of death vpon him,
Ther is a Litter ready lay him in't,|& driue towards Douer frend,
Where thou shalt meet|both welcome & protection,take vp thy
If thou should'st dally halfe an houre,his life | with thine (master,
And all that offer to defend him | stand in assured losse,
Take vp the King|and followe,me that will to some prouision
Giue thee quicke conduct. (G4v7–14; 3.6.88–97)

This instance of relineation (twice using the ampersand) saved two verse lines, the average amount achieved by the forty-two such interventions made in Okes's printing shop. As column G records, altogether 330 lines of verse were affected, resulting in a print space saving of 74 lines. Examination of the relevant passages shows that the purely mechanical methods of reducing space already considered (contracting words, using numerals and ampersands, turning line endings over or under) were regularly combined with relineation to save a line or two, as here:

Lear. No *Regan*, thou shalt neuer haue my curse,
{Thy}tēder{hefted}nature shall not giue | {thee}[42]or'e (burne
To harshnes,her eies are fierce,but thine|do cōfort & not

Tis not in thee'to grudge my pleasures, to cut off my
To bandy hasty words, to scant my sizes, (traine,
(F1r31–35; 2.4.170–175)

In that passage the compositor managed to squeeze six lines into five. In the following speech by Lear he was able to reduce seven lines to six by using two tildes, two ampersands (one of them unnecessary), a turn-down, and a numeral instead of a number (see Plate 2):

Lear. You owe me no subscription, why thenlet fall your horrible
Here I stād your slaue,'a poore infirme weak & (plesure
Despis'd ould man,but yet I call you seruile
Ministers,'that haue with 2 .pernitious daughters ioin'd'
Your high engēdred battel gainst a head'so old & white
As this, O tis foule. (F4r20–25; 3.2.18–24)

The result is an ugly piece of printing, but by such systematic exploitation of typographical means Okes managed to compress many more lines than anyone could have expected into the space constraints of his paper estimate. A printer's miscalculations "by desperate appliances are reliev'd."

On four occasions Okes's compositors mistakenly set prose as verse, affecting forty lines of text. Examination of the contexts show that the compositors either forgot to change the setting of their stick or could not be bothered to do so.[43]

"Continuous Printing"

Early modern compositors generally set each utterance by a different speaker as a separate line, with its own speech prefix. To save space, Okes's compositors—or else the pressman imposing the pages on the stone—often set two half-lines, each with its own speech prefix, as one. As column H records, whoever was responsible did so on twenty occasions, saving a total of fifty-six lines. On one occasion they even managed to combine two half-lines by absorbing the fag-end of Edgar's preceding line:

Edg. I would not take this from report, it is , and my heart breakes at it. *Lear.* Read. *Glost.* What! With the case of eyes
(I4r11–12; 4.6.141–144)

(No room was left for the question mark.)

Henry Woudhuysen recently commented on the frequency in the *Lear* Quarto of what W. W. Greg called "continuous printing." As Greg observed, "In many plays, especially when the compositor is pressed for space, short speeches of two or three words may occasionally be found tucked in on the same line as the end of the previous speech, in verse and prose alike. . . . The irregularity varies widely, from only occasional to almost regular."[44] While Jonson's use of this practice verged on the regular, Woudhuysen endorsed Greg's view that in general "irregular continuous printing tends to suggest compositorial anxiety about space," for it is "more . . . marked towards the play's end." As for the 1608 *Lear* Quarto, Woudhuysen computed that "[t]wenty-five of the play's seventy-nine pages contain continuous printing," while the last three pages of text contain some fourteen instances of this practice, a clear sign that "the compositor was trying to save space."[45] Here are two examples of this rather undignified crowding at the play's tragic climax, in Lear's speech over the body of Cordelia:

I know when one is dead and when one liues,
Shees dead as earth, lend me a looking glasse,
If that her breath will mist or staine the stone,
Why then she liues. *Kent.* Is this the promist end.
Edg. Or image of that horror. *Duke.* Fall and cease.
(L3v11–15; 5.3.261–265)

{*Kent.*}[46] Breake hart,I prethe breake. *Edgar.* Look vp my Lord.
(L4r20; 5.3.312–313)

Perhaps the most damaging instance of continuous printing for modern readers is the climactic moment of Lear's recognition of Cordelia:

nor I know not
Where I did lodge last night,doe not laugh at me,
For as I am a man, I thinke this Ladie
To be my child *Cordelia.* *Cord.* And so I am.
(K2v11–14; 4.7.67–69)

Having squeezed her reply into that line and placed one or more spacing quads in the middle to hold the type together more firmly, inadvertently creating a blank space (in Moxon's derogatory term, a "pigeon-hole") Okes's compositor had no room for Cordelia's characteristically simple but eloquent reduplication, which the Folio retained: "I am. I am." Fortunately, the compositor found room for her matching repetition a few lines later: "No cause, no cause" (K2v20).

Stage Directions Omitted or Not Displayed

In all Elizabethan play texts stage directions play a crucial part, first for the actors and spectators at a theatrical representation and subsequently for the reader. In Elizabethan play texts entrances were normally set on a separate line, in the center of the page; exits were sometimes given a separate line, but were mostly set at the right margin, the simple direction "*Exit*" often following a full line. But in the Folio *2 Henry IV*, as we have seen, to save space Compositor B several times had to set an entrance to the right of short lines, while in the 1598 Quarto of *1 Henry IV*, where Wise had to reduce the play's length from ten-and-a-half sheets to ten, his compositor squeezed stage directions into the text, prose or verse, on more than twenty occasions.

The Quarto text of *King Lear* omits six entrances and twenty-five exits.[47] It contains fifty-six properly displayed stage directions, totaling fifty-six lines of text. As Column I records, on thirty-five occasions exits are set in the text, and in only two instances (B4v11; F3r5) are they displayed in a separate line. To save space, Okes's compositors often set an entrance stage direction not on a separate line but within the text, sometimes incongruously, as in these instances:

Lear. No I will be the pattern of all patience *Enter Kent.*
I will say nothing. (F4r33–34; 3.2.36–37)

Lear. Make no noise,make no noise,draw the
curtains,so,so,so,
Weele go to supper it'h morning, so,so,so, *Enter Gloster.*
(G4v3–4; 3.6.84–85)

Okes's compositors resorted to this expedient on eighteen occasions, saving a line each time. As we have seen, perhaps due to an oversight, on three occasions they retrieved a missing entry by setting the character's name in the margin. When "necessity" demanded, two stage directions could be crammed into one line. In this example, having run two lines together, the compositor still found himself short of space to accommodate the final direction, which had to be turned down, and thus appears to belong with the first line of the scene following, with Kent's parting from the eponymous Gentleman encroaching on Cordelia's search for Lear:

When I am knowne aright you shall not greeue,
Lending me this acquaintance, I pray you go | along with me.
Enter Cordelia, Doctor and others. *Exit.*
Cor. Alack tis he, why he was met euen now
(I1r33–36; 4.3.53–55; 4.4.1)

Conversely, at a climactic moment in the desperately crowded concluding pages, Okes's compositors divided one stage direction into two half-lines set in the text at the wider measure (see below; the two measures switch without warning):

Duke. Great thing of vs forgot,
Speake *Edmund*, whers the king, and whers *Cordelia*
Seest thou this obiect *Kent.* *The bodies of Gonorill and*
Kent. Alack why thus. *Regan are brought in.*
(L3r25–27; 5.3.238–240)

And again on the next leaf (see Plate 6):

Duke. He knowes not what he sees, and vaine it is,
That we present vs to him. *Edg.* Very bootlesse. *Enter*
Capt. Edmund is dead my Lord. *Captaine.*
(L4r6–8; 5.3.294–296)

Only an urgent need to save space would bring a compositor to this pass. Of course, Shakespeare's manuscript may not have recorded every stage direction, but compared to the Folio text, the 1608 Quarto lacks a necessary exit on twenty-five occasions. The compositors would hardly have saved much space by cutting these, because exits were not set on a separate line. However, they would certainly have saved space by omitting six entrances and setting a further eighteen within a text line—that is, if these directions were in the manuscript copy from which they worked.[48]

The Question of Measure

We can gain a better understanding of the problems facing Okes's compositors if we return to my earlier observation regarding the unpredictable variations in the width of the printed page. As I briefly noted, of the Quarto's seventy-nine pages containing printed matter, twelve are set at the width or "measure" that Nicholas Okes deemed appropriate for the verse in this play, that is, 80–81 millimeters. In these pages the compositors succeeded in justifying the right-hand margin to achieve a regular layout, albeit with an unusual number of turned lines. A further thirty-four pages are set at the width that Okes deemed appropriate for prose: 93–94 mm, the maximum page width in this volume. It was normal for play texts to use a narrow and a wide setting respectively, for verse and prose, with the compositor changing his measure from wide to narrow, or vice versa, as the medium changes. The unusual feature of Okes's 1608 *Lear* Quarto is that on thirty-three pages it uses a mixture of both settings, narrow and wide.[49] We can tell this from the use of turned lines. When Joseph Moxon described the procedure for setting the measure, or width, of a line of type, he distinguished between setting from printed copy and setting from manuscript. In the former case, the compositor "Sets or Composes the fullest Line he finds in his Copy" and adjusts the composing stick accordingly. In the latter he considers the density of the handwriting, "whether it be throughout of an equal siz'd Hand, or whether part be close Written and part wide Written." Having made his decision "he Composes one line in his Measure: The Matter he Composes he chuses out of that part of his Copy that in his Judgment . . . is most indifferently [equally] Written, between Wide and Close, as being such as his whole Copy, one part with another, will likeliest Come-in alike with."[50] That must have been no easy task for Okes, setting as he was from a messy authorial manuscript, and he clearly underestimated the measure of Shakespeare's hand, since he used many more turn-overs in setting verse than other Jacobean printers (see p. 116). In the wider measure (93–94 mm) we could expect a compositor not to need turn-overs, since he could simply run on prose passages from one line to the next. Okes, however, even at this maximum width, was forced to turn lines, both in verse and prose.

This unpredictable switching between narrow, wide, mixed, or hybrid settings has aroused discussion among bibliographers, directed more to explaining how Okes created this range of settings rather than why he did so. As with so many features of this text, W. W. Greg was the first to notice and account for it, in an essay published in 1936. Greg noted a typographic feature that is "found only in quartos, and is particularly common in *Lear* . . . the use of two distinct measures (i.e. line-lengths); the wider being usually reserved for prose, and another narrower one for verse." He argued that "the compositor actually used two composing-sticks of different lengths," since "he frequently turned over long lines of verse although there was plenty of room to print them out in the width of the page."[51] Greg pointed out that "when printing verse on the wide page of the quarto it was necessary to fill out most of the lines with a large number of quads," or blank types; when the compositor produced "a column of type narrower than the full measure of the page [he] made up the difference in the galley with furniture," that is, blanks. Greg noted the most unusual feature of Okes's Quarto: "it is not always whole pages that are in wider or narrower measure: the width of the column of type sometimes alters within the page. There are in *Lear* no less than nineteen pages that can be proved to be set partly in wide and partly in narrow measure, and the actual number is no doubt greater." In a footnote Greg listed the nineteen pages that showed two different measures, adding that "the remaining forty-eight pages of text are ostensibly in wide measure, but in no less than twenty it seems probably that part was actually set in the narrow measure, though in the absence of turn-overs or the like no definite evidence is available."[52] Greg's total would therefore be thirty-nine "mixed" pages: mine is the more conservative thirty-three.

Greg's identification of this typographic feature in the 1608 *Lear* was obviously correct, but D. F. McKenzie gave the most convincing explanation of the mechanics of printing involved, focusing on Okes's *Lear.* Drawing on his own experience in hand-setting books of poetry, McKenzie explained that the readiest answer to the problem of setting texts of varying widths on the same page "is to leave the composing-stick set to the wider measure, using it as necessary for long lines, but indenting it wherever possible by adding large quads at one end."[53] McKenzie had rediscovered a method described by Moxon as "indenting the stick," a necessary procedure when setting an ornamental letter at the beginning of a chapter or when adding marginal notes. On such occasions the compositor would fill out the blank space by the use of "Quotation Quadrats" of the appropriate size, "so exactly Cast that he shall not need to Justifie them either with Spaces or other helps."[54] McKenzie noted that the two line lengths in Okes's *Lear* Quarto, 80–81 and 93–94 mm, were equivalent to a 20 em and a 23 em measure, respectively.[55] As he pointed out, the difference between the two is "regularly 3-ems," a difference that "results, not from a change of measure, but from the compositor's indenting his stick by using a quad which, running up the head of the stick, served to indent two, three, or four text lines at a time." Adrian Weiss has helpfully commented that when compositors produced a narrower measure by setting "a stack of quads of one size . . . against the right cheek of the stick in advance of setting a line of verse," they created "a right margin defined by an imaginary vertical line at the end of the longest lines in a group."[56] (In my copy of the Quarto facsimile I have found it helpful to draw a pencil line joining all instances of the short measure, used either singly or mixed with the wide setting.)

McKenzie pointed to the most frequently visible effect of indenting in Q1 *King Lear*, the abbreviated spelling "daugter" (E3v11), which ensured that the verse line would just fit within the 80 mm measure. The need to justify the line within the space left by the indenting quads explains the presence of abbreviated word spellings. In the 1608 Quarto as published, the compositors were forced to contract several words to justify lines set in the narrow measure. They removed the letter "l" in "swels" (E4r2) and twice in this line: "With him I wil keep stil, with my Philosopher" (G3r24). They removed an "e" from "her's the place" (I2v6) and "don," (K4v9), and wrote "sory" (E2v29) and "ingratful" (F1r22, having to turn up the next word, "top"). Needing to justify pages set to the narrow measure, Okes's compositors also abbreviated names already abbreviated in speech prefixes.[57] They abridged "*Lear.*" to "*Lea.*" (F2v11), "*Kent.*" to "*Ken.*" (G3r25; also having to reduce spacing before the speech prefix), "*Stew.*" to "*Ste.*" (I2r27), and "*Cord.*" to "*Cor.*" (K4r14; also needing a turned line). As in many other cases, space-saving devices could be combined, as here:

> *Glo.* The King is in high rage, & wil I know not whe-
> *Re.* Tis good to giue him way, he leads himselfe.(ther.
>
> (F3r15–16)

That instance used an ampersand, a turned-down line, and an abbreviated speech prefix.

McKenzie also made an important observation on the psychology of managing spacing in this manner: "knowing that he can juggle the indenting quads breeds a confidence in the compositor that can lead to oversights not likely if the measure were fixed to the shorter length and the extra words just had to be fitted in there and then."[58] McKenzie's illustration of a compositor's overconfidence leading to "a serious error" is Edmund's specious explanation of why he had sent the captured Lear and Cordelia to prison, a passage where, as we have seen, the proof corrector of Q retrieved some missing words from Shakespeare's manuscript:

> *Bast.* Sir I thought it fit,
> To send the old and miserable King to some retention, and ap-
> Whose age has charmes in it whose title more, (pointed guard,
> To pluck the common bossome of his side,
>
> (K4v21–24; 5.3.45–49)

The rest of this page is set at the narrower width of 80 mm, marked by the comma after "retention." As McKenzie observed, in the uncorrected Quarto the original line "justified itself nicely within the 20 ems. With his stick already indented for the next line or two, the compositor failed to alter the quads to take in the extra words," which had to be added at proofing. McKenzie found another instance of compositorial oversight caused by using an indented stick on K1r, a particularly messy page. When Edgar (as Poor Tom) kills Oswald and intercepts Goneril's letter to Edmund, McKenzie noted that the stage direction "*He dies*" (K1r24) is correctly placed in the "3-em space to the right" of a sequence of verse lines set at the 80 mm measure. Thirteen lines are set in the narrow measure (21–33), involving a turned-up line and this ugly compression: "deathsmā" (30). In fact, the stage direction occurs outside the measure, at the extreme setting of the wide measure used twice on this page (1–20, 34–38), and looks to me like an afterthought. I agree with McKenzie, however, that the stage direction "*A letter*," which was omitted in the uncorrected Quarto,[59] was wrongly added later (K1r33) "within the shorter line-length."[60]

Between them, Greg and McKenzie clarified the mechanics of printing as regards the use of two measures in Q1 of *King Lear*. However, neither considered what I have called "the dynamics of typesetting," which would lead us to inquire why Okes produced so many pages mixing both measures. In one or two instances we can posit an accidental omission of text that was subsequently corrected during proofing, as can be seen from Greg's collation of variant copies; however, that explanation cannot account for the majority of these cases. To understand their cause, we must revert to Peter Blayney's argument that, although Okes chose not to set by formes, "in another sense the whole text must have been cast off, in that the number of sheets it was to fill had been predetermined. . . . [I]t can be assumed that there was an ever-present awareness of the need to fit about a tenth of the text into each sheet, and *this may have affected the setting from time to time*."[61] I have italicized those words to bring out the contradiction between that somewhat casual concession and Blayney's preceding phrase: "an ever-present awareness of the need to fit about a tenth of the text into each sheet." I suggest that Okes's workmen in fact had an "ever-present anxiety" to adjust print space to text space. To set the eight pages of a Quarto sheet from a messy authorial manuscript, without any guide to the amount of text to be accommodated on each page, would have been a constant strain. The most striking evidence of the pressure that the compositors were under comes precisely in those pages where Okes mixed narrow and wide settings for reasons not implicit in the "matter" of the play, as Moxon might describe it. Where Shakespeare switches from passages or whole scenes written in verse to a sequence of prose, the move from the narrow to the wide setting is given by the author's text.[62] When one or more characters in a scene speak verse, while others speak prose, a mixture of narrow and wide measures is appropriate.[63] But there are many instances in the 1608 *Lear* of the compositor switching from the narrow to the wide measure for no other reason than to squeeze more text on the page. An early example of this ad hoc adjustment of the measure comes in the opening scene, when Cordelia, invited to exceed her sisters in flattery, offers the fateful response, "Nothing my Lord":

> (againe.
> *Lear.* How, nothing can come of nothing, speake
> *Cord.* Vnhappie that I am, I cannot heaue my heart into my mouth,I loue your Maiestie according to my bond,nor more nor lesse. (B2r17–21; 1.1.90–93)

The narrow measure finishes at Lear's "speake," with the turned-up word "(againe" being set within the 20 em line. To save space, the compositor then turned Cordelia's speech into prose, but gained nothing in the process. That he used the wide measure in an attempt to accommodate more text is confirmed by examination of verse passages above and below this more easily visible use of prose. In

Regan's flattering speech ("Sir I am made of the selfe same mettall . . ."), the compositor adjusted the lineation to reduce eight verse lines to six (B2r2–7), a device that he used again in Cordelia's self-defense ("Good my Lord, | You haue begot me, bred me . . ."), where he reduced ten verse lines to nine (B2r24–32).

From our examination of analogous instances in other Quartos, as in the Folio, we can recognize these as typographical adjustments designed to solve a local space problem. In the 1608 Quarto of *Lear*, however, the local almost becomes universal: a majority of pages show signs of interventions disturbing normal printing practices. Examples of regular layout can be found, such as in the passage where Goneril and Regan are left behind onstage.[64] They "descend" to prose, in line with Shakespeare's stylistic convention of distinguishing private from public utterances, and the compositor correctly switched from the narrow to the wide measure, which he maintained until the end of the scene on the facing page (B4v33–C1r13). However, he then retained the wide setting for the following scene (1.2), Edmund's first soliloquy, where he reduced twenty-two lines of verse to fourteen of prose (C1r15–28). This retention of the wide setting is more than a matter of convenience to the compositor—not having to change the setting of his stick—but is clearly the result of an overall need to save space. Similarly, when the disguised Kent explains to Cornwall why he has attacked Oswald, he intentionally descends to prose for some plain speaking:

> *Kent.* To goe out of my{dialect}[65] which you discommend so much,I know sir,I am no flatterer,he that beguild you in a plain accent, was a plaine knaue, which for my part I will not bee, though I should win your displeasure, to intreat mee too't.
>
> (E2r24–27; 2.2.109–110)

After these four lines in prose, which are appropriately set in the wider measure, the medium reverts to verse and the narrow measure. But to accommodate the last line of the page, Kent's angry outburst, "None of these roges & cowards | but *AIax* is their foole" (124–125), the compositor was forced to use an ampersand, run two verse lines together, and set to the full 90 mm width. As he continued setting on the following page, he set the first twelve lines in the wider measure, compressing six lines of verse into five, before being able to revert to the narrow measure (with one line turned under) for the remainder of the page.

As we study the unpredictable oscillation between the narrow and wide measures, we gain the distinct impression that Okes and his compositor were not fully in control of the printing process. For a long period they played safe, simply using the wider measure for seventeen consecutive pages, covering sheets C, D, and the first page of E. These are the most crowded pages in the Quarto, accommodating a large amount of Shakespeare's text by the brutal expedient of setting verse as prose and making several omissions. When the compositors reverted to the narrow setting for verse scenes, on all too many occasions they were forced to set several verse lines as prose to save space. Whether or not the compositor could only make a rough estimate of the amount of text he could fit into the print space, the result is a disconcerting switch between narrow and wide measures, as the printed text mingles verse and prose without any inherent artistic motivation. The Folio preserves Shakespeare's careful distinction between the two media, unlike the Quarto, which abandoned it whenever space was tight. Some characters, such as the Fool and Edgar in his disguise as Poor Tom, speak mostly prose, but when verse characters such as Cordelia, Edgar, or Kent descend to prose it is a clear sign of a compositor suddenly realizing that he needs to save space.

In the scene where Kent pleads with Lear to take shelter from the storm, he begins in verse (F4v1–8), but for his second speech, "Alacke bare headed" (3.2.60–67), the compositor suddenly switched to the wide measure, reducing eight lines of verse to six of prose (F4v20–25), before reverting to verse for Lear's anguished realization, "My wit begins to turn." But a few lines later he had to set the Fool's four lines of rhyme—"Hee that has a little {tiny}[66] witte, | with hey ho the wind and the rain"—as three lines of prose (34–36), as if to finish the page by a given point. He again reduced Kent's verse to prose on the following page (G1r).

Disguised as Poor Tom, Edgar speaks prose both to Lear and to Gloucester, but in his asides, directed at the audience, he reverts to verse and his own persona. Edgar's first aside in the "mad trial" scene is correctly printed as verse:

Edg. My teares begin to take his part so much,
Theile marre my counterfeiting. (G4r24–25; 3.6.60–61)

In the scene where he tends his blinded father (4.1), Edgar's first three asides are also in verse (H2r35–37; H2v14–15, 17–18). For the fourth, however, the compositor suddenly reverted to the wider measure, changing verse into prose and saving a line:

Edg. How should this be,|bad is the trade that must play the foole to sorrow|angring it selfe and others, blesse thee maister. (H2v29–30; 4.1.37–39)

When Gloucester, believing that he is on "th'extreame verge" of Dover cliff, has jumped to his wished-for death, the compositor had to convert Edgar's worried reaction, as his father lies senseless, into prose and the wider measure, managing to save three lines in the process:

Edg. Gon sir, farewell, | and yet I know not how conceit{may}[67] robbe the treasurie of life, when life it selfe | yealds to the theft (I3r2–3; 4.6.41–48)

Cordelia is a verse character, but she, too, can be reduced to prose when "necessity" demands:

Cord. O looke upon me sir,|and hold your hands in benediction o're me, | no sir you must not kneele. (K2v2–3; 4.7.56–58)

If not reducing her to prose, the compositor could deploy another recurrent space-saving device used by Okes and his fellow printers: running Cordelia's verse lines together:

Cor. O my deer father restoratiō hang | thy medicin on my lips,
And let this kis|repaire those violent harmes that my two sisters |
Haue in thy reuerence made. (K2r8–10; 4.7.25–28)

By using the wider measure Okes saved one line. As should now be evident, the cause of these myriad small adjustments was the constant anxiety to adjust text space to print space.

Whoever examines the Quarto will see that several of the passages already discussed were set in the wider measure either at the end of a page (Kent's "roges and cowards," the Fool's rhymes) or at its beginning (Edgar's misgivings, Cordelia's wish to be blessed). There are further examples of a wider measure being used in both positions.[68] In some instances passages are compressed both at the end of one page and the beginning of the next, as in Lear's anger that Cornwall and Regan have not greeted him on his arrival at Gloucester's house. In the last three lines of this page the compositor converted verse to prose:

> *Glost.* My deere Lord, | you know the fierie qualitie of the
> Duke,| how vnremouable and fixt he is | in his own Course.
> *Lear.* Vengeance, death,plague,confusion,| what fierie quality,
> (E4r36–38)

On the next page the compositor continued at the wider measure (the Quarto showing some disturbance of the text) as Lear now appeals to be allowed to see his daughter and son-in-law:

> why *Gloster,Gloster,* | id'e speake with the Duke of *Cornewall*,and
> his wife. |
> *Glost.* I my good Lord.
> *Lear.* The King would speak with *Cornewal,*| the deare father |
> Would with his daughter sp eake, commands her seruice |
> Fierie Duke, tell the hot Duke that *Lear,*
> (E4v1–6; 2.4.90–104)

In this exchange, whether inadvertently or (as I shall argue) by design, the compositor twice omitted verse lines, abbreviating Shakespeare's text (the Quarto omissions are enclosed between pointed brackets):

> <*Glo.* Well my good, I haue inform'd them so.
> <*Lear.* Inform'd them? Do'st thou vnderstand me man?>
> *Lear.* The King would speak with *Cornewal* . . .
> (98–99; TLN 1373–1374)

and a few lines later he removed this line from Lear's outburst:

<Are they inform'd of this? My breath and blood. >
(103; TLN 1379)

A similar use of the longer measure at the end of a page and the start of the one following, combined with the reduction of verse to prose and "continuous printing," can be seen in Cornwall and Regan's vicious questioning of Gloucester (H1r25–H1v11).

Evidently Okes and his compositors switched to the wider measure to save space. Yet they did not achieve as much as they may have hoped by using this resort, and on numerous occasions they were obliged to use another space-saving device, turning a line over or under to prevent the text from running on and occupying an extra line. In Kent's quarrel with Oswald, the compositor correctly used the wide measure for the prose passages, but decided to keep it for the verse following. There, however, having adjusted Kent's speech so as to save a line, the knock-on effect of this change made him turn up the final word, in what Moxon would have termed a "botch":

Reneag,affirme,and turne their halcion beakes
With euery gale and varie of their masters, (epeliptick
Knowing nought like{dogges}[69] but following,|a plague upon your
Visage,|smoyle you my speeces, as I were a foole?
(E1v31–34; 2.2.78–81)

In Lear's address to the elements, the compositor suddenly switched to the full width to gain space, accommodating more verse by realignment, but nonetheless had to turn a line down in an equally ugly manner:

I neuer gaue you kingdome,cald you children,
You owe me no subscription, why thenlet fall | your horrible
Here I stād your slaue,|a poor infirm weak & (plesure
Despis'd ould man,|but yet I call you seruile
(F4r19–22; 3.2.17–20)

With that turn-over and other awkward adjustments (running two words together at "thenlet," using a tilde at "stād," followed by an ampersand), the compositor managed to reduce Lear's speech from twelve to ten verse lines. However, he must have realized that he would need to save more space, so he turned the Fool's rhymes—"the Codpeece that will house | before the head, has any | . . ." (F4r 27–30; 3.2.27–34)—into prose, thus saving an additional four lines. As examples mount up it is clear that for practical purposes the page must have been the unit of composition, with problems accumulating as the compositor reached the last two pages of the quire or gathering: F4r (the last page of the inner forme) and F4v (the last page of the outer forme). There he may have inherited a problem from the preceding page of the inner forme (F3v), which ends with Kent dismissing the Gentleman in their search for the king:

> Ile this way, you that, he that first lights
> *Enter*
> (F3v38)

The first line on F4r should begin with the stage direction "*Enter*," but it proved to be the last line of Kent's speech:

> On him,hollow the other. *Exeunt* (3.1.54–5)
> *Enter Lear and Foole.*
> *Lear.* Blow wind & cracke your cheekes,rage,blow
> (F4r1–3; 3.2.1)

Having to fit in one more line than expected led to this awkward page break. It is significant that, as with the other examples given by Greg and Blayney, the disturbance occurs at the end of a page.

The space constraints under which Okes and his compositors were working frequently led them to "o'er-flow the measure." Having chosen to set the "mad trial" scene at the wide measure (93–94 mm), the compositor mistakenly set Poor Tom's speech as verse—at least, he gave the first word of each line a capital letter—and then had to resort first to a tilde and next to a turn-over:

Edg. The foule fiend haũts poore *Tom* in the voyce of a nigh-
Hoppedance cries in *Toms* belly for two white herring, (tingale,
(G4r1–2; 3.6.29–30)

Further down that page—once again, the penultimate one of the gathering—he mistakenly set Lear's prose as verse, again using initial capitals, and was again forced to turn a line awkwardly:

(her
Lear. Then let them anotomize *Regan*, see what|breeds about
Hart is there any cause in nature that|makes this hardnes,
(G4r35–36; 3.6.76–78)

On the following page, despite having compressed the ten lines of Gloucester's speech into eight, he still had to turn down the line at "take up thy ‖ master" (G4v10–11; 3.6.92).[70] Further down the page he set a prose line to the full measure, but still had to turn up a word: "shew him this ‖ (letter," that word being uncomfortably inserted at the end of the opening stage direction (G4v34–35; 3.7.1). Similarly on the next page, the compositor was forced to use two turned lines in a prose speech: "keep you our sister ‖ (company" (H1r1–2)—the word "company" wastefully occupying a line on its own—and "where you are ‖ (going" (H1r5; 3.7.7, 9). The luckless compositor also needed a turn-over involving (most unusually) two words in Gloucester's indignant but futile protest, in verse already set to the wide measure usually reserved for prose:

Glost. Naughty Ladie,|these haires which thou dost rauish
from
Will quicken and accuse thee, I am your host. (my chin|
(H1r33–34; 3.7.37–39)

On the final page of this gathering Okes's compositor again found that the wide measure was not wide enough and on three occasions was forced to use a turned line to fit the text extent into the print space available:

But O Poore *Gloster*ˡ lost he his other eye. (answer,
Gent. Both, both my Lord,ˡthis letter Madam craues a speedy
Tis from your sistcr. *Gon.* One way I like this well,
(H4v1–3; 4.2.81–83)
(King,
Alb. *Gloster* I liueˡto thanke thee for the love thou shewedst the
And to reuenge thy eyes . . . (14–16; 4.2.94–95)
(of griefe.
Kent. Did your letters pierce the queene to any demonstratiō
(26–27; 4.3. 9–10)

The last line, Kent's question, is in fact in prose and could quite properly have been run on into the next line. But on this page, where the compositor had already resorted to unusual measures to compensate for having realigned the verse, no more space was available.

Knowing what it means when a Jacobean printer suddenly shifts from the narrow to the wide measure, and taking into account the simultaneous use of other space-saving devices, we can chart the varying amounts of pressure that Okes came under as printing progressed. Of the eight pages in sheet F, five justify the page at the narrow measure,[71] and three are set wide, yet still overrun the measure on five occasions. In sheet H only one page is set to the narrow measure (H3r), and keeps within the allotted space by using three turn-overs. In sheet I also, only one page is set narrow (I2v), using two turn-overs. In the remainder of this sheet, which Blayney described as "arguably the worst sheet in the whole book," almost half of which was set by Compositor C, local "necessity" caused him to set several lines beyond the wide measure[72]:

What we are come about,and by no meanesˡwill yeeld to see his
(daughter.
(I1r20–21; 4.3.40–1)
Mes. News Madam,ˡthe Brittish powers are marching hither-
(ward.
(I1v18–19; 4.4.20–1)

Okes's employees seem to become increasingly stretched for space in sheet K, on which no pages are set narrow. Three pages are set wide, but nonetheless overrun the measure. As we have seen, in January 1608, Okes employed a second compositor ("C"), an apprentice, and Blayney has valuably identified their respective stints.[73] The new man found himself in difficulties again in the middle of K1v where, to compress the text at a point where two scenes overlap, each showing a child tending its parent, he resorted to the wider measure, but still had to chop up verse lines to fit:

> *Glost.* And woes by wrong imaginations loose
> The knowledge of themselues. *A drum a farre off.*
> *Edg.* Giue me your hand|far off me thinks I heare the beaten
> Come father ile bestow you with a friend. *Exit.* (drum,
> *Enter Cordelia, Kent and Doctor.* (thy goodnes,
> *Cord.* O thou good *Kent* how shall I liue and worke|to match
> My life will be too short|and euery measure faile me.
> (K1v15–21; 4.6.284–286; 4.7.1–3)

That is probably a typical example of an inexperienced compositor using turn-overs in two consecutive lines, and some master printers would have insisted on the lines being reset. Despite these botches, and three times compressing the verse by realignment, lower down the page Compositor C had to switch measure again, but still there was an overrun:

> (nature,
> *Cord.* O you kind Gods | cure this great breach in his abused
> (32–34; 4.7.13–15)

When Compositor B returned to his typesetting stint he found himself compelled to use the same devices to save space and still had to turn lines up or down, despite having chosen the wide measure.[74] On page K3r he resorted to an unusual practice in two lines where he had run together the end of a speech by Regan and Edmund's reply (see Plate 4). In both cases he aligned the end of Edmund's speeches with the right-hand margin, using the wide measure to the utmost.

In the process he left gaps in the text, botches that Moxon called "pigeon holes." As William Proctor Williams has observed, these gaps represent spacing quads inserted into the middle of the line, rather than at the end, to hold the block of type more firmly in position.[75]

According to Blayney's analysis, Compositor C set the last five-and-a-half pages of the 1608 Quarto. We soon find him compressing the text in the middle of the page, but having to leave some unsightly spaces:

> *Alb.* Stop your mouth dame,|or with this paper shall I stople
> it,|thou worse then any thing, reade thine   owne euill, | nay no
> tearing Lady ,I perceiue you know't. (me for't.
> *Gon.* Say if I do,the lawes are mine not thine,|who shal arraine
> (L2r15–18; 5.3.155–159)

Compositor C turned those speeches into prose, running verse lines together and setting to the full measure, as he did again here, managing to save two lines in the process:

> Let sorow split my heart if I did euer | hate thee or thy father.
> (L2r38; 5.3.178–179)

But comparison with the Folio reveals that he saved two other lines by a more desperate measure: omitting parts of Shakespeare's text. In Edmund's speech, where he complacently agrees to accept Edgar's challenge, one whole line has been dropped (Quarto omissions are set between pointed brackets):

<What safe, and nicely I might well delay> (5.3.145; TLN 3100)

And in Albany's reply to Goneril, after "it" the words < "hold Sir" > (156; TLN 3113) have been left out. Together with earlier instances and with many more to be discussed, these adjustments are signs that the words, phrases, and lines omitted in the 1608 Quarto of *King Lear* were sacrificed to save space.

Consideration of the choice of measure, whether short or full, has turned out to be unexpectedly significant. Peter Blayney evidently realized this fact thirty years ago, but unfortunately never followed it up.[76] My examination of the Quarto's unpredictable shifts from narrow to wide settings has shown that the expansion of the page depth still failed to accommodate all the text estimated for that page. The typesetting practiced by Okes and his compositors in the 1608 *Lear* can best be described as directionless. Every page presented a fresh set of problems, each of which was solved typographically by shifting to the wide setting, by setting verse as prose, by relining verse to reduce its extent on the page, or by using an abnormally high number of turned lines and other mechanical devices, as we have seen. Okes managed to print *King Lear* within the ten-and-a-half pages he had estimated, but only by constantly manipulating the print space, and, as I shall show in the next chapter, occasionally reducing the text by omissions.

Space Saving in Contemporary Shakespeare Quartos

My argument that Nicholas Okes used desperate remedies to solve the space problem caused by having ordered too little paper can be tested by comparing his *King Lear* with three other contemporary Shakespeare Quartos: *Hamlet* (1605), *Troilus and Cressida* (1609), and the second Quarto of *King Lear* (1619).[77] For each play I made a word count of the complete text (in electronic form), including speech prefixes and stage directions but excluding running titles. This produces a larger total than if one were to count only the words spoken by the characters, but since I use the same measure for each play this method seems legitimate. The total sheet count is given in column B of Table 1. In column C I give the total number of printed pages for each play, and column D gives the word count. Column E shows the result of dividing the word total by the page total, from which we can see that the 1608 *Lear* Quarto, at 333 words per page, is the most densely printed. The 1604/05 *Hamlet* Quarto has only 302 words per page, whereas the 1609 *Troilus and Cressida* has slightly more (307). The 1619 Pavier Quarto of *King Lear* adds stage directions omitted in Q1, expands others, and inserts some words into the text (recovering a two-word speech in 4.6). But at the same time, as Doran noted, its printing shows "a certain amount of carelessness that leads to the omission of several necessary words and even in one case of a line (5.3.146)."[78] It has approximately the same word count as the 1608 Quarto, but since Pavier and Jaggard wisely allowed twelve sheets for the play, instead of Okes's ten-and-a-half, the 1619 Quarto could spread the text over eighty-five pages, at 311 words per page, resulting in a much more comfortable reading experience.

As for the typographical adjustments used to justify a line of verse or to accommodate a prose speech without running over into an extra line, I counted the four most common devices used in these texts: tildes, ampersands, lines turned up or down, and numbers shown as numerals rather than letters. (I leave the task of counting unspaced medial commas to other hands, but a cursory glance at any of the three other Quartos shows nothing like the density of compression that Okes achieved.)

The 1605 Quarto of *Hamlet* has often been criticized for its many textual inaccuracies, with most of the blame previously falling on the compositors. Recent scholarship agrees that the copy itself—an autograph in Shakespeare's hand that had been partly marked up for the theater—is to blame.[79] In terms of typography and layout, however, James Roberts produced a commendably tidy and spacious text. There is not a single "botch," to use Moxon's criteria, until page 32, by which time Okes's *Lear* had made several dozen. There are occasional signs of cramped space, probably due to inaccurate casting off, as in the last line of a page ending with a prose speech by Hamlet to Polonius, where the compositor had to use two ampersands and omit two spaces, in order to finish before the catchword:

> purging thick Amber,&plumtree gum,& that they haue a plen-||
> ||tifull
> (F1r)

Roberts used the ampersand more than any other space-saving device—thirty times in prose but also three times in verse—on each occasion to justify a long line:

> They foole me to the top of my bent, I will come by & by
> (H4v)
> Two thousand soules, & twenty thousand duckets (K3r)
> When our deepe plots fall, & that shoulde learne vs (N1r)

Table 1 Space Saving in Four Jacobean Quartos

A	B	C	D	E	F		G		H		I		J	K
					Tilde		&		Turned lines		Numerals			
Text	Sheet total	Page total	Word total	Words p. page	V	P	V	P	V	P	V	P	Savers total	Per page
Q2 *Hamlet* 1605	13.5	99	29,864	301.7	2	2	3	30	1	4	0	0	42	0.4
Q1 *Lear* 1608	10.5	79	26,402	333.2	25	20	15	22	60	5	2	3	151	1.9
Q *Troilus & Cressida* 1609	11.5	88	27,050	307.4	2	6	3	11	4	12	0	0	38	0.4
Q2 *Lear* 1619	12	85	26,409	310.7	2	12	2	25	4	0	0	2	37	0.4

V = Verse

P = Prose

It is no accident that all three verse instances occur in Hamlet's part, the longest in the play. He is also the cause (so to speak) of most of the prose ampersands, twenty-six of thirty falling in his speeches. In some cases the ampersand was needed to prevent a line of prose from overrunning and disturbing the whole page.[80] Looking at the frequent occurrences of the ampersand, it seems at first as if the *copia verborum* with which Shakespeare endowed Hamlet had to be typographically abridged on the printed page. However, in several cases there would have been enough space to print the word "and" in full.[81] These superfluous ampersands may be a sign either that a compositor setting prose needed to take precautions from the outset or else that he had no compunctions about using this resort.

Roberts made sparing use of the other standard space-saving devices. He used a tilde only once, to justify a long verse line:

> *Ham.* I see a Cherub that sees thē, but come for England
> (K2v)

In prose passages, the tilde served the same function, used at the last moment to avoid an overrun, both for Hamlet

> *Ham.* Bid the players make hast. Will you two help to hasten
> thē. (G4r)

and for the gravedigger, in a line ending "thēselues" (M2r). Roberts was seldom obliged to turn a long line over. The only verse instance comes in Hamlet's graveside quarrel with Laertes, a line that the Folio divided (TLN 3055–3056):

> *Ham.* Thou pray'st not well , I prethee take thy fingers
> For though I am not spleenatiue rash (from my throat,
> Yet haue I in me something dangerous (M4v)

In sequences of prose Roberts used the turn-over three times (F1v, F3r, M3r) and once in a prose speech placed between two passages of verse (F3v). On seven occasions he combined an entry with part of a verse line,[82] but in general he allowed ample room for stage directions, setting them with white space some thirty-five times.

George Eld's 1609 Quarto, *The Famous Historie of Troylus and Cresseid*, uses slightly fewer space-saving devices than Roberts's *Hamlet*, but distributes them more evenly. Eld used the ampersand three times to justify a long verse line:

> Good armes,strong ioints,true swords,& great *Ioues* accord
> (C2r)
>
> *Cres.* Teare my bright haire,& scratch my praised cheekes,
> (H2v)

In one of these instances the compositor had to combine an ampersand with a turned-up line to set an unusually long verse:

> (by ioint.
> I have with exact view perusde thee *Hector*, & quoted ioynt
> (I4r)

The compositor used the ampersand more freely in prose, as did the printing houses for all four Quartos. In some cases its use solved a minor typographical crisis, as in this speech by Pandarus, whose name was also abbreviated to two letters so as not to overrun the page:

> *Pa.* Asses,fooles,doults,chaff & bran,chaff & bran, porredge after meate , I could liue and die in the eyes of *Troylus*,nere‖
> ‖looke
> (B2r)

Eld deployed other devices to solve local typographical difficulties, such as the tilde in long verse lines:

> *Vli.* What hath she done Prince that cā spoile our mothers.
> (K4r)
>
> *Troy.* Words,words,meere words,no matter frō the heart,
> (L2v)

In prose the tilde is less conspicuous, but its use four times within three lines (E1v) suggests another local difficulty, perhaps due to an error in casting off copy.

The space-saving device used most often by Eld's compositor was the turned line, in further instances of overlong verse lines, pointing to an unequal relationship between text space and print space. As so often, the beginning of a speech, with the speaker's name indented, caused problems:

> *Aga.* Princes:what griefe hath set these Iaundies ore your
> (cheekes?
> (B3r)
> (row.
> *Nest.* Ha ? by this white beard Ide fight with thee to mor-
> (I3v)

That example is one of several in this play where the compositors produced hypermetrical verse lines, as again here:

> (*Phoebus,*
> Modest as morning, when shee coldly eyes the youthfull
> (C2r)

Eld's compositor turned lines more often in prose (twelve times as against four in verse); on one occasion a turn-over occurred twice in three lines (D1r), which might have been due to an error in casting off copy. Although Eld managed to fit *Troilus and Cressida* into the eleven sheets he had bargained for, there are some indications of pressure on space, such as the presence of "continuous copy" or printing two speeches in one line. Given the amount of (often scabrous) repartee in this play, especially in the scenes between Cressida and Pandarus, and between Thersites and Achilles' entourage, it made economic sense to run short speeches together, and Eld did so both in verse and prose (nine, and forty times, respectively). On the same basis he combined stage directions with speeches twelve times. One particularly crowded page (K2r) has two entrances run into the remainder of a speech, five instances of continuous copy, and one turn-over. Despite this evidence of compression, Eld's total use of the four typographical space-saving devices was a mere 38 in 88 pages, comparable with that of James Roberts in *Hamlet* (42 in 99 pages), both averaging 0.4 space savers per page. Nicholas Okes's accumulation of 148 such devices in the 79 pages of his 1608 *King Lear*, or nearly five times as many, shows how poorly he had estimated the amount of print space he would need for that text.

When Jaggard and Pavier set out to reprint *Lear* in 1619 (with the false date "1608"), as part of a plan to reissue nine Shakespearean Quartos, they had divided aims. On the one hand they were trying to imitate Q1, reproducing some more or less distinguishing features of the original. They copied the setting of the title page, retaining the four blocks of type in varying fonts, with a mixture of roman and italic, while abbreviating the colophon, which now reads simply "Printed for Nathaniel Butter. 1608." Okes had recycled part of the title-page setting to produce the title on the first text page: they did the same. Okes had cramped the last three pages of text (L3r, L3v, L4v) in order to leave the final page blank—as was his wont, reducing verse to prose, running short speeches into the same line, crowding stage directions and speeches together. Jaggard did the same, unfortunately ruining what had been a quite presentable piece of printing up to this point.

Although one of their goals was to produce a "mock-up" of the 1608 Quarto, with some intention to deceive or mislead purchasers, Jaggard and Pavier's other goal was to undo Okes's extreme crowding of the text on the page. Where his text had a blank leaf preceding the title, amounting to a half-sheet, with the text extending from B to L3v, Pavier and Jaggard had no blank leaf, the title page forming [A1], with the text extending from A2 to L4r. Both texts end on L4r, but the 1619 version begins on sheet A, not B. Okes had estimated ten-and-a-half sheets: they made good his mistake by allowing twelve sheets for their *Lear*. Apart from the pages that copy the 1608 Quarto, their 1619 version offers a comfortable reading experience. They allowed thirty-seven lines per page, as against Okes's thirty-eight, and their ample use of white space around stage directions (not only for entrances) on thirty occasions gives the reader's eyes the chance to relax. Since the compositors were setting from the 1608 Quarto, without access to Shakespeare's text as preserved in the King's Men promptbook, they had no choice but to reproduce Okes's reduction of verse to prose, together with his relining of the verse, to cram in additional lines per page. Studies of Q2 by Madeleine Doran and Richard Knowles have illuminated the printing process and the sporadic attempts by Jaggard and his compositors to correct errors and improve layout.[83] Knowles showed that the quarto was set by formes, so that "accurate casting-off of Q1 copy must have been relatively easy." This allowed the compositors to copy the appearance of Q1, closely following its line length for both prose and verse.[84] Since Knowles did not know of Blayney's work on Q1 when he published this article, we can add that Jaggard, setting by formes and with an adequate supply of both type and spaces, was able to avoid the narrow verse setting that Okes used (mostly 80 mm, as against Q2's 94–95 mm).

We can extend the work of Doran and Knowles by examining Jaggard's treatment of the space-saving devices that Okes had used in Q1. A side-by-side comparison of the two Quartos reveals a systematic reduction in all four categories of space savers. Where Okes's compositors had been forced to use the tilde twenty-two times in verse lines, Jaggard's men did so only twice. In Q1 Edmund reports that it is hard to guess the enemy's strength "By diligent discouery but your hast'is now vrg'd on you." (K3v18). The verse line in Q1 at this point is unusually long (93 mm, as against 86 mm in Q2). In order to justify the line, Jaggard's compositor removed the apostrophe in "vrgd"; however, he still had to use a tilde for "diligēt" and even omit the full stop, two uncharacteristic decisions (K3r37). Kent's attempts to make Lear recognize his true identity in the final scene had caused Okes's compositor to run two lines together and set the third unusually long (100 mm):

Kent. If Fortune bragd of two she loued or hated,
One of them we behold. *Lear.* Are you not *Kent?*
Kent. The same your seruant *Kent*, where is your servant
Caius, (L3v32–34)

In Q2 the compositor set all three speeches on separate lines:

Kent. If Fortune bragd of two she loued or hated,
One of them we behold.
Lear. Are you not *Kent?*
Kent. The same your servant *Kent*, wher is your seruāt *Caius?*
(L3v25–28)

Having replaced the concluding comma with a question mark, in order to justify the line (at a width of 94 mm) he shortened the spelling of "where" to "wher," but still had to use a tilde. Both Doran and Knowles noted that a different compositor set the last three sheets, with "a marked change to more carefully lined verse, more freely emended readings, more careless mistakes."[85] His colleagues, setting sheets A to H, had removed the eighteen tildes that Okes had used in verse, and the new man continued their clean up, removing an additional four tildes in sheets I to L. But in these two instances a local lack of adequate print space, together with a reluctance to remove the spacing around commas, caused him to reintroduce a device that all three compositors had outlawed.

Where Okes had deployed the tilde nineteen times in prose, Jaggard's compositors did so only once (B2r10). Using the longer line length (94 mm) Okes's compositor had run verse lines together for Gloucester's complaint at Regan's violence:

Naughty Ladie,these haires which thou dost rauish from
Will quicken and accuse thee, I am your host. (my chin
(H1r33–34)

Having no independent text, the Q2 compositor preserved the compressed layout of the verse, but turned the line up, not down:

(my chin,
Glost. Naughty Lady, these haires which thou dost rauish frō
Will quicken and accuse thee, I am your host:
(G3v28–29)

Although the Q2 compositor used the maximum line length (100 mm) and reducing the spelling of "Ladie" to "Lady," his disinclination to set commas without spacing, coupled with his use of more space between words, left him one letter short at the line ending, so he replaced the "m" of "from" with a tilde.

Addressing another type of "botch" in the copy text, Jaggard's compositor decisively reduced the number of ampersands that Okes had used in verse, eliminating fourteen instances and leaving only two. In Q1 Regan's hypocritical words to her "good old friend" Gloucester are set at the maximum width for this page (91 mm):

> Lay comforts to your bosome,& bestow your needful councell
> To our busines,which craues the instant vse. (*Exeunt.*
> (D4v37–38)

Using a wider setting, Jaggard's compositor left spaces before and after the ampersand, but had insufficient room to substitute "and." However, enjoying the luxury of an extra line per page, he was able to set the stage direction for Regan on a separate line, also correcting it to the singular "*Exit*" (D2r37). The other verse ampersand taken over from Q1 also occurs at the end of a page in Q2. In the 1608 Quarto, Lear's anger at not having been greeted by Cornwall and Regan included one hypermetric line, for which Okes's compositor had to use both an ampersand and a turn-down:

> This act persuades me,that this remotion of the Duke
> Is practise (& her
> (E4v14–15)

On this occasion the Q2 compositor chose the longer spelling "acte," forfeited a space after the comma, managed to avoid the turn-down, but still had to use the ampersand (E2r37–E2v1).

In resetting *King Lear*, although Jaggard practically eliminated the ampersand in verse, like other Jacobean printers he had no misgivings about using it in prose. In the 99 pages of *Hamlet* Roberts printed 30 ampersands in prose passages; for the 1608 *Lear* Okes used it 22 times in 79 pages; for the 1609 *Troilus and Cressida* Eld used it 11 times in 88 pages; for the 1619 *Lear* Jaggard used it 25 times in 85 pages. Of these, 9 were repeated from Q1, 16 newly introduced. As in other Jacobean quartos, on several occasions an ampersand would not have been necessary, there being enough space for the word "and."[86] Neither Roberts nor Eld used numerals for numbers, but in attempting to copy Q1 by setting Edmund's first soliloquy as prose, Jaggard's compositor kept one numeral, but had to add a second: "some 12. or 14. moone-shines lag of a brother" (B2r26), where Q1 had "twelue" (C1r18).

The biggest numerical change that Jaggard's printing house made to Q1 *Lear* concerned turned lines. Richard Knowles stated that in Q2 "a few turnovers and turn unders are carried down and indented to make a separate part-line."[87] This is true, but Okes's 1608 Quarto had contained sixty turn-overs in verse and five in prose. In 1619 Jaggard eliminated all of the prose usages and reduced those in verse to four only. By my count, Jaggard's compositors indented the turn-over to form a separate line on nine occasions.[88] In some cases they adjusted the verse lineation, shifting the turned word(s) down into the line following, with the risk of ruining the meter of both lines.[89] In most cases Jaggard was able to accommodate the turned word(s) within the proper line because he was using a wider measure for the verse setting. Where Okes had varied between a width of 81 mm and 95 mm, due to an inadequate supply of spacing quads, from sheet C onward Jaggard's compositors were able to shift from 94 to 95 mm.[90] They certainly exerted themselves to minimize unsightly turn-overs. In the Folio, as Prosser observed, there are very few instances of two-word turn-overs. In Q1 *Lear* Okes was frequently guilty of this "botch," as Moxon termed it. Where Okes had turned up two words "(the Dukes," (G1r6), Jaggard's men reduced that to just one, "(Dukes," (F3r10). They managed to reduce Q1's turned-up "(*Burgūdy.*" (B4v9) to just "(*gundy.*" (B1v15); they restored Q1's turned-down "(& her" (E4v15) to its proper line, but had to retain the ampersand (E2r37). The compositor of Q1 had to abbreviate the turned-down word by using a tilde:

> Into this scattered Kingdome, who alreadie wise in our
> (negligēce,
> (F3v15–16)

Jaggard's compositor shortened the spelling of two words, managing to do away with both the turn-over and the tilde, but at the cost of the final comma:

> Into this scatterd Kingdom, who already wise in
> our negligence (F1v15)

Omitting a comma is a small offense, but on some occasions, to avoid a turnover, Jaggard's compositors were forced to delete a word.[91] Compare

> (appeare,
> Q1 *Kent.* Why fare thee well king,since thus thou wilt
> (B3r35–36)
> Q2 *Kent.* Why fare thee well King, since thou wilt appeare
> (A4v2)

There Jaggard's compositor used the maximum width (100 mm), but preferred to omit the word "thus" rather than turn the line. As I have observed, for early modern printers the author's text was a flexible, not an absolute entity. We see that again here:

> (rude wind
> Q1 *Alb.* O *Gonoril*,you are not worth the dust which the
> (H3v26–27)
> Q2 *Alb.* O *Gonorill*, you are not worth the dust which the winde
> (H2v3)

Jaggard's compositor set this line at 96 mm, but deleted "rude" in order to retain his spacing.

> Q1 Ere they shall make vs weepe ? wele see vm starue first,
> (come.
> (K4r36–37)
> Q2 Ere they shall make vs weepe? Weele see em
> starue first. *Exit* (K4r25)

In the above lines, the compositor avoided the turn-over, restored the needed stage direction, but omitted Lear's decisive "come." In all three instances the Q2 compositor simply abbreviated Shakespeare's text to avoid making a turn-over, omitting the words "thus," "rude," and "come." These are not particularly serious losses, but they do show that, as a material object, the text of *King Lear* was subject to many depredations by the craftsmen who produced it, including deletions made to avoid a typographical solecism.

This analysis of three Shakespeare Quartos contemporaneous with Okes's 1608 *Lear* shows that other Jacobean printers sometimes used typographical space-saving devices out of "necessity." But their relatively infrequent use in the 1605 *Hamlet* and the 1609 *Troilus and Cressida* (0.4 instances per page), and the diligent efforts made by Jaggard to purge his *Lear* of Okes's excesses, reducing them from 148 to 37 (also resulting in 0.4 instances per page), also proves that they regarded them, as Moxon did a few decades later, as expedients to be avoided wherever possible. But then, none of the three was under the same space pressure as was Okes, having to cram into every page twenty to thirty more words than they did. Not having allowed himself enough paper, something had to give. Unfortunately, that necessity also affected Shakespeare's text.

Summary

In Appendix 2 I itemize the nine types of space-saving devices that I have identified in the 1608 Quarto, amounting to a total of 413 lines. On the seventy-nine pages available to them Okes's compositors managed to accommodate 3,252 lines of text (using the Folio lineation)[92] and 55 lines of stage directions, a total of 3,307 lines at an average of 41.9 lines per page. Thus, to accommodate the 418 lines saved by one or other form of cutting and scraping, Okes would have needed another ten pages to print the full text. In total, then, he ought to have estimated eighty-nine pages of text (one blank) together with four pages of preliminaries, a total of ninety-three pages. Thus, like Jaggard in 1619, he should have allowed a comfortable twelve sheets for the whole Quarto, not ten and a half. Okes sold his author and his readers short, creating for bibliographers, textual critics, and editors four centuries later a series of problems that have given rise to many misleading literary-critical or aesthetic arguments. But now we can dispense with the range of theories produced to explain these various deformations of the text in the Quarto of *King Lear:* Okes simply had too little paper.

An examination of the data collected in Appendix 2 will confirm my argument that the compositors' problems with space began long before the final gathering. Column K shows that Okes and his men, by manipulating their presentation of Shakespeare's text, saved just 22 lines on the initial sheet B; on C they raised the total to 42; on the eight pages of sheet D (1.4.149–2.1.128), with more intense exertions they reached the massive total of 89 lines saved, using all the devices available to them: turning verse into prose (saving 61 lines), relining verse (1 line), "continuous printing" or running half-lines together (7 lines), compressing or omitting stage directions (4 lines), and omitting 16 lines of Shakespeare's text. The prosification here (1.4) mostly affects the Fool's part, beginning on C4v, where the compositor reduced ten rhymed lines to five of prose, and continuing on D2v, where he compressed four of the Fool's rhyming lines to two of prose. But the felt need to save space here was so pressing that Okes's compositor B took the drastic step of turning into prose four speeches by Goneril and five by Lear, saving 34 lines (D1v–D2v). There is no contextual artistic justification for these changes (as there would be later, with Lear's relapse into madness), the only possible explanation being the need to save space. In the following scene (2.1) compositor B, again without any artistic warrant, reduced to prose a long sequence of verse spoken by Edmund, Gloucester, and Cornwall (D3v–D4r), saving a further 21 lines. Such a massive degree of compression, only a quarter of the way through the text, must have been caused by the equivalent of a typographical panic attack.

Having saved 148 lines in setting the first three sheets, Okes and his compositors could relax somewhat. In the next three sheets (E–G) they made fairly even cuts, of 34, 34, and 33 lines respectively, saving 97 lines. But anxiety set in again with sheets H and I, on which they managed to save 41 and 46 lines, respectively, and continued for the final two sheets, where the compositors managed to save 34 lines on K and 49 on the seven pages of L. Looking at these figures it becomes clear that the final sheet was by no means the one with most space saved, as some scholars have suggested, since its amount of lines saved is equaled by that in sheet I and massively exceeded by that in D, which contains nearly twice as much text. Evidently Okes's realization that he had seriously underestimated the available space for printing *King Lear* had registered on his compositor with the final page of sheet C, where the casting off was terminated. Although set seriatim, the 1608 Quarto displays the same space-saving techniques that miscalculated cast-off copy does. The easiest way to save space was by turning verse into prose, which accounts for more than a third of the total lines saved (145 out of 413), followed by relining the verse (saving 85 lines), "continuous printing" or setting two speeches on one line (saving 56 lines), manipulating the stage directions (saving 30 lines), and—most drastically—leaving out passages of Shakespeare's text (saving 102 lines). In the next chapter I analyze the omissions they made to see whether they did so on the basis of any consistent principles.

4

Nicholas Okes Abridges It

ALTHOUGH OKES's compositors assiduously manipulated Shakespeare's text to save as much space as possible, their efforts were insufficient, and they had to resort to the most effective but most damaging type of space saving available to early modern compositors, the curtailment of the text, ranging from single words to whole lines of verse or prose. As we have seen, due to a serious miscalculation in casting off copy for the Folio Histories, when Compositor B set 2 *Henry IV* he had to make urgent adjustments to compress the text, including "leaving something out." Eleanor Prosser's acute analysis of these adjustments showed that on many occasions he omitted a single word, on a few occasions he left out two or more words, and once—at a particularly awkward juncture—he omitted four entire lines. Prosser established that the cuts had been made by comparing the Folio text with the Quartos from which it was set. My analysis takes a different direction, comparing the 1608 Quarto of *Lear* with the fuller text as preserved in the Folio. The cumulative significance of my analysis of the eight other types of text manipulation made by the Quarto compositors leads me to the confident conclusion that these omissions were deliberate.[1] Apart from a few possibly accidental omissions, they were space-saving cuts made in Okes's printing shop, and not passages subsequently added to the Folio text either by Shakespeare or anyone else. The serious discrepancy between what I have called text space and print space led to a constant cutting of the text, spread out across the entire Quarto. The number of lines cut on each sheet is as follows—B: 13, C: 12, D: 16, E: 14, F: 16, G: 9, H: 6, I: 6, K: 2, L: 9—an average of 10.2 lines per sheet. The only visible principle that the compositors followed seems to have been "save where you can."

The bibliographical evidence of systematic cutting in the Quarto has never been properly investigated, and I present my findings in full here. As a practical exercise, the easiest way to make such cuts would have been for an abridger to work through the manuscript and mark passages for exclusion.[2] That seems a far more rational way of doing things than expecting a compositor to leave out words and lines as he goes along, which could only confuse him. For the *Lear* Quarto, I suggest that Okes himself acted not only as proof corrector, a normal role for the master printer, but also as abridger, reading through the text in advance and making whatever cuts he could. First, as we have seen, Charlton Hinman observed that the compositor would not have been the only person in the printing house making decisions about "justifying," which might also involve shortening a text when necessity called for it. Second, Okes must have told his compositors about the problem, instructing them to save space by all possible typographical adjustments. Third, whatever space the compositors had saved, additional economies could be made in the process of "imposition." Commenting on an earlier version of this chapter (having accepted my argument that Nicholas Okes abridged the 1608 Quarto), W. P. Williams helpfully pointed out that certain adjustments would be made by the pressman when he imposed the set type into pages in the formes:

> These would have been such things as setting parts of a shared pentameter line on the same type line, moving around stage directions, and so on. Although these three sets of actions and actors all are aimed at achieving the same end—making it fit—they would have been conducted at distinct times and places in the shop. The abridger has the whole ms. before him when he makes his cuts; the compositors will be dealing with the small number of lines that their sticks will hold at any one time (prob-

ably 7 or 8 lines) . . . ; the stone hand is dealing with long columns of set type, tied up with string, which he has to make into pages and fit into the skeleton formc.[3]

In abridging the play, Okes made 89 separate cuts, 25 of which involved omitting between 1 and 15 lines of verse or prose, making a total saving of 102 lines, compared to the Folio. The majority of the Folio cuts—34 out of 54 (63 percent, as against the Quarto's 30 percent)—were of longer passages. It is easy to see the advantage gained by the abridger when cutting entire lines of text. But it is surprising to discover that the vast majority of cuts made were of a few words only: 16 of them involved one-word omissions, 25 were of two words, 10 of three words, 10 of four words, 2 of five words, and 1 of seven words. These 64 cuts saved a mere 143 words, at an average of 2.2 words per omission, the equivalent of 18 lines of verse. We can endorse Alice Walker's judgment that "what is missing from the quarto seems . . . too pointless to represent a coherent effort to shorten the play."[4] Evidently Okes was aware of the need to save space by whatever means and started to do so on the verso of the first page (B1v). Thereafter, cuts were made on 48 of the total of 79 pages. Studying the location of these cuts on the page will enable us to identify some patterns and to discover the principles by which they were made.

If we reconstruct the process by which Okes tried to fit this messy manuscript into the space available, several consistent principles emerge. Cutting of repetitious or redundant material took two forms. First, in any instance of a word or words being repeated, the repetition was likely to be deleted, however important it might seem to modern sensibilities. This was an operation that could easily be performed, with little forethought. But such local cuts did not always result in the saving of entire lines, so more care had to be expended to achieve this goal. Looking over the abridger's shoulder, we can see him engaged on the second and harder task, establishing a scale of importance, so to speak, assessing which parts of a speech could be cut without affecting its dramatic function. If a speech consisted of a main and a subordinate clause, he could cut the latter. If it included digressions to apparently unrelated topics, they could be excised. If it contained a descriptive element but also formulated an order or request, the description could be omitted. If a speech did not seem to be addressing anyone on stage (as in soliloquies or asides to the audience) or did not receive a reply from any other character, it could be left out. In effect, to make these longer deletions the abridger had to establish a ranking order of semantic importance and dramatic function. I attempt to identify the underlying rationale for their omission by grouping them into separate categories, although some passages could be classified in several ways.

Accidents and Puzzles

This category includes the inadvertent cutting of words due to carelessness, as in the loss of a single word on E1r, where adequate space was available. (Words enclosed within pointed brackets < . . . > are found in the Folio but not in the Quarto text; words enclosed within square brackets [. . .] are found in the Quarto but not in the Folio; words enclosed within curly brackets { . . . } are variant readings.)

> *Stew.* Helpe,ho,murther,helpe.
> *Enter Edmund with his rapier drawne, Gloster the Duke and Dutchesse.*
> *Bast.* How now, whats the matter? <Part.>
> (E1r35–38; 2.2.43–44; TLN 1116–1118)

There would be no reason for omitting that word, other than an oversight; the Folio preserves it. Another instance where a single word has been lost occurs in what Gloucester intends to be his last speech:

> My snurff and loathed part of nature should
> Burne it selfe out, if *Edgar* liue, O blesse, <him>,
> Now fellow fare thee well. *He fals.*
> (I2v37–I3r1; 4.6.39–41; TLN 2478–2480)

Significantly, both these instances entail the loss of a word in the last line of the page, which therefore does not serve as a catchword;

these pages' catchwords are, respectively, "*Kent.*" and "Now." Compositorial inattention probably caused the loss of the last word in this line:

> *Gent.* O here he is, lay hands vpon him sirs, your most deere
> (I4v4; 4.6.188–189; TLN 2631–2632)

Examination of the Quarto at this point shows that the compositor set this speech, like Lear's preceding and following speeches, as prose, using the wide measure and full out to the right-hand margin, so that he had no room for a turn-over line. The pressure on space here was so acute that he even had to leave out the period ending that sentence, an expedient that Prosser noted in the Folio text of *Much Ado.* The whole page is crowded, with verse set as prose and two instances of "continuous printing." Thanks to the Folio, we can recover the word following "deere" that Okes's compositor was forced to leave out for lack of space—namely "Daughter"—the most important word in the sentence, which is otherwise unintelligible. Further down this page the compositor had to omit a word to justify the line and, following what I have called the semantic principle, chose the word of least importance:

> *Lear.* I will die brauely like a <Smugge> bridegroom, what?
> I will be Iouiall, come, come, I am a King my maisters,
> know you that.
> (I4v12–13; 4.6.198–200; TLN 2640–2642)

Fortunately, the Folio preserved that remarkable qualifying epithet "smug."

Other instances of inadvertent omission occur in Edmund's incrimination of his brother, where the cuts were probably due to eye-skip or inattention:

> *Bast.* . . . haue you not spoken gainst the Duke of *Cornwall*
> ought . . . haue you nothing said | vpon his partie against the
> Duke of *Albany,* | aduise your---<selfe.>
> *Edg.* I am sure on't not a word.

Bast. I heare my father coming,pardon me in{cunning},[5]
I must draw my sword vpon you, | <Draw,> seeme to defend
your selfe, now quit you well,
(D3v21–28; 2.1.25–30; TLN 953–962)

At line 24 Okes's compositor, presumably unable to read the word "selfe" in Shakespeare's manuscript, left the sentence without a predicate, setting three hyphens, as if Edmund had intended not to complete his sentence (the rhetorical figure *aposiopesis*). However, rhetoric specified definite motivations for breaking off an utterance, as we can see from its correct use elsewhere in *Lear.*[6] The more likely explanation is that the compositor's eye inadvertently picked up the clause ending "your selfe," just below. The omission of "Draw" in the last line quoted may have been due to inattention rather than to save space, since Edmund's speech ends with enough space for a half-line.

A related series of cuts were made not out of carelessness but probably out of desperation, involving words or longer utterances that puzzled Okes and his employees. They can surely be excused for not understanding many of the cryptic words and expressions that Shakespeare used for the disguise of Edgar as Poor Tom. Seemingly obeying the principle "when in doubt leave it out," in 3.4 they simply omitted the following puzzles: "Humh" and "O do, de, do, de, do de" (G1v; TLN 1828, 1839); "Sayes suum, mun" (G2r; TLN 1879); and "*Sesey*" (TLN 1880)—although they had no problem with Edgar's rustic expressions "Chill," "voke," "chud," "Vortnight," and "chevuore ye" (K1r11–16). In one instance, however, puzzlement with Tom's diction led to an unfortunate omission, in his first appearance to Lear on the heath:

Lear. That thou mayst shake the superflux to them,
And shew the heauens more iust.
<*Enter Edgar, and Foole.*
<*Edg.* Fathom, and halfe, Fathom and halfe; poore *Tom.*>
Foole. Come not in here Nunckle,her's a spirit,helpe me, helpe mee.

Kent. Giue me thy hand, whose there.
Foole. A spirit, <a spirite,> he sayes, his nam's poore *Tom.*
(G1v18–23; 3.4.35–43; TLN 1816–1824)

Although seemingly obscure in its use of a sailor's terminology ("fathom and halfe"), Edgar's line must have existed in Shakespeare's manuscript; otherwise the Fool would not have known his assumed identity. The language of mad Lear was not as difficult as that of the beggar, but the compositors still omitted expressions that they did not understand, such as "i'th'clout" (I3v; TLN 2539) and "Sa, sa, sa, sa." (I4v; TLN 2645). In Edmund's transition from direct address to the audience, in which he reveals his destructive plans, to a feigned concern for Edgar's welfare, the Quarto omits four terms of musical notation:

Bast. O these eclipses doe portend these diuisions. <Fa, Sol, La, Me.>
(C2v11; 1.2.136–137; TLN 466)

The abridger probably failed to recognize Edmund's pun on "divisions"—that is, as G. K. Hunter glossed it, "(1) Conflicts—of father against son, etc . . . ;(2) musical 'divisions'—counterpoint against plainsong," which had further significance to the initiated in the sequence of notes that Edmund sings.[7]

Before progressing, I would like to remind the reader of the implications of my argument: that the fuller version of *Lear* found in the Folio derives from the complete text as it existed in Shakespeare's manuscript. In the normal course of events he would have handed his manuscript to the theater house scribe for him to prepare the Booke and copy out the actors' parts. Subsequently Butter purchased the no longer needed manuscript from the company and Okes printed it, being forced to shorten the text to accommodate it within the ten sheets of paper he had estimated. On this reading of the evidence, the passages not found in the Quarto are *omissions* made by Okes in the winter of 1607–1608 in the course of printing the Quarto. The contrary interpretation, held by the Two Versions theorists, believes that the passages found only in the Folio represent *additions* made subsequently by Shakespeare (in 1609–1611, it is claimed), as deliberate expansions of the text, designed to remedy some perceived shortcoming. I believe that the evidence collected here makes the latter hypothesis untenable. To argue that the Folio represents additions made to clarify the situation or characters would mean that what I have described as cuts in the mad speech of Lear, or in the assumed idiolect of Poor Tom, were later additions. But in a text already overlong and verbally dense, why would anyone wish to add such puzzling utterances as "Humh"; "O do, de, do, de, do de"; "Sayes suum, mun"; "*Sesey*"; and "Sa, sa, sa, sa"? What possible motive could they have had to do so?

Verbal Repetition

The most frequent target for the abridger was verbal repetition. As we saw from the cuts in the Folio text of *2 Henry IV*, necessitated by a major error in casting off copy, the repetitions of the garrulous Doll Tearsheet and the imminently senile Justice Shallow were consistently shortened or eliminated to accommodate the text space within the print space. In *Lear* also, no matter how important repetitions may have been to Shakespeare in conveying a speaker's deliberate emphasis or in charting the rising temperature of a dispute, anything that seemed redundant to Okes's abridger was dispensed with. Thus, in the speech just quoted, where the Fool first sees Poor Tom, the abridger cut the Fool's frightened repetition of "a spirite." Altogether sixty-four smaller cuts were made in the 1608 Quarto, averaging two words each, including many instances of repetition.

If we look at Edmund's first soliloquy (set as prose in Q) through the abridger's eyes we can see why he cut some of the repetitions:

> *Bast* . . . why bastard? wherfore base . . .
> why brand they vs with base, base bastardie? <Base, Base?>. . . .
> well the legitimate *Edgar*, I must haue your land, our Fathers loue is to the bastard
> *Edmund*, as to the legitimate, <fine word: Legitimate.> well my legitimate, if this letter
> speede,and my inuention thriue, *Edmund* the base shall tooth' legitimate. (C1r18–28; 1.2.6–21; TLN 340–355)

To modern Shakespearians the abridger deleted a small but significant aspect of the bastard's mentality—the way he holds up for scornful inspection the words and concepts that deny him social acceptance, as if he could so deprive them of meaning and power.[8] Of course, the understanding that modern scholars have of Shakespeare's text far exceeds that of Okes and his employees, for whom these were just words surplus to purpose. Indeed, it is hard to imagine Shakespeare, or anyone else, subsequently inserting two additional instances of "Base" and one of "Legitimate" into what is already a long speech.

In some cases Shakespeare's manuscript included insignificant repetitions that could be omitted without visible loss to the sense. In the scene between Gloucester and his two sons, the abridger made a number of small space-saving cuts, some of little significance; here he cut just two words from Edgar's forged letter, read out by his father:

> *Glost.* This policie <and reuerence> of age makes the world bitter to the best of our times
>
> (C1v14–15; 1.2.46–47; TLN 382–383)

That cut removed a tautology; it seems unlikely that Shakespeare, or anyone else, would have felt the need to add those two words here.

Sensitivity to character or theatrical context cannot be expected of a printing house that was trying to squeeze into ten sheets of paper a text that would have needed a fifth as much again. As a punishment for his assault on Oswald, Cornwall and Regan put Kent in the stocks, where Lear discovers him. In setting type for this scene the compositor knew that space was at a premium and began his compression by running six speeches into three lines:

> *Lear.* Whats he, that hath so much thy place mistooke to set thee here?
> *Kent.* It is both he and shee, your sonne & daugter.
> *Lear.* No. *Kent.* Yes.
> *Lear.* No I say, *Kent.* I say yea.
> *Lear.* No no, they would not. *Kent.* Yes they haue.

Lear. By *Iupiter* I sweare no,
<*Kent.* By *Iuno,* I sweare I.
Lear.> they durst not do't,
(E3v9–15; 2.4.12–22; TLN 1286–1297)

Kent's riposte is witty, and in character, since it shows him once again challenging Lear's reliance on pagan authority, as he had done earlier:

Lear. Now by *Appollo,*
Kent. Now by *Appollo* King thou swearest thy Gods
(in vaine.
(B3r16–18; 1.1.160–161: TLN 172–174)

Okes, however, was concerned neither with consistency of character nor with subtle verbal effects: the things that mattered most to him were saving space while retaining a coherent sequence of events. In the scene where Lear has arrived at the house of Cornwall and Regan, expecting to be greeted by them, a verb that occurred three times in succession was ripe for cutting:

Lear . . . why *Gloster,Gloster,* i'de speake with the Duke of
*Cornewall,*and his wife.
<*Glost.* Well my good Lord,I haue inform'd them so.
<*Lear.* Inform'd them? Do'st thou vnderstand me man.>
Glost. I my good Lord.
Lear. The King would speake with *Cornewal,*the deare father
Would with the daughter sp eake, {commands, tends,}[9] seruice,
<Are they inform'd of this? My breath and blood:>
(E4v1–5; 2.4.96–103; TLN 1372–1379)

Lear's disbelieving repetition of "inform'd" conveys his anger at the unpleasant experience of being kept waiting, particularly for a king used to having his wishes instantly fulfilled ("Let me not stay a jot for dinner, goe get it readie . . ."). It is an integral part of Lear's feeling state—anger on the one hand and on the other some kind of attempt to be conciliatory, presenting himself as "the deare father" who, in the Folio reading that exactly catches his divided state, "commands, tends, seruice." It seems to me unlikely that a reviser would think of adding the anger, and the repetition, after the event.

In the hands of a printer short of space, any repetition was liable to be cut, as we see again with Lear's awareness of the first signs of madness. Shakespeare introduced this symptom using the traditional medical terms:

> *Lear.* O how this mother swels vp toward my hart,
> {*Hysterica*}[10] *passio* downe thou climing sorrow,
> Thy element's below,where is this daughter?
>
> (E4r2–5; 2.4.56–58; TLN 1372–1379)

As Lear becomes even angrier, the symptoms recur. The Quarto reads:

> *Lear.* O my heart, my heart.
> *Foole.* Cry to it Nunckle,as the Cokney did to the eeles, when she put vm it'h pâst aliue,she rapt vm ath coxcombs with a stick, and cryed downe wantons downe
>
> (E4v21–24; 2.4.121–125)

Fortunately the Folio preserves the correct text: "Oh me my heart! My rising heart! But downe." (TLN 1397). As modern readers may well complain here, the abridger's dislike of repetition cut something integral to the sense, for both the words "rising" and "downe" refer to the symptoms of hysteria that Lear had just recorded ("swels vpward," "climing"), which are echoed at a bawdy level by the Fool's punning reference to the phallic eels squirming in the pie: "downe wantons downe." Proponents of the Two Versions theory would have us believe that in Shakespeare's original version Lear's exclamation read, as it does in the Quarto, "O my heart, my heart," a curiously vapid and inarticulate utterance, and that the author subsequently returned to it and made three separate insertions. He first added "me" before "my heart"; then he inserted "rising" preceding the repetition of "my heart"; and he followed those two insertions with "But downe," finally achieving a regular blank verse line:

> O me my heart! My rising heart! But downe.

That seems to me utterly improbable.

Once we are alerted to his methods we notice how the abridger pounced on any obvious verbal repetition as if by a reflex action. (Where today fuller versions of films are reissued as "the director's cut," the *Lear* Quarto deserves to be known as "the abridger's cut.") At times his zeal in deleting even single word repetitions could leave the text in disarray. In betraying his natural father to whatever punishment Cornwall and Regan may devise, Edmund feigns embarrassment:

> *Bast.* How malicious is my fortune, that I must repent to bee iust? this is the letter he spoke of,which approues him an intelligent partie to the aduantages of *France*, O heauens that his treason were <not>, or not I the detecter.
>
> (G3v2–5; 3.5.9–13; TLN 1979–1983)

Having noticed the repetition of "not," the editor, or compositor, removed the first instance and ruined the sense. He made a similar deletion in one of Lear's mad speeches, when Cordelia's servants try to catch and tend for him:

> *Gent.* You shall haue any thing.
> *Lear.* No seconds, all my selfe, why this would make a man <a man> of salt to vse his eyes for garden waterpots, I and laying Autums dust.
>
> (I4v8–11; 4.6.194–197; TLN 2638–2640)

I imagine that the abridger would have had a better knowledge of English grammar than to have marked up this as a redundant repetition; more likely, the compositor (probably the apprentice "C") took his own initiative to save space. On this page he used two instances of continuous printing and set a long passage of verse as prose (4.6.184–207), saving five lines in the process. He made two cuts in Lear's role, one deleting the word "Smugge," as we have seen, and the other in the mad king's revenge plan:

> It were a delicate stra-
> tagem to {shoo}[11] a troupe of horse with felt <:Ile put't in
> proofe,> & when I haue stole Vpon these sonne in lawes,
> then kill,kill,kill,kill,kill,kill.
> (I4r38–I4v2; 4.6.184–187; TLN 2626–2629)

If we were asked to shorten that speech with the minimum loss to sense, we might well choose to omit those four words.

Unnecessary Cuts

Examination of the Quarto cuts shows that in several cases the compositors used various forms of abridgement without saving any space. This fact has been held up as counterevidence by scholars who maintain that the omissions were either accidental or were in fact "additions" made by Shakespeare in revising a play with which he had become dissatisfied. We have noticed this phenomenon several times in studying other abridged texts, with cuts made on a page that did not always have the desired effect. Here, I suggest that, as well as making cuts marked in advance by the abridger, the compositors had been instructed to save space wherever possible. Following this plan they made local cuts in situ, so to speak, even though no space was thereby saved. As we have seen, on several occasions verse speeches were turned into prose without saving space.[12] The compositors even used some of the "mechanical" devices, as I have called them, on pages where adequate space was available. Inspection of the context shows that neither the tildes for "beatē" (D3r28; 1.5.42) and "cānot" (G2v34; 3.4.148), nor the ampersands at "weak &" (F4r21; 3.2.20) and "& in the end" (H2r21; 3.7.101) were needed. This point reinforces my argument that two types of cutting were used: Okes's abridger marked up passages for cutting in advance, while the compositors applied their range of space-saving devices during the setting of type.

That Okes was aiming to delete repetitions to save space is shown by instances where enough room would have been available to include the omitted phrase. Thus Lear's decisive rejection of Burgundy's appeal to receive Cordelia with the agreed dowry was shorn of a repetition that emphasizes his decision:

> *Lear.* Nothing, I haue sworne. <I am firme.>
> (B4r28; 1.1.245; TLN 269)

By the strict criterion of saving all available space that repetition adds nothing to the sense. However, on this page (set at the narrow measure, with two turn-overs) half the line is empty, leaving enough room for the full text, so the space-saving process must have been set up in advance.

The abridger also cut some trivial phrases in Kent's punishment of the Steward's insubordination:

> *Kent.* Come sir <arise, away,> ile teach you differences, away, away, if you will measure your lubbers length againe, tarry, but away, <goe too,> you haue wisedome<, so>.
> (C4r34–36; 1.4.89–92; TLN 619–621)

Committed to shortening the text, the abridger duly omitted the least important words. However, inspection of this page shows that more than enough space (three-quarters of a line) remained to accommodate the six words omitted. This again suggests that the abridgement was marked up before printing began and then dutifully followed by the compositor, although it would not have been needed. In theatrical terms, we might object, those repetitions are needed for the stage business, but to the abridger a repetition was a repetition and took up unnecessary space.

In a later scene, Lear's disastrous confrontation with Goneril, the compositor, having chosen the wide measure and saved a great deal of space by the drastic means of reducing more than one hundred verse lines to prose, would have had enough room to include the single word he decided to omit:

> *Lear.* It may be so my Lord, harke *Nature*,heare deere God-desse, <heare:>suspend thy purpose
>
> (D2r24–25; 1.4.274–276; TLN 788–790)

We recognize Lear's habit of authority in the way he imperiously repeats his summoning of Nature three times over.[13] However, to the abridger a repetition was a repetition and it had to go, even though cutting it destroyed a rhetorical figure (*epanalepsis*, by which the same word occurs at the beginning and end of a sentence or verse line). The final line of this speech is only half full. A few lines later another verse speech was set as prose, although there would have been enough room for this deleted phrase, evidently thought to be redundant. The Quarto reads:

> *Lear.* . . . . yea, i'st come to this?|<Ha? Let it be so.> yet haue I left a daughter,
>
> (D2v8; 1.4.304–305)

The Folio reads "Ha? Let it be so. | I haue another daughter" (TLN 823–824). The phrase omitted in the Quarto marks a conscious decision on Lear's part to dispense with Goneril and to turn to Regan. His illusion that his second-born daughter will treat him in the way he thinks he deserves shows us that Lear has yet to register her true nature. But to the abridger the phrase added nothing either to the sense or to the immediate dramatic situation and so could be safely omitted.

Unanchored Utterances

Another coherent principle that Okes's abridger observed was to omit any utterances that were not anchored in the text—that is, not eliciting a reply by another speaker. If they were not sufficiently relevant for a listener to answer them, he may have reasoned, they could be safely omitted. One such instance was the Fool's trick question concerning the social categories "gentleman" and "yeoman":

Foole. Prithe Nunckle tell me, whether a mad man be a Gentleman or a Yeoman.

Lear. A King, a King,

<*Foole.* No, he's a Yeoman, that ha's a Gentleman to his Sonne: for hee's a <mad Yeoman that sees his Sonne a Gentleman before him.>

<*Lear.*> to haue a thousand with red burning spits come hiszing in vpon them.

(G3v25–28; 3.6.9–15; TLN 2007–2014)

Lear, obsessed with his own grievances and impotent wish for revenge, failed to answer the Fool's witticism, so the abridger removed it. He applied the same principle in the scene where Kent finally persuades Lear to rest:

Kent. Now good my Lord lie here <and rest> awhile.

Lear. Make no noise, make no noise, draw the curtains, so, so, so, Weele go to supper it'h morning, so, so, so, *Enter Gloster.*

<*Foole.* And Ile go to bed at noone.>

Glost. Come hither friend, where is the King my maister.

(G4v3–5; 3.6.82–86; TLN 2041–2045)

The first cut there removed a slight redundancy (since to lie down is to rest), but it also cropped a pentameter line of one foot.[14] The abridger's omission of the Fool's parting line ("And Ile go to bed at no one"), doubtless directed at the audience, demonstrates the same principle—that if a speech does not receive a reply from another character it can be dispensed with as unimportant.

Another type of unanswered and thus unanchored utterance—by definition—is the aside. Since *King Lear* was the first play he printed, Okes may have been unaware of the theatrical convention of direct address. In Edgar's shattering reunion with his father, when the tension between reality and role playing becomes too much for him to bear, he utters words apparently unrelated to the context, which were duly excised:

Glost. Sirrah naked fellow.
Edg. Poore *Toms* a cold, *[aside.]* I cannot {daub}[15] it farther
Glost. Come hither fellow.
Edg. *[aside.]*<And yet I must.>
Blesse thy sweete eyes, they bleed.
Glost. Knowst thou the way to Douer?
(H3r6–10; 4.1.51–55; TLN 2240–2245)

Like all modern editors, I have indicated Edgar's two asides to the audience. Although this is a relatively recent editorial convention, unknown at that time, Okes's fellow printers included asides as part of the text. Edgar's first speech to the audience was retained as having some kind of relevance, but the second is clearly unrelated to the words that precede and follow it and was therefore cut. The abridger's principle of omitting speeches within a scene to which no one replies applies equally to exit lines, as in Edgar's tending and consoling his father:

Giue me thy hand, come on.
Glost. No farther sir, a man may rot euen here.
Edg. What in ill thoughts againe men must indure,
Their going hence, euen as their coming hither,
Ripenes is all come on.
<*Glost.* And that's true too. *Exeunt.*>
(K4r5–9; 5.2.7–11; TLN 2930–2936)

Revisionist critics who imagine that the lines omitted in printing are later additions have developed complicated theories about deliberate changes in characterization on Shakespeare's part, supposedly designed to rebalance the emotional level of the play. My explanation is simpler and more coherent: the abridger judged that these lines were not essential to the character or to the dramatic situation and could be omitted without damaging either.

As one looks at each omission in its typographical and theatrical context one can follow the abridger picking out for deletion utterances that are not syntactically anchored in the surrounding linguistic texture—interjections, qualifications or digressions, often of a single line, as here:

Lear. Pray doe not mocke <me>,
I am a very foolish fond old man,
Fourescore and vpward,
<Not an houre more, nor lesse:>
and to deale plainly
I feare I am not in my perfect mind,
(K2v4–7; 4.7.58–62; TLN 2813–2818)

Two Versions theorists would need to ask themselves why Shakespeare, or anyone else, would have added the redundant line, "Not an houre more, nor lesse," at this crucial point in the action.

In the subplot scenes where the rivalry between Goneril and Regan for the love of Edmund starts to destroy the fortunes of all three, the abridger made a few small cuts, one line here, another there:

Gon. Decline your head: this kisse if it durst speake
Would stretch thy spirits vp into the ayre,
Conceaue and far you well.
Bast. Yours in the ranks of death. <*Exit.*>
Gon. My most deere *Gloster*,
<Oh, the difference of man, and man,> (are dew
to thee a womans seruices
{A foole vsurps my bed.}[16]
(H3v19–24; 4.2.22–28; TLN 2290–2298)

Much as the modern reader would regret losing that line, we must admit that the abridger was consistent in his principles, deleting a commentary line while retaining the main clause surrounding it. In Regan's tardy declaration of commitment to Edmund (Goneril has already given her poison), the abridger cut one line:

Reg. Lady I am not well, els I should answere
From a full flowing stomack. Generall
Take thou my souldiers, prisoners, patrimonie,

<Dispose of them, of me, the walls is thine:>
Witnes the world that I create thee here
My Lord and maister.
(L1r10–14; 5.3.73–78; TLN 3016–3021)

The omitted verse repeats the sense of the line preceding and includes a metaphor ("walls," meaning something like "the citadel of my heart") that may have puzzled the abridger.

Following his tactic of removing short utterances that broke up a more significant speech, the abridger cut an interjection from Goneril a few lines later that, to the attentive reader, conveys both her disgust at Albany's control of the situation and her powerlessness to affect it:

Alb. If you will mary, make your loue to me,
My Lady is bespoke,
<*Gon* . An enterlude.>
Alb. thou art arm'd *Gloster*,
<Let the Trumpet sound:>
If none appeare to proue vpon thy head,
(L1r26–28; 5.3.88–90; TLN 3033–3038)

However, since Albany ignores Goneril's remark, out it goes. When Edmund, glorying in his newly acquired legitimacy, fatally accepts Edgar's challenge, the abridger picks out for deletion the one line not absolutely necessary to the sense:

Bast. In wisdome I should aske thy name,
But since thy outside lookes so faire and warlike,
And that thy being some say of breeding breathes,
<What safe, and nicely I might well delay,>
By right of knighthood, I disdaine and spurne
(L2r2–5; 5.3.142–146; TLN 3097–3101)

However much we might deplore the omissions that Okes's abridger made, we must admit that he managed these one-line deletions for the most part skillfully. If we did not have the Folio as an independent witness no one would have noticed these cuts.

Major Omissions

But more space needed to be gained, and from first to last the abridger of the 1608 Quarto was on the lookout for longer passages to delete. As I have suggested, he found them in speeches containing expansive writing, where the speaker elaborated a point, got lost in a subordinate clause, or digressed. Two Versions theorists may argue that these are additions made by Shakespeare between 1609 and 1611, but they cannot explain why, in a play text already far too long for performance, he should have wanted to add passages that elaborate a point without developing it or forwarding the action. A further consideration, ignored by those who believe that Shakespeare revised the play, concerns the diction of the passages surrounding the omissions. As far as I know, the relevant criterion was first set out by E. K. Chambers in 1930. Commenting on *Richard III*, a play that also exists in two differing texts, Chambers made an observation highly relevant to this discussion. The Folio text of *Richard III* contains some 230 lines not found in the Quarto, Chambers noted, of which "about half are in six considerable passages. . . . They form parts of long speeches or long sections of dialogue, do not differ in style from the rest of the play, fit in without awkward joints, and in some cases leave the context abrupt or less effective when omitted."[17] That notion of the homogeneity of style within the whole of a passage, including the omitted lines, is an important criterion. If additions had been made at any point in the period between the play's first performance in 1606 and the printing of this section of the Folio in 1622, we might expect to find variations of style, since Shakespeare's grammar, syntax, and prosody continued to develop. But none have been identified.

Turning to these larger cuts, I have shown that the abridger was on the alert to remove repetitions, over-expansive utterances, digressions, and verbal elaborations of a point that added neither to the meaning of a scene nor to its dramatic function. The role of Lear offered several opportunities for such cuts, especially in the opening scene. The abridger started his work with Lear's periphrastic, self-regarding speech introducing the gift ceremony of which, as he has planned it, he would have been the chief beneficiary, spending his declining years in the "most opulent" part of his kingdom, looked after by his favorite daughter:

> *Lear.* Meane time we will expresse our darker purposes,
> The map there; know we haue diuided
> In three,our kingdome; and tis our {fast}[18] intent,
> To shake all cares and busines of our state,
> Confirming them on yonger yeares, <while we
> <Vnburthen'd crawle toward death. Our son of *Cornwal,*
> <And you our no lesse louing Sonne of *Albany,*
> <We haue this houre a constant will to publish
> <Our daughters seuerall Dowers, that future strife
> <May be preuented now.>
>
> (B1v14–18; 1.1.36–45; TLN 41–50)

The abridger first cut the qualification by which Lear enlarged on his decision to abicate with the self-pitying pathos of "crawle toward death." Next he removed the apparent elaboration of "Our son of *Cornwal,* | And you our no lesse louing Sonne of *Albany*": however, these are essential markers for the theater audience to identify the characters whom Lear addresses, his sons-in-law. They are named subsequently, but only as spouses: Lear refers to "thine [Goneril's] and *Albanies* issue" (66) and to "*Regan*, wife to *Cornwall*" (68), but it is not immediately clear to the audience who they are. To an abridger unfamiliar with the theater, Lear's speech may have seemed verbose, but it is vital to the business of the scene.[19]

When Lear initiates the serious action of dividing his kingdom, he identifies the two rivals for Cordelia's hand, France and Burgundy, who are not yet onstage. Lear then begins a straightforward verbal imperative ("tell me my daughters"). However, as if the first-person pronouns had reminded him of himself, he immediately interrupts the onward flow:

> The two great Princes *France* and *Burgundy,*
> Great ryuals in our youngest daughters loue,

Long in our Court haue made their amorous soiourne,
And here are to be answerd, tell me my daughters,
<(Since now we will diuest vs both of Rule,
<Interest of Territory, Cares of State)>
Which of you shall we say doth loue vs most,
That we our largest bountie may extend,
Where merit doth most challenge it,
Gonorill our eldest borne, speake first[.]
(B1v19–26; 1.1.46–54; TLN 50–59)

Here the abridger made a clean and metrically skillful excision, removing that tautological parenthesis, which refers back to Lear's earlier self-presentation, "we Vnburthen'd crawle toward death," without damaging the sense of the action taking place. (If you have decided to give away your kingdom it is obvious that you are parting with "Rule . . . Territory . . . State"; that goes without saying.)

When Lear advertises his second daughter's generous portion, he embarks on a series of parallel "with" clauses that offered the abridger another easy option for omission:

Lear. Of al these bounds,euen from this line to this,
With shady forrests, <and with Champains rich'd
<With plenteous Riuers> and wide skirted meades,
We make thee Lady (B1v35–37; 1.1.63–66; TLN 68–71)

Had the Folio text not survived, we would never have known that Lear had also promised Regan "Champains rich'd" and "plenteous Rivers."

Having approved of Goneril and Regan's love declarations, Lear comes to the climax of a gift ceremony that he has debased into a kind of auction, showing pleasurable anticipation as he turns to Cordelia:

Lear. . . . but now our ioy,
Although the last,not least in our deere loue,
<The Vines of France, and Milke of Burgundie,
<Striue to be interest.>

What can you say to win a third, more opulent
Then your sisters. <speake.>
Cord. Nothing my Lord.
<*Lear.* Nothing?
<*Cord.* Nothing.> (againe.
Lear. How, nothing can come of nothing, speake
(B2r13–18; 1.1.82–90; TLN 88–96)

The abridger's first cut was innocuous, because Lear's identification of the two suitors' rich possessions, although entirely in keeping with his high style up to this point, is not essential to the action. The single imperative, by which Lear had ordered the two elder daughters to make their pitch ("Goneril . . . speake first," "Regan . . . speake"), is, strictly speaking, redundant here, since Lear has just asked Cordelia a question, which she proceeds to answer. (The Quarto's omission of "speake" makes sense as a cut, but does it make equal or better sense as an addition?) The abridger's third cut removed two of the five repetitions of "Nothing," a deplorable loss in our eyes, but wholly consistent with Okes's need to save a great deal of space, due to having miscalculated the amount of paper he would need.

As the abridger worked through this opening scene he found other phrases that could be judged redundant, as here:

Lear. . . . the barbarous *Scythyan*,
Or he that makes his generation
Messes to gorge his appetite
Shall <to my bosome>
bee as well neighbour'd,pittyed and relieued
As thou my sometime daughter.
(B2v7–11; 1.1.116–119; TLN 123–127)

On a strict evaluation, that phrase might be considered tautologous, since the "bosom" or heart was taken to be the location of all human feelings, so out it went. Conversely, to imagine Shakespeare adding it to an already lengthy scene would call in question any sense of artistic economy. Little is gained by omitting it; nothing would be gained by adding it. The abridger then took out a single line in which the two "loving" sons tried to intervene between Lear and Kent:

> *Lear.* Vassall, recreant.
> <*Alb. Cor.* Deare Sir forbeare.>
> *Kent.* Doe, kill thy Physicion,
> And the fee bestow vpon the foule disease
> (B3r18–20; 1.1.161–164; TLN 175–178)

Their intervention was ineffective, since no other character responded: as we have seen several times, speeches that are not taken up by the person addressed are ripe for cutting.

Shakespeare's fullness of invention in this play posed a severe challenge to the abridger: he had to decide which passages were not absolutely necessary either to the sense or to the dramatic context. In the fateful scene where the bastard Edmund deceives his natural father into thinking that Edgar is planning to kill him, Gloucester justifies this horrible allegation to himself in terms of judicial astrology, but too expansively for the abridger:

> *Glost.* These late eclipses in the Sunne and Moone portend
> no good to vs, though the wisedome of nature can reason thus
> and thus, yet nature finds it selfe scourg'd by the sequent effects,
> loue cooles, friendship fals off, brothers diuide,in Citties mu-
> tinies, in Countries discords, Pallaces treason, the bond crackt
> betweene sonne and father;
> <This villaine of mine comes vnder the
> <prediction; there's Son against Father, the King fals from
> <byas of Nature, there's Father against Childe. We haue
> <seene the best of our time. Machinations, hollownesse,
> <treacherie, and all ruinous disorders follow vs disquietly
> < to our Graues.> find out this villaine *Edmund*, it shal
> loose thee nothing, doe it carefully
> (C2r26–31; 1.2.103–115; TLN 433–445)

The abridger made his cut at the point where Gloucester applies the general theory of planetary influence to the specific instance of this family, on a one-to-one basis, as if he were just grasping its significance. Perhaps the abridger found the application too obvious; in any event, he once again cut to the action: "find out this villaine *Edmund*."

In the subsequent conversation, where Edmund tells Edgar about his father's anger, Shakespeare conveyed the dissembler's hypocrisy through his curiously affected diction:

> *Bast.* Parted you in good tearmes? found you no displeasure
> in him by word or countenance?
> *Edg.* None at all.
> *Bast.* Bethinke your selfe wherein you may haue offended
> him, and at my intreatie,forbeare his presence ,till some little
> time hath qualified the heat of his displeasure, which at this in-
> stant so rageth in him,that with the mischiefe,of your person it
> would scarce allay.
> *Edg.* Some villaine hath done me wrong.
> *Bast.* Thats my feare
> <,I pray you haue a continent
> <forbearance till the speed of his rage goes slower: and as
> <I say, retire with me to my lodging, from whence I will
> <fitly bring you to heare my Lord speake : pray ye goe,
> <there's my key : if you do stirre abroad,goe arm'd.
> <*Edg.* Arm'd, Brother?>
> *Bast.* brother, I aduise you to the best, [goe
> arm'd] (C2v28–38; 1.2.166–171; TLN 488–493)

The abridger noticed that the second part of Edmund's speech repeats what he has already said—in effect, "lie low until your father's anger has died down"—and was not essential to the action. (He also removed the not strictly necessary repetition of "arm'd," but retained the final injunction, "goe arm'd," omitted in the Folio.) Edmund's style is homogeneous throughout, for Shakespeare conveys his affected, insincere concern for his brother's safety—we know how insincere he is, having just seen and heard "the bastard" vowing to supplant "the legitimate"—in the same artificially extended metaphors that Edmund had used to Gloucester a few lines earlier:[20]

> . . . *forbeare* his presence, till some little time hath *qualified* the *heat* of his *displeasure*, which at this instant so *rageth* in him, that with the *mischief*, of your person it would scarce *allay*. (C2v32–35; 1.2.160–164; TLN 482–485)

The passage omitted in Okes's printing shop repeats the injunction to "forbear" and recycles the extended metaphor for Gloucester's anger (here italicized), which is now varied from heat to motion: "I pray you have a continent *forbearance* till the *speed* of his *rage* goes *slower*." Once again, we have two options: either this speech was "all of a piece" at the time of its composing, or Shakespeare returned to it five or more years later and neatly matched the stylistic trait he had created to embody Edmund's hypocrisy. Those who choose the latter explanation then have to answer the awkward objection that, while it is understandable that cuts could have been made in Okes's printing house out of necessity, there would be little point in anyone adding such lines, insignificant in content, to Edmund's speeches or to those of Lear and Gloucester. It is not as if the Quarto text needed enlarging, either for theatrical representation or for printing. Like the Folio version, it was always far too long to be performed in the time available on a winter's afternoon in an open-air London theater. The cuts in the 1608 Quarto were made to save space in consequence of Okes's potentially disastrous underestimate of the paper quantity.

Examination of further cuts made throughout the play supports this explanation of the Quarto omissions. In Act 1, scene 4, Okes's compositor evidently realized how short he was of space. This scene occupies six pages (C4r–D2v; see Plate 1 in Appendix 1); in the 38 lines of each page he managed to squeeze in 35, 49, 39, 48, 53, 46, and 37 lines, as compared to the full Folio text, resulting in a series of uncomfortably crowded pages. In addition to various forms of compression the abridger made a few small cuts in Kent's part, starting with the soliloquy in which he announces his intention to serve Lear:

> *Kent.* . . . now banisht *Kent*, if thou canst
> serue where thou dost stand condem'd,

<So may it come,> thy maister whom thou louest
shall find {thee}[21] full of labour

(C3v2–4; 1.4.4–7; TLN 534–537)

The omitted clause was hardly significant for either the character or the dramatic action, but the speech ends with an empty half line, suggesting that the cut had been indicated ahead of type-setting. In the servant's confirmation of the disrespectful behavior that Lear and his followers now receive, Okes's abridger was able to cut two words, this time weakening the sense:

Servant . . . . . ther's a great abatement, <of kindnesse> apeer's as well in the generall dependants, as in the Duke himselfe also, and your daughter. *Lear.* Ha, say'st thou so?

(C4r10–12; 1.4.60–62; TLN 589–591)

In the following scene between Lear, Albany, and Goneril the abridger made a few local cuts, gaining little space in the process:

Lear. {Woe}[22] that too late repent's, O sir, are you come? is it your will <, speake Sir!> that wee prepare any horses,ingratitude! thou marble harted fiend, more hideous when thou shewest thee in a child, then the Sea-monster,

<*Duke.* Pray Sir be patient.

<*Lear.*> detested kite, thou {lyest}[23]my traine, {are}[24] men of choise and rarest parts

(D2r12–15; 1.4.257–263; TLN 769–776)

Once more, the abridger decides that if a character does not respond to a direct address ("speake Sir!"), then words having no "uptake" may be omitted. When Albany subsequently addresses Lear ("Pray Sir . . .") and Lear takes no notice of him, then that speech can also be cut. An examination of this page in the Quarto, one of the most densely printed in the whole play, explains why poor Albany loses another not absolutely vital line:

Duke. My Lord, I am giltles as I am ignorant.
<Of what hath moued you.>

Here, at least, Lear does reply, but only momentarily, for his mind is elsewhere:

It may be so my Lord, harke *Nature*, heare deere Goddesse,
suspend thy purpose, . . .
(D2r23–25; 1.4.274–276; TLN 786–790)

While making these small cuts in 1.4 the compositor did his utmost to gain space through other means, saving thirty-eight lines by reducing verse to prose, and another four lines by relineation. But the abridger must have felt that more cuts were needed, for when, after Lear has stormed off, Goneril tries to anticipate any criticism that her husband might make of her callous treatment of her father, the Quarto simply omits thirteen lines:

<*Gon.* This man hath had good Counsell,
<A hundred Knights?
<'Tis politike, and safe to let him keepe
<At point a hundred Knights: yes, that on euerie dreame,
<Each buz, each fancie, each complaint, dislike,
<He may enguard his dotage with their powres,
<And hold our liues in mercy. Oswald, I say.
<*Duke.* Well, you may feare too farre.
<*Gon.* Safer then trust too farre;
<Let me still take away the harmes I feare,
<Not feare still to be taken. I know his heart,
<What he hath vtter'd I haue writ my Sister:
<If she sustaine him, and his hundred Knights
<When I haue shew'd th'vnfitnesse.
<*Enter Steward.*
How now Oswald?> (1.4.322–333; TLN 842–857)

As with the previous passages considered, it is clear that the need for space, all too visible throughout the printing of this scene, motivated

Okes to cut these lines. They do contain information relevant to the plot, namely that Goneril has written to her sister to warn her of their father's violent reaction to their calculated offense; however, the abridger noticed that Goneril repeats this matter to Oswald a few lines later:

Gon. What Oswald, ho. *Oswald.* Here Madam.
Gon. What haue you writ this letter to my sister?
(D2v22–23; 1.4.334; TLN 858)

The converse explanation, that they were added in 1610–1611 by Shakespeare himself, is again open to the objection that it makes no sense to expand the play at this point, where the on-stage action is perfectly comprehensible.

Having cut the hypocrisy of Edmund as he elaborated his insincere warning to Edgar, the abridger did the same for Regan, in the scene where she attempts to justify Goneril's cold-hearted behavior:

Lear. [. . .] Beloued *Regan*,
Thy sister is naught, oh *Regan* she hath tyed,
Sharpe tooth'd vnkindnes, like a vulture heare,
I can scarce speake to thee, thout not beleeue,
Of how {deprau'd}[25] a qualitie, O *Regan*.
Reg. I pray sir take patience, I haue hope
You lesse know how to value her desert,
Then she to slacke her dutie.
< *Lear.* Say? How is that?
<*Reg.* I cannot thinke my Sister in the least
<Would faile her Obligation. If Sir perchance
<She haue restrained the Riots of your Followres,
<'Tis on such ground, and to such wholesome end,
<As cleeres her from all blame.>
Lear. My cursses on her.
Reg. O Sir you are old . . .
. . . .
Therfore I pray that to our sister, you do make returne,
Say you haue wrong'd her Sir
(E4v34–F1r10; 2.4.133–152; TLN 1411–1432)

We know, as Lear does not, that Regan has already received Goneril's letter urging her to disabuse their father of any entitlement he may feel due to him, so the reader or theatergoer will recognize her hypocrisy here, excusing Goneril of the charge of having been deliberately provocative. However, the abridger saw that this was another instance of a character not responding when addressed ("My curses on her," Lear says, brooding on Goneril's treatment of him), so he deleted her insincere vindication. The style is homogeneous throughout, as Regan smoothly deploys counterfactual conditionals ("I haue hope | You lesse know how to value her desert, | Then she to slacke her dutie"; "I cannot thinke my Sister in the least | Would faile her Obligation. If Sir perchance | She haue restrained . . ."). I can see no discontinuity in her diction that might point to an addition or revision five years or more later, nor any reason to add this long prevarication.

The abridger's principle of omitting speeches to which there is no uptake explains his handling of this passage earlier in the scene:

> *Kent* . . . . Your sonne and daughter found this trespass worth
> This shame which here it suffers.
> <*Foole.* Winters not gon yet, if the wild Geese fly that way,
> <Fathers that weare rags, do make their Children blind,
> <But Fathers that beare bags,shall see their children kind.
> <Fortune that arrant whore,nere turns the key toth' poore.
> <But for all this thou shalt haue as many Dolors for thy
> <Daughters, as thou canst tell in a yeare.>
> *Lear.* O how this mother swells vp toward my hart
> (E3v38–E4r2; 2.4.44–55; TLN 1320–1328)

Because Lear, troubled by his sense of incipient breakdown, takes no notice of the Fool's admonitory rhymes, the abridger could consign them to the waste bin.

The abridger's wish to reduce repetition can be seen in this omission from the second storm scene:

> *Lear.* No I will weepe no more, in such a night as this!
> <To shut me out? Poure on, I will endure:

<In such a night as this?>
O *Regan*, *Gonorill*,your old kind father (lies,
Whose franke heart gaue you all, O that way madnes
Let me shun that, no more of that.
(G1v3–6; 3.4.17–22; TLN 1797–1802)

To have a six-word phrase ("in such a night as this") repeated within three lines clearly triggered the abridger's sense of superfluity. Similarly in this passage there was one repetition too many:

Kent. Good my Lord enter.
Lear. Prethe goe in thy selfe, seeke thy {own}[26] ease
This tempest will not giue me leaue to ponder
On things would hurt me more, but ile goe in,
<In Boy, go first. You houselesse pouertie,
<Nay get thee in; Ile pray, and then Ile sleepe. {*Exeunt*}[27] >
Poore naked wretches, where so ere you are
That bide the pelting of this pittiles night,
How shall your house-lesse heads, and vnfed sides
(G1v7–13; 3.4.22–30; TLN 1803–1811)

The abridger noted the duplication of "goe in thy selfe" in line 23 by "ile goe in" (line 25), followed two lines later by "In Boy, go first" and "get thee in." However important these comforting repetitions are to both readers and theatergoers in establishing Lear's newfound awareness of other people's suffering, they were repetitions and could be deleted. Given that Lear appears to begin his address to "You houselesse pouertie" at line 26, then repeats the word "house-lesse" in line 30, we can understand why the abridger omitted those two lines. We may deplore these cuts, but it is thanks to the survival of an independent copy of Shakespeare's manuscript, as reproduced in the Folio, that we even know of their omission from the Quarto.

Despite the seemingly hopeless task to which Nicholas Okes had set himself and his employees by underestimating the quantity of paper needed, to a reader not having access to the 1623 Folio their pruning was largely unobtrusive. In the following passage, where

Edgar is seen again in his own persona, the abridger made another perfectly logical cut:

Enter Edgar.
Edg. Yet better thus, and knowne to be contemnd,
Then still contemn'd and flattered to be worst,
The lowest and most deiected thing of Fortune
Stands still in {esperance},[28] liues not in feare,
The lamentable change is from the best,
The worst returnes to laughter, <Welcome then,
<Thou vnsubstantiall ayre that I embrace:
<The Wretch that thou hast blowne vnto the worst,
<Owes nothing to thy blasts. >
Enter Glost. led by an old man.
Who's here,my father {poorlie, leed}[29] world,world, O world!
(H2r29–35; 4.1.1–10; TLN 2179–2190)

Edgar congratulates himself on having survived at the degree zero of human experience and is trying to deduce a consolation from his ordeal—"Welcome then . . ."—when something far worse occurs. But the attentive reader can see that the idea expressed in the first long sentence, stretching over six lines, is repeated in the next, shorter sentence, as Edgar moves from a general observation to a deduction from it. This is just like Gloucester's two-part observation on "the late eclipses," and it was perfectly consistent of the abridger to remove the second member of the two.

The abridger applied the same principle to Lear's searing denunciations of social injustice, crammed into densely packed prose in both Quarto and Folio:

thou rascall beadle hold thy bloudy hand, why dost thou lash that whore, strip thine owne backe,thy bloud hotly lusts to vse her in that kind for which thou whipst her, the vsurer hangs the cosioner,through{tattered}[30]raggs,smal vices do appeare,robes & furd-gownes hides all, <{Plate sinne}[31]with Gold, and <the strong Lance of Iustice,hurtlesse breakes : Arme it in

<ragges, a Pigmies straw do's pierce it. None do's offend,
<none, I say none, Ile able 'em; take that of me my Friend,
<who haue the power to seale th'accusers lips. >
get thee glasse eyes, and like a scuruy po-
litician seeme to see the things thou doest not
(I4r24–29; 4.6.160–172; TLN 2603–2614)

Perfectly consistent, the abridger omitted the sequence where the king elaborates on his insight and turns from concrete instances of lust and corruption to the abstractions of "sinnes" and "Iustice." If one were set the task of omitting four or five lines from that speech that would probably be the least damaging cut.

In the final scene, although sorely pressed for space, Okes's abridger preferred to set verse as prose, reline the verse, or run two speeches into one line, rather than cutting the text. We must be grateful for that much relief. He made two small cuts in Lear's part, the first innocuous:

Lear. . . . I am old now,
And these same crosses spoyle me, who are you?
Mine eyes are not othe best, ile tell you straight.
Kent. If Fortune bragd of two she loued or hated,
One of them we behold.
Lear. <This is a dull sight,> Are not you Kent?
Kent. The same your seruant *Kent*,where is thy seruant *Caius?*
(L3v20–34; 5.3.278–284; TLN 3243–3248)

Always on the lookout for repetitions, the abridger balked at two references within four lines to Lear's failing eyesight. Having realized the pressing need to fit the final 38 lines of Shakespeare's text into the 35 lines of the remaining page—given that Okes liked to keep the verso of the final leaf blank, and wanted a decent size "*FINIS*" (see Plate 6, Appendix 2)—either the abridger or the compositor excised some repetitions that did not seem essential. Choosing the wide measure, and regrettably reducing several speeches to prose, this is how Lear's final words appears in the 1608 Quarto:

Lear. . . . O thou wilt
come no more, neuer,neuer, neuer, pray you vndo this button,
thanke you sir, O, o,o,o. *Edg.* He faints my Lord, my Lord.
(L4r17–19)

The abridger's final cut, understandable enough, perhaps, would have been the unkindest, had it not been for the Folio's preservation of an independent authentic text, with proper verse divisions. It would have been a huge loss to not have had Lear's desperate gesture toward Cordelia's lips, whatever he thought he saw there:

Lear. . . . Thou'lt come no more,
Neuer,neuer,neuer,neuer,neuer.
Pray you vndo this Button. Thanke you Sir,
Do you see this? Looke on her? Looke her lips,
Looke there, looke there. *He dies.*
(5.3.308–312; TLN 3279–3283)

Surely, no one can seriously think that Shakespeare or anyone else would have added the two instances of "neuer" necessary to fill out what would otherwise have been a defective blank verse line, or would have added the characteristically emphatic four-fold repetition of "Looke." These were always integral parts of Lear's language, in Shakespeare's text. Such divergences between the two texts, like all the other evidence we have been examining, point to the necessity that Nicholas Okes was under, having been taken short in a printer's main material, paper.

Afterword

The research and writing of this book stretched over several years (with interruptions), and for much of that time I believed that I was the first reader of *King Lear* to suggest that, in printing the quarto, Nicholas Okes had deliberately compressed and cut the text to save space. The feeling of originality when working on such a well-known play is exciting, but also worrying: if nobody else had reached this conclusion then perhaps I was just being eccentric? Fortunately, or otherwise, I came across two earlier scholars who had anticipated me.

In a seldom-cited essay contributed to the *Festschrift* for T. M. Parrott, Edward Hubler—subsequently known for his work on Shakespeare's *Sonnets*—gave a coherent account of the metrical irregularities in the 1608 Quarto in terms of decisions made in the printing house.[32] Hubler began by challenging the dominant theory of Chambers and Greg, that Okes's *Lear* was a reported text, and that therefore (in Greg's words) "the printer had before him a copy that was entirely undivided metrically," together with the related theory that, due to a stenographical report, "the verse-lining [is] almost a complete wreck."[33] Hubler argued that the various types of irregularities found in the 1608 Quarto were not due to a reporter but could be "attributed to the printer's office." Hubler itemized the main forms of irregularity, giving statistics (although not always accurate):[34]

> A quarter of *Lear* is prose, and these lines are correctly set up as prose in the Quarto. But there are five hundred lines of verse set up as prose, and sixty-one lines of prose set up as verse. . . . Of the verses which the *Lear* Quarto sets up as verses it is important to remember that 1,580 verses are lined correctly and that 650 are lined incorrectly. Much of the Quarto lining, two-thirds of it, is good, and in agreement with the Folio. The good lining is found in passages varying in length from one to sixty-five lines. The last 145 lines of the fourth scene of the second act have very few mislinings. . . . The verses which are mislined in the *Lear* Quarto are definitely verses which are mislined, and anyone who has read a little poetry may easily restore them to their proper lining.[35]

Madeleine Doran had already observed that much of the verse in the Quarto was correctly lined, a fact which shifted the onus of blame from the copy (as the exponents of the reported text theorized) to the compositor.[36] But Hubler was the first to offer an explanation: "The mislining consists in the lengthening and crowding of lines for the purpose, I think, of conserving space."[37] Hubler quoted Lear's final speech in the first scene—"For we | Have no such daughter" (B4v7–10; 1.1.262–266; TLN 287–291)—which takes up five lines in the Folio, but only four in the Quarto, and argued that "the mislining did not exist in the Quarto copy but is rather the work of a compositor intent upon compressing his text into as small a space as possible." Whereas some bibliographers treat the text as a neutral object in value-free terms, Hubler was not afraid to pass judgment on Okes's work:

> The First Quarto is a wretched piece of printing . . . The many printer's mistakes and the hasty corrections suggest what these observations bear out; that is, that the printers of the First Quarto were unwilling to spend much time or money on the publication of the book. They compressed the text into a small space, corrected some of the errors, and when it did not suit their convenience to consult the manuscript in the correction of still other errors, they changed the readings as best they could. The whole business was a hasty and economical venture.[38]

Credit must be given to Edward Hubler, writing in 1932, for anticipating Peter Blayney's demonstration of Okes's poor workmanship, published in 1982.

Hubler cited several convincing examples of space saving. He compared the 1608 Quarto both with the 1619 reprint and with the Folio regarding this "example of concentrated compression" (discussed earlier, p. 112):

And woes by wrong imaginations loose
The knowledge of themselues. *A drum a farre off.*
Edg. Giue me your hand far off me thinks I heare the beaten
Come father ile bestow you with a friend. *Exit.* (drum,
Enter Cordelia, Kent and Doctor. (thy goodnes,
Cord. O thou good *Kent* how shall I liue and worke to match
My life will be too short and euery measure faile me.
(K1v15–21; 4.6.283–4.7.2; TLN 2738–2749)

As Hubler observed, "Not allowing for spacing before and after stage directions, the Folio takes up [twelve] lines. A modern version would take eleven lines, the Second Quarto takes ten, the First Quarto only seven. Again it will be observed that the First Quarto preserves the correct lining when there is no occasion for changing it, as in the first two lines and the line beginning, 'Come father.'"[39] A further consequence of mis-lineation was that the compositor, by running the initial half-line into the one following, created a knock-on effect, already noted by Chambers: "In the First Quarto I find forty-two lines of six feet or more which are long because the compositor has set up the half line with which the speech begins and the following line as one line. There are ninety-seven lines which are long because the compositor has set up the half line with which a speech ended and the preceding line as one line. And there are one hundred and one lines which are long because the compositor has set up three lines of verse in the space of two, or four in the space of three."[40] This feature of Q1 could not be explained by theories of deficient lineation, as Hubler showed: "Sometimes when the fraction of the line was long the compression of it disturbed the lining for three or four lines. The compositor, however, always worked back to the correct lining as soon as he could, indicating that he had no doubt about what the correct lining should be." Hubler's demonstration of how the compositor "was able to save the space of a line" by rearranging the lineation justified his deduction that "all but a very few lines were lengthened to this end."[41]

Finally, Hubler turned to the compositors' mis-lineation of verse as prose, having calculated that "[o]f the mislined verses of the Quarto, five times as many are set up as prose as are mislined in any other way. The length of these passages varies from two lines to two hundred and thirty. . . . One of the strongest reasons for thinking that these mislinings are the deliberate work of the compositor is the fact that four of these shorter passages are rhymed." Hubler cited the rhymed verse (quoted earlier on p. 79) by which Poor Tom offers to scare away all dogs—"Be thy mouth, or blacke, or white, tooth that poysons if it bite" (G4r28–34; 3.6.64–75; TLN 2023–2030)—as "bibliographical evidence" that "the compositor recognized these verses" as such, but "did not want to align them in the usual manner."[42] To begin with, he "printed the two verses of the rhymed couplets on one line. He has set up the first word of each line with a capital. The first three lines could be subjected to this treatment and still appear as verse, but the two verses which went to make up the last line were too long to be placed on one line, and he continued the verse on the following line as prose." Hubler printed the whole speech and then commented on the typographical devices that were used to save space: "As very often happened when the compositor was intent upon compression, he used the tilde for the *n* and the symbol *&* for *and.* I submit that there is conscious purpose in such mislining as this. I take these mislined rhymes as very strong evidence of the fact that these mislinings are not the work of a stenographer, for he would be a very dull stenographer indeed who did not recognize a rhyme when he heard one."[43]

Hubler had undoubtedly made his case that the typographical irregularities in the 1608 *Lear* were due not to errors in reporting, whether shorthand or longhand, but to deliberate decisions taken in Okes's printing house. The only step that he could not take was to recognize any coherent typographical intent in this process:

> I have not meant to suggest that the compositor of the First Quarto carefully and consistently planned to save space by thoughtfully arranging the type upon the page. He was much too careless a fellow, and the printing of the book was much too hasty a project, for that. I mean to say only that he was under the compulsion of turning out as compact a volume as he could. *Perhaps he was instructed to set up the type to fit a given number of pages, and when he saw an opportunity to effect a saving, he took advantage of it.* That he worked without much forethought is evident from a small number of cases in which mislinings do not conserve space. These inefficient mislinings are few. They consist of a half-dozen passages of prose set up as verse, and eleven passages of verse set up as prose in which no saving is effected. In view of the many cases of misalignment which did conserve space, and considering the slovenly work on the Quarto as a whole, I do not think these cases are too many to fall within the margin we must allow for the printer of so carelessly published a book.[44]

This judgment anticipates with uncanny accuracy both the far more extensive bibliographic analysis of the 1608 *Lear* in the context of

Okes's printing house practices that Peter Blayney produced fifty years later, and the independent textual analysis I have presented here. The passage I italicized shows a scholar on the brink of realizing a major insight, which he failed to follow up. Hubler reiterated his point that the mis-lineation could not

> be explained on the theory of a stenographic report because the irregularities of the Quarto are often found in other books which were not reported. The errors of the Quarto differ from the errors of other books more in quantity than in kind, and if a thing can happen once without a reporter, it can happen several times. The irregularities of the Quarto are more numerous because the book is a singularly bad piece of printing. Whatever may be said of my explanation, it has the virtue of being based on observable bibliographical data.[45]

That is indeed a major consideration, to be borne in mind when we review the Two Versions theory, for which observable bibliographic data are completely lacking. If Edward Hubler's argument had been fairly assessed by one or more bibliographical authorities at the time when it appeared, the textual history of the 1608 *King Lear* Quarto would have been totally different. Unfortunately, his essay was reviewed by Sir Walter Greg, the self-appointed guardian of *Lear*'s text, in such a manner as to dismiss it from serious consideration.[46] I hope that this discussion may give to Hubler some of the credit he deserved. As he modestly concluded, "These are simple matters which have been overlooked, doubtless because of their simplicity."

The other scholar who suggested that the Quarto omissions were deliberate was Gwynne Blakemore Evans, who threw out this idea twice, if only in passing. Reviewing Peter Blayney's groundbreaking study in 1984, Evans commented,

> Although a good deal has recently been written in support of Q1 and F1 as authoritative independent versions, I must admit to remaining unconvinced. Neither text can really stand on its own, the folio even less perhaps than the quarto, and the so-called changes in F1 in several of the characters (for example, Edgar and Albany) appear to me exaggerated. Apart from the

> roughly one hundred lines and part-lines unique to F1, *which, for a variety of reasons, may well have been omitted in Q1*, I see nothing in the F1 cuts beyond the capacity of a competent company book-keeper / reviser, intent, for the most part, on shortening the play.[47]

I italicize the tantalizing evidence that Evans had already considered the possibility that the passages existing only in the Folio were not added subsequently, but merely restored omissions made by the Quarto. Five years later, reviewing the Oxford Shakespeare, Evans took issue with the editors' approach to what they designated as "two-text plays" and their "two interrelated postulates," which made him "very uneasy": "(1) that Shakespeare was regularly given to revising his work; (2) that where there are two substantially variant versions of the same play, one of which can be associated with performance by Shakespeare's company, the theatre version is to be preferred because it preserves Shakespeare's final revision. Compelling evidence for both these postulates is tenuous, particularly for the second."[48] In the analogous case of *Hamlet*, Evans argued that the 217 lines found in the second Quarto (1604–1605; printed from "Shakespeare's holograph foul papers") but omitted in the Folio, represent cuts that may have been "forced on Shakespeare by the demands of playing time or the interference of his fellow actors." At all events, "these omitted lines were originally an integral part of Shakespeare's conception of the play." As for the supposed "additions," Evans objected that "a number of them are almost certainly omissions from Q2 rather than later additions to F1." Evans briefly discussed the similar claims that Taylor had made for *King Lear*—that the Folio text was, like *Hamlet*, "an acting version preserving Shakespeare's final revision"—but dismissed the case, for the time being, as "not proved."[49]

Evans returned to the text of *Lear* in the second *Riverside* edition, revising his "Note on the Text" to discuss "the new 'two-*Lear*' theory."[50] He acknowledged the obvious facts that the Folio text "differs in several ways from the Q1–2 text; it omits some 288 lines or part-lines, adds some 133 lines or part-lines; differs in a substantial number of substantive readings (single words and phrases . . .), and handles the war theme more diplomatically by getting rid of Q1–2 references to Cordelia's attempt to rescue Lear as a French invasion of England." Referring to the "group of critics" who had claimed that the Folio text "must be considered a separate play in its own right," Evans objected that

> the premise on which the proponents of the two-*Lear* theory build their case—that the F1 text represents Shakespeare's own revision of the play as it appears in Q1–2—is, so far as any hard evidence is concerned, grounded on subjective interpretations of the 'facts' by critics, who, taking Shakespeare's full involvement as a given, discover exaggerated indications of a planned revision even in the most trifling differences, none of which, except perhaps, but not necessarily, for the lines unique to F1 *(a number of which, however, are almost certainly due to omissions by the Q1 compositors)*, are not beyond the capability of an intelligent, but careless, book-keeper.[51]

Readers will note that, in the interval between his Blayney review of 1984 and the revised *Riverside* thirteen years later, a significant change can be seen in the crucial italicized passages, referring to the lines unique to the Folio as representing Quarto omissions. Evans shifted from an expression of possibility—"may well have been omitted in Q1"—to one of near conviction: "are almost certainly due to omissions by the Q1 compositors." Having started work on this book some years after his death, it is a matter of keen regret to me that I was unable to ask Gwynne Evans to elaborate his case. However, I hope that I have marshaled enough evidence to substantiate it.

PART 2

The Folio, 1623

5

One Play, One Manuscript, Two Printed Books

MOST CURRENT THEORIES about the text of *King Lear*, as found in the 1623 Folio, hold that it derives from exemplars of the First and Second Quartos that had been marked up by reference to a theatrical text. As I have argued, such theories are untenable, since they would involve thousands of handwritten markings in the margins and elsewhere on the page that would soon become illegible. The dissenting position, by Madeleine Doran in 1931, argues that the Folio was set up in part from direct consultation of a theatrical manuscript preserving Shakespeare's original text. This would mean that both the Quarto and Folio represent two differing versions of the same underlying text. A common thread in both cases is the nature of Shakespeare's handwriting and spelling, which I now briefly review.

The Quarto and Shakespeare's Manuscript

Shakespeare's handwriting began to attract the attention of scholars as they studied documents containing his six genuine autograph signatures: the three on his will, the one on his deposition in the Belott-Mountjoy suit in May 1612, and the two attached to the conveyance and mortgage of the Blackfriars gatehouse in March 1613.[1] A further stimulus to research was given by Richard Simpson's suggestion that a play manuscript in the British Library contained a scene in Shakespeare's hand.[2] This is the collaborative play (Harleian MS 7368), containing the Booke of *Sir Thomas Moore*. In this manuscript thirteen of the twenty-two leaves are in the hand of Anthony Munday, as W. W. Greg first showed, with five other writers contributing various "Additions": Hand A is Henry Chettle, Hand B is Thomas Heyword, Hand C is the playhouse bookkeeper or scribe; Hand E is Thomas Dekker; and Hand D, who wrote the insurrection scene (Addition IIc) is Shakespeare, according to Simpson.[3] A leading handwriting expert confirmed the ascription in 1916, and most of the reliable authorities since then have agreed.[4] The relevance of this document to the text of *King Lear* concerns the relationship between an author's handwriting and spelling. If we could determine that relationship we would be able to recognize the kind of mistakes that a compositor might make. If Shakespeare's *k* was hard to distinguish from his *b*, for instance, or his *a* from his *u*, this would produce a particular type of misreading.

The obvious objection is that the more stages through which Shakespeare's manuscript passed the less likelihood that his distinctive spellings would be preserved. In 1923 John Dover Wilson overcame this difficulty by comparing spelling in the *Moore* manuscript with that of fifteen authentic Shakespeare Quartos, which had been "produced by some nine or ten different printing-houses over a space of twenty-nine years." As Wilson argued, when "we find the same types of misprint and the same peculiarities of spelling recurring throughout, it is safe to attribute them to the one constant factor behind them all—the pen of William Shakespeare."[5] Wilson returned to this topic some years later in his remarkable study of the manuscript of *Hamlet*, where he emphasized the connection between "Shakespeare's penmanship" and his "archaic orthography" as the cause of compositors misreading his manuscript and creating "graphic error."[6]

Wilson divided the commonest misprints into five classes, starting with minim letters, those made by a single downstroke of the pen, such as *m*, *n*, *u*, *i*, *c*, *r*, and *w*. As he noted,

> the large number of compositor's errors in words containing such letters prove that Shakespeare must have been more than

> ordinarily careless in his formation of them, that he did not properly distinguish between the convex and concave forms, and that he often kept no count of his strokes, especially when writing two or more minim-letters in combination. For example, we have 'game' for 'gain' *(Oth.)*, 'might' for 'night' and 'sting' for 'stung' *(Lear)*, 'sanctity' for 'sanity', and 'the most' for 'th' in-most' *(Ham.)*, 'vncharmd' for 'unharmed' and 'fennell' for 'fe-male' *(Rom.)*, 'where' for 'when' (*Oth.* and *Lear*) and 'when' for 'where' (2 *Hen. IV*).

In the three pages of the *Moore* manuscript the "excessive carelessness of the pen" makes it "difficult to distinguish *w* from *r* . . . or *r* from *n*," while "the letters *m* and *n* are very often concave in form." The "writer's besetting sin is a neglect to count the strokes of such letters, especially when they appear in combination," such as "*un* with five minims."[7] Wilson itemized four other types of misprint in the authentic Quartos resulting from carelessness in Shakespeare's calligraphy. First, compositors misread *a* for *o*, due to "Shakespeare's habit of sometimes leaving the top of his *a* open, or conversely of curving the initial minim of his *u* so that it appears to be an ill-formed *a*," a habit that resulted in such misprints as "coach" for "couch" *(Oth.)*, "raine" for "ruin" *(Ham.)*, and "sure" for "sale" *(Rom.)*. Second, compositors confused the letters *e* and *d*, which in English secretary hand differ only in scale, resulting in such misprints as "end" for "due" *(Son.)*, "some" for "fond" *(Rom.)*, "and" for "are" *(Lear)*. In Shakespeare's Addition to *Sir Thomas Moore* "instances of similar carelessness . . . occur in almost every other line." Third, compositors could not distinguish between Shakespeare's small-scale *e* and *o*, producing such typical misprints in the authentic Quartos as "these" / "those," "now" / "new," and "thou" / "then." Finally, Wilson noted instances of compositors printing *a* for *o*, generally where a minim letter follows—for example, "frame" for "from" and "hand" for "home"—but also where "no minim letter occurs to account for the confusion." Thus we find "obiect" for "abiect" in *Troil.*, "lodes" for "ladies" and "O light" for "alight" in *Lear*, and "cost" for "cast" in *Hamlet*.

Wilson followed this analysis of the five most common Quarto misreadings explainable by "Shakespearian orthography" with an appendix listing parallel spellings between the three pages of Shakespeare's Addition to *Sir Thomas Moore* and the authentic Quartos, divided into thirty categories, from which I pick out examples from the Quarto of *Lear.*[8] Shakespeare frequently doubled the final consonant of a word, generally after a short vowel. In the *Moore* Addition we find "loff" (9) for "loaf," "gott" (68, 80), "chidd" (73), "sytt" (77), "gospell" (88), "cutt" (120), "slipp" (122), "whett" (134), and "doggs" (135). In the 1608 Quarto of *Lear* we find "ruffe" (G1r26), "dogge" (I4r23), and "gotte" (L2r33). In both the *Moore* manuscript and the authentic Quartos, Shakespeare sometimes omitted the final mute *e* after *c*. Hand D writes "obedyenc" (39, 94,113), "insolenc" (81), "offyc" (98), and "ffraunc" (121). This unusual spelling accounts for the misprints "intelligence" for "intelligent" (*Lear* H1r6), "pallat" for "pallace" (*R. J.* 5.3.107), and "ingredience" for "ingredient" (*Oth.* 2.3.311). Shakespeare omitted the final *e* after *n*, as with "on" for "one" in the Addition (68, 83), a spelling found eight times in the Quartos. He also dropped *e* after *r*, as in "y'ar" (*Lear* I3v3; K2r32), "wer't" (*Lear* H4r21), and "wherin" (*Lear* F3v2).

Many of the spellings in Hand D's portion of the *Moore* manuscript were already old-fashioned in the early 1600s, as Wilson noted.[9] For example, where the choice existed between *-s* and—*ss(e)* endings, Shakespeare "generally preferred the former (*-s* had come in early in the 16th century and was going out at the end of it)."[10] In the *Moore* Addition we find "stilnes" (52) and "trespas" (124). In *Lear* we find *trespas* (E3v38), *addres* (B3v8), *bluntnes* (E2r11), *business* (C2r22), *breefnes* (D3v18), and *plainness* (B3r3). The second Quarto (1619) and the Folio (1623) changed all—*s* spellings to *–ess(e)*, almost without exception.[11] In Elizabethan spelling *c* and *t* were interchangeable before *-ion*, *-ient*, *-ial:* "*c* was the early form, which *t* was superseding." In the *Moore* manuscript Shakespeare wrote "infeccion" (14) and "adicion" (118), as in *Lear* "addicions" (B2v27). In Shakespeare's spelling *-ay* could be substituted for *-ey*, giving "obay" three times in *Moore* (100, 116, 146), three times in *Lear* (G2r16, G2v34, H4r22), and twice in *Hamlet*. He also substituted *ai* for *ei*, spelling "waight" in *Moore* (7), in *Lear* (L4r32), and in the *Sonnets* (50.6). Shakespeare regularly interchanged diphthongs, spelling *ea* for *ei* or *ie*—thus, "perceaue" in *Moore* (92) and "perceau'd" (*Lear* E3v33)—or using *ea* for *e;* thus, "heare" for "here" in *Moore* (62) and in *Lear* (E4v36). He also wrote *oo* for *o:* in *Moore* (76) we find "to the" written as "tooth" and in *Lear* as both "too'th" (F1r4) and "toth" (L3r33). In both the *Moore* Addition (51) and in *Lear* Shakespeare abbreviated "by the" to "byth" or "bit'h" (E3v6, K4r29).

The significance of Wilson's work, as Madeleine Doran quickly saw, was that it provided evidence that the 1608 Quarto of *King Lear* must have been set directly from Shakespeare's manuscript. She cited additional examples in the 1608 Quarto to illustrate his main categories of misreadings:

> Examples of minim misreadings are . . . *might* for *night* (B2v1), *festuant* for *festinate* (H1r5), *flechuent* for *fleshment* (E2r36), *snyted* for *suited* (E1r13; evidently spelled *suyted* in the manuscript). The misreading of *u* as *a* is found in *crauing* for *cunning* (D4v26) and in *warbling* for *mumbling* (D4v34); of *a* as *u* in *gull* for *gall* (C4v17) and in *starre-blusting* for *starre-blasting* (G1r38). *E* and *d* have frequently been mistaken for one another, as in *heard* for *heare* (D4v16), *circled* for *circle* (L2r35) *praise* for *prais'd* (D2v30), *and* for *are* (D2r15) *and* for *one* (K4v1).[12]

Doran noted several instances of *o* misread as *a*, including *clat-pole* for *clot-pole* (C4v38) and *dayes* for *dogges* (E1r33), and underlined the significance of these misreadings in the 1608 Quarto: "If, as Professor Wilson thinks, *a* mistaken for *o* is a peculiar characteristic of Shakespeare's handwriting, we have evidence of his hand in the manuscript for the quarto, namely, in the misreadings *con* for *can* (D3r8), *tottered* for *tattered* (I4r27), *lou'd* for *bare* (H1v16), *night more* for *nightmare* (G2v11), *O light* for *alight* (G2v13), *bedlom* for *bedlam* (H2r23), and *deptoued* for *depraued* (E4v38)."[13]

Unlike many modern Shakespeare scholars, Madeleine Doran had received training in the history of the English language and was familiar with changes in pronunciation between Middle English and those of Shakespeare's day. She cited contemporary scholarship to define the old-fashioned nature of the spelling (and, by inference, pronunciation) of Q1, pointing out that the Second Quarto (1619) systematically modernized Shakespeare's orthography only eleven years later.[14] She noted that the 1608 *Lear*, like the authentic quartos, displays "an interchange of *ea*, *ie*, *ei*, and *e*, regardless of the quality of the long *e* sound" and observed that "*oo* is sometimes used in *King Lear*, as it frequently is in the other quartos, for the old open *o*, as in *foord* [G1v32], or for a short *o*, as in *strooke* [F1r20] (F *stroke;* modern *struck*), instead of being reserved for the old close *o* which had moved up to the sound of Germanic *u*."[15] Having acknowledged her debt to Dover Wilson, she went beyond him, pointing to "a characteristic of the first quarto of *King Lear* that he had not noticed as occurring in the other quartos"; that is, "the spelling *ou* to indicate the old open *o*, e.g., *ould* [B3r1; F4r22], *could* (i.e., cold), *vnfould* [B4v26], *hould* [B2v7; C3r35; D1v1]. Two combinations frequently occurring in the other quartos, *ow* for *ou*, and *ew* for *ieu* and *ue*, occur in *King Lear* in *hower* [*howers*, K1v26; *howerly*, I4v27], *adew*, *reuennew*, *crewell* (i.e., cruel)." As Doran reviewed Wilson's findings and added her own, she noted a number of individual spellings that linked the 1608 *Lear* with other authentic Quartos, establishing its closeness to Shakespeare's final manuscript and further refuting the case for it being a reported text. (I add within square brackets the number of times each word occurs.)

> The addition of mute *e* at the end of a syllable to indicate length of the preceding vowel was coming to be an established usage; but this *e* is often omitted in the Shakespearean quartos. In Q1 of *King Lear* such spellings as *ther's* [13], *her's* (i.e., here's) [3], *wher's* [6], *whereupon* [1], *safty* [2], *vnprizd* [1], *past* (i.e., paste) [1], *wast* (i.e., waist) [1], *wholesome* [1], *nam's* [1], *y'ar* [2], *far ye well* [1] are frequent. A single instead of a double medial consonant, frequent in the quartos, is also common in *King Lear*, e.g., *mary* [3], *cary* [4], *sory* [2], *tary* [1], *vilaine* [1] . . . *Ck* for *k* after *n* occurs in *vnckle* [2] and *truncke* [2].[16]

John Dover Wilson and Madeleine Doran collected enough evidence from handwriting and spelling to establish that the 1608 Quarto was set from Shakespeare's foul manuscript.

Subsequent studies of Shakespeare's handwriting and spelling strengthened the evidence that the 1608 Quarto of *King Lear* was set from an authorial manuscript. Giles Dawson partly corrected and extended the findings of Maunde Thompson in an important essay, based on a comparison of Shakespeare's handwriting with "a collection of Elizabethan and Jacobean letters and documents . . . written by 250 writers."[17] Dawson noted that "the man who wrote Hand D was given to such carelessness in writing the letters *b* and *d* that they looked, respectively, like *t* and *e*," while his "carelessly written *k*" could be taken for a *b* or an *l*, but seldom for a *k*. Where forty other writers all gave *k* "one general shape, Shakespeare was in this respect an eccentric making no effort to conform to the common usage of his day. In the signatures of his that have survived and can be seen clearly, no two specimens of the *k* are made in the same way." The variations in forming the *k* found in the signatures and 147 lines of Hand D, Dawson concluded, "provide strong evidence that one and the same hand wrote both."[18]

Additional evidence linking the *Moore* manuscript with Shakespeare's authentic Quartos was provided by A. C. Partridge, a scholar who had a wide knowledge of textual scholarship and the history of the English language.[19] Partridge studied the orthography of the *Moore* additions and the Quartos of *Venus and Adonis*, *The Rape of Lucrece*, and the *Sonnets*. In these extensive discussions Partridge established the authenticity of several Shakespearian spelling preferences also found in the 1608 Quarto of *King Lear*, such as the double *oo* for *o; ou* for *oo* and *u; ea* for *ee* and *e; ee* for *ea* and *e; ai* for *e; ew* for *ie, u, e,* and *ow;* and the frequent use of *in-* for *en-*. The multiple instances of all these spellings found in the *Moore* manuscript and the Quartos of Shakespeare's narrative poems leave little doubt that these shared spellings identify the copy used for the 1608 Quarto of *Lear* as Shakespeare's manuscript.

In his edition of the 1608 Quarto of *King Lear*, Jay L. Halio endorsed Madeleine Doran's demonstration that Q was "printed from Shakespeare's manuscript and not from a pirated copy."[20] Halio cited the identification of authorial spellings made by Doran and Dover Wilson and added further instances, including the omission of a terminal *e* in such words as "haste" ("Hast," L3v1) and "taste" ("tast," F3r10, L1r31, L4r14). Further indications of manuscript provenance include a marked tendency to use *-ea-* for *-ei-*, *-ie-*, or *-e-*, as in "ceaze"

(B4r35), "perceau'd" (E3v33), "pearce" (D2v31), "fleash" (E1v2), "tearmes" (C2v28; F1v23), and conversely in such spellings such as "deere" (for "dear, B2r8) [16 instances], "neerely" (B4v31), "apeer's" (C4r10), "cleerest" (I3r35). Halio also noted the frequent use of initial *in-* for *en-*, as in "intire" (B4r23), "inioy" (C1v19), "intreat" (F3r17 [5 instances]), "inough" (I4r7,33, twice), "indure" (K3r17, K4r7), and "indur'd" (H1v17). In addition to these and other authorial spellings Halio pointed out that "some curiously separated syllables, probably the result of penmanship, may be Shakespearian." He cited these instances: "all waies" (B1r20), "many fould" (D4r5), "so phisticated" (G2r38), "how ere" (H4r20), "a hight" (I3r17), "a squint" (L1r9), and "Sweet hart" (G4r27). Halio concluded that these and other linguistic details, such as the use of contractions, "point to a holograph source."[21] In his invaluable discussion of the variant readings in surviving copies of the 1608 Quarto, W. W. Greg still held the belief that it contained "an often inferior text," "a reported text, obtained from actual performance presumably by some method of shorthand," a text that is "in some way corrupt," indeed seriously corrupt," and "in general a very inferior version" of the play.[22] His scholarly evaluation would have been very different had he known, as we do now, that it was set directly from Shakespeare's manuscript.

The Folio and the "Booke"

Once a dramatist had delivered the manuscript of his play the theater company could begin processing it for its purposes. Their scribe would begin preparing the parts for each of the main actors, copying out their roles and adding cue lines from the speeches immediately preceding and following.[23] He would then begin to make the "Booke," the company's master version of the play that would be used during rehearsals and at performances by the "bookkeeper" or "book-holder," whose job was to ensure that actors kept to the text and to help them should they forget their lines. We used to know a lot more about this document than we know now.[24] Two influential scholars of the twentieth century, R. B. McKerrow and W. W. Greg, formulated a plausible theory of what a "promptbook" should contain. It should be perfectly clear and consistent, with no ambiguities. It should mark every entrance and exit; it should denote the speaking characters through a regular and unchanging set of speech prefixes; stage directions should specify exactly what was to be done on stage and how many actors should be involved; any loose ends left by the dramatist should be tidied up. If these conditions were met, more or less, then bibliographers could classify the text in question as having been prepared by the theater company, and it would be edited accordingly. If they were not met, a crucial set of deductions would follow. If entrances and exits were missing; if speech prefixes for the same character were inconsistent or included the name of an actor performing that role; if speech directions were "permissive," specifying an undefined number of actors ("Enter two or three"), or formulated in the imperative ("Ring the bell"); or if the text had incomplete speeches or revisions without deletions, then that text would be classified as having derived from the dramatist's "foul papers," a term thought to have been widely used in the early modern theater to describe the manuscript as supplied by the dramatist. Such a text occupied a superior place in the theoretical hierarchy and would have its own status for an editor. This system was designed not for readers but for editors, providing a rule of thumb by which they could establish different degrees of authority to texts of each kind.

Unfortunately, as we now know, that theory was a modern construct, conceived at some distance from the surviving manuscripts. A counterargument has been developing in recent times, led by William B. Long and Paul Werstine, and has come to fruition in a comprehensive study by the latter.[25] Werstine has examined with forensic exactitude the evolution of Greg's theories, which were influenced in part by McKerrow's work but also differed from his, and has traced a disturbing series of self-contradictions and inconsistencies.[26] Werstine devoted two chapters to the concept of "foul papers," in which he reconstructed the context in which the term first appeared and argued that it had a specific meaning that cannot be generalized into an all-purpose term for authorial manuscripts.[27] As he summed up this part of his critique, the proper historical sense of the term is its use "in relation to the term 'Fair copy': that is, 'foul papers' refers to a MS that is to be or is being or has been fair-copied. Contrary to Greg's assumption, 'foul papers' need not refer exclusively to authorial drafts, whether these are messy or not." Although the two terms are relational, he argued, they are not "neutral: "'foul papers' has a pejorative sense, referring to a[n] MS set in opposition to another, somehow superior MS, the 'fair copy.'"[28] Although Werstine's argument is forceful, Ernst Honigmann cited several contemporary usages where "'foul' papers, sheets, etc. was a term in general use, and not confined to the theatre," connoting any kind of draft preceding the first fair copy, and "refers more often to the roughness of the text than its incompleteness."[29] Scholars may continue to use this term without endorsing related and inappropriate theories.

The second part of Werstine's critique is even more far-reaching in its implications for students of early modern drama. He has made a prolonged study of the surviving nineteen theatrical manuscripts and three annotated quartos, all of which "contain annotation for stage production, usually, in the case of the MSS, in other hands than those in which the main text is inscribed."[30] With constant reference to these witnesses, Werstine disproves every assumption made by McKerrow and Greg concerning the ways in which the bookkeeper is supposed to have treated authorial manuscripts.[31] As he sums up this part of his argument, playhouse texts are very different from the promptbooks that appeared much later in theatrical history, on which the McKerrow-Greg expectations were based:

> In early modern playhouse texts character designations can vary more and be rendered more ambiguously, rather than less so, after theatrical personnel have prepared a text for the stage. Bookkeepers' versions of stage directions, some of which can be indefinite, permissive, or petitory, can be less reliable as a guide to or record of who entered at a particular juncture in performance than the stage directions playwrights furnished. Playhouse manuscripts also sport the loose ends, false starts, unresolved conclusions, and alternative passages of dialogue once thought peculiar to authorial texts.

As for the appearance of actors' names in printed texts, once taken to be a sure sign of a dramatist's "foul papers," Werstine shows that "there is abundant empirical evidence of the introduction into playhouse manuscripts of actors' names by bookkeepers, and not one instance of an actor's name written in an authorial hand."[32] These two chapters, taken in conjunction with an appendix detailing "Characteristics of Gregian 'foul papers' in playhouse texts," correct seventy years' misapprehension of the nature of authorial copy.[33]

The significance of this revolution in scholarly assumptions for *King Lear*, and other play texts is that it can encourage us to look for signs of an author's continuing presence in plays printed from a theatrical manuscript. Where Greg believed that a company would be unwilling to part with the Booke of a play to a publisher, since it contained the license for acting, Werstine counters that "it hardly seems impossible that a playhouse MS might serve as printer's copy" and cites the evidence of one play that appeared in print with its license actually reproduced in the printed text.[34] As he observes, a time there was before the "empirically invalid textual categories" of "foul papers" and "promptbooks," an age of innocence when A. W. Pollard studied authorial play manuscripts and "concluded, incontestably, that acting companies sometimes possessed and used in performance copies in the dramatists' own hands."[35] Pollard had contested the theory that playwrights usually "handed their plays to the companies in fair copies written for them by scriveners," citing the evidence provided by several plays in the British Museum library that the companies had obtained a license from the Master of the Revels "by submitting to him the play as written by the author, or authors, sometimes in pretty rough manuscript, and with passages written on slips and pasted in." Further, also contrary to some opinions, Pollard showed that "plays endorsed with the licence for their public performance might be handed over to the prompter, and by him converted into prompt copies."[36] Pollard concluded that "in some cases Shakespeare's own autograph of a play may have been the copy supplied to its first printer," and since "in other cases we find an autograph manuscript used as a prompt copy" then "at least some of the First Quartos were set up from prompt-copies."[37] Pollard's argument that plays were regularly printed from authorial manuscripts that had served as the company's Booke is valid not only for the authorized Quartos but also for the Folio, in which eighteen of Shakespeare's plays appeared for the first time. In the spirit of Pollard, but newly instructed by Werstine, we can now see that all those texts are, to some degree or other, hybrids, possessing characteristics that resist Greg's division into separate categories of authorial and theatrical. It follows that the Booke of *King Lear*, as delivered to Jaggard in 1623, may also contain traces of Shakespeare's original manuscript, as delivered in 1605.

How would we recognize such traces? The most important evidence that Jaggard and his compositors had access to a theatrical Booke directly derived from Shakespeare's manuscript is that they were able to correct the many instances of verse mis-lineation and of verse set as prose created in the 1608 Quarto and copied by that of 1619. As we saw in Chapter 3, Okes's compositors managed to reduce Lear's address to the elements from seven lines to six, by using two tildes, two ampersands, a turn-under, and a numeral instead of a number:

> You owe me no subscription, why thenlet fall your horrible
> Here I stād your slaue,a poore infirme weak & (plesure
> Despis'd ould man,but yet I call you seruile
> Ministers, that haue with 2 .pernitious daughters ioin'd
> Your high engēdred battel gainst a head so old & white
> As this, O tis foule. (F4r20–25; 3.2.18–24)

Being able to consult the Booke containing Shakespeare's original text, Jaggard's Folio editors could omit all the space-saving devices and restore the proper punctuation and lineation:

> You owe me no subscription. Then let fall
> Your horrible pleasure. Heere I stand your Slaue,
> A poore, infirme, weake, and dispis'd old man:
> But yet I call you Seruile Ministers,
> That will with two pernicious Daughters ioyne
> Your high-engender'd Battailes,'gainst a head
> So old, and white as this. O, ho! 'tis foule. (TLN 1673–1679)

If we consider the established theory that the Folio was set from a marked-up copy of Q1 or Q2, in this instance that would have involved at least some two dozen separate marginal instructions by the editor, as we can imagine them:

> separate "thenlet"/ /divide line after "fall"/ /capital letter for "Your"/ / insert period after "pleasure" and correct spelling/ capital letter for "Heer" / /remove tilde in "stād"/ /divide line after "Slaue" and capitalize "A"/ /insert commas after each of these words: "poore infirme weak"/ / replace "&" with "and"/ /divide line after "Ministers,"/ /replace "2 ." with "two"/ /remove tilde in "engēdred"/ / divide line after "head," and capitalize "So"/ / replace "&" with "and"/ /for "O tis" read "O, ho! 'tis"/ /capitalize "Slaue," "Seruile," "Ministers," "Daughters," and "Battailes"/

Many of these corrections could be made with the usual printer's marks, of course, but given that this passage fills about one vertical inch of text (2.5 cm), with a left-hand margin of less than a half-inch (1 cm) and a right-hand margin perhaps twice as wide (although "plesure" is set outside the measure), the resulting corrected page would be extremely crowded or even illegible.[38] Moreover, every line on this page would require from one to five corrections. Writing the *Iliad* in a nutshell might be easier.

Although W. W. Greg once airily remarked that he could easily mark up a copy of Q1 for the Folio printers, other scholars have been less sanguine.[39] Hardin Craig, arguing that the Folio text had been set from the theatrical Booke, flatly asserted that it would be "a mistake to think that the folio was set up from a printed quarto that had been corrected from a stage manuscript, since more than two thousand changes, some of them long, would have been necessary, and they simply could not have been legible if made on the soft paper of an Elizabethan quarto."[40] Similarly, J. M. Nosworthy dismissed Alice Walker's theory that an editor might have marked up a copy of the unauthorized 1603 Quarto of *Hamlet* to serve as the text for the authorized replacement in 1604–1605, expressing disbelief that the printer, James Roberts, would have sanctioned

> [a] tedious and laborious process whereby a collator transferred to the comparatively restricted margins of Q1 all the corrections

> and additions that were necessary to convert its version of Act I into that presented in Q2. The kind of copy that would have resulted can only be described as a compositor's nightmare compared to which fair would be too foul an epithet for the foulest of foul papers. It may be said that this whole doctrine of marked quartos serving as printing-house copy is one that calls for the most rigid control.[41]

This is an important caveat, to be recalled when we examine the Two Versions theory in Chapter 8.

Thanks to their possession of the Booke, Jaggard's Folio compositors were able to undo what Okes's men did out of "necessity," returning prosified verse to its original Shakespearian state. In Chapter 3 I quoted the speech by Goneril that Okes reduced to prose and crammed into sheet D, beginning,

> *Gon.* Not onely sir this, your all-licenc'd foole, but other of your insolent retinue do hourely carpe and quarrell, breaking forth in ranke & (not to be indured riots,) Sir I had thought by making this well knowne vnto you, to haue found a safe redres, but now grow fearefull by what your selfe too late haue spoke and done, that you protect this course, and put on by your allowance, which if you should,the fault would not scape censure, nor the redresse, sleepe, which in the tender of a wholsome weale, might in their working doe you that offence, that else
>
> (D1v5–13)

This glibly evasive speech appears in the Folio as the verse that Shakespeare wrote:

> *Gon.* Not only Sir this, your all-lycenc'd Foole,
> But other of your insolent retinue
> Do hourely Carpe and Quarrell, breaking forth
> In ranke, and (not to be endur'd) riots Sir.
> I had thought by making this well knowne vnto you,
> To haue found a safe redresse,but now grow fearefull
> By what your selfe too late haue spoke and done,

That you protect this course,and put it on
By your allowance, which if you should, the fault
Would not scape censure,nor the redresses sleepe,
Which in the tender of a wholesome weale,
Might in their working do you that offence,
Which else were shame,that then necessitie
Will call discreet proceeding. (TLN 712–725)

It is past belief that a compositor having little formal education could correctly reline Goneril's smooth and hypocritical verse by his own efforts alone. Thanks to the Booke containing a faithful record of Shakespeare's intentions, the Folio compositors were able to restore his verse as he had written it.

The Folio's restoration of the play's careful division between verse and prose is the single most important proof that it relied on the Booke as its main authority. The accuracy with which it preserved this large-scale feature of Shakespeare's text is repeated on the smaller scale of textual readings. Jaggard's compositors were evidently more able to decipher some of his characteristic letter forms than were those employed by Nicholas Okes. I cannot claim that the Booke supplied by the King's Men was actually in Shakespeare's hand, but whichever scribe had copied it did so accurately and his hand may have been easier to read than Shakespeare's. Although Jaggard's compositors consulted both Quartos, there is strong evidence that the manuscript copy represented by the Booke constitutes an independent textual witness to what Shakespeare wrote.

This truly revolutionary argument was first made by Madeleine Doran in 1931, in a pioneering study that was unjustly marginalized by W. W. Greg and consequently ignored by all who deferred to his considerable authority.[42] Doran realized that both the First Quarto and the Folio derived from the same authorial copy when she noticed that the type of verbal error most abundantly represented in Q1 is "that comprising misreadings of a manuscript." In fact, she judged, "Exclusive of the many instances which are allowable readings if considered by themselves, but which, when compared with the folio, appear to be manuscript misreadings of the correct readings given in that text, there are upward of one hundred and twenty-five errors in Q1, which seem to have been caused by failure on the part of the printer to decipher his manuscript correctly."[43] Further study of the relationship between the two texts led Doran to conclude that "the first quarto was printed from Shakespeare's original manuscript, and that the folio represents the prompt-book, which had been transcribed from the original and subsequently revised and shortened." She added this important corollary: "It will therefore not be quite correct to speak of the manuscript for the folio as independent of the manuscript for the quarto; it is rather a different one."[44]

The first stage in her argument that the Folio derived from a different manuscript from that behind the quartos was the observable fact that

> the folio gives correct readings for most of the errors in both of the quartos. A certain number of obvious misprints could have been corrected by the printer, as was done in Q2, for example, *my robbe* to *may rob* (I3r2), *snurff* to *snuffe* (I2v37), *euer inch* to *euery inch* (I3v26). But of the great number of manuscript misreadings in Q1, correction could not have been made without reference to a good text. The good readings in F are not conjectural emendations, as were so many in Q2, but the readings which were evidently in the manuscript from which Q1 was printed, and which were misread by the printer of that text.

As she pointed out, where Q1 reads *on speed fort* [I4v2]), emended in Q2 to *on speed for't*, Folio reads *On speedy foot* [TLN 2657]; *vnder excesse* [Q H3r26] is replaced by *vndoo* [TLN 2255]; *deseruing thine honour* [H4r10] by *discerning* [TLN 2306]; *snulbug* [G2v27] by *Smulkin* [TLN 1919];[45] *stands still in experience* [H2r32] by *esperance* [TLN 2182]; *Bring oyle to stir* [E1v29] by *fire* [TLN 1150]; *accent teares* [D2r30] by *cadent* [TLN 799]; *low seruice* [E3r30] by *low Farmes* [TLN 1268], and so forth—all of them correct readings derived from Shakespeare's manuscript as preserved in the company's Booke.[46] Doran illustrated the difference between the conjectural emendations of the Second Quarto and the Folio's preservation of the correct manuscript readings by quoting Lear's angry retort to Goneril's description of his Knights as a "disordred rabble": "Detested kite, thou list my traine, and men of choise and | Rarest parts" [D2r15–16]. The compositor or editor of Q2 simply "fixed on the word which appeared to be wrong and found a substitute for it which gave a satisfactory sense: 'thou *lessen* my traine and men of choise and rarest parts' [C3r36–37]. The folio, on the other hand, supplies the original reading, from which the errors in Q1 arose by a misreading of the manuscript and a consequent misinterpretation of the sense on the part of the printer: 'thou *lyest.* | My Traine are men of choice, and rarest parts' [1.4.262–263; TLN 775]." In this, as in many other cases, Doran argued, "the folio gives not only a good reading, but a reading which is evidently original."[47]

The misreadings of authorial copy in the 1608 Quarto sometimes converge to produce completely puzzling sequences, such as the scene where Gloucester, tied to a chair by Cornwall and Regan, is forced to explain why he has sent the king to Dover. Madeleine Doran quoted this passage from the corrected forme of sheet H in the Quarto, placing the readings from the uncorrected sheet within square brackets, and juxtaposed it with the Folio text. The Folio text gives eight variant readings, italicized in both of these excerpts. Doran commented, "Even in its corrected form in Q1, there is much in the passage that is unintelligible."

QUARTO

Glost. Because I would not see thy cruell nayles
Pluck out his poore old eyes, nor thy fierce sister
In his [aurynted] annoynted flesh *rash* borish phangs,
The Sea with such a storme [of his lou'd] *on his lowd* head 59
In hell blacke night indur'd, would haue [layd] *bod* vp
And quencht the [steeled] stelled fires, yet poore old heart,
Hee *holpt* the heauens to *rage*,
If wolues had at thy gate *heard* that *dearne* time
Thou shouldst haue said,good Porter turne the key,
All cruels else *subscrib'd* but I shall see
The winged vengeance ouertake such children.

(H1v13–23; 3.7.56–66)

FOLIO

Glou. Because I would not see thy cruell Nailes
Plucke out his poore old eyes : nor thy fierce Sister,
In his Annointed flesh, *sticke* boarish phangs.
The Sea, with such a storme *as his bare* head,
In Hell-blacke-night indur'd, would haue *buoy'd* vp
And quench'd the Stelled fires:
Yet poore old heart, he *holpe* the Heauens to *raine.*
If Wolues had at thy Gate *howl'd* that *sterne* time,
Thou should'st haue said, good Porter turne the Key:
All Cruels else *subscribe:* but I shall see
The winged Vengeance ouertake such Children

(TLN 2128–2138)

As Doran observed, "*of his lou'd*," the uncorrected Quarto reading in line 59, "could be a manuscript misreading of *as his bare*," since mistakes involving the letters *a* for *o*, *s* for *f*, *r* for *u*, and *e* for *d* "are not uncommon; *b* misread as *l* occurs again in *layd* for *buoy'd*. Of the first misreading, the printer of Q1 has attempted an emendation; of the second, he has blundered his correction. In both these instances the folio furnishes the undoubted original; its readings are not conjectural emendations of the errors in Q1."[48] This is a crucial point, establishing the Folio as an independent witness deriving from Shakespeare's manuscript as preserved in the Booke. Extending her argument, Doran noted, "*Rash* and *sticke*, *rage* and *raine*, *dearne* and *sterne* are variant pairs, either of which gives a satisfactory sense. The folio printer might have substituted *rain* for *rage*, but *rash* and *dearne* are sufficiently striking for him to have attended to particularly. *Stick* is a commonplace word which he might have substituted for one he did not understand; but *sterne* appears to bear a somewhat unusual sense, not likely to have come from a printer."[49] The Folio reading is an instance of "sophistication," in the technical bibliographic sense, namely the "disingenuous alteration or perversion of something; conversion into some less genuine form; the alteration of a literary text in the course of copying or printing."[50] Many commentators have taken the Folio's replacement of *dearne* (concealed, dark, and evil) by *sterne* to be an analogous sophistication made by an editor (as Doran noted, the change is not likely to have come from a printer). That passage "illustrates the type of error for the correction of which the folio must have drawn upon a good manuscript text."[51]

Other misreadings in the Folio prove that it was set from a manuscript, not a printed book. "Positive proof" for this conclusion, Doran claimed, "lies in the fact that among the fresh errors in the folio text—that is, erroneous readings where the corresponding readings in Q1 are correct—are a number of manuscript misreadings."[52] Setting aside ordinary misprints in the Folio, omissions and substitutions such as a printer might have made whatever the nature of his copy, Doran argued that some significant

> errors in F could have been caused, like many in Q1, only by the misreading of manuscript. If a compositor had a correctly printed word before him, why should he set an incorrect word whose form in Elizabethan handwriting resembles the written form of the correct word? . . . There are half a dozen or more errors in the folio which could have arisen in no other way and a number more which might be accidental misprints or printer's substitutions, but which may be most plausibly accounted for as misreadings of a manuscript.[53]

One of her most striking instances of the Folio compositors' misinterpretation of manuscript copy comes from Kent's angry denunciation of Oswald. The misreadings in Q1 are italicized:

QUARTO

such smiling roges as these,
Like Rats oft bite those cordes in twaine,
Which are to *intrench*,to *inloose* smooth euery passion
That in the natures of their Lords rebell,
Bring oyle to *stir*, snow to their colder moods,
Reneag, affirme,and turn their halcion beakes
With euery gale and varie of their maisters,
Knowing nought like *dayes* but following,

(E1v26–33; 2.2.73–80)

Doran pointed out that the folio corrects the misreadings of the quarto, but adds three fresh errors, here italicized:

FOLIO:

such smiling rogues as these,
Like Rats oft bite the holy cords a twaine,
Which are t'intrince, t'vnloose: smooth euery passion
That in the natures of their Lords rebell,
Being oile to fire, snow to the colder moodes,
Reuenge, affirme, and turne their Halcion beakes
With euery *gall*, and varry of their Masters,
Knowing naught (like dogges) but following:

(TLN 1146–1153)

In line 77, she argued, "*Being* is probably due to misreading; *r* is mistaken for *e* in the misreading of Q1, *lyed* for *tyred* (i.e., tired; C1r23). An Elizabethan *e* would not ordinarily be mistaken for *l* (as in *gall* for *gale*)" in line 79, but Doran could cite "two instances in Shakespeare in which it has been so mistaken, namely, *sellingly* for *feelingly* (Q2 *Hamlet*, 5.2.113), and *melts* for *meets* (Q1 *Troil.*, 1.3.110)." As she noted, "*Reuenge* [l. 78] has every appearance of being a misreading of *reneag;* it has more than one letter misprinted for another, yet the result is not a printer's pi but an actual word whose form in Elizabethan handwriting resembles *reneag.*"[54] A similar mistaking of *n* for *u* is found later in this scene, where in the uncorrected Quarto the compositor printed *ausrent* (E2v3), altered by the proofreader to "miscreant," as against the Folio reading "ancient" (2.2.126), evidently derived from the copy text supplied by the King's Men in 1622.[55] As for the Folio's "tintrince, t'vnloose" (l. 75), compared to the Quarto's "to intrench, to inloose," where Greg had deduced that "the corrector, with an idea of mending the meter reduced *to* in both case to *t'*, oblivious of the fact that in the first it stands for *too*,"[56] Doran replied, "The fact that the manuscript misreadings occur in the folio close by this reading shows that it is not a blundered correction of the misreading in the quarto, but a reading derived, perhaps in slightly altered form, from the manuscript itself."[57] Madeleine Doran added more instances confirming her diagnosis that the Folio text, with alterations made both by the theater company and the printer, had been set from a later version of the same manuscript that had been used for the Quarto.[58]

Doran's interpretation was strengthened by P. W. K. Stone in his somewhat eccentric study. Among the Folio's "gratuitous errors" he itemized "misinterpretations of manuscript 'copy,'" such as Cornwall's report that "since I came hether, which I can call but now, I haue heard strange newes" [D4r36–37], which the Folio set as "strangenesse" [2.1.87; TLN 1025–1026]. Stone observed that the nature of the mistake, "the substitution of an unacceptable, though not nonsensical, reading for another closely resembling it orthographical form," suggests that this is not an instance of the compositor miscopying the Quarto reading, but rather of misreading "*strange newes* . . . as it appeared, perhaps erratically spelt, in some manuscript version of the text," perhaps as "*strange nes*."[59] Although Stone rejected Doran's case that Q and F derived independently of each other from the original, he accepted her evidence that the Folio contained many instances of misreading from a manuscript where the Quarto had read the same word correctly. I select a few of these instances, giving the Folio misreading first: *painting* (2.4.31; TLN 1307) for *panting* (E3v25); *spirits* (2.1.76; TLN 1013) for *spurres* (D4r27); *Iustice* (3.4 80; TLN 1861) for *iustly* (G2r18); *tight* (3.6.70; TLN 2027) for *tike* (G4r31); *slaues* (4.1.68; TLN 2253)) for *stands; walk'd* (4.6.17; TLN 2452) for *walke* (I2v12); and *enraged* (4.6.71; TLN 2516) for *enridg'd* (I3r23).[60]

Unexpected support for Doran's argument that the Quarto and Folio texts derive from the same manuscript was provided in 1949 by G. I. Duthie in his book on Elizabethan shorthand, which proved that none of the systems available in 1608 was able to reproduce language of any complexity as uttered in a theatrical performance. Wanting to prove that the copy behind the 1608 Quarto could have been taken down in longhand, Duthie listed a series of "Q readings explicable as misreadings of corresponding F words in longhand."[61] He proceeded to cite no less than seventy-four instances where an error in the Quarto, as compared to the correct reading in the Folio, "may very well be due to a misreading of longhand," thus presenting strong evidence that the Quarto and Folio texts of *Lear* were set from the same manuscript.[62] Many of his examples concern misreadings in other authentic Quartos that had already been used as evidence of a common manuscript source by Madeleine Doran, whose work was apparently unknown to Duthie. These include instances already discussed, including Q *first* F *fast* (1.1.137), Q *gull* F *gall* (1.4.112), Q *crauing* F *cunning* (2.1.29), and Q *dayes* F *dogges* (2.2.74). Duthie repeatedly reconstructed how the compositors of Q1 misread the handwriting in their copy. In many of his instances of Q variants being due to misreading of longhand, once Duthie had deciphered the original reading in "the copy for Q," it turned out to be identical with the F reading. These instances confirm that the Folio compositor was setting text from a manuscript, not from the printed Quarto.

As I noted in the Preface, advocates of the theory that the Folio represents Shakespeare's revision of the Quarto dismissed any idea that there could have been a "lost archetype" behind both texts, and in the Oxford Shakespeare proclaimed that that notion had "collapsed."[63] My response was that Shakespeare's manuscript is indeed lost, like the vast majority of early modern playbooks, but that it survives in both the Quarto and Folio, despite the vagaries they suffered in the printing house and in the theater. The distinguished literary critic and Shakespeare scholar, Sir Frank Kermode, strengthened that conclusion in commenting on the Oxford Shakespeare's treatment of some textual cruces in *King Lear*.[64] As we have just seen, Kent's diatribe against Oswald includes this savage comparison:

such smiling roges as these,
Like Rats oft bite those cordes in twaine,
Which are to intrench to inloose (E1v26–28; 2.3.23–25)

The Folio reads:

such smiling rogues as these,
Like Rats oft bite the holly cords a twaine,
Which are t'intrince, t'vnloose (TLN 1146–1148)

Kermode expressed disbelief that Shakespeare ever wrote "intrench," explaining his reasons in a model of critical elucidation:

> Nor do I believe that "holly" or "holy" is the result of revision. The rats bite the knots because they are too complicated, too

> intricate, to untie; they aren't trying to dig out with their teeth cords that have buried themselves into something—a far vaguer idea, conveying nothing of stout bonding by a complication of cords. Moreover the cords were surely always "holy." The word makes for better meter, though that cannot be decisive in a text prone to metrical irregularities, as *Lear* is. Much more certain is the fact that without "holy" the simile loses what must have been its original force: rats like Oswald are not the enemies of any old cords, but of those that bind friends, families, societies in sacred obligation. The origin of these cords may well be Ecclesiastes 4:12, "a threefold cord is not quickly broken" . . .

He concluded that "a version of the text containing 'intrince' lies behind both Q, which misunderstood it, and F, which didn't, and which even, at some cost in elision, made a regular pentameter of the line. The F version cannot derive from the Quarto tradition," and must have "survived in a manuscript tradition." Kermode gave examples of other readings "which most have existed in some pre-Q version recorded by F," namely Shakespeare's manuscript. He drily wondered "whether that collapsed archetype might not after all be shorne up," and his acute remarks show that the revisionists' diagnosis of collapse was premature.

Earlier in this chapter I presented the evidence that the 1608 Quarto contains many characteristic Shakespeare spellings and that some of its errors were due to the compositors having been unable to read his handwriting. Some readers might find it unlikely that Shakespearian spellings survived into the Folio, which indeed modernized his orthography in many cases. But an important essay by the late Trevor Howard-Hill compared the spelling of some unusual words in the Folio and in both Quartos, testing his impression that "compositors much more frequently adopt copy spellings of unfamiliar words than change them."[65] He analyzed more than a hundred spellings in the Folio text of *Lear*, together with speech prefixes, and demonstrated that a significant number did not correspond to those in either Q1 or Q2, proving that both Compositor B and the inexperienced Compositor E had access to "an authoritative manuscript," probably "a current transcript of the promptbook," which they collated with a copy of Q2. This explanation would account for the Folio's "mélange of forms indicative of *both* manuscript and typographical origin."[66] The term "mélange" corresponds to the word "hybrid" that I used earlier to describe the Booke, with its mixture of authorial and theatrical readings. In 2008 Richard Knowles endorsed the work of both Doran and Howard-Hill in rejecting claims by Gary Taylor and other revisionists "that a marked-up Q2, instead of or in addition to Q1, was printer's copy for F1." Having made his "own computer-aided comparison of the three texts," Knowles could assert with some authority that "such claims are untenable; F rejects some 1,300 substantive readings found in Q2, and seems to accept a mere 90. Moreover . . . the F readings could all have been arrived at independently by such natural means as the substitution of obviously correct readings for Q1 misreadings. Both F compositors obviously derive their substantive readings from elsewhere—i.e., from a manuscript, not from Q1 or Q2."[67]

The case made by Madeleine Doran, and endorsed by Howard-Hill and Knowles, has recently been revived and strengthened. In the first issue (1993) of his parallel text edition of the play René Weis maintained a divided position on the Two Versions thesis, but in its revised edition (2010) he came down firmly in favor of "the traditional concept of a unified text of *Lear*."[68] Weis pointed to "a wider pattern of variant readings by Q and F that are, often demonstrably, guesses at the same manuscript word or phrases. They include, from the opening lines of the play, 'first' / 'fast', 'Confirming' / 'Conferring' (later 'confirmed' / 'conferred')."[69] Others instances of the two texts giving variant readings are less obvious, such as Edgar's plan to disguise himself as a beggar and seek charity "from low Farmes, | Poor pelting villages, Sheepes-Coates, and Milles" (2.3.17–18). As we have seen, for "Farmes" the Quarto reads "seruice" (E3r30), apparently a quite different word. However, as Weis points out,

> in the original spelling of 'farmes' in foul papers they may have looked more alike . . . since in secretary 'f' and 's' are easily confused, all it needs for the two readings to merge almost entirely is for 'ui' to be misread for 'm', which is easily done; at which point the two words become virtually indistinct. If 'service' and

'farmes' are variant readings of the same copy, then 'farmes' is probably what Shakespeare wrote given the context: 'farmes, / Poor pelting villages, sheepcotes and mills.'[70]

Weis gives other examples to support his claim that "with most *Lear* variants there are sound palaeographic reasons for arguing that Q and F are guessing at the same reading," such as Edmund's explanation to Edgar that "in crauing, I must draw my sword vpon you" (D3v26), for which the Folio correctly reads "in cunning" (2.1.29). As Weis commented, here "the divergences arose from a conjunction of minims, the closeness of 'c' and 'r' in secretary, and the fact that 'u' was often written 'v' and vice-versa (i.e. 'crauing' / 'cunning'). Also, Shakespeare's 'a' in his deed signature for the 1613 Blackfriars Gatehouse is open.[71] If this was a regular feature of his hand it would push 'craving' and 'cunning' ever closer together while accounting more broadly for the number of 'a' / 'u' confusions in printed texts set from his foul papers."[72]

We have seen many instances of misreading in the two texts that Doran described as "variant pairs, either of which gives a satisfactory reading," such as the mad king's assurance (in the Quarto) that "they cannot touch mee for coyning" (I3v7). Here the Folio reads "crying" (4.6.83; TLN 2530), which is either a misreading by the compositor setting from the transcribed play book or else an alteration by Jaggard's editor, who failed to understand Lear's meaning. Weis makes the crucial point that "while both readings make sense and look similar, only one of them reproduces what Shakespeare wrote," in this case the Quarto.[73] It follows that several variant readings which, according to exponents of the Two Versions thesis—that the Quarto and Folio are substantially different versions—represent "stylistic nuancing by a reviser" are in fact different scribal interpretations of the same word, only one of which can be correct. In his denunciation of Edgar to Gloucester, Edmund alleges that he found his brother standing "in the darke,his sharpe sword out, *warbling* of wicked charms, coniuring the Moone to stand's auspicious Mistris" (D3v34–36); the Folio reads "Mumbling" (2.1.39; TLN 973). Although some editors regard the Quarto reading as "legitimate and correct,"[74] Weis points out that

> [t]he two words only differ in their first three letters, 'War' versus 'Mum', sharing the participial '*-ling*' after '*b*'. Given the possibility of vowel confusion in Shakespeare's hand here, the presence of '*r*' and the minims 'u' and 'm', and the closeness of W / M in some hands (in type they are turned versions of each other), Q and F are more likely to be guesses at the same manuscript than an instance of revision. If so, then 'Mumbling' is preferable to Q's reading as it carries a charge of huggermugger and covertness: after all, according to his brother, Edgar is stealthily ('in the dark') evoking the powers of the night, 'conjuring the moon'. Shakespeare's other uses of 'Warbling' (in for example *Lucrece* and *A Midsummer Night's Dream*) are lyrical and associated with singing, as the word still is in modern usage.[75]

A close attention to handwriting forms in the *Moore* manuscript and the authentic Quartos can solve many textual problems. Following Dover Wilson and Doran, Weis based his analysis on known features of Shakespeare's handwriting, such as his eccentric form of the letter *k*, which, as Giles Dawson showed, could easily be taken for a *b*.[76] In the Quarto Curran tells Edmund of the "eare-bussing arguments" that suggest "likely warres" between Albany and Cornwall (D3v7). The Folio reads "ear-kissing" (2.1.8; TLN 926), the reading preferred by modern editors. Another instance of a *k* / *b* misreading is the Quarto's version of Gloucester's despairing words:

> As flies are toth' wanton boyes,are we toth' Gods,
> They bitt vs for their sport. (H2v27–28; 4.1.34–35)

The Folio compositor, probably working from the scribal copy of Shakespeare's manuscript that had been made for the 1606 promptbook, could provide the authentic reading:

> As flies to wanton Boyes, are we to th'Gods,
> They kill vs for their sport. (TLN 2221–2222)

We must agree with Weis that "F's readings are almost invariably superior to Q's . . . when the two are demonstrably guessing at the same word(s) or phrase(s)."[77] In the uncorrected Quarto Lear refers to "this crulentious storme," which the printer altered to "tempestious storm" (G1r30), a tautology; "F's reading 'contentious' (3.4.6; TLN 1786) is undoubtedly correct and evidently guesses at the same manuscript readings as Qa." So many of the variants are "palaeographically as well as metrically close as in . . . 'blast her' / 'blister', or in 'experience' / 'esperance'," that "they emphatically point to a single original."[78]

René Weis's independent study has confirmed Doran's argument that the Quarto edition of *King Lear*, printed in the winter of 1607–1608, was set from Shakespeare's manuscript, while "the 1606 promptbook lies behind F." In turn, this implies that "F's readings have independent authority from Q and existed *before* the printing of 1608, sharing its foul-paper source" as copied afresh by the playhouse scribe.[79] Furthermore, "not only is it likely that the copyist of the promptbook knew Shakespeare, but Shakespeare would also have acted in this version of the play," and "would undoubtedly have spotted, and set right, nonce words in a promptbook transcribed from his own writing."[80] I happily join Weis in celebrating a pioneering scholar:

> The reappraisal of the evidence here marks a return above all to the bibliographical study of the printed texts of *Lear* by Madeleine Doran. More than any other, her interpretations of the evidence provided by Q and F underpin integrated versions of Shakespeare's greatest play. She writes persuasively about the intimate links at source between the manuscripts behind Q and F; they may be separated by fifteen years in print, but only a few months at most intervene between foul papers (Q) and promptbook (F).[81]

We can be confident that the text purchased by Nathaniel Butter from the King's Men in 1607, before printing began, was the complete authorial draft, imperfectly preserved in the 1608 Quarto. We can also be sure that the text delivered by the King's Men to Isaac Jaggard in 1622 derived from the same manuscript, probably with alterations made by the company for theatrical performance. What Jaggard did with that manuscript must concern us next.

6

The Folio Editors Regularize Shakespeare

To modern readers the Shakespeare First Folio is a monument, both in its dimensions and for what it contains. It has an "iconic" existence, having been revered and sought after by book collectors since the early nineteenth century. We naturally assume that the reverence we feel for it must have been shared by those who collaborated on its production. The manuscript of a major author in our time would be treated with great respect and care. But these are anachronistic expectations. In Shakespeare's age a dramatist sold his work to the theater company who could do what they liked with it, cut and rearrange scenes, and shorten or omit roles. When the theater company sold it to a printer, it was his property, and he could treat it as he wished. His respect for the text might be greater than those who adapted it for performance, but he was free to edit it so that it conformed to his printing-house style. This is a familiar process in our time, but our expectation of the editor's role differs greatly from early modern practices. Modern publishers employ copyeditors and proofreaders to oversee the transformation of an author's manuscript into a printed book, correcting typographical errors and achieving consistency in spelling, punctuation, and footnote referencing according to a "house style." A publisher's individual set of stylistic and grammatical regulations might cover the choice between alternative spellings ("judgment" or "judgement"), the use of capital letters, abbreviations, and other relatively minor matters of presentation, sometimes following a standard authority, such as *The Oxford Guide to Style*, *The Chicago Manual of Style*, or those produced by academic organizations like the MHRA and the MLA. In the early modern period, however, different practices prevailed. Whereas a modern writer is able to check the work of copyeditors and proofreaders before a book is printed, in Shakespeare's time printing-house changes were generally made without consulting the author. Whatever the author's preferences, the printer and his compositors regarded spelling and punctuation as within their remit. For our taste, they often damaged poetry and dramatic verse with their indiscriminate or insensitive pointing, inserting commas at the end of many lines, for instance. But printers also employed workmen to act as editors who intervened in other areas. They would expurgate oaths, in line with official injunctions before plays were performed, but they would also make a series of noncompulsory changes based on notions of grammatical correctness (regularizing the use of relative pronouns, for instance, or ensuring the concord of singular and plural), speech decorum (omitting vulgar or colloquial expressions), or even aesthetic considerations (correcting "irregularities" in blank verse).

Modern readers need to be aware of this practice since it adds a nonauthorial layer to the text. Shakespeare scholars have long been aware that the first Folio is marked by such interventions. One need look no further back than Sir Edmund Chambers and his epoch-making synthesis and critique of Shakespeare scholarship up to 1930, Chambers often observed that the Folio editors were guilty of "sophistication," a word used in the older sense of a "deceptive alteration" or "corruption of something, conversion into a less genuine form, *spec.* the alteration of a text in the course of copying or printing."[1] Chambers made the general point that most, probably all, of the reprinted texts in the First Folio "have undergone some modification beyond what can be attributed to the compositors," changes made by an editor or "improver."[2] Having compared the Folio versions of Quarto texts, he identified considerable departures from the originals' in "orthography, elision, punctuation, and capitalization," drawing particular attention to the use of elisions, the running together of two words in such a way as to affect the meter.[3] In addition to these areas, Chambers noted that the process of sophistication is also traceable in the diction. "There may be some tendency to eliminate dialectal, colloquial, or merely unusual words and archaic inflexions. The use of 'a' for 'he', 'of' or 'on' seems to meet with particular disapproval. Even puns are misunderstood or disliked. Trifling grammatical solecisms in moods and cases are removed. Adverbial adjectives give way to adverbs. There are substitutions of 'thou' for 'you' and of 'mine' for 'my' and of 'my' for 'mine' before a vowel or consonant respectively."[4] Having noted a number of such sophistications, Chambers stated, "It is not at all clear that we need look beyond the compositors," ruling out the possible agency of either an author or an editor. When he subsequently discussed the relationship between the Quarto and Folio versions of *Lear*, Chambers judged that "[t]he texts are substantially derived from the same original. There are a good many verbal variants, and where one is clearly wrong, the better reason, except for a dozen or score of cases, is in F. Subject, therefore, to its usual sophistications, F must have the preference where the variants are indifferent."[5]

Chambers made some well-informed observations as ever, but no scholar pursued the question of the nature and extent of editing carried out in the Folio. Greg, in his summation of the editorial work in Shakespeare, made a number of comments in passing, often critical. He refers to the "incompetence" and "clumsiness of the editor" of one quarto, who was "rather fussy but incompetent"; another play's editor was "superficial," overlooking many "irregularities"; the Folio's editing of *Hamlet* "was at times competent and even adroit, at times bungled and ineffective"; *Othello* suffered from "the usual sophisticating hand of its editor," who was "interfering."[6] But Greg was undecided as to whether Jaggard employed an editor as such. He stated that the Folio text of *Love's Labour's Lost* "was set up from Q with the usual printing-house corrections and corruptions . . . That the text received some editorial attention appears from a rather unsuccessful attempt to reduce speakers' names to order, and there may have been some emendation. There is nothing that would be beyond the scope of an intelligent press reader, but there is elsewhere little to justify the assumption of the presence of such a person in Jaggard's office."[7] Yet earlier Greg had declared that, "apart from works seen through the press by their authors, no book of the time had greater care and labour bestowed on its editing than did the First Folio of Shakespeare's plays."[8] Indeed, he found it "more likely that the editing was in the hands of the players rather than the stationers, for it was they who had access to the material and were in a position to estimate its value," and he suggested that the most likely person would have been "the book-keeper of the King's company."[9] Yet it seems more likely that the theater's interest in this project ended with its sale of the manuscripts to the printers. Greg continued to vacillate as to whether the editing of individual plays had been carried out by a "book-keeper," a "literary reviser," a "collator," a "transcriber," or a "scribe of rather careless habits"—but then, "the workings of a scribe's mind are often queer."[10] Greg never gave sustained attention to the Folio editors, and these scattered remarks left the subject in a still more confused state. No scholar attempted to fill this lacuna, and as late as 1983 Paul Werstine could justly complain that, "Unlike the Folio compositors, the Folio editors have received almost no attention; they therefore remain shadowy figures. Yet no play in the Folio is a simple reprint of an earlier printed text, no play thought to have been set from quarto copy contains only compositorial variants from printed copy."[11] Werstine stated that "a modern editor of any Folio play can ill afford to ignore the earliest of Shakespeare's editors," but I would argue that the same holds for every serious student of Shakespeare. The transmission of his plays is a matter too important to be left to textual scholars.

The editors of the Shakespeare First Folio—we must think of them in the plural, since the book took eighteen months to print—had for eighteen plays both a Quarto (in some cases more than one) and a manuscript, probably the theater's Booke, and for eighteen plays only a manuscript source. We can tell that they collated printed and manuscript copy, but often in a careless or perfunctory manner.[12] Their routine tasks included correcting typographical errors in the printed text, editing stage directions, clearing up ambiguities and inconsistencies in the naming of characters, and dealing with theater cuts. Some of these tasks were followed, others ignored, fortunately for posterity. However, the Folio editors who prepared the text for printing did not stop there, but imposed their own linguistic and stylistic preferences on Shakespeare's text. As Madeleine Doran showed, when Jaggard's printing house issued the Second Quarto of *Lear* in 1619, the person responsible for editing it changed Shakespeare's word order to suit his own preferences. So did the Folio reviser, as one instance can illustrate:

Q1 for thee oppressed King *am I* cast downe,
My selfe could else outfrowne false Fortunes frowne,
F For thee oppressed King *I am* cast downe,
My selfe could else out-frowne false Fortunes frowne.
(K4r15–16; 5.3.5–6; TLN 2944–2945)

The Folio editors took pains to regularize grammatical concord. Where the corrector of Q2 "occasionally made a singular noun plural or a plural noun singular," Doran counted "as many as fifty" such grammatical changes in the Folio text of *King Lear*.[13] When Goneril declares, in the Quarto text, "Sir, I do love you more then words can weild the matter" (1.1.56), the Folio corrector substituted "word," making the noun singular. In fact, the verb form "wield" would have been correct for either singular or plural, and "words" would have been more appropriate in the context of rival speeches, given the standard distinction in rhetoric between *res* (matter) and *verba*.[14] Elsewhere he changed both noun and verb:

Q1 Nor are those empty harted whose low,sound
Reverbs no hollowness.
F Nor are those empty hearted, whose low sounds
Reverbe no hollownesse.
(B3r7–8; 1.1.153–154; TLN 163–164)

The Quarto reading, "sound," describes a general phenomenon; the Folio version, "sounds," particular instances of it. Neither of the Folio changes was grammatically necessary.

The Folio corrector of *Lear* also altered the text to suit his own grammatical preferences in the choice of particles, as Doran noted: "*Toward* is regularly *towards* in Q1, *toward* in F. *Sometimes* is always *sometime* in Q1, more often *sometimes* in F. The adverb *besides* is *beside* in Q1, *besides* in F."[15] He also followed what historians of the English language have established as the grammatical norm of the 1620s for the endings of the third-person singular, replacing *doth* with *does*.[16] Thus Gloucester's question to Edmund: "(Q1: *Hath*) *Has* he never before sounded you in this busines?" (1.2.69–70; TLN 404). The Folio reviser imposed on the text his own concept of grammatical rectitude concerning verb forms. Where the 1608 Quarto used the subjunctive form of the second-person singular, the Folio changed it to the indicative, as in these two instances. Q reads "if thou *love* me, tell me"; F changes it to "*lov'st*" (2.2.6; TLN 1086). Q1 reads "whom I will beat into clamorous whyning, if thou *denie* the least sillable of the addition"; F substitutes "*deny'st*" (2.2.23–4; TLN 1096–1097).

As we study the systematic changes made by the Folio editor, extending far beyond grammatical correctness, we realize the fundamental difference between the two versions of *Lear*. The Quarto reproduces Shakespeare's manuscript, designed for acting, while the Folio edits a theatrical text for readers. In recent years the Folio text has been favored by editors of the Oxford Shakespeare, who claim that it is nearer to the theater's acting versions as found in the promptbook, and thus represents "the more theatrical version of each play."[17] The uncomfortable fact ignored by proponents of "theatrical" versions is that all Folio texts went through the hands of the scribes, editors, and compositors employed by William Jaggard and his son Isaac. The influence exerted on the Folio text by the scribes, in particular Ralph Crane, has been well studied by the late Trevor Howard-Hill and others, while the compositors' work has also attracted excellent scholarly studies.[18] But scholars have yet to recognize the editors as an influence on Shakespeare's text, not always for the good. Properly evaluated, the Folio is not so much a "theatrical" as a "post-theatrical" text, designed for readers.

One striking demonstration of the difference between an acting and a reading edition is the Folio editors' treatment of word elision. In theatrical performances actors will adjust the enunciation of words to fit them to the underlying meter and rhythm, introducing elisions where needed. But the Folio editor seems to have been bothered by such evidence of the interpreters' freedom to elide words as required and felt that they ought to be contracted for the benefit of those readers of the "Complete Works" who liked their verse to scan. This is the only conclusion to be drawn from Doran's demonstration that the Folio text of *Lear* regularly contracts forms that are uncontracted in the 1608 Quarto. As she observed,

> Both contracted and uncontracted forms, where the meter requires contraction in pronunciation, are found in Q1. This circumstance does not necessarily injure the authority of the text. Abbott gives several pages of readings the frequent appearance of which in contracted form shows that they might be elided in pronunciation although often written in the full form. But contraction occurs so frequently in F that it may be understood as a principle of form in that text of the play; nearly always when a full form appears in Q1 which requires, for metrical reasons, to be elided in pronunciation, the contracted form is given in F.[19]

The Folio editors subordinated the needs of actors, who know where to elide to preserve rhythm, to those of readers, who need to have such cases spelled out, and the text was altered to suit the latter. We can judge for ourselves from the examples that Doran collected of "contractions of the definite article accompanied by a preposition, or of a pronoun or adverb followed by *is*, *are*, or an auxiliary verb" that the contractions were designed to produce regular decasyllabic lines. (Examples from Q1 are enclosed within angled brackets.)

Under *<the allowance> th'allowance* of your great aspect,
(2.2.106; TLN 1181)
Thy halfe *<of the kingdome> o' th' Kingdome* hast thou not forgot,
(2.4.180; TLN 1464)
Why not *<by the hand> by' th' hand* Sir? How have I offended?
(2.4.195; TLN 1485)
Duke. *<What is> What's* the matter, Sir?
(1.4.295; TLN 811)
<Thou hadst> Thou'dst shiver'd like an egge: but thou do'st
breath: (4.6.51; TLN 2493)

The Folio "transcriber" was not immune from mistake, as this erroneous contraction shows:

> *Bast.* There's my exchange, what in the world <*he is*> *hes*
> That names me Traitor, villain-like he lies,
> (5.3.97–8; TLN 3045)

As Doran noticed, "There is sufficient room on the right-hand margin" of this Folio page "for the printer to have used the full form; his habit of contraction here may have betrayed him into the blunder."[20] Altogether Doran counted ninety-two cases in which F contracts the lengthened form of Q1 and about thirty-one cases in which F expands a contraction in Q1. Such attempts to "correct" Shakespeare's diction have consequences for the meter that were not always beneficial. One instance of contraction makes a verse line more regular:

> *Lear.* <*Yar*> *You are* a spirit I know, where did you dye?
> (4.7.48; TLN 2799)

However, I would argue that Shakespeare did not necessarily intend to write a regular pentameter line here. "Yar" gives a slurred effect that might be more appropriate for someone who has just awoken from a deep sleep. Elsewhere, as Doran rightly judged, the "habit of contraction" changes the rhythm of a speech, making it less colloquial:

> *Lear.* Deny to speake with me?
> <*th'are*> *They are* sicke, <*th'are*> *they are* weary,
> (2.7.88; TLN 1361–1362)
> In fellow there <*in't*> *into th'* Hovel; keep thee warm.
> (3.4.174; TLN 1955)

Doran drew attention to a more serious consequence for Shakespeare's artistry in verse: in the Folio text "the *-est* ending of the second person singular is often contracted at the end of a line, where it may be thought that Shakespeare intended a feminine ending" (that is, with an extra, eleventh syllable, often more expressive). Consider these examples:

> Thou out of Heavens benediction *<comest> com'st*
> (2.2.161; TLN 1238)
> Why nature needs not what thou gorgeous *<wearest> wear'st*
> (2.4.269; TLN 1569)

If we read the first of those lines aloud, we may well prefer the Quarto reading, the Folio's conjunction of three consonants ("com'st") making pronunciation awkward; in the second the collocation of sibilants in "gorgeous wear'st" is equally awkward and unrhythmical. Conversely, a change of an opposite kind sometimes occurs: an expanded form in the folio produces a feminine ending, not necessarily intended by Shakespeare:

> No tearing Lady, I perceive you *<know't> know it.*
> (5.3.158; TLN 3115)

Which of the two options is that of the dramatist? (I would prefer the more urgent contracted form.) As we shall see, many other changes made by the Folio editor affected Shakespeare's verse. Doran noted that the 1608 Quarto, set from Shakespeare's manuscript, frequently uses "the possessive forms *my* and *thy* . . . before a noun beginning with a vowel. In the folio they are consistently altered, when they occur before a vowel, to *mine* and *thine*, e.g., '*thy* eyes' to '*thine* eyes.'" Apparently reluctant to conceive of an editor as such, Doran suggested that "this alteration may have been made by the transcriber of the folio manuscript, or possibly even by the printer, in accordance with a fixed rule of form." The Folio corrector followed the example of Q2, also printed by the Jaggards, in altering "the dialectal pronoun *a* to *he* and the conditional conjunction *and* to *if*," but he pursued the latter change less keenly than his predecessor.[21]

At this point the modern reader may wonder whether Jaggard's employees really had the authority to make these changes. Madeleine Doran was willing to conceive that some of the smaller changes represented the preferences of a compositor, but when considering the evidence she had collected of the Folio's systematic alterations to Shakespeare's use of relative pronouns, she balked at the notion of a printer's employee assuming such a responsibility: "The alteration under certain conditions of the relative *that* in Q1 to *which*, *who*, or *whom* in F is so frequent as to indicate a deliberate policy of revision. For these substitutions, however, I think it was not the printer who was responsible, but probably Shakespeare himself."[22] Doran justified this conclusion by reference to E. A. Abbott's discussion of Shakespeare's use of relative pronouns.[23] However, modern historical linguistics has established that Shakespeare conformed to older usage patterns, which did not yet distinguish relative pronouns according to whether they referred to inanimate or animate antecedents. In plays written after *Lear* Shakespeare could still use "*which*" with a personal antecedent; as in "that slaue | *Which*" (*Coriolanus*, 1.6.39–40), or "*whom*" with a nonpersonal antecedent, as in "the Elements | Of *whom* your swords are tempered" (*Tempest*, 3.3.62).[24] The modern system of relativization was standardized in the course of the seventeenth century, and such changes in the Folio were undoubtedly the work of Jaggard's editors, not Shakespeare.[25]

In her analysis of the relation between the Quarto and Folio texts of *King Lear*, made more than eighty years ago, Madeleine Doran drew attention to a series of changes, designed to make the meter more regular, that definitely rule out Shakespeare as the corrector. The expressive range of Shakespeare's verse in *King Lear* is huge, the opening scene alone displaying at least four registers for the king (smug satisfaction in the gift ceremony, stunned inexpressiveness when Cordelia refuses to flatter, cold formality in disowning her, and unbridled violence in cursing Kent), and two for Goneril and Regan (fawning verse until they are rewarded, heartless or ruthless prose thereafter). By this point in his career Shakespeare could express many registers in verse responding to the pulse of the action without necessarily keeping to the regular ten-syllable line. But the Folio editor, either troubled by irregularity per se or concerned for the reader's convenience, made several adjustments to make the prosody more regular. Doran believed that some of the smaller variants in the Folio regularizing the meter can be attributed to the printer, such as this one:

Rule in this *<kingdome> Realme*, and the gor'd state sustaine.
(5.3.321; TLN 3295)

But Doran detected a different agency at work in the following instance, where "the substitution of a synonym has been accompanied by the expansion of a contracted form, evidently with the purpose of preserving the meter":

Q1 *Duke.* Why dost thou call him knaue,*what's his offence.*
F *Corn.* Why do'st thou call him Knaue?
What is his fault? (2.2.89; TLN 1162–3)

Doran found there "an element of consciousness in the substitution that makes it appear to be the result of deliberate revision."[26] I agree with her conclusion, but doubt that Shakespeare made the change. The Folio's grammatically tidy separate question, "What is his fault?" may be metrically regular, but it is a limp phrase, unsuited to Cornwall's "fiery" temper. Doran failed to notice further evidence that the Quarto reading ("what's his offence?") was Shakespearian. Cornwall, having received no answer from Kent to his question, repeats the same colloquial wording to Oswald: "What's the offence you gave him?" (2.2.114; TLN 1190).

Doran strengthened her case for the Folio having made a deliberate alteration of Shakespeare's text to achieve prosodic regularity by citing "variants which are different but equally suitable in meaning, and both of which answer to the requirements of the meter," as in this instance:

my loue's
More *<richer> ponderous* then my tongue.
(1.1.77–78; TLN 83–84)

Cordelia's word "ponderous" is so familiar to most readers from editors having regularly chosen the Folio reading that it may not have occurred to us to question it. Although Shakespeare uses it elsewhere, it seems to me that a polysyllabic Latinate word is hardly appropriate to Cordelia's plain-spokenness, especially in the context of her three brief asides to the audience, which otherwise consist of one- or two-syllable words.[27] The modernizing Folio editor, I suggest, introduced the phrase "more ponderous" in preference to the Quarto's old-fashioned double comparative "more richer." Yet the monetary term "richer" picks up both Goneril's claim to love Lear "Beyond what can be valued rich or rare" (1.1.57), and Regan's assertion that she is made of the "same metal" as her sister and prizes herself at "her worth" (69–70). Few, if any, of the Folio's "improvements" were for the better.

Writing some thirty years after Madeleine Doran, P. W. K. Stone agreed with her diagnosis of the 1623 Folio as an edited text, but differed by exonerating Shakespeare of all responsibility:

> The person responsible for editing and revising the Q text was not Shakespeare. The number of errors remaining in F is enough to arouse suspicion. Far more significant, however, is their nature. We cannot plausibly suppose an author so forgetful of his original intentions that he would fall into obtuse mistakes and misconceptions of the kind we have noticed. Still less can we suppose that Shakespeare would have baulked at the many difficulties and obscurities we find glossed over or hesitantly tinkered with. When baffled by a garbled passage he would surely, like any other writer, have rewritten it entirely rather than rest satisfied with an unsuccessful attempt to recover it. The reviser's work, in short, is too conscientiously aimed at restoration and repair, and is too ineffectual in achieving that aim, to be mistaken for that of the author himself. If Shakespeare did not himself undertake the task of revision, then we may plausibly assume that he was not available to do so. The date, therefore, at which it was accomplished is unlikely to have preceded his retirement from the theater in 1613.[28]

After that cogent argument, it is disappointing to discover Stone speculating that, "in all probability after that date, a copy of Q, together with the manuscript 'copy' which . . . must have been obtained from the publisher, was handed to another dramatist with a commission to convert it into a usable text. We must assume that the work was entrusted to an experienced writer, since for all his errors of misunderstanding and carelessness he carried it out in the main intelligently and skilfully." Stone's belief that some other Jacobean dramatist must have been entrusted with these revisions led him into an unprofitable discussion of his identity, excluding Jonson and Fletcher "on grounds of style" and declaring Massinger the likely person "who undertook the revision of *King Lear*."[29] I ignore Stone's speculations about the reviser's identity, while reviewing his useful analysis of the types of change that were made. In general terms, he indicated that

> [t]he F text shows, on comparison with Q, a great deal of regularisation of grammar, syntax and idiom. Not all of it is necessary or even correct, but it betokens the reviser's fastidiousness in such matters. He valued a smooth style, and was liberal with small "improvements" of wording and arrangement. Where he replaced a (satisfactory) reading of Q with his own choice of word, it was sometimes to substitute the current for the uncommon, e.g. *sticke* for *rash* (3.7.58); *sterne* for *dearne* (3.7.63); *stop* for *stople* (5.3.155).

The reviser, Stone argued, sometimes altered Shakespeare's text "for a gain in emphasis, e.g. *falls* for *stoops* (1.1.151); *condemne* for *dislike* (1.4.365); *Coward* for *caytife* (2.1.64). The stronger word, needless to say, is not always the more effective." On other occasions the reviser amended Shakespeare's text "simply because he preferred one word to another: *strike* for *smite* (3.2.7) is an example which may stand for a considerable number." Stone acutely observed that the reviser "had, too, a strong sense of logic, and many of his corrections and expansions were clearly dictated (not always advisedly) by his suspicions of irrationality in the original text."[30] In his denunciation of corruption, Lear sees that

> Through tottered rags, *smal* vices do appeare,
> Robes & furd-gownes hides al (4.6.164–5; TLN 2607–8)

The Folio reviser changed *smal* to *great* and so "misunderstood the point in a rather literal way." Other changes show that the reviser's sense of scale differs from Shakespeare's.[31] Although I cannot follow

Stone in his belief that Massinger performed this function, he certainly proved that "[t]he person responsible for editing and revising the Q text was not Shakespeare."[32]

The most comprehensive analysis of the textual changes made in the Folio *Lear* has been made by Richard Knowles for his forthcoming New Variorum edition, the fruit of twenty-five years' study.[33] Knowles summarized the work of earlier scholars, approving Madeleine Doran's observation that the Folio changed several particles merely on the grounds of personal preference (*towards* > *toward*, *sometime* > *sometimes*, *beside* > *besides*), but added a variant she missed: "*farther* (TLN 1639, 2241, 2467, 2931) is consistently changed . . . to *further*, the preferred form elsewhere in Q1, Q2, and F." Doran worked long before bibliographical analysis had identified the two compositors responsible for setting the Folio *Lear*, the experienced B and the apprentice E, to whose account most of the errors and resulting corrections to the text can be charged.[34] Recent scholars, notably Paul Werstine, building on and updating Doran's findings, have been able to evaluate these two compositors' varying performance for what it might reveal about the text from which they worked. As Werstine pointed out, "Both B and E changed *towards* to *toward*, and, in one instance (TLN 938), [compositor] E apparently followed manuscript copy in setting *toward*, since this line is missing from the second quarto. Thus the *toward* variants must derive from copy, not from the compositors," a point that strengthens the case for the Folio having been in part set from Shakespeare's manuscript.[35] By contrast, as Knowles noted, "the modernizations of *a* to *he* by both compositors (TLN 585, 897, 1473, 1947, 2215, 2515) are all anticipated in Q2, they may reflect only Jaggard's house style."[36] Both Werstine and Knowles endorse earlier scholars' observation that the Folio compositors reversed some preferences, such as the older and newer spellings of *hath* / *has*, and made others inconsistently: "in Q1 (and Q2) *thy* is frequently used before a vowel; in F it is changed by both compositors to *thine* in almost half of the cases (TLN 167, 181, 676, 1804, 2346, 2580, 2595, 2597)." But they noted a striking consistency in the Folio's treatment of relativization. Werstine observed that "*Lear* is almost unique among the Folio tragedies in preferring *who[m]*, *where*, and *which* to quarto copy *that*."[37] Knowles documented the varying input of the compositors:

> *That* in Q1 (and Q2) is changed to *which* by both compositors (TLN 259, 724, 733, 761, 781, 816, 1316, 1350, 2654, 3188), *that* is altered to *who* or *whom* (TLN 235, 1146, 2911, 2985, all E), B corrects *whom* to *Who* (825) and *Who* to *Which* (2232) while E alters *What's* to *Who's* (1616), and both men ignore Q2 changes of *which* (3077, 3228). . . . Virtually none of these changes serves any purpose in the theater, many are trivial, and some verge on the pedantic. While it is impossible to rule out authorial correction, they are both inconsistent with Shakespeare's known style in Q1 and more rigidly regular in matters of grammatical usage than he customarily was. They seem more likely to reflect the habits of a scrivener whose profession it was to turn rough drafts into smooth copy.[38]

Knowles attributed these changes to a scribe, but if so that employee was filling the role of an editor, however defined. Knowles gave a similar explanation for the use of a contracted form of the auxiliary "would," where the consistency in the Folio spelling supports the case for a professional scribe:

> In Q1 I *would* is variously abbreviated *I'd*, *id'e*, and *ide*, in Q2 the abbreviation is uniformly *ide;* in F, in passages set by both compositors, the term is uniformly (except for TLN 520 *I'de*) spelled *I'ld* (TLN 637, 913, 1009, 1157, 1372, 1392, 2151, 2205, 3208). Compositor E never uses this form elsewhere in F1. . . . In plays that B set from authorial papers . . . his usual form is *I'de.* In uniformly using *I'ld* in *Lear* the two compositors seem to be following neither their own nor Shakespeare's preference but the spelling of their copy, which is apparently scribal.

If so, compositor B must have acted on his own initiative, emending the text in un-Shakespearean ways: "In the stints of both compositors, the quartos *'vm* or *them* is changed to *'em* (TLN 908, 1399 twice, 1845, 2014, 2549 twice, 2698; cf. F-only 2611); . . . this abbreviation is virtually absent from the good quartos and from F1 plays set from author's papers, and appears in F exclusively in plays now thought to be set from transcripts."[39] The Folio also introduces "the evidently un-Shakespearian contractions *o' th'*, *i'th'*, and *th' hast.*" The use of apostrophes with *has* (*ha'* or *ha's*) is almost never found in authentic Shakespearean quartos, and whereas Shakespeare preferred the spelling *O*, the preponderant form as used in both Quarto texts of *Lear*, Knowles points out that "in F this has been changed by both compositors to *Oh*" (twelve instances quoted). Where both Quartos agree in spelling *the*, "Compositor B elides to *th'* 12 times and E 24 times." In the Folio *Lear*, therefore, the compositors "were following neither quarto copy, nor their own preferences nor . . . Shakespeare's prevailing usage outside of plays set from transcripts."[40] One last instance of scribal—or editorial—intervention in the Folio concerns the spelling of a character's name. Where the Quartos consistently spell *Gonorill* both F compositors consistently spell *Gonerill.* Knowles can find "no evident reason whatsoever to change the spelling *Gono-*, standard in all the sources, to F's unique *Gone-*. This inexplicable and thoroughgoing alteration suggests a scribe who mistakenly or carelessly started spelling the name one way in his transcript and kept doing so throughout." Unless unexplored documentary evidence turns up, in the present state of scholarship it is impossible to be sure how much authority a Jacobean scribe possessed. We cannot tell whether the person(s) who introduced so many changes into the Folio text of *King Lear* did so with or without Isaac Jaggard's knowledge and approval. To repeat Peter Stone's observation, these changes were certainly not made by Shakespeare. Earlier I described the Folio text as "post-theatrical": it might also be termed "post-Shakespearian."

Although Doran, Stone, and Knowles, writing between 1930 and 2011, identified the majority of editorial changes made by the Jaggards in Q2 and F, my own study of the variants between Q1 and the Folio adds some further types of change. Some of these categories overlap with each other. Richard Knowles has drawn attention to the many occasions on which the Folio editors intervened in Shakespeare's text by omitting words, contracting word forms, and even adding words. Knowles suggested that those changes were partly intended to regularize Shakespeare's meter.[41] In making omissions they consistently deleted colloquial expressions, often monosyllabic, at the beginning of lines, such words or phrases as "Sir," "How," "Well," "Why," "Now," "Come sir," "Nay," and "O." These are what I would call "way-in phrases," interjections by which the speaker calls for the listener's attention before delivering the core message. They include the following instances, where I have italicized the omission:

Q *Sir* I am made of the selfe same mettall that my sister is, (B2r2)
F I am made of that selfe-mettle as my Sister, (TLN 74)
Q *How*, nothing can come of nothing, speake againe. (B2r18)
F Nothing will come of nothing, speake againe. (TLN 96)

Q *Goe to, goe to*, mend your speech a little, (B2r22)
F How, how Cordelia? Mend your speech a little, (TLN 100)

Q *Well* let it be so, thy truth then be thy dower, (B2r37)
F Let it be so, thy truth then be thy dowre: (TLN 115)

Q *Doe*, kill thy Physicion, (B3r19)
F Kill thy Physition, (TLN 177)

Q *Why* fare thee well king, since thus thou wilt appeare, (B3r36)
F Fare thee well King, sith thus thou wilt appeare, (TLN 194)

Q *Sir* will you with those infirmities she owes, (B3v21)
F Will you with those infirmities she owes, (TLN 221)

Q *Goe to, goe to*, better thou hadst not bin borne,
Then not to haue pleas'd me better. (B4r17)
F Better thou had'st
Not beene borne, then not to haue pleas'd me better. (TLN 256–257)

Q *Very* well Madam. (C3r31)
F Well Madam. (TLN 524)

Q *Come sir*, I would you would make vse of that good wisedome (D1v19)
F I would you would make vse of your good wisedome (TLN 730)

Q *Come sir*, this admiration is much of the sauour (D1v34)
F This admiration Sir, is much o'th' sauour (TLN 746)

Q *Now* I prithee daughter do not make me mad, (F2r9)
F I prythee Daughter do not make me mad, (TLN 1512)

Q *Alack sir*, you cannot see your way. (H2v2)
F You cannot see your way. (TLN 2198)

Q *Then prethee* get thee *gon*, (H2v33)
F Get thee away: (TLN 2228)

Q *O* know my name is lost (L1v19)
F Know my name is lost (TLN 3073)

Q *nay* no tearing Lady, I perceiue you know't. (L2r16–17)
F No tearing Lady, I perceiue you know it. (TLN 3115)

By omitting these introductory phrases the Folio editors maintained a more formal linguistic register, suitable for a reading public, at the cost of a realistic feature of everyday communication in such common phrases as "Goe to, goe to" and "Come sir." They also achieved metrical regularity.

The Folio editor's dislike of colloquialisms also extended to personal pronouns used in connection with verbs, where either part could be deemed redundant. That was the apparent motivation for the following cuts:

Q What mean'st *thou* by this? (E2r23)
F What mean'st by this? (TLN 1184)

Q Pray *you* doe not sir, I haue watcht and trauaild hard, (E2v32)
F Pray do not Sir, I haue watch'd and trauail'd hard, (TLN 1231)

Q Must be content to thinke you *are* old, and so, (F2r26)
F Must be content to thinke you old, and so, (TLN 1530)

Q Whose franke heart gaue *you* all (G1r5)
F whose franke heart gaue all, (TLN 1800)

Q As flies *are* toth' wanton boyes, are we toth' Gods, (H2v27)
F As Flies to wanton Boyes, are we to th'Gods, (TLN 2221)

Q Pardon *me* deere madame, (K1v26)
F Pardon deere Madam, (TLN 2756)

Q Feare *me* not, shee and the Duke her husband. (K3r19)
F Feare not, she and the Duke her husband. (TLN 2863)

Q Tis most conuenient, pray *you* goe with vs. (K3r38)
F 'Tis most conuenient, pray go with vs. (TLN 2877)

In one instance the Folio preserves a personal pronoun omitted by the Quarto compositors on a page where space saving was needed, as can be seen from the stage direction at the end of Lear's speech:

Q pray now forget and forgiue,
I am old and foolish. *Exeunt. Manet Kent and Gent.*
(K2v27–28)
F Pray *you* now forget, and forgiue,
I am old and foolish. *Exeunt*
(TLN 2842–2843)

Other instances of Folio alterations removing apparent superfluities include the following:

Q Is it *no more* but this, a tardines in nature, (B4r19)
F Is it but this? A tardinesse in nature, (TLN 258)

Q you and your fellow *seruants*, i'de haue it come in question, (C3r24–25)
F You and your Fellowes: I'de haue it come to question; (TLN 520)

Q haue you not spoken gainst the Duke of Cornwall *ought*,
(D3v21–22)
F Haue you not spoken 'gainst the Duke of Cornewall?
(TLN 953)

Q In the restoring his bereued sence, he that *can* helpe him
(I1v6)
F In the restoring his bereaued Sense; he that helpes him
(TLN 2359)

We seem to be dealing with an officious editor who thought he could improve Shakespeare's style.

Other Folio variants show the editors achieving metrical regularity by leaving out semantically insignificant words, such as "the," "sir," "now," "of," "very," "ho," "yet," and "his." The following examples show this type of alteration:

Q goe to the creating *of* a whole tribe of fops (C1r23–24)
F Goe to th' creating a whole tribe of Fops (TLN 348)

Q ile write straight to my sister to hould my *very* course
(C3r34–35)
F Ile write straight to my Sister to hold my course (TLN 527)

Q Bring forth the stockes *ho?* (E2v1)
F Fetch forth the Stocks? (TLN 1203)

Q Say you have wrong'd her *Sir?* (F1r10)
F Say you have wrong'd her. (TLN 1432)

Q Not altogether so *sir*, I looke not for you yet, (F2r22)
F Not altogether so, I look'd not for you yet, (TLN 1526–1527)

Q Is this well spoken *now?* (F2r29)
F Is this well spoken? (TLN 1532)

Q You owe me no subscription, *why* then let fall (F4r20)
F You owe me no subscription. Then let fall (TLN 1673)

Q Wherefore to Douer *sir?* (H1r12)
F Wherefore to Douer? (TLN 2127)

Q Oh I am slaine my Lord, *yet* haue you one eye left (H2r2)
F Oh I am slaine: my Lord,you haue one eye left (TLN 2156)

Q bad is the trade that must play *the* foole to sorrow (H2v29–30)
F Bad is the Trade that must play Foole to sorrow (TLN 2224)

Q I madam, in the heauinesse of *his* sleepe, (K2r2)
F I Madam: in the heauinesse of sleepe, (TLN 2772)

Q Meane you to inioy him *then?* (L1r15)
F Meane you to enioy him? (TLN 3022)

Q the aduersarie I come to cope *with all.* (L1v21)
F the Aduersary I come to cope. (TLN 3075–3076)

Q Here comes Kent *sir.* (L3r19)
F Here comes Kent. (TLN 3181)

Q and thou no breath at all, O thou *wilt* come no more (L4r18–19)
F And thou no breath at all? Thou'lt come no more (TLN 3279)

Without exception the Quarto readings are more colloquial and often more emphatic: "*yet* haue you one eye left" and "Meane you to inioy him *then?*" carry an extra level of expressiveness than the Folio's more decorous revisions, intended for a reading public.

In some instances the Folio editors seem to have exercised their aesthetic judgment by substituting semantically significant words, not always for the better:

Q Neuer afflict your selfe to know the cause, (D2r36)
F Neuer afflict your selfe to know *more of it:* (TLN 806)

Q Thou may'st deserue, or they purpose this vsage (E3v19)
F Thou *might'st* deserue, or they *impose* this vsage (TLN 1301)

Q No Regan, (F1r31)
F *Neuer* Regan: (TLN 1440)

Q me on paine of their displeasure, neither to speake (G1r3–4)
F me on paine of *perpetuall* displeasure, neither to speake (TLN 1756)

Q the vsurer hangs the cosioner, through tottered raggs, smal vices do appeare, (I4r26–27)
F The Vsurer hangs the Cozener. Thorough tatter'd *cloathes great* Vices do appeare: (TLN 2606–2607)

Again, the Folio editorial choices are not the happiest. The revised line "Neuer afflict your selfe to know *more of it*" substitutes three colorless words for the more substantial noun, "the cause"; while "tatter'd *cloathes*" may be more decorous than "tottered rags," it is far less expressive.

Clear examples of the Folio editors' personal stylistic preferences are the transpositions of word order:

Q Oh I am slaine my Lord, yet haue you one eye left (H2r2)
F Oh I am slaine: my Lord, *you haue* one eye left (TLN 2156)

Q Good madam be by, when we do awake him, (K2r4)
F *Be by good Madam* when we do awake him, (TLN 2774)

Reviewing these groups of variants, we can see that the Folio editors may have been trying to produce regular iambic pentameters, but often weakened Shakespeare's language: "yet haue you one eye left" is more metrical and more expressive than "*you haue* one eye left."

Stage Directions

Modern readers would never notice the great majority of these alterations unless they compared the Quarto and Folio texts side by side. But one category of alteration is clearly visible, the treatment of stage directions. Scholars have noted that the Folio directions are much more consistent than in the Quarto, and such regularization was previously thought to have been the work of the bookkeeper. Thanks to the work of Paul Werstine and W. B. Long we know that surviving theater manuscripts were anything but tidy. But the Folio includes some plays in which stage directions have been "scrupulously regularized" when compared with their appearance in the Quarto, such as 2 *Henry IV* and *King Lear.* In both plays, according to Werstine, the stage directions are "remarkable for the near perfection they exhibit in repairing deficiencies in the Quarto so as to include the entrance of all necessary characters, no matter how insignificant." Such "relative completeness and regularization are unusual in actual playhouse texts," he observed, and was unlikely ever "achieved within the playhouses themselves. Thus, while the cuts evident in Folio *Lear* . . . may very well testify that somewhere in [its] provenance there is the playhouse, the regularization of stage-directions and / or character designations cannot easily be traced to the same source. Instead, it strongly suggests intervention by an extra-theatrical agency."[42] Perhaps Jaggard had employed, for some plays, an unusually alert editor, even one with theatrical experience. It is disappointing that at this late stage in Shakespeare studies we still have no detailed study of editorial procedures across the whole Folio.

The Folio's changes to *Lear,* however, suggest that regularization has been bought at a price. If we compare the opening stage direction we notice a striking difference.

> Q *Sound a Sennet, Enter one bearing a Coronet, then Lear, then the Dukes of Albany, and Cornwell, next Gonorill, Regan, Cordelia, with followers.* (B1v9–11)
>
> F *Sennet. Enter King Lear, Cornwall, Albany, Gonerill, Regan, Cordelia, and attendants.* (TLN 37–38)

The Quarto direction is evidently conceived from the viewpoint of a writer who knows the text and what will happen later in this scene. As Wilfrid Perrett noticed in 1904, this and other stage directions in the Quarto

> correspond more closely to the actual performance as directed by Shakespeare than those printed in the 1623 collective edition. . . . Plainly a coronet is needed at 1.1.139; but it is there needed for purpose no one could have foreseen. In high rage at Cordelia's answer the king impetuously changes his plan, disowns his favourite daughter, gives her intended dower to the two dukes, and together with the whole land thus bestowed, his kingly power; and announcing the conditions on which he does so, adds: "which to confirm, | This coronet part between you."

Having noted the silence or puzzlement of editors on this point, Perrett asked, "Now why should a coronet be borne in at the head of the procession, preceding the king himself? It cannot be a symbol of his majesty, for Lear is traditionally represented as wearing his crown, and this is but a coronet, which is quite a different thing . . . The explanation is that *the coronet was intended for Cordelia*."[43] While scholars legitimately discuss the differences between the two texts Perrett did well to remind us that Shakespeare would have been fully involved during the performances at the Globe, so that the Quarto directions are both authorial and directorial (to use a modern term).

Many of the Quarto directions are "clearly visualized," as Greg observed.[44] Presumably the King's Men knew which stage properties and actions would be appropriate, so that the actual stage business in their performances would have corresponded to the directions given in the Quarto. But the modern reader—and editor—would regret losing the helps to visualization given by that text and excised in the Folio. "*Enter Bastard solus*" (C1r14; 1.2.1) is rather more expressive of an authorial conception or a character's purposeful intention than the Folio's "*Enter Bastard*" (TLN 334). "*Enter Edmund with his rapier drawne*" (E1r36; 2.2.44) is both more vivid and more informative than "*Enter Bastard*" (TLN 1117). "*Enter Gloster brought in by two or three*" (H1r22; 3.7.28) may be vague, but it offers more help to visualizing him being delivered for punishment than "*Enter Gloucester and Seruants*" (TLN 2088). In the fatal dispute between Cornwall and his servant, outraged by Gloucester's blinding, the reader is helped by the Quarto direction for the men to "*draw and fight*" (H1v36; 3.7.78), omitted by the Folio. And we are duly horrified at its description of Regan's ruthless intervention: "*Shee takes a sword and runs at him behind*" (H2r1; 3.7.80), incomparably more expressive than the Folio's laconic "*Killes him*" (TLN 2155). The actor playing blinded Gloucester will know what to do, but the reader is grateful for the Quarto's description of his actions as he hopes to meet his longed-for death on the Dover cliffs: "*He kneeles*" (I2v32;4.6.34) and "*He fals*" (I3r1; 41), both omitted in the Folio. For a Jacobean audience or reader there could be few stage directions more disturbing than "*Enter Lear mad*" (I3v6; 4.6.80) and "*Exit King running*" (I4v16; 204), for which the Folio's "*Enter Lear*" and "*Exit*" (TLN 2526, 2645) seem pallid substitutes. Visualization produces a greater response from reader or spectator in this direction, which brings out Lear's vulnerability and Cordelia's protectiveness: "*Enter the powers of France ouer the stage, Cordelia with her father in her hand*" (K3v34–35; 5.2.0), for which the Folio merely gives the characters' names. The reality of Goneril's off-stage suicide is brought home to us by the direction "*Enter one with a bloudie knife*" (L3r8; 5.3.222), quite missing in the Folio's "*Enter a Gentleman*" (TLN 3169). Many readers will have encountered these directions in modern editions and may be surprised to discover that they come from the often disparaged Quarto, not from the supposedly authoritative Folio. Although Jaggard and his editors altered many aspects of Shakespeare's text, seemingly for the convenience of readers, it is in fact the Quarto produced by Nicholas Okes, with all its faults, which brings us closer to Shakespeare's play as he conceived it.

7

The King's Men Abridge a Tragedy

King Lear is Shakespeare's most complex, most carefully designed play. He went to unusual lengths in consulting multiple treatments of the story. He took much from *The True Chronicle History of King Leir*, which was performed at the Rose Theatre in April 1594 and entered in the Stationers' Register a month later but not published until 1605, doubtless as an attempt to cash in on the success of *King Lear*.[1] Wilfrid Perrett, in his unsurpassed study of the story of King Lear—from folk tale to Geoffrey of Monmouth and in more than fifty intermediate versions preceding Shakespeare—showed that, for the main plot the dramatist also consulted Holinshed's *Chronicle*, *The Mirror for Magistrates*, Spenser's *Faerie Queene*, William Warner's *Albion's England*, and other sources.[2] Most inventively, to that story of a father wronged by two of his three daughters Shakespeare added a subplot from Sidney's *Arcadia* concerning the Paphlagonian king, who was "deceived by his bastard, Plexirtus, blinded, cast out, and brought to the brink of suicide. The good son, like Cordelia, returns from exile, and with foreign help thwarts the efforts of Plexirtus to murder him and his father."[3] Shakespeare skillfully interwove that story with his main plot, with a slight delay, as it were, so that the doings of Goneril and Regan are a step ahead of those by Edmund, but lead to the same outcome. In an uncanny parallel movement the children who have been benefited by their parents reciprocate by giving them up to death and mutilation. As Edgar learns of how Lear has been treated by his daughters his recognition echoes ours: "He childed as I fathered" (3.6.110).

Whoever experiences *Lear* fully, whether by reading or seeing it performed, will notice many instances where each plot casts light on the other. One element with far-reaching consequences is that of a rupture in relationships caused by real or apparent harm, where the injured party denounces and rejects the suspected person. In the opening scene Lear does this twice, first with Kent and then with Cordelia. When he experiences the ingratitude of Goneril and Regan, Lear would wish to be able to banish them; unable to do so, he banishes himself from their society. Meanwhile Gloucester, deceived into regarding Edgar as a parricide, has put a price on his head. Subsequently Goneril and Cornwall put both Gloucester and Lear in the same category, a human being to be hunted down and punished. The result of these ruptures is that characters are forced out of the milieu in which, at the start of the play, they would have expected to remain. Kent and Edgar forfeit both society and identity, having to disguise to evade capture and punishment. Lear exiles himself, together with the Fool. Cordelia goes to France with her husband, but returns in a hopeless attempt to save her father.

The further result of these multiple displacements is that the action takes place in many different places, more than in any other Shakespeare play. At any given point we can be asked to imagine the separate locations of Lear and his court; of Goneril and Cornwall; of Regan and Albany; and of Gloucester and Edmund, all these people in their normal dwelling places. Out in the open country, enduring rain and tempest, we see Kent, Lear, and the Fool together; Edgar alone; Edgar disguised as Poor Tom, joining the other fugitives; Gloucester tending Lear, at the risk of his own life; Kent twice engaged in conversation with an unnamed "Gentleman"; Edgar tending blinded Gloucester; Edgar killing Oswald. We hear of Cordelia returning from France long before we see her. All these characters traverse many spaces, familiar and strange. In the final scene, set on a battlefield where all the conflicts in the play meet their resolution—an appropriate setting for the decline of humanity into a level below animality—all the characters are reunited and meet their end, just or unjust.

Given the fragmentation of relationships and living spaces that Shakespeare has brought about, communication becomes a problem. Goncril and Regan exchange letters to coordinate their inhospitable treatment of Lear; Lear writes a letter announcing his futile wish to change his residence from Goneril to Regan; Edmund forges a letter by Edgar and gets him disinherited; Cordelia writes a letter to Kent expressing her concern and hopes to help; and Goneril writes a letter to Edmund offering him an adulterous relationship, just like the one in which he was begot. Edgar intercepts her letter and reads it aloud, documenting the latest instance of the individual's desire for personal gratification at the expense of those to whom they are indebted, visible in all the doings of Goneril, Regan, Cornwall and Edmund since the opening two scenes. Edgar delivers the letter to Goneril's husband Albany, exposing her duplicity, just before the three evil children's schemes implode.

With the action dispersed into so many locales, characters are constantly asking the whereabouts of others, increasingly so in the later stages of the play. Such inquiries can be answered accurately (Lear is indeed roaming the fields near Dover), but at other times characters can only report rumors (Kent hears a report that Lear is supposedly in Germany). This is a familiar plot function that narratologists term "notification," whereby characters are used to convey information necessary for the reader or spectator to understand what is happening.[4] Shakespeare's use of these two modes of communication, written and oral, together with his wonderfully assured interweaving of plot lines, gives this play a complex unified structure. At any one point in the action we know where each of these characters is, more or less, and what they are doing. If we were to highlight their position in every scene, whether on or off stage, each in a different color, we would have a bundle of multi-colored strands. To cut though this unity at any point would break essential links in the narrative, with damaging effects to the whole structure, as Shakespeare planned it. But the King's Men attempted the task.

At some point between the first performance of *King Lear* in 1606 and its appearance in the 1623 Folio, a number of passages that had appeared in the 1608 Quarto were cut. According to my computations, 54 omissions were made, 7 of them involving more than 10 lines. The most extensive cut was the omission of a whole scene (4.3), totaling 56 lines, where an eponymous "Gentleman" informs Kent (and the audience) of the intensity of Cordelia's grief and anger on learning about how her sisters have treated Lear, together with a report of her father's "sovereign shame" at his treatment of her. The next largest cuts were in 3.6, the scene where mad Lear "arraigns" Goneril and Regan, which lost 40 lines (17–56), and in 4.2. Here the theater abridger cut Albany's speeches expressing disgust at the two daughters' evil (31–50, 62–69), as well as Goneril's taunting replies (53–87), a total of 34 lines. In 5.3 the theater company cut Edgar's report of his reunion with Kent, totaling 18 lines (205–222), and in 1.4 it removed some of the Fool's mockery of Lear, amounting to 16 lines (140–155). In 3.1 the company made two cuts, excising nine lines in which the Gentleman describes Lear defying the storm (7–15) and 13 lines of Kent's opaque account of the French force that has landed, with instructions to head for Dover (30–42). There are shorter cuts, from one to nine lines, in twenty-seven other scenes. Altogether, by my count, 288 blank verse lines were omitted.[5] Comparison of the two texts reveals that in twenty scenes the Folio also made many smaller cuts, from one to five words, losing fifty-nine words in all.

The standard explanation for the Folio omissions, since at least 1875 when Nikolaus Delius, the great German scholar, made the first analysis in modern times of the play's textual problems, is that they reflect a text shortened for theatrical performance.[6] Having dealt with the Quarto omissions in some detail, Delius found it easier to explain the cause of the "much more considerable" omissions in the Folio text, since their function was clear: "Their object is merely to shorten the drama, which may have proved too long for representation. The reason of these cuts in the Folio is, that it was edited from a later theatre MS."[7] E. K. Chambers agreed with Delius both as to the agents of the abridgement and its nature. Chambers also noted that the omissions in F include "some printer's errors" and that others may be due to the censor. "But in the main we probably have to do with ordinary theatrical cutting. It is not unintelligent, affecting chiefly narratives of episodes in France and elsewhere away from the main action, . . . some dialogue between servants . . . , a bit of poetic description," and "Edgar's sententious rhymes." As to the agent responsible, Chambers judged it "idle to ask whether Shakespeare himself or a colleague made these cuts. They point, of course, to the use of stage-copy for F."[8] Other scholars agreed that the cuts were made by the King's Men.[9] The alternative, as Delius saw, would be that "Shakespeare revised the text of *King Lear* . . . with his own hand," an opinion that Delius refuted by means of cogent arguments concerning the effect of all the major omissions.[10] I shall also argue that the cuts were made for theatrical reasons, that they damage the play, and that Shakespeare did not make them.

Whereas the cuts made in Nicholas Okes's printing shop in 1607–1608 were mainly of shorter passages, ranging from one to seven words (63 of the 91 cuts were of this size), the majority of the Folio cuts—34 out of 54 (63 percent, as against the Quarto's 30 percent)—were of longer passages. Their nature and placing strongly suggest cuts made for theatrical reasons. Eric Rasmussen, in a valuable discussion of "Theatrical Cutting," compared the cuts in the Folio text of *King Lear* to those in *Hamlet* and in Middleton's *The Second Maiden's Tragedy*, of which the manuscript, now in the British Library (Lansdowne MS 807), is "the only extant playbook of a play performed by the King's Men when Shakespeare was an active member of the company" and is thus "directly relevant" to the cutting of Shakespeare's plays. As Rasmussen showed, the distribution of the cuts within the two Shakespeare tragedies "is nearly identical," the major omissions falling in Acts 3–5, which indicates that "the cuts were made in order to shorten each play by abbreviating the second half," a practice continued by modern theater directors. In *Hamlet*, "lines are generally cut from the middle of long speeches," two of which "were originally more than twenty lines long, and two were originally longer than thirty lines." In *The Second Maiden's Tragedy* the "reviser also generally marked cuts in the middle of speeches," five of them in lengthy speeches, and "only twice simply deleted the end of a speech."[11] Rasmussen pointed out the striking difference, that "in *Lear* lines are generally cut from the end of speeches, and, following the same principle, larger cuts simply remove the conclusions of scenes."[12] The type of "internal cutting" found in both *Hamlet* and the *Second Maiden*'s playbook, Rasmussen observed, is that still used in the modern theater. By contrast,

> the method of cutting in *Lear* resembles that performed by newspaper editors who assume that their reporters have structured their articles in a 'pyramidal form' (most important information first, least important last) and so cut from the end if the story needs to be shortened. Obviously, dramatists do not write according to these rules. Certain principles of closure absent from the journalist's work are nearly always present in the playwright's: fifth acts are frequently more important than fourth acts; the climax of a scene may be more essential than the opening. One cannot simply cut from the end of the play, or a scene, or even a speech with any assurance that a passage's structural position indicates its relative significance.[13]

Since all three plays were subjected to cutting by the King's Men, the difference between them may point to a change of personnel at some point, although no evidence has survived. Rasmussen's comments on the damaging effect of "pyramidal" cutting will prove highly pertinent when we begin to analyze the longer cuts.

The person normally responsible for making cuts was the bookkeeper. In an important study of the surviving early modern playhouse manuscripts Paul Werstine has shown that "casting plays is a major, if customary, responsibility of the bookkeeper that can often be achieved only by cutting roles, sometimes from the play as a whole, sometimes only from particular scenes. In carrying out this task, the bookkeeper often changes the manuscript only insofar as serves his immediate purpose, without taking care to tidy up after himself by eliminating every trace of the playwright's original intentions that are being sacrificed to theatrical exigency."[14] It is precisely the working of theatrical exigency that accounted for the large omissions that bookkeepers made. As Werstine showed, in the anonymously published *Edmund Ironside* the bookkeeper "slices out a pair of roles"; someone from the "playhouse personnel" cut out the servants in a scene of Anthony Munday's *John a Kent and John a Cumber;* Edward Knight cut one role in Massinger's *Beleeue as you list*, "artfully merging him with" another character. But Knight's involvement was not limited to deletion, for he twice added "a seemingly missing character," one of whom is just "brought on later in the scene," while the other "is not required by the dialogue or action." In Edward Sharpham's *The Fleire* theatrical annotation "takes out not just one but several roles," while the "adaptation for playing" made by the scribe Ralph Crane in Massinger's *Sir John van Olden Barnavelt* "is unusual only for the number of roles that are conflated or otherwise altered." These instances of bookkeepers making considerable alterations to a dramatist's text may seem alarming to the modern reader, predisposed to regard a play as the author's creation, but they reflect the balance of power and responsibility within a theatre company. Although Werstine praises some bookkeepers who "make well-informed cuts of roles by intervening in plays' dialogue," he notes that in other cases their "cutting and telescoping of roles produce more complex results."[15] The person who cut *King Lear* deserves little praise.

Not all the cuts in the Folio text of *Lear* are theatrical; some may be due to the compositors and editors employed by Jaggard's printing house. (Omissions from the Folio text, as compared to the Quarto, are enclosed in square brackets; omissions from the Quarto are in angled brackets; variant readings are in curly brackets.) To begin with the smaller cuts, one of these may indeed have been accidental:

> *Gon.* the obseruation we haue made of it hath [not] beene
> little (1.1.289; TLN 314–315)

It would be a self-contradiction for Goneril to affirm that she and Regan have made an "observation" of their father's impetuous behavior, but only a "little" one. Similarly, with the assurance given to Cordelia about Lear's recovery from mental disturbance:

> *Gent.* Be by good Madam when we do awake him,
> I doubt [not] of his Temperance. (4.7.22–23: TLN 2774–2775)

The Folio compositor's omission of "not" ruins the whole point of this reassuring remark. Other smaller cuts may have been either editorial or compositorial, such as Lear's injunction to his second daughter:

> *Lear.* Our deerest *Regan*, wife of *Cornwall?* [, speake]
> (1.1.67; TLN 73)

This omission ruins the symmetry by which Lear orders Goneril to "speake first" (54), then Regan, and then Cordelia (86). Whoever omitted the imperative verb here was not paying attention to Shakespeare's design.

Convergence

Despite their divergent intentions, the Quarto and Folio abridgers often converged on the same passages of text, each sacrificing some of Shakespeare's verbal richness. As Gloucester absorbs the malicious lies about his legitimate son fed him by his bastard, each abridger cut differently:

> *Glo.* O strange and fastned Villaine,
> Would he deny his Letter, <said he?> [I never got him,]
> (2.1.77–78; TLN 1015–1016)

Here I feel that the Quarto abridger made the better choice, retaining "I never got him." This is a shocking denial of parentage, and one that links the subplot and main plot, echoing Lear's angry attempts to disown his children, first Cordelia (1.1.109–119), then Goneril (1.4.232–234), and finally Regan (2.4.219–225). In the scene where Goneril denies Lear the satisfaction of keeping "a hundred knights and squires" by dismissing fifty of them, his hurt expresses itself in "hot tears, which break from me perforce," before he regains self-control and reaches a moment of decision:

> Old fond eyes,
> Beweepe this cause againe, Ile pluck ye out,
> And cast you with the waters that you loose
> To temper Clay. [yea, i'st come to this?] <Ha? Let it be so.>
> (1.4.301–304; TLN 820–823)

The Quarto and Folio abridgers each cut a few words, the Folio abridger making the better choice here by cutting Lear's shocked question but retaining the king's resolve to accept Goneril's rejection. This shows that he still believes that Regan will accept him with love, a delusion soon to be dispelled. Modern editors rightly restore both speeches. The Quarto and Folio abridgers, each working to a different agenda, converged again in the scene of Lear's first quarrel with Regan.

Enter Albany.
Lear. Woe, that too late repents: [O sir, are you come?]
Is it your will <,speake Sir?> [that wee] Prepare {my}[16] horses,
Ingratitude! thou Marble-hearted Fiend
(1.4.257–259; TLN 768–771)

Presumably Okes cut "speake Sir" since it duplicated "O sir" just before, and then misread "my" as "any." He probably added the words "that wee" in order to make a coherent sentence, since it would be inconceivable that Lear should defer to Albany about any matter concerning his retinue. The Folio abridger made a different cut and also restored Lear's characteristic imperative.

When Lear has quit his unloving daughters for "The tirrany of the open night," Quarto and Folio abridgers each omitted a repetition. In this instance Okes chose the longer cut:

Lear. No, I will weepe no more; in such a night, [as this!]
<To shut me out? Poure on, I will endure:
<In such a night as this?> O *Regan*, *Gonerill*,
Your old kind Father, whose franke heart gaue all
(3.4.17–21; TLN 1797–1800)

Whoever shortened the promptbook for the King's Men also omitted several of Lear's verbal repetitions, characteristic of Shakespeare's old men:

Lear. O let me not be mad, not mad sweet Heauen; [I would not be mad,] Keepe me in temper, I would not be mad.
(1.5.46–47; TLN 918–919)
Lear. Make no noise, make no noise, draw the Curtaines:
so, so,[so,] wee'l go to Supper i't'h morning. [so,so,so,]
(3.6.83–84; TLN 2041–2042)

Lear. No Seconds? All my selfe?
Why, this would make a man, <a man> of Salt
To vse his eyes for Garden water-pots.
[I, and laying Autums dust.] (4.6.194–197; TLN 2638–2640)

The previous omissions were of simple repetitions, but in cutting this reference to a further use for water the Folio editor may have judged the line obscure, as the mad Lear elaborates on a private joke. The most important addition, perhaps, comes in Lear's final speech:

Lear. Pray you vndo this button. Thanke you Sir,
<Do you see this? Looke on her? Looke her lips,
<Looke there, looke there.> [O, o, o, o.] <*He dies.*>
(5.3.310–312; TLN 3281–3283)

Happily, the Folio editor, while eliminating the fourfold groans, probably substituted by Okes or his compositors, retained the manuscript's fourfold repetition of "looke" (deemed superfluous by the Quarto's abridger), leaving us Lear's last, ambivalent gesture, either of despair or—more likely, I have always thought—of deluded hope that Cordelia lives.

Losing the Plot

Looked at in isolation, we may agree with Chambers that some of the Folio cuts are "not unintelligent." However, every cut sacrifices something from Shakespeare's careful design, with its interweaving of multiple plot threads. The omissions imposed on this carefully planned whole so often leave awkward lacunae in the text, destroying carefully worked out elements of plot and motivation, that they cannot have been made by the author. If we credit Shakespeare with having made the Folio omissions it would mean that on many occasions he was undermining his own design.

I begin with a general observation concerning dramatic preparation. Some Jacobean dramatists (such as Webster and Fletcher) often introduced elements of surprise into their plots—unprepared developments in the action or unmotivated reversals in their characters' goals and desires. Shakespeare's dramaturgy worked in the opposite manner, preferring to prepare the audience for what will happen, enabling them to recognize and respond to developments that have been flagged in advance. There are exceptions, of course, such as the unexpected death that overclouds the ending of *Love's Labor's Lost*, or the statue scene in *The Winter's Tale*, where we are made to share the ignorance of Leontes and Perdita that the statue of Hermione is not real, so that we, too, feel their shock of surprise at her being alive, with all its release of pent-up guilt and emotion. (The ending of *King Lear* may be a surprise to those who know other versions of the story, but it is entirely coherent, given the interplay of these characters, agents, and victims.) In general, Shakespeare helps us to look ahead into what will happen—or, sometimes, to what characters think will happen.

The person who abridged *Lear* for the King's Men, and whose cut version survives in the Folio, did not have this longer view. Several of his omissions destroy Shakespeare's careful anticipation of what is about to unfold. One damaging series of cuts affected Shakespeare's careful charting of the off-stage preparations by Cordelia to rescue her father, which run in parallel with events in the play before us. Act 3, scene 1 includes a long conversation between Kent and a Gentleman about the French forces sent to rescue Lear, in which Shakespeare makes Kent adopt an evasive style to communicate mysterious hints about the rumored division between Albany and Cornwall. The Quarto abridger chose to omit eight lines, which the Folio kept:

Kent. Sir, I do know you,
And dare vpon the warrant of my {note}[17]
Commend a deere thing to you. There is diuision
(Although as yet the face of it is couer'd
With mutuall cunning) 'twixt Albany, and Cornwall:
<Who haue, as who haue not, that their great Starres
<Thron'd and set high; Seruants, who seeme no lesse,
<Which are to France the Spies and Speculations
<Intelligent of our State. What hath bin seene,
<Either in snuffes, and packings of the Dukes,
<Or the hard Reine which both of them hath borne
<Against the old kinde King; or something deeper,
<Whereof (perchance) these are but furnishings.>

(3.1.17–29; TLN 1626–1639)

The first sentence of the omission eddies away, not explaining the nature of the division between Albany and Cornwall, but deflecting to a generalization about the servants of men in power. Kent evades a straight forward utterance with a flurry of relative pronouns ("who," "who," "who," "Which," "What," "Whereof"), then sets up two alternative explanations without resolving them: "What hath bin seene, | Either in . . . | Or . . . or something deeper, | Whereof (perchance) these are but furnishings." The style here becomes the thing it describes, the indeterminate workings of rumor. The Quarto chose to omit those lines, but retained the transition, where Kent decisively dispels rumor with fact: "But true it is . . . ." The Folio, however, made the opposite and less astute choice, omitting this crucial passage:

[But true it is, from *France* there comes a power
[Into this scattered kingdome, who alreadie wise in our
[Haue secret feet in some of our best Ports, (negligēce,
[And are at point to shew their open banner.
[Now to you, if on my credit you dare build so farre,
[To make your speed to Douer, you shall find
[Some that will thanke you, making iust report
[Of how vnnaturall and bemadding sorrow
[The King hath cause to plaine,
[I am a Gentleman of blood and breeding,
[And from some knowledge and assurance,
[Offer this office to you.
Gent. I will talke further with you.
Kent. No, do not:
For confirmation that I am much more
Then my out-wall; open this Purse (F3v14–29; 3.1.30–47)

Both texts retain the closing dialogue between Kent and the Gentleman.

By omitting these thirteen lines the theater bookkeeper left a damaging gap in the plot, as Delius pointed out:

> Still more indispensable is the second passage, in which Kent informs the nobleman of the arming of France, and the im-

> pending landing of a French host, and sends him to Dover, to the friends of Lear who are there. The actors overlooked the fact that the omission of this passage renders that which follows incomprehensible. How could the nobleman find Cordelia, and deliver Kent's message to her, if he did not know that she was with the French army at Dover? Naturally such a palpable error cannot have emanated from Shakespeare, who better understood the plan of his drama.[18]

Richard Knowles has added more detail to this diagnosis, judging that "the absence of the Quarto lines from Folio makes hash of the sense."[19]

It has always seemed to me that the existence of the two halves of Kent's speech, one in each of the authoritative texts, juxtaposing rumor and reliable news, suggests that it was originally a whole unit, differently cut by the Quarto printer (who made the better choice) and the theater bookkeeper. The hinge line is Kent's "But true it is . . . ." It follows, as René Weis has forcefully argued, that 3.1 "constituted the strongest textual evidence afforded by the two printed versions in support of a single original text of *Lear*; that Kent's lines in Act 3 scene 1 may make sense only if Q and F are seamlessly joined just as they were in editions of *Lear* . . . before 1986"—that is, before the editors of the Oxford Shakespeare fulfilled the Two Versions project by presenting the Quarto and Folio texts as separate entities.[20]

For his largest and most damaging cut to the multiple plot lines the playhouse abridger omitted the whole of 4.3, a conversation between Kent and a Gentleman that picks up their previous conversation in 3.1. This time the Gentleman brings surprising news, that the French king has unexpectedly returned home, information that the theater bookkeeper regarded as dispensable. In his commentary Delius underlined the essential function of this scene in removing any concern that Jacobean readers or spectators might feel at the presence of a foreign ruler on English soil, and he brought out its connection to an earlier scene in the play:

> The actors cheerfully omitted this explanatory scene between Kent and the nobleman, as superfluous, because in it nothing is done, but something only talked of. And yet so essential is it to

> Shakespeare's plot, that we have every reason to be thankful to the editor of the Quartos for having preserved it to us. It must be explained why the King of France, Cordelia's husband, who would only have been an encumbrance to the farther intentions of the poet, disappears, so to speak, from the play. Cordelia disappears still more entirely at the beginning of the drama. It probably appeared right to the poet, to prepare the audience for the re-appearance on the stage of this character who plays so important a part in the last portion of the tragedy. The nobleman, whom Kent, in an earlier part of the play (Act III, sc. 1), had sent to Cordelia, is expected to give an account of the Queen's reception of himself, and of the intelligence he brought of Lear and his elder daughters. This is the direct reference to that earlier scene, which the actors considered superfluous, and therefore omitted.[21]

As we will see in Chapter 8, the Two Versions theorists, convinced that every Folio omission was made by Shakespeare, in effect reproduce the theater company's practice of cutting passages where "nothing is done, but something only talked of."

Reducing Iteration

In working out the interactions and conflicts between human beings that constitute the stuff of drama, a skillful dramatist will make sure that playgoers—and, later, readers—fully understand what the characters say and why they behave as they do. To achieve these goals, a dramatist will have to fill out characters' definition by repeating certain details of their personality and motives, in greater or less detail according to their importance. We may call this process "iteration." In this play Shakespeare's fullness of invention registered with clarity and intensity the distinct desires and motives of eleven major characters—Lear, Kent, Cordelia, Goneril, Regan, Cornwall, Albany, Gloucester, Edmund, Edgar as himself and disguised as "Poor Tom," and the Fool. For each of them we are left in no doubt as to their overt motives and, in several cases, of their covert motives, as revealed to each other in conversation or to the audience in asides and soliloquies.

Confronted with this richness, the theater abridger went about his business by reducing the amount of iteration, removing passages that, as Delius put it, he "supposed to be not indispensable." One of the remarkable stylistic features of *King Lear* is Shakespeare's fertility of invention, creating an immediately identifiable idiolect for at least seven of those characters: Lear, Cordelia, Kent, the Fool, Edgar, Poor Tom, and Edmund. (Only *Hamlet* equals it in the linguistic differentiation of characters.) A striking instance of a particular idiolect created for this play is the Fool's cross-questioning of Lear, where the clown's usual repertoire of jests and riddles is given a new thematic function, constantly reminding Lear of his folly in giving away his kingdom. Shakespeare developed this invention with so much persistence that the King's Men felt able to omit this exchange:

> *Foole.* Do'st know the difference my Boy, betweene a bitter Foole,and a sweet one?
> *Lear.* No Lad, teach me.
> *Foole.* [That Lord that counsail'd thee to give away thy land,
> [Come place him heere by mee, doe thou for him stand,
> [The sweet and bitter foole will presently appeare,
> [The one in motley here, the other found out there.
> [*Lear.* Do'st thou call mee foole boy?
> [*Foole.* All thy other Titles thou hast giuen away, that thou wast borne with.
> [*Kent.* This is not altogether foole my Lord.
> [*Foole.* No faith, Lords and great men will not let me, if I had [a monopolie out, they would have part on't, and Ladies too, they [will not let me haue all the foole to my selfe, they'l be snatching;] Nunckle, giue me an egge, and Ile give thee two Crownes.
> (C4v31–D1r7; 1.4.140–156; TLN 667–671)

That piece of jesting includes a contemporary allusion to the abuse of monopolies, a social injustice frequently criticized in the reigns of Elizabeth and James I. Taylor has argued that its omission in the Folio was due to censorship, but that seems unlikely, given the frequency of such complaints elsewhere in the literature of the time.

(Nor is it probable that the Fool's bawdy joke on "snatching," alluding to his "bauble," referred to "fool" in the sense of "custard," and was omitted lest it offend ladies of the court.[22]) This seems to me a simple theatrical cut, of a passage that does not advance the action and reiterates points already made in the Fool's exposure of Lear's folly.

If that cut was made merely to shorten a passage deemed inessential, the theater abridger worked on a related principle, cutting words that are preparatory to deeds. He seems to have felt that behavior represented on stage could be left to speak for itself and that speeches leading up to or commenting on that behavior could be dispensed with. Preparing us for the scene where Goneril will deny Lear his full complement of knights and squires, Shakespeare prefixed a conversation with her steward in which she reiterates her unity with Regan in the tactics of denial, an iteration cut by the theater abridger:

> *Gon.* If he distaste it, let him to my Sister,
> Whose mind and mine I know in that are one,
> [not to be ouerruld; idle old man that still would manage those
> [authorities that hee hath given away, now by my life old fooles
> [are babes again, & must be vs'd with checkes as flatteries, when
> [they are seene abusd,remember what I tell you.]
> Remember what I have said.
>
> (C3r27–30; 1.3.14–20; TLN 521–523)

Those lines may have been sacrificed as not advancing the action, but the omission leaves a lacuna. They add reinforcing detail of the extent of Goneril's callous contempt for her father ("old fooles are babes again"), as it will shortly issue into action:

> *Gon.* And let his Knights have colder looks among
> you: what growes of it no matter, aduise your fellowes so,
> [I would breed from hence occasions, and I shall, that I may
> speake,]
>
> (C3r32–34; 1.3.22–25; TLN 525–527)

Shakespeare explicitly makes Goneril explain her motives, which she carries out in the following scene. His dramaturgy generally preferred preparation, oblivious though the Folio abridger may have been to such considerations.

In eliminating iteration, the person(s) who made these cuts to the King's Men promptbook reduced certain emphases made by Shakespeare but without wholly eliminating them from the text. Gloucester's sentimental self-image as a loving father survives, despite the excision of this passage:

Glost. He cannot bee such a Monster.
[*Bast.* Nor is not, sure.
[*Glost.* To his father, that so tenderly and intirely loues him,
[heauen and earth!] *Edmund* seeke him out: winde me into him
(C2r18–21; 1.2.94–98; TLN 427–428)

However, by this omission the theatrical abridger lost the shock effect as the deceived father moves in one breath from the sentimental self-image of the loving parent (echoing Lear's self-representation)—"that so tenderly . . . loues him"—to the ruthless "winde me into him," with its associations of Machiavellian insinuation, gaining someone's confidence in order to manipulate them.

Shakespeare's fullness of expression in *King Lear* was such that many passages provide incremental detail, adding substance to an idea or emotion to make sure that the audience fully realizes its significance. For a theater company looking to shorten a play this *copia verborum* simplified the cutting process, since a whole block of speech could be omitted, stretching over several lines. This was a quite different approach from that used by the Quarto abridger. At the end of Act 2 we saw Lear leaving Gloucester's castle as night falls and the storm breaks: "the {bleak}[23] windes | Do surely ruffle" on a bare and exposed landscape; " 'tis a wild night." The next scene gives us Kent meeting a Gentleman and inquiring after Lear, where the Folio abridger chose to omit nine lines:

Kent. I know you: Where's the King?
Gent. Contending with the fretfull Elements;

Bids the winde blow the Earth into the Sea,
Or swell the curled Waters 'boue the Maine,
That things might change, or cease [, teares his white haire,
[Which the impetuous blasts with eyles rage
[Catch in their furie,and make nothing of,
[Striues in his little world of man to outscorne,
[The too and fro conflicting wind and raine,
[This night wherin the cub-drawne Beare would couch,
[The Lyon, and the belly pinched Wolfe
[Keepe their furre dry, vnbonneted he runnes,
[And bids what will take all.]
Kent. But who is with him?
(F3r31–F3v6; 3.1.3–15; TLN 1618–1623)

This "description of Lear's mad defiance of the unchained elements," Delius objected, is "so essential to the delineation of the whole situation, that it is impossible that Shakespeare should have omitted it."[24] This report also prepares us for Lear's imminent appearance: "Blow windes, & crack your cheeks; Rage, blow | You Cataracts, and Hyrricano's spout" (3.2.1–2), which an audience would otherwise find puzzling (if they are able to hear these lines in a modern theater using modern sound effects).

The longest role in the play is that of Lear himself, so it is not surprising that the bookkeeper of the King's Men judged that several of his speeches could be shortened. The affected pose that Lear strikes in his first encounter with Goneril—"Who is it that can tell me who I am?"—a pose that ironically echoes Regan's judgment, "yet he hath ever but slenderly known himself" (1.1.294), is truncated with this omission, leaving an unmotivated question:

Lear. Who is it that can tell me who I am?
Foole. *Lears* shadow.
[*Lear.* I would learne that, for by the markes of soueraintie,
[knowledge, and reason, I should bee false perswaded I
[had daughters.
[*Foole.* Which they, will make an obedient father.]
(D1v 28–32 1.4.232–235; TLN 743–744)

The two characters' speeches are interlocking. Lear's second speech follows on from his first, and the Fool's second speech refers back to his first speech: the cut makes Lear's next line to Goneril—"Your name, faire Gentlewoman?"—seem abrupt and unprepared for. Lear's exit line in this scene contains a reinforcing repetition that the playhouse editor also decided to omit:

> *Lear.* Thou shalt finde,
> That Ile resume the shape which thou dost thinke
> I haue cast off for euer. [thou shalt I warrant thee.] <*Exit*>
> *Gon.* Doe you marke that [my Lord]?
> (D2v10–13; 1.4.308–310; TLN 827–829)

A small detail, but this phrase underlines the impotence of Lear's threats, "To take't again perforce" (1.5.39).

The Structure and Integrity of *King Lear*

If we consider the playbook omissions, as recorded in the Folio, from the viewpoint not of character and role but of their position within the play's structure, two patterns emerge. In terms of the number of omissions—counting those of at least a half-line—Acts 1 and 4 suffered the most, each with eleven cuts, followed by Act 5 (eight cuts), Act 3 (six cuts), and Act 2 (four cuts). But if we evaluate the cuts according to the number of lines left out, then Act 4 can be seen as the greatest loser, with one whole scene (4.3) being sacrificed and cuts made to four other scenes, totaling 116 lines. Next comes Act 3, which lost 88 lines, followed by Act 1 (40), Act 5 (35), and Act 2, which lost a mere 7 lines. Looked at in terms of the play as a whole the cuts in Acts 3 and 4 were the most serious and most damaging. We might need to qualify Rasmussen's point, that "fifth acts are frequently more important than fourth acts; the climax of a scene may be more essential than the opening."[25]

Abbreviating a work of art intended for performance reveals two conflicting claims: on the one hand, those of a theater or opera company that is governed by contingencies of cost, practicality, and the availability of specific performers, and, on the other, the artistic intentions of the dramatist or composer. A work of art is an ecosystem:

damage it at one point, and it will suffer unforeseen consequences somewhere else. The cuts in the Folio text of *Lear* that we have so far examined cause little harm to our experience of the play. Few readers or theatergoers familiar with the full text as found in the 1608 Quarto would even notice their absence. But some of the larger cuts raise more serious problems. In one of his outstanding studies of nineteenth-century Italian opera, Philip Gossett described the genre as being partly based on separate "numbers"—recitatives, solos, duets, and so forth—which were always liable to cutting, depending on day-to-day conditions in a particular opera company. As he rightly observed, "not every musical or dramaturgical element in a work is crucial to our perception of that work's integrity. When we make a decision about cuts in the modern performance of an opera, we are making a judgment about integrity. The more we believe in the work's integrity, the more hesitant we will be about making cuts."[26] Much musical evidence survives as to which elements have been judged to be fragile, and thus disposable, some of the cuts being made by the composers themselves, as Gossett observed: "Most cuts introduced by thoughtful performers in the nineteenth century and in the modern world are not arbitrary manipulations of unstable texts, but rather attempts to eliminate elements considered to be least significant or characteristic for a work's aesthetic integrity and historical position. In deciding which cuts to countenance in modern performance we must determine how far to allow this elimination to proceed. At what point do such cuts distort the work?"[27] Such considerations were evidently not uppermost in the minds either of the Jacobean playhouse abridger, but Nikolaus Delius gave them full expression a century and a half ago. Having "weighed the external evidence against Shakespeare's participation in the abridgment of *King Lear*," Delius conceded that

> care has been taken to spare as much as possible, and only to cut out such passages as are merely ornamental, and are not necessary for the plot, or for the development of the characters. But there is a great difference between the actors' idea of what is necessary, and the poet's. The actors see in the play merely a certain number of leading and secondary characters to be divided amongst them, and to be separately studied according to

> the taste of the individual. The poet views his play as an edifice, out of the architectural structure of which no part can be taken without damaging the whole building. Shakespeare himself certainly did not consider any part of his *King Lear* superfluous; if he had, he would not have written it.[28]

Setting aside the unkind words about actors (today we should have to substitute directors), that is a wonderfully cogent statement of an artist's concern for the whole of his creation.

Self for Other; Self versus Other

The cuts made by the King's Men in their promptbook for *Lear* included several that distorted the play by removing elements vital to its aesthetic integrity and historical meaning. The cuts made in Acts 3 and 4 damaged the vital connection in the world of this play between the destruction caused by human evil and the positive responses that it produced, expressed both as words and deeds: moral outrage at evildoers, and active charity, the wish to tend and protect sufferers. The unique characteristic of *King Lear* among Shakespeare's tragedies is its polarization of human behavior into extremes of egoistic destructiveness and altruistic help. (In the other mature tragedies there are many who destroy, but hardly any who comfort or assist those suffering.) The cuts made by the theater company harm the play's moral structure at both extremes.

As commentators on this play have often shown, Shakespeare assiduously established a current of imagery associated with the evil daughters.[29] It originates in the mouth of Lear, describing the actions of Goneril and Regan in terms of ferocious animals. Goneril's ingratitude is "More hideous . . . | Than the Sea-monster" (1.4.259–261), and "sharper than a Serpents tooth" (288–289). To Lear, Goneril is a "Detested Kite" (262), and he fondly imagines that when Regan hears how her sister has treated him, "with her nailes | Shee'l flea ["flay"] thy Wolvish visage" (307–8). To Regan he complains that Goneril "hath tied | Sharpe-tooth'd unkindnesse, like a vulture here" (2.4.134–135), and "strooke me with her Tongue | Most Serpent-like, upon the very Heart" (160–161).

Shakespeare has thus developed a coherent series of metaphors to describe Goneril and Regan from Lear's viewpoint. This may seem like an old-fashioned piece of literary criticism, but we should remind ourselves that metaphors are more than rhetorical devices: they embody ethical judgments that define a human being. Earlier in the play Kent confirmed our instinctive feeling that Lear's anger toward Cordelia was all out of proportion, an impetuous but unjustified anger that made him first disown his daughter and then his most loyal servant. But as the action develops, the inhumanity of the two daughters and of their willing accomplice, Cornwall, becomes so apparent that the beast-like analogies turn out to be appropriate. Initially, Lear's anger at his daughters' ingratitude may have seemed extravagant or merely the anger of a disappointed father, "but the time gives it proof." In the scene of Gloucester's blinding, Shakespeare gives the victim the same feral terms to describe Regan and Goneril:

> *Glou.* Because I would not see thy cruell Nailes
> Plucke out his poore old eyes, nor thy fierce Sister,
> In his Annointed flesh, {rash}[30] boarish phangs,
> (H1v 13–15 3.7.56–58; TLN 2128–2130)

Having ensured that Gloucester would not see anything again, with his dying breath Cornwall orders "that eyelesse Villaine" to be turned out and the servant who has fatally wounded him to be thrown "Upon the dunghill' (3.7.95–97). Shakespeare shows the two remaining servants dealing with the aftermath of these fatalities. The Folio abridger cut this exchange:

> *Corn.* *Regan*, I bleed apace,
> Vntimely comes this hurt. Giue me your arme. *Exeunt.*
> [*Seruant.* Ile neuer care what wickednes I doe,
> [If this man come to good.
> [2 *Seruant.* If she liue long, & in the end meet the old course of death, women will all turne monsters.
> [1 *Ser.* Lets follow the old Earle, and get the bedlom
> [To lead him where he would, his madnes
> [Allows it selfe to any thing.
> [2 *Ser.* Goe thou, ile fetch some flaxe and whites of egges to apply to his bleeding face, now heauen helpe him. *Exit.*]
> (H2r17–27; 3.7.99–107; TLN 2175–2176)

By omitting these lines the King's Men abridger damaged Shakespeare's design in two respects, first its narrative function. As René Weis observed, "the servants' comments in Q are needed above all to explain the movement of the plot," for otherwise the reader or spectator is "given no indication at all of how and why he and the 'bedlam' . . . should meet in 4.1."[31] More seriously, the abridger weakened two important elements in the play's ethical structure as Shakespeare conceived it. After Lear and Gloucester, here is a third person whose moral outrage at the behavior of the evil daughters can only express itself in terms outside the realm of humanity: if Regan lives out her natural life unscathed by "The winged vengeance" that Gloucester hopes for, by that time "women will all turne monsters." (In Elizabethan moral and social attitudes women were not often considered to be agents of violence. "Unsex me here," Lady Macbeth appeals to the spirits, to destroy her essential nature. She suppresses it during the murder but it comes back to haunt her.) Further, the omission deprives the play of another instance of human charity responding to human destructiveness. The two servants find someone to lead Gloucester wherever he wants to go, and apply "flaxe and whites of egges to . . . his bleeding face," the treatment recommended by Renaissance physicians for eye injuries.[32] Omitting this scene unbalances the play's moral structure, for here is a humane reaction to evil, albeit only able to cure a wound.

Lear and Gloucester, unable to tell the difference between good and evil, undergo much suffering, mental and physical, and register profound changes in their attitude to life. Up to the point where he ceded power to Goneril and Regan, Lear had enjoyed a monarch's privilege in a feudal society, where his word was law. The concept of justice had never occurred to him. It is only when he is exposed to the fury of the elements that the existence of human evil and the need for a just society enter his consciousness:

Tremble thou Wretch,
That hast within thee undivulged Crimes
Vnwhipt of Iustice. Hide thee, thou Bloudy hand;
Thou Periur'd, and thou Simular of Vertue
That art Incestuous. Caytiffe, to peeces shake
That vnder couert, and conuenient seeming

Ha's practis'd on mans life. Close pent-vp guilts,
Riue your concealing Continents, and cry
These dreadfull Summoners grace. I am a man,
More sinn'd against, then sinning.
(3.2.49–60; TLN 1704–1713)

Shakespeare gives Lear a wide scope for indictment of crimes in general, including some pertinent to this play, yet adds the concluding sentence to show that Lear's egoistic concern for his own grievances blinds him to the suffering of others. That awareness begins a few moments later:

Lear. My wits begin to turne.
Come on my boy. How dost my boy? Art cold?
I am cold my selfe . . .
Poore Foole, and Knaue, I haue one part in my heart
That's sorry yet for thee. (3.2.68–72; TLN 1722–1728)

Across the next three scenes Shakespeare shows us Lear's divided concern. Uppermost is "the tempest in my mind" at his daughters' "Filiall ingratitude," with the desire for justice: "But I will punish home" (3.4.12–16). At the same time we see him beginning to realize the extent of human suffering, uttering a prayer for "houselesse pouertie" and all "Poore naked wretches," with the recognition "O I haue tane | Too little care of this" (3.4.26–33). The encounter with Poor Tom is a turning point, suspending compassion for others and driving him back into the causes of his own suffering:

Ha's his Daughters brought him to this passe? Couldst thou
saue nothing? Would'st thou giue them all? . . .
. . . .
. . . nothing could haue subdu'd Nature
To such a lownesse, but his vnkind Daughters.
Is it the fashion, that discarded Fathers,
Should haue thus little mercy on their flesh
(3.4.63–73; TLN 1844–1854)

Some editors, and actors, have attempted to give the last two lines a straightforward meaning by imagining Lear "sticking pins into his mortified arms."[33] But to me it suggests that Lear's wits have indeed turned, so much so that he inverts cause and effect: it is the daughters who have had "thus little mercy" on their "discarded Fathers." At all events, they again become the focus of his anger:

> Now all the plagues that in the pendulous ayre
> Hang fated o'er mens faults,light on thy Daughters.
> (3.4.67–68; TLN 1848–1849)

I have retraced these familiar stages in Lear's experience to bring out the care with which Shakespeare has created the association between his daughters' crimes and his wish for punishment. Lear's denunciation of "undivulged Crimes" and the "Caytiffe" who, "vnder couert, and conuenient seeming | Ha's practis'd on mans life" seemed general and undefined two scenes ago, but it becomes shockingly immediate as we register new information from the world outside, where unseen events run in parallel with those we see on stage. When Kent explains that Lear's "wits begin t'vnsettle," Gloucester replies: "Can'st thou blame him? | His Daughters seeke his death" (3.4.162–163; TLN 1941–1943). This notification of threatening developments elsewhere gives the audience and reader a new sense that Lear's obsession with his daughters' crime and punishment is fully justified. The culmination of Lear's insistent but powerless wish for retribution emerges in the most unlikely context of the hovel where he shelters with Poor Tom and the Fool. Each of the outcasts from society pursues his own preoccupations. Poor Tom is haunted by "*Frateretto*," the Fool poses a riddle, "whether a madmen be a Gentleman or a Yeoman" (3.6.7–10). Oblivious to both, demented Lear envisages a truly satisfying punishment:

> To haue a thousand with red burning spits
> Come hizzing in vpon 'em. (TLN 2013–2014)

Just at this point the theater abridger cut forty lines from the Quarto text:[34]

> [*Edg.* The foule fiend bites my backe,

[*Foole.* He's mad, that trusts in the tamenes of a Wolfe, a hor-
[ses health, a boyes loue, or a whores oath.
[*Lear.* It shalbe done, I wil arraigne them straight,
[Come sit thou here most learned Iustice,
[Thou sapient sir sit here, no you shee Foxes—
[*Edg.* Looke where he stands and glars, want'st thou eyes, at
[trial madam come ore the bourne *Bessy* to mee.
[*Foole.* Her boat hath a leake,and she must not speake,
[Why she dares not come,ouer to thee.
[*Edg.* The foule fiend haũts poore *Tom* in the voyce of a nigh-
[Hoppedance cries in *Toms* belly for two white herring, (tingale,
[Croke not blacke Angell, I haue no foode for thee.
[*Kent.* How doe you sir? stand you not so amazd, will you
lie downe and rest vpon the cushings?
[*Lear.* Ile see their triall first, bring in their euidence, thou
[robed man of Iustice take thy place, & thou his yokefellow of
[equity, bench by his side, you are ot'h commission, sit you too.
[*Ed.* Let vs deale justly sleepest or wakest thou iolly
[shepheard,
[Thy sheepe bee in the corne, And for one blast of thy minikin
[mouth, thy sheepe shall take no harme, Pur the cat is gray.
[*Lear.* Arraigne her first, tis *Gonoril*, I here take my oath
before this honorable assembly kickt the poore king her father.
[*Foole.* Come hither mistrisse, is your name *Gonorill.*
[*Lear.* She cannot deny it.
[*Fool.* Cry you mercy, I tooke you for a ioynt stoole.
[*Lear.* And heres another whose warpt lookes proclaime,
[What store her hart is made on, stop her there,
[Armes,armes, sword, fire, corruption in the place,
[False Iusticer why hast thou let her scape?]

(G3v29–G4r11; 3.6.17–57)

The theater abridger cut these lines from the most extraordinary scene in English drama up to this point (or perhaps since), in which Shakespeare follows out the characteristic thought patterns and language he has created for all three outcasts, together with Kent in his role as comforter. Theater audiences, who have to comprehend each character on his own terms, will realize with some surprise that, of the three, it is Lear who is making the most sense. We know, as he does not, that Goneril and Regan are planning his death, so that the trivial accusation of Goneril having "kickt the poore king her father" may stand as a marker for the much more sinister harm she intends.

The 1608 Quarto preserves the unity of this scene, with the imagined trial as Lear's only means of confronting and denouncing these "shee Foxes"—linking up with the earlier descriptions of Goneril and Regan as ferocious animals. The theater abridger most unfortunately omitted this crucial episode, in which Lear sets up his crazy trial and reveals the "reason in madnesse," as Edgar describes it, creating such an uncanny effect as he identifies the ongoing sources of his suffering. The Folio abridger stopped cutting here, but preserved the comments of Edgar and Kent. Shakespeare intended these to articulate our reactions to this painful scene, but in Jaggard's cut version they follow immediately upon Lear's initial wish for revenge:

> *Lear.* To have a thousand with red burning spits
> Come hizzing in vpon 'em.
> *Edg.* Blesse thy fiue wits.
> *Kent.* O pitty: Sir, where is the patience now
> That you so oft have boasted to retaine?
> *Edg.* My teares begin to take his part so much,
> They marre my counterfeiting.
> (3.6.15–16, 57–61; TLN 2013–2019)

The compassionate reactions of Edgar and Kent read strangely given the discrepancy between their intense sympathy and what Lear has—or rather, has not said. The bystanders' reactions seem "in excess of the facts," in no proportion to Lear's single utterance. The cut, whereby compassion exists without suffering, leaves a hole in this scene. And because the abridger omitted all reference to the imagined trial, those who only have access to the Folio text will be confused when Lear continues the arraignment:

Then let them Anatomize *Regan*: See what
breeds about her heart. Is there any cause in Nature that
make these hard-hearts (3.6.76–78; TLN 2033–2035)

In Lear's mouth "then" means "next," but in the absence of Goneril's "arraignment" it would be truly puzzling. Seventeenth-century readers of the Folio may have taken this apparently inconsequential comment to be an instance of a madman's incoherence, but Shakespeare's complete text, as preserved by the 1608 Quarto, shows that he achieved a far more difficult task: to show a substratum of coherence in Lear's anger at "filial ingratitude." We should be grateful to those eighteenth-century editors who took the logical step of restoring Shakespeare's original conception of this scene.

In reducing "iteration," as I have called it, the theater abridger damaged other parts of Shakespeare's careful design. Gloucester returns at the end of this scene and insists on urgency—"I haue oreheard a plot of death vpon him"—having arranged for a litter to carry Lear to Dover and to hoped-for safety. Shakespeare makes Kent, ever the faithful servant, object that moving Lear at this point will disturb his recovery.[35] Nonetheless, he agrees, asking the Fool to help:

Glou. Take vp, take vp,
And follow me, that will to some prouision
Giue thee quicke conduct.
[*Kent.* Oppressed nature sleepes,
[This rest might yet haue balmed thy broken sinewes,
[Which, if conuenience will not alow stand in hard cure,
[Come helpe to beare thy maister, thou must not stay behind.
Glou. Comc,come,away. *Exeunt.*
(G4v15–18; 3.6.97–101; TLN 2054–2056)

Cutting those lines robs us of this instance of Kent's deep care for Lear and of our perception that the Fool is also a carer and helper. The theater abridger further damaged Shakespeare's coherent balance between cruelty and compassion by cutting Edgar's soliloquy concluding this "arraignment" scene:

[*Edg.* When we our betters see bearing our woes:
[We scarcely thinke, our miseries, our foes.
[Who alone suffers, suffers most ith' mind,
[Leauing free things and happy showes behind,
[But then the mind much sufferance doth or'e scip,
[When griefe hath mates, and bearing fellowship:
[How light and portable my paine seemes now,
[When that which makes me bend, makes the King bow.
[He childed as I fathered,*Tom* away,
[Marke the high noyses and thy selfe bewray,
[When false opinion whose wrong thoughts defile thee,
[In thy just proofe repeals and reconciles thee,
[What will hap more to night,safe scape the King,
[Lurke, lurke.] G4v20–33; 3.6.102–115)

Shakespeare wrote this speech in rhyming couplets to underline its nature as a self-consolation, building on the well-known saying, *Solamen miseris socios habuisse doloris.*[36] Where some Victorian editors had dismissed this speech as an interpolation, Delius defended it by reference to the dramatist's interweaving of the two plots:

> [T]he poet lays great stress on the parallelism existing between the families of Lear and Gloucester, and takes this opportunity of again impressing it upon his audience. A mere interpolator would hardly have known of this peculiar tendency of the poet, or have carried it out so thoroughly, and in so pregnant a manner, as in the few but completely Shakespearian words—'he childed as I fathered'. For the same reason, it is more than improbable that Shakespeare should have cut out this passage, thereby thwarting his own purposes.[37]

Further, the soliloquy shows Edgar optimistically anticipating the time when he will be proved guiltless.

The theater abridger not only cut important passages showing altruistic help but he also made large and more damaging cuts in Shakespeare's presentation and denunciation of egoistic destructiveness, expressed in two encounters between Albany and Goneril. In the opening scene of the play Albany speaks only once, intervening with Cornwall, as Lear's anger against Kent threatens to issue out in violence: "Deere sir forbeare" (1.1.162). We see Albany briefly later in this act, in the scene where Goneril provokes Lear to towering rage and denunciation—"Degenerate Bastard, Ile not trouble thee" (1.4.252). Albany acts as peacemaker: "Pray Sir be patient," and declares himself "guiltlesse" and "ignorant | Of what hath moued you" (273–274; TLN 786–787). Since we have seen Goneril, in an earlier scene, ordering her steward to assume "a pose of weary negligence" towards Lear, we take Albany at his word, as the first signs appear of a rift in values between husband and wife: "I cannot be so partiall *Gonerill*, | To the great loue I beare you"—only for her to silence him: "Pray you content" (1.4.311–313; TLN 831–833). Albany mutters his doubts about Goneril's behavior (328), but she dismisses them in terms that serve to define her as much as him:

no, no, my Lord,
This milky gentlenesse, and course of yours
Though I condemne not, yet vnder pardon
You are much more at task for want of wisedome
Then prais'd for harmefull mildnesse.

(337–41; TLN 864–868)

The metaphor "milky gentlenesse" sounds contemptuous in Goneril's mouth, but it carries inalienable associations with nature and nurture, as in *Macbeth.* Her equally contemptuous term, "harmefull mildnesse," is in fact an oxymoron, a conjunction of opposites suggesting that, for Goneril, any "mildnesse" would damage the "wisdom" of self-enrichment. As Francis Bacon wrote in his essay on selfishness, "Wisdom for a man's self is, in many branches thereof, a depraved thing. It is the wisdom or rats, that will be sure to leave a house somewhat before it fall. It is the wisdom of the fox, that thrusts out the badger, who digged and made room for him. It is the wisdom of crocodiles, that shed tears when they would devour."[38]

Shakespeare fully exposes us to the inhumanity of Cornwall and Regan, but he keeps Albany off stage for thirteen scenes (1.5–4.2), totaling 1,348 lines, more than a third of the play. When we hear of him next it is through Goneril, welcoming Edmund to her palace and expressing surprise that "our mild husband | Not met vs on the way." Her Steward describes him as "neuer man so chang'd," who merely smiled at hearing of "the Army that was Landed" (4.2.1–6; TLN 2268–2272). But Oswald's account of Albany's reaction to the next piece of news marks a turning point in the play:

Of Gloster's Treachery,
And of the loyall Seruice of his Sonne
When I inform'd him, then he call'd me Sot,
And told me that I had turn'd the wrong side out (6–9)

Goneril responds only to the first part of Oswald's report, dismissing her husband as a coward: "It is the Cowish terror of his spirit | That dares not vndertake" (12–13). But when Albany appears, he shows that he has finally understood his wife's evil, and he expresses his newfound disgust. Unfortunately, the theater abridger cut the lines that follow, which therefore do not appear in the Folio text:

Oh *Gonerill*,
You are not worth the dust which the rude winde
Blowes in your face. [I feare your disposition
[That nature which contemnes {its}[39] origin
[Cannot be bordered certaine in it selfe,
[She that her selfe will sliuer and disbranch
[From her materiall sap, perforce must wither,
[And come to deadly vse.
[*Gon.* No more, the text is foolish.
[*Alb.* Wisedome and goodnes,to the vild seeme vild,
[Filths sauor but themselues, what haue you done?
[Tigers, not daughters, what haue you perform'd?
[A father, and a gracious aged man
[Whose reuerence even the head-lugd beare would lick.
[Most barbarous, most degenerate, haue you madded,
[Could my good brother suffer you to doe it?

[A man, a Prince, by him so benifited.
[If that the heauens doe not their visible spirits (come
[Send quickly downe to tame these[40] vild offences, it will
[Humanity must perforce pray on it self like monsters of
(the deepe]
(H3v27–H4r7; 4.2.29–50)

Evidently wishing to move forward the play's action at this point, the theater bookkeeper also cut seven lines from Goneril's contemptuous response, beginning "Milkeliuer'd man." The cut includes her attempt to bring Albany's attention back to the army that has landed: "Wher's thy drum?*France* spreds his banners in out noyseles land" (50–59). The gap that opens up between Albany and Goneril is an important sign that human goodness has not entirely vanished, and it redefines the play's moral balance. The theater bookkeeper, however, went on cutting:

Gon. Oh vaine foole.
[*Alb.* Thou changed, and selfe-couerd thing for shame
[Be-monster not thy feature, wer't my fitnes
[To let these hands obay my bloud,
[They are apt enough to dislecate and teare
[Thy flesh and bones, how ere thou art a fiend,
[A womans shape doth shield thee.
[*Gon.* Marry your manhood mew (H4r 20–26; 4.2.61–68)

To Albany, who told Oswald that he had "turn'd the wrong side out," Goneril seems "changed and self-couered," the past participles conveying his sense that she has debased and occluded her own nature as a human being. He reinforces his verdict by the reflexive construction, "Be-monster not thy feature," where the noun "monster," twice used in connection with Lear's daughters, is converted into a verb.[41] To the audience and reader, however, who are fully aware of Goneril's true nature, she has not changed at all.

This crucial exchange establishes Albany as a moral authority, the only character in the play able to make ethical judgments on human depravity. Since he has been outside the action for so long he brings a fresh perspective, which Shakespeare uses to define the damage that Goneril and Regan have done to themselves. They have destroyed their own nature as human beings, as if a tree branch could forcibly separate itself from the main stem and roots, without whose sustaining "sap" it will not only die but also become an instrument of death. Readers and theatergoers who had to rely on the Folio version would miss, in Albany's severely abridged speech, passages of central importance in the moral structure of *King Lear* as Shakespeare designed it, completing his polarization of good and evil, with Goneril, Regan, and Edmund as the three remaining destructive egoists and Albany as their chief opponent. Unfortunately, Shakespeare's postponement of Albany's reentry into the play coincided with the theater bookkeeper's wish to shorten performance time.

In addition to cutting thirty-five lines in this scene (4.2), the playhouse abridger then omitted the whole of 4.3, another drastic cut that upsets the moral and emotional balance of the play. This scene consists of a dialogue between Kent and a Gentleman having three focal points. First, as we have seen, it records the sudden return of the French king to his country. Second, with a rather simple "feed" question from Kent, Shakespeare can depict the mixed emotions of Cordelia as she received news of her sisters' brutal treatment of their father:[42]

[*Kent.* Did your letters pierce the queene to any demonstration
[of griefe.
[*Gent.* I sir she tooke them, read them in my presence,
[And now and then an ample teare trild downe
[Her delicate cheeke, it seemed she was a queene over her
passion,
Who most rebell-like, sought to be King ore her.
[*Kent.* O then it moued her.
[*Gent.* Not to a rage, patience and sorow strove,
[Who should expresse her goodliest you haue seene,
[Sunshine and raine at once, her smiles and teares,
[Were like a better way those happie smilets,
[That playd on her ripe lip seemd not to know,

[What guests were in her eyes which parted thence,
[As pearles from diamonds dropt in briefe,
[Sorow would be a raritie most beloued,
[If all could so become it.] (H4v27–I1r1–3; 4.3.9–24)

The Gentleman's rather affected description of the conflict between "patience and sorrow" in Cordelia's reaction is in the same genre—"a reporter's account of intense emotions he has witnessed offstage," as we might call it—that we find in *The Winter's Tale* just before the most important reunion, that between Leontes and Hermione.[43] Not wanting to dilute the audience's experience of that great moment, Shakespeare precedes it with a report of the lesser but also highly emotional reunions of Leontes with Polixenes, then with Perdita, and finally describes the mixture of emotions in the bystander Paulina. In the same way, Shakespeare prepares us for the climactic reunion between Lear and Cordelia with this report, which also serves to define the reasons for Cordelia's return. The scene serves above all to distance her from the politics of invasion: she is there out of love and filial duty.

Kent's next "feed" question suddenly brings Cordelia closer to us:

[*Kent.* Made she no verball question
[*Gent.* Faith once or twice she heau'd the name of father,
[Pantingly forth as if it prest her heart,
[Cried sisters, sisters, shame of Ladies sisters:
[*Kent*, father, sisters, what ith storme, ith night,
[Let pitie not be beleeft there she shooke,
[The holy water from her heauenly eyes,
[And clamour moystened her, then away she started,
[To deale with griefe alone.] (I1r4–12; 4.3.25–33)

This is a wonderfully imagined representation of Cordelia's moment-by-moment response as she learns of Lear's humiliations, struggling to give her feelings words ("heav'd . . . | Pantingly forth"). As she registers what Goneril and Regan have done to Lear, with only Kent to help him, her coherence breaks down into a series of unconnected phrases: "Cried sisters, sisters, shame of Ladies sisters. | *Kent*, father, sisters." Here the basic kinship terms of the family echo accusingly as she registers shock at her sisters' behavior, but in terms typifying her reserve when it comes to revealing her feelings—"shame of Ladies"—before withdrawing, to express her grief in private.[44] This passage is important to the play's emotional and moral design, showing both Cordelia's deep love for her father and her difficulty in articulating it. When Lear has been brought to safety and is recovering from his mental chaos, helped (in the Quarto) by the healing power of music, Cordelia expresses her realization of what her father must have suffered, exposed to the storm:

> *Cor.* Was this a face
> To be oppos'd against the iarring windes?
> [To stand against the deepe dread bolted thunder,
> [In the most terrible and nimble stroke
> [Of quicke crosse lightning to watch poore *Perdu*,
> [With this thin helme]
> (K2r13–18; 4.7.30–35; TLN 2782–2783)

By cutting four lines the theater abridger weakened our recognition of her filial love. Eloquent while her father is asleep (this is almost her longest speech in the play), when he awakes, recognizes her, and begs forgiveness, she can only echo the simplest phrases, "And so I am: I am"; "No cause, no cause" (4.7.69, 74; TLN 2826, 2833).

To return to 4.3, the final element lost when the theater abridger omitted this scene is the most important "notification" of an off-stage event in the whole play. In his down-to-earth manner Kent gives us this account of a crucial change in Lear's moral and emotional state:

> [*Kent.* Well sir, the poore distressed *Lear*'s ith towne,
> [Who some time in his better tune remembers,
> [What we are come about, and by no meanes will yeeld to see his (daughter.
> [*Gent.* Why good sir?
> [*Kent.* A soueraigne shame so elbows him his own vnkindnes,

[That stript her from his benediction turnd her,
[To forraine casualties gaue her deare rights,
[To his dog-harted daughters, these things sting
[His mind so venomously that burning shame detaines him
[from *Cordelia.*
[*Gent.* Alack poore Gentleman.]

(I1r18–27; 4.3.38–47)

This passage links up with those earlier moments where Lear realizes that he has misjudged and mistreated Cordelia. His first words about her, following his angry disowning, were "I lou'd her most, and thought to set my rest | On her kind nursery" (1.1.122–123). After his first rebuff by Goneril, Lear had exclaimed:

O most small fault,
How vgly did'st thou in *Cordelia* shew?
Which like an Engine, wrencht my frame of Nature
From the fixt place: drew from my heart all loue,
And added to the gall. O *Lear*, *Lear*, *Lear*!
Beate at this gate that let thy Folly in,
And thy deere Iudgement out. (1.4.266–272: TLN 779–785)

In the scene following, amidst a series of quips and riddles from the Fool, Lear mutters to himself: "I did her wrong" (1.5.24). From this point on Shakespeare involves Lear fully in the cruelties that Goneril and Regan put upon him, so that every mention of his "daughters" refers to them alone. It is not until 4.3, fourteen scenes and 1,450 lines later, that we hear of Lear referring to Cordelia again.

Among the many changes to Lear's personality brought about by his experience outside society is the new emotion of shame. In moral philosophy, to feel shame is to recognize that one has done wrong, and it shows the presence of some relic of virtue. A popular handbook of Renaissance moral philosophy defined shame as "the keeper of all vertues," especially temperance and justice. Although it "seemeth to be a hurtful passion in the soule," the author wrote, it is a sign of some "good nature. Therefore shamefastnes is to be nourished and much made of. For so long as it remaineth in any mans spirite, there is good hope to be conceived of him. . . . A fault is lessened through shame, as it is made greater by contention."[45]

In the polarized world of this play, the fact that Lear can feel shame puts him at the opposite pole to that occupied by Goneril, Regan, and Edmund. As our moralist put it,

> He that is troubled to the quicke through a sharpe reprehension for the reformation of his manners, and yet is nothing restrayned thereby, nor full of sweate and blushing for shame, which causeth heate to ascend into the face of every one well borne, but remaineth inflexible and unmooveable, smiling, and jesting thereat, such a one I say, giveth a great argument of a very blockish and senceles nature, which is ashamed of nothing, by reason of his long custome and confirmation in doing evill.

In contrast to shameless people—such as Cornwall, Goneril, Regan, and Edmund, who have "a very blockish and senceles nature," hardened in evil—when a good person "is ashamed that he hath offended, we are to hope well of his amendment."[46] Lear is evidently experiencing the emotions that La Primaudaye describes: "troubled to the quicke," feeling the "heate" that ascends "into the face of every one well borne" at the recognition of his faults: "these things sting his mind | So venomously that burning shame detained him from Cordelia." Lear's shame is a sign that he is recovering both his sanity and his moral sense, even though the immediate effect of it, as we see from Kent's report, is to render him more distraught. When father and daughter are reunited, it will be on a new basis, where Lear's remorse and admission of wrongdoing will lead to Cordelia's forgiveness. To omit this essential prelude to their reconciliation is to leave a hole in the ethical and emotional design that Shakespeare so carefully created.

In the play's later stages the theater abridger made several shorter cuts, none as damaging as those in the scenes of Lear's "trial," Albany's denunciation of Goneril, or the report of Cordelia's grief and Lear's shame. It was probably not to speed up the action that the theater abridger shortened this exchange between Regan and Edmund:

Reg. Do you not loue my Sister?
Bast. In honour'd Loue
Reg. But have you never found my Brothers way,
To the fore-fended place?
[*Bast.* That thought abuses you.
[*Reg.* I am doubtfull that you haue beene coniunct and bosom'd with hir, as far as we call hirs.]
Bast. No by mine honour Madam.
(K3r12–17; 5.1.19–14; TLN 2856–2861)

Perhaps the Folio editor was disturbed by this glimpse of a woman's transgressive sexuality. If so, and to even things out, he also cut Goneril's disclosure of her all-consuming desire for Edmund:

Enter with Drum and Colours, Albany, Gonerill, Soldiers.
[*Gon.* I had rather loose the battaile, then that sister should loosen him and mee.]
Alb. Our very louing Sister, well be-met:
(K3r21–22; 5.1.18–20; TLN 2865)

In the to and fro of the final battle sequence the abridger cut a passage in which Shakespeare further defines Albany as a good man and a worthy future ruler. Justifying his decision to take up arms in a just cause, he makes a *profession de foi* both to ethical standards ("honest") and to defending his country:

Alb. Sir, this I heard, the King is come to his Daughter
With others, whom the rigour of our State
Forc'd to cry out. [where I could not be honest
[I neuer yet was valiant, for this busines
[It touches vs, as *France* inuades our land
[Not bolds the King, with others whome I feare,
[Most iust and heauy causes make oppose.
[*Bast.* Sir you speake nobly.]
Reg. Why is this reasond?
(K3r24–31; 5.1.21–28; TLN 2866–2869)

Having cut Albany's statement of principle, the abridger left Regan's question without an apparent cause.[47] It is impossible to believe that a dramatist of Shakespeare's experience would make such crude cuts to a play on which he had expended so much care and imaginative energy.

The King's Men employee also omitted Edmund's hypocritical explanation of why he has sent Lear and Cordelia to prison, communicated in devious, evasive language, matching the insincerity of Goneril and Regan:

> *Bast.* With him I sent the Queen:
> My reason all the same, and they are ready
> Tomorrow, or at further space, t'appeare
> Where you shall hold your session.
> [at this time, wee sweat and bleed,
> [The friend hath lost his friend and the best quarrels
> [In the heat are curst, by those that feele their sharpnes,
> [The question of *Cordelia* and her father
> [Requires a fitter place.]
> *Alb.* Sir, by your patience,
> I hold you but a subject of this Warre,
> Not as a Brother. (K4v25–34; 5.3.51–59; TLN 2994–3000)

That omission leaves Albany, in the Folio text, rebuking Edmund for apparent insubordinate behavior that we have not witnessed. Earlier, we saw Edmund glorying in his power to have whichever sister he pleases and planning to use the confusion of war to frustrate "the mercie" that Albany "intends to *Lear* and to *Cordelia*" (5.1.65–69). A smaller cut, but one that will be regretted by readers and theatergoers who have recognized in *King Lear* an unsystematic but nevertheless profound exploration of human nature, occurs when Edmund suborns a Captain to kill his defenseless prisoners:

> *Cap.* Ile do't my Lord.
> *Bast.* About it,and write happy, when th'hast done,
> Marke I say instantly, and carry it so

As I haue set it downe.
[*Cap.* I cannot draw a cart, nor eate dride oats,
[If it bee mans worke ile do't.] *Exit Captaine.*
(K4v8–13; 5.3.30–39; TLN 2978–2981)

That sardonic reply is the last of several instances in the play of Shakespeare dwelling on the extremes of human nature, the permeable fault-line that he has exposed between man and beast. But this willing servant of evil does not live to "write happy," for Lear kills him.

A more substantial omission was Edgar's narrative to Albany of two momentous events that have occurred beyond our ken. The Folio retains his account of how he had comforted the blinded Gloucester and finally revealed his true identity, at which his father's heart had "Burst smilingly" (5.3.180–200; TLN 3144–3162). But the theater bookkeeper omitted Edgar's description of his reunion with Kent, probably to shorten the performance time:

Alb. If there be more, more wofull, hold it in,
For I am almost ready to dissolue,
Hearing of this.
[*Edg.* This would have seemd a periode to such
[As loue not sorow, but another to amplifie too much,
[Would make much more, and top extreamitie
[Whil'st I was big in clamor, came there in a man,
[Who hauing seene me in my worst estate,
[Shund my abhord society, but then finding
[Who twas that so indur'd with his strong armes
[He fastened on my necke and bellowed out,
[As hee'd burst heauen,threw {him}[48] on my father,
[Told the most pitious tale of *Lear* and him,
[That ever eare receiued, which in recounting
[His griefe grew puissant and the strings of life,
[Began to cracke: twice then the trumpets sounded
[And there I left him traunst.
[*Alb.* But who was this.
[*Edg.* *Kent* sir, the banisht *Kent*, who in disguise,

[Followed his enemie king and did him seruice
[Improper for a slaue.]

(L2v28–L3r7; 5.3.203–222; TLN 3166–3168)

When he wrote those lines Shakespeare was not concerned with the contingencies of playing time in an open-air theater. Rather, he was following out the moral imperatives of Kent's code of friendship and service, even to a king who had earlier declared himself his "enemie." In the play's closing moments Kent's great loyalty to Lear goes unrecognized by his master, but we have seen it and know what it means.

Evaluating the theater abridger's work, we can agree that the numerical majority of his cuts do not substantially damage either our understanding of individual characters or the play's overall design. However, his severe abridgements of Lear's demented "arraignment"; his omission of the servants' tending blinded Gloucester; of Albany's denunciation of Goneril and Regan's inhuman behavior; and, most damaging of all, the complete loss of 4.3, depicting Cordelia's grief for her father's sufferings and Lear's remorse at having disowned her—cuts totaling 140 lines—leave major gaps in the play's moral and emotional structure. Other, far less significant scenes were left untouched, for reasons that we can only guess at. For instance, the Folio text preserves in full Kent's taunting of Oswald, briefly at first, when the steward insults Lear (1.4.86–92), but then at great length when he meets him again at Gloucester's house. Kent begins with a volley of insults and physical violence, and follows them with a lengthy denunciation of "such smiling rogues as these," corrupt servants who "turn every gale and vary of their masters" (2.2.1–80). He caps this aggression with a resolute defiance of Cornwall—"I serue the King, on whose imployments I was sent to you" (128–129). Clearly, Shakespeare needed adequate provocation to account for Kent being put in the stocks, but this scene of 173 lines could easily have been shortened without any great loss. Many readers and theatergoers would gladly exchange much of this business for the four scenes so damagingly cut. At this point in time one can only guess at the theatrical contingencies that led to these relative priorities: perhaps the Kent-Oswald scene was a crowd pleaser, or perhaps the actor playing Albany at this period was unconvincing, or perhaps the theater abridger wanted to hurry the play's action on to its climaxes. Whatever the cause, the result severely damaged the play as Shakespeare had constructed it.

An early surviving text of Quintilian's great *Institutio Oratoria* is known to classical scholars as a "*mutilus*," lacking large parts of the text.[49] That text dates from the ninth century and has suffered the many depredations of time. The Folio text of *King Lear* falls in the same category, but the King's Men mutilated a perfectly sound copy of the play for their own theatrical purposes. At no point can Shakespeare be considered as the agent who destroyed his own design.

PART 3

The One *King Lear*

8

The "Two Versions" Revisited

THE TWO VERSIONS theory was launched by Michael Warren in 1968,[1] elaborated in 1980 by Steven Urkowitz in a monograph,[2] and in 1983 reached its apotheosis as a specially commissioned volume edited by Gary Taylor and Michael Warren, with an introduction by Stanley Wells, called *The Division of the Kingdoms*.[3] This group makes the following claims:

1. That Shakespeare revised the Folio text of *King Lear*, making it a distinctly different play from the Quarto.
2. That Shakespeare made cuts in order to speed up the action and make it more "theatrical."
3. That Shakespeare omitted passages from the Quarto that were "redundant" or "disposable" in his eyes.
4. That Shakespeare omitted passages from the Quarto in order to change the characterization of Edgar and Albany.
5. That Shakespeare's responsibility for the Folio cuts can be proved on textual grounds.

Readers who have followed the argument of this book, and the evidence presented, may feel tempted to skip this chapter, bearing in mind that Shakespeare died in 1616 and could have had no part in either the Second Quarto (1619) or the Folio (1623). But that would be to miss a case study of the extremes of ingenuity that critics can be forced into when lacking any material evidence. Readers would also miss the cogent refutations of the revisionist theory made by a number of independent scholars, including William Carroll,[4] Robert Clare,[5] Philip Edwards,[6] William Elton,[7] Gwynne Blakemore Evans,[8] Andrew Gurr,[9] Ernst Honigmann,[10] Frank Kermode,[11] Richard Knowles,[12] Ann Meyer,[13] Kenneth Muir,[14] Sidney Thomas,[15] Marion Trousdale,[16] Brian Vickers[17] and Paul Werstine.[18] The significance of my term "independent scholars" will become clear in the course of this discussion as I deal with the revisionist beliefs in sequence.

1. That Shakespeare Revised the Folio Text of *King Lear*, Making It a Distinctly Different Play from the Quarto

Michael Warren argued that "Q and F *King Lear* are sufficiently dissimilar that they . . . should be treated as two versions of a single play."[19] Steven Urkowitz claimed that the Folio text "represents a careful and dramatically sensitive revision of the Quarto, and that the revision could have been made by no one other than Shakespeare himself."[20] In his preface to the revisionists' manifesto Gary Taylor announced that its contributors had been chosen, and its essays solicited, in order to consider "the hypothesis that both texts represent independent versions" of the play, each having "an independent integrity."[21] Stanley Wells spoke for them all in asserting that there are "two versions of the play, each consciously and distinctly fashioned."[22]

The relevant response to these claims is that the two texts have in fact suffered "coincidentally independent omissions," in the words of Stanley Wells.[23] I have argued, I hope persuasively, that the printer omitted the 102 lines found in the Folio, while the theater company omitted the 285 lines found in the Folio. The cuts were made on different occasions, for different purposes, but, remarkably enough, the deficiencies in each text can be supplied by the other, as if they had formed a unity at the beginning. There is, nonetheless, a prior consideration: what is the truth of Warren's claim that the two texts "are sufficiently dissimilar" to be "treated as two versions"? How much is "sufficient"? MacDonald Jackson, a member of the Two Versions group, mentioned in passing that there are "2,825 lines of *Lear* common to Q and F."[24] It is difficult to see how two versions of a text sharing 90 percent of the same lines could be described as "different." That might be conceivable if they contained both additions and excisions, with material being shifted around. But Richard Knowles pointed out that, if the Folio *Lear* is "a second authorial revision of the play," as the Two Versions theory claims,

> it is remarkable for its limited means of revision. Except for cutting, which could be theatrical rather than authorial, the major substantive changes in F are usually additions of a line or more to existing Q speeches, generally designed to expand or clarify motive or meaning, and hundreds of small verbal changes; most of these changes are explainable as editorial, scribal, or compositorial error, correction, or sophistication, and the vast majority of them make no practical difference. There are in Folio *Lear* no new scenes, characters, or episodes; no rearrangements of plot or scenes or speeches; no omissions or renaming of named characters; no new speeches to introduce new themes or different motives. The few reassignments of speeches have seemed to editors to be in most cases either errors or the correction of errors. Though revisionist critics have made the most of existing differences between the two texts, the fact is that, except for cuts and local additions of lines and an occasionally significant verbal substitution, the speeches and actions of the characters remain on the whole unchanged. Most remarkably, virtually no speech of any length seems to have been either wholly reworked or replaced by a different one.[25]

The Two Versions theorists have ignored these fundamental objections, as they have ignored all substantive criticisms of their claims. If Shakespeare really had revised this play it is hardly conceivable that he would have been content to do so merely by making cuts. In the two undisputed revisions that I discussed in Chapter 2, those to *Romeo and Juliet* and *A Midsummer Night's Dream*, he added new material. The "right happy and copious industry" that John Webster attributed to him would surely have invented anew.[26]

The unavoidable, and so far unanswered objection to the Two Versions theory concerns the impossibility of knowing who was responsible for the Folio omissions. As Richard Knowles memorably put it, "Scholars have often imagined that they can discern a genuine Shakespearean line, but how does one recognize a genuine Shakespearean cut? Only Shakespeare can have written some lines, we believe, but anyone can delete any line in any canon."[27] One obvious candidate for the deletions is Edward Knight, bookkeeper of the King's Men, as some scholars have suggested.[28] Proponents of the Two Versions theory, however, rejected out of hand the possibility that the theater company made the cuts, not Shakespeare. Wells led the way by dismissing any idea that the passages omitted from the Quarto text were "forced upon the author by vulgar theatrical exigencies—length, censorship, theatrical practicality."[29] The pejorative term "vulgar" there is expected to do a lot of work in place of an argument. Wells surely knows that theatrical exigencies affect every production in planning and often in performance. Indeed, he had earlier claimed "that, to a considerable degree, the Folio represents actual theatrical practice."[30] It is hard to see how the Folio can represent "actual theatrical practice" in one context, but not in another: here Wells the advocate overcame Wells the scholar. The same position was expressed with more vehemence by Gary Taylor. At one point Taylor conceded the existence of "several unanswered questions about the authority of whole categories of Folio variants. The Folio text may contain actors' interpolations, theatrical alterations made for practical reasons, errors and sophistications accumulated during the course of its transmission."[31] But within a few pages he had established to his own satisfaction that it is "most unlikely" that either "theatrical interpolation" or "unauthorized theatrical alterations . . . contaminated the Folio text," and he energetically denied that the Folio omissions were, as he put it, "dictated by hack-theatrical consideration," or to satisfy "vulgar theatricalism," or made "for vulgarly theatrical motives," or "prompted by 'illegitimate' theatrical considerations."[32] If all such arguments were indeed "demonstrably implausible," based on "a pyramid of unsubstantiated and improbable speculations," one wonders why Taylor should expend so much energy refuting them, without even thinking it necessary to confront the arguments for theatrical cutting made by previous scholars.

To construct their theory, the revisionists had to hermetically isolate the Folio text from contact with any other hand than Shakespeare's over a period of several years. As Knowles observed in a later critique,

> The question is not whether there was revision—of course there was—but who did it, and when, and why. If some or all of the F changes (excluding the corrections of obvious errors) were made by various members of Shakespeare's company, or by one or more hired revisers, or by a censor, or by scribes and compositors, at one or more times between the rough-draft version (ca. 1605–6) in Q and the prompt-book version printed in the 1623 Folio a decade after Shakespeare had retired from the theater, then such variants [cannot be authorial].

The "bi-textual critics," as Knowles christened them, claim that the promptbook version lying behind the Folio was Shakespeare's considered revision. Knowles responded that "this is just bluffing or wishful thinking: we do not know for a certainty even when the changes were made, and if they were made in the decade between his retirement and the publication of F, or in the seven years after his death, then they were not even made with his knowledge let alone his consent or blessing."[33] These objections, too remain unanswered.

2. That Shakespeare Made Cuts in Order to Speed up the Action and Make It More "Theatrical"

In effect, the Two Versions theorists found themselves in the unenviable position of having to endorse cuts that the King's Men had made out of theatrical expediency. To do so they had to find literary-critical arguments (there being no textual evidence) to legitimize the theater company's omissions. In canonizing the Folio text as Shakespeare's final conception of *King Lear*, the revisionists tried to justify many of its choices on a superficial argument, the dramatist's supposed desire to "speed up the play." Michael Warren praised the Folio omission of one section, since "the play is shortened and speeded by the loss from 3.6 and the opening of 4.1 of about 54 lines (three minutes of playing time at least)."[34] This would be a trivial reduction of the performance length in comparison to the value of the material omitted. On the Folio's omission of Edgar's report to Albany of his cathartic meeting with Kent (5.3.205–222), Warren commented, "The removal of this speech . . . speeds the last act by the elimination of material of no immediate importance to the plot."[35] This is to use a very narrow concept of plot as a mere series of "events," dismissing other essential elements in drama and downgrading passages where, as Delius put it, "nothing is done, but something only talked of."

Discussing the quarrel between Albany and Goneril (4.2.29–70), Urkowitz noted, "Forty lines in the Quarto are reduced to only twelve in the Folio," an omission that, he claimed "increases the excitement," resulting in a "vigorous and theatrical" scene: "It is fierce and quick."[36] In an essay on the war in *King Lear*, admired by Two Versions theorists but subjected to devastating criticism by independent scholars, Gary Taylor attributed an "apparent motive" to the Folio, and hence Shakespeare, namely "[t]o strengthen the structure of Act 4, in the inevitable anticlimax which follows Gloucester's blinding. The Folio has done this by cutting superfluities (4.3, much of 4.2, the ending of 4.7) and strengthening the narrative line, largely by accelerating and clarifying the movement toward war."[37] I do not recognize any "anticlimax" after Gloucester's blinding: rather, audiences and readers of the Quarto text are in a state of shock, having been unprepared for the sadistic cruelty of Cornwall and Regan, stunned by two sudden deaths, and partly relieved at the compassion shown toward the blinded Gloucester by Cornwall's remaining servants (3.7.99–107; Folio omits).

Taylor's essay shows that the revisionist endorsement of the Folio has the inevitable consequence of disvaluing the Quarto. By splitting *King Lear* into two supposedly separate and incompatible entities the revisionists relied on the adversarial technique of the Greek and Roman courtrooms, epideictic rhetoric, with its opposed poles of praise and blame, *laudatio* and *vituperatio*.[38] Taylor claims that the Folio, "by cutting superfluities,"—omitting passages ending 3.6 and 3.7, and the whole of 4.3—"strongly establishes the narrative momentum, and helps sustain the play through the long, leisurely scenes at Dover."[39] What are these "long, leisurely scenes"? Presumably the whole of Act 5, which older editors set in "[t]he British camp near Dover," with the sudden emergence, and implosion, of the destructive love triangle of Goneril, Regan, and Edmund; Edgar's reappearance *in propria persona;* the challenge to Edmund; the capture and imprisonment of Lear and Cordelia; Edmund's plot to have them secretly murdered; the duel and Edgar's victory . . . and so on, with a further 150 lines of climactic action to come. These scenes are neither long nor leisurely, but the revisionist agenda of elevating the Folio and disparaging the Quarto did not permit these theorists to give accurate accounts of the play. In Taylor's opinion, what the Folio sacrifices is for the most part eminently

> dispensable. The narrative prelude to Cordelia's return (4.3) is hardly necessary; it is much more immediately satisfying to hear and see Cordelia than to be told about her. Elsewhere, the Folio consistently omits backward-looking reflection on what has happened, so as to throw the emphasis forward on to what will happen. We surely no longer need to be told, by Edgar or the two servants or Albany or Cordelia, what to think of the two sisters' treatment of Lear and Gloucester. Albany need not go on at such length in 4.2 in order to "motivate" his eventual repudiation of his wife in 5.3; so horrendous are the events of acts 2 and 3 that we will easily infer that Albany's feelings are similar to our own. If Albany speaks so vehemently and at such length as he does in the Quarto, we may rightly object that his delay in changing sides becomes inexplicable.[40]

A critic who can make this casual evisceration of Shakespeare's carefully constructed dramatic design in *King Lear*, denigrating long sequences as disposable superfluities, has lost contact with the play and should seek some other occupation. Taylor was blind to the significance of Shakespeare's deliberate articulation of moral disgust in these two scenes, expressed first by Cornwall's servants and then by Albany in denouncing the crimes of Regan, Cornwall, and Goneril. Taylor, like other revisionists, had a regettably narrow conception of "plot." Thus Albany's denunciation of Regan could only be intended "to 'motivate' his eventual repudiation" of her (one can only wonder what those scare quotes are meant to express), and could have no significance in itself. Along with other Polonius-like revisionists, Taylor complained about the number of lines in the Quarto text that Shakespeare devoted to these crucial scenes: "Albany need not go on at such length"; "Albany speaks . . . at such length"; the question of who leads the French army is "a matter discussed at curious length [in 4.3], which the Folio omits."[41] Like the King's Men abridger, the Two Versions theorists evidently had a short attention span.

The revisionists' concern with "dramatic momentum" left them unable to cope with moral issues fundamental to this play. Confronted with the sequel to Gloucester's blinding, the horror expressed by the servants at the inhumanity of Cornwall and Regan, and their compassion for the victim, Urkowitz summarized the ending of 3.7 in these terms: "A dramatic coda, including an exchange of moral sentiments and a plan to aid Gloucester, appears in the Quarto version of this scene."[42] This comment empties the scene of any human or moral significance. To reduce it to "an exchange of moral sentiments" echoes modern press releases ("a full and frank exchange of views") and reveals a disturbing lack of empathy. As for the scene between Albany and Goneril (4.2), ruthlessly shortened in the Folio, Shakespeare used it to mark Albany's belated recognition of the inhumanity that characterizes Cornwall, Goneril, Regan, and Edmund:

> If that the heauens doe not their visible spirits
> Send quickly downe to tame these vild offences, it will come
> Humanity must perforce pray on itself like monsters of the
> deepe. (H4r5–7; 4.2.47–49)

Urkowitz's account of their confrontation reads like a bad plot synopsis: "The duke and duchess have been exchanging abusive remarks about one another's general human worth"—taking up a neutral position, as if Albany and Goneril were of equal moral stature, engaged in a domestic quarrel over which an observer should remain neutral.[43] It is because of his profound sense of moral outrage that, as the steward reports, Albany—"neuer man so chang'd"—dismissed the wider political situation:

> I told him of the Army that was Landed:
> He smil'd at it. I told him you were comming,
> His answer was, the worse. Of Glosters Treachery,
> And of the loyall Seruice of his Sonne
> When I inform'd him, then he call'd me Sot,
> And told me I had turn'd the wrong side out
> (4.2.4–9; TLN 2270–2276).

Despite Taylor's objection that "his delay in changing sides becomes incredible," Albany does not change sides politically. He is the sole surviving nobleman and de facto leader of the English army against a foreign invasion: to "change sides" would be to ally himself with the French. He changes sides morally, putting himself in opposition to Goneril, Regan, Edmund, and their followers, all who have "turn'd the wrong side out." That is the whole point of this scene.

The dubious element in the revisionists' case is the supposed advantage of "accelerating" the action of *King Lear.* Several independent scholars have criticized their notion of theatricality. William Carroll commented that "[t]he language of speed" dominates their praise of the Folio cuts as producing a " 'narrative excitement' . . . which apparently did not exist in Q," but objected:

> To say that a deletion leads to a faster playing time of the surviving material is merely a tautology. How could it not? *Every* omission necessarily results in streamlining and acceleration; what is not effectively shown is why this acceleration and streamlining are really virtues. Indeed, the very metaphors used by these scholars—positives like 'streamline' and 'accelerate' rather than, for example, 'abort' or 'truncate'—beg the question of the argument.

The revisionists' praise of the Folio for its greater "speed," Carroll concluded, diminished the whole nature of drama: "What all these assertions about 'narrative' or 'dramatic' momentum, of 'more urgent and rapid' dramaturgy, have in common is an implicit poetics of drama which exalts simplicity of structure and speed of performance over complexity and difficulty, an assumption which I doubt can be proven in relation to the greatest Elizabethan and Jacobean drama."[44] As Frank Kermode once observed, the scene where mad Lear meets blind Gloucester, "although it is the boldest effort of imagination in Shakespeare, has no *narrative* value."[45] If speed had been their main goal the King's Men might well have omitted that scene, together with most of those involving the Fool and Poor Tom.

William Carroll's commentary well reveals the deficiencies of the revisionists' need for speed. But their concept of theatricality is a post facto rationalization of the Folio omissions, which are in fact theatrically impractical. Where Urkowitz and Taylor had endorsed the theater company's omission of the dialogue between Cornwall's servants after Gloucester's blinding, Kenneth Muir, an eminent schholar with theatrical experience, vigorously denied it. Muir replied first as a literary critic, keenly aware of the ethical issue and how any humane audience would react to the blinding with moral disgust: "the various comments by the good characters on the deeds of the evil ones are felt by the audience to be a necessary expression of our sense of outrage. The multiple choric effects of the speeches of sympathetic characters are an essential part of Shakespeare's method. To cut them out will leave us feeling deprived, if not in a moral vacuum."[46] Second, Muir cited his own experience as an actor and director. In the two productions in which he had taken part, when the servants' dialogue was omitted,

> we found on both occasions that after the blinding, and despite an interval between Acts 3 and 4, Gloucester had very little time between his exit in Act 3 Scene 7 and his reappearance in Act 4 Scene 1 to change his clothes or put on a cloak and to have his eyes bandaged. Even with the additional two-and-a-half lines in Edgar's opening soliloquy, Gloucester has only fourteen lines in the wings if we stick to the Folio text. It is not enough. Apart from its dramatic value, the dialogue between the servants is a theatrical necessity. Either the cut was made accidentally by the Folio compositor, or the cut was not Shakespeare's.[47]

4. That Shakespeare Omitted Passages from the Quarto That Were "Redundant" or "Disposable" in His Eyes

Committed to justifying the Folio text as Shakespeare's final conception of *Lear*, the revisionists had to defend its drastic treatment of two scenes: the omission of 4.3, amounting to fifty-five lines, and its cutting of fifty-eight lines in 3.6, the scene where the mad king imagines that Goneril and Regan are present in a hovel on the heath. I begin with the omitted scene, in which an unnamed Gentleman informs Kent of three important events that, since Shakespeare could not represent them on stage (unless he had invented the cinema), had to be reported. The dramatist keeps us informed that the French king has returned to his country, leaving a deputy in charge of the soldiers accompanying Cordelia; that Cordelia has been searching for her father, distraught with grief at his treatment by her sisters; and that Lear is so affected with "burning shame" at his treatment of Cordelia that he is unwilling to meet her. Having claimed that the Folio omissions "could have been made by no one other than Shakespeare himself," Urkowitz necessarily approved the Folio's total suppression of 4.3, but then had to find a post facto justification for it.[48] In his patronizing judgment, "[t]he dramatic material found in 4.3 has many of the qualities found in the coda to 3.7; it is of poetic interest, but in the plot it is at best forgettable and at worst seriously misleading. When the scene is cut the play improves."[49] Few, if any readers or theatergoers will share Urkowitz's judgment that this scene, as Shakespeare wrote it, may have "poetic"—rather than dramatic?—"interest," but is otherwise "forgettable" or "misleading" (in what way?). Such disparaging comments on the Quarto may be the unavoidable consequence of the Two Versions thesis that the Folio is Shakespeare's revision, but they nonetheless represent the collapse of literary criticism as a response to a work's ethical and emotional design. If you cannot feel the intensity of Cordelia's love and of her father's shame, even in a report, you are not responding to *King Lear*. Urkowitz concluded this chapter by praising the Folio's "theatrical" cuts as having been made in order "to bring the text into accord with important theatrical values—concision, contrast, and surprise."[50] These may be inappropriate aesthetic criteria for

Shakespeare's dramaturgy, but in any case the cuts were made at the expense of other no less theatrical, and human values—moral outrage at evil, compassion at suffering, and a readiness to help those in need, whatever the risk. When we go to the theater we do not leave our ethical values at home.

The Folio's cuts, I have argued, were made by a bookkeeper working for the King's Men, for local production purposes, and did serious damage to the play's design and meaning. This point has been well made by Robert Clare, a literary scholar with professional theater experience.[51] Clare commented that just because the first two sections of 4.3, giving news of the French king's departure and Cordelia's feelings for her father, "describe the developing action rather than obviously advancing it, the revisionists seem to think that both of them may therefore be summarily dismissed. Urkowitz says of the first that 'the interpolation of 4.3 into the text of a performing script of *King Lear* creates serious dramatic problems not found in the Folio.'"[52] (By what privileged insight can Urkowitz claim that this scene was "interpolated"? His belief that, according to Two Versions dogma, the scene is irrelevant makes him imagine that someone has inserted it, a curious form of wish fulfillment.) Urkowitz itemizes three "serious dramatic problems" caused by the Quarto's 4.3. First, he complains that when we next see Lear in the reunion with Cordelia (4.7) "though he has ample opportunity to express the 'shame' ascribed to him, he does not."[53] Clare dismissed that complaint by simply quoting Lear's words to Cordelia:

> If you haue poyson for mee I will drinke it,
> I know you doe not loue me, for your sisters
> Haue as I doe remember, done me wrong,
> You haue some cause, they haue not. (K2v16–19; 4.7.71–74)

Second, Urkowitz objects that Kent's report that "the poor distressed *Lear*'s ith towne" (4.3.38) "contradicts lines at the beginning of 4.4," where Cordelia has her soldiers search "euery acre in the hie growne field" for him (4.4.7). Anyone who reads the play moderately attentively will realize that Lear's wandering outside the town is the precise consequence of the shame he feels, which makes him avoid Cordelia. While correcting Urkowitz's mistaken conception of the dramatic sequence, Clare drew attention to a wider issue, concerning what I have called "notification," the delivery of information about what is happening elsewhere. Clare agreed that "4.4 'contradicts' 4.3," but "for the simple and entirely appropriate reason that to do so advances the drama. Just when we have been told that Lear is safely arrived in Dover, and so believe that he is on the verge of being brought to Cordelia, we learn that he has in fact slipped away, and is vulnerable again. Peripeteia is not a contradiction, and in *Lear* it is used widely and to great effect."[54] When this scene is omitted, as it was in the Royal Shakespeare Company (RSC) productions of 1990 and 1993, the result proved confusing. As Clare described it,

> the audience cannot properly appreciate what Kent is trying to do: that is, to continue what he began at the start of Act 3, using the agency of the Gentleman to attempt to reunite Lear and Cordelia. Kent must be certain of Cordelia's feelings towards her father before he delivers him into her hands. Unlike his revisionist critics, he is taking nothing for granted. The need to meet his agent again in 4.3, to confirm that Lear will be safe with this daughter at least, is the only conceivable reason for Kent to have left the king unattended. What he does not anticipate, is that Lear will meanwhile go off again on his own to be encountered by Gloucester and Edgar (in 4.6). Without 4.3, the audience must wonder why Kent should have abandoned Lear, since he exited from 3.6 with the king in his care.[55]

Once again a scholar with theatrical experience can dismiss a revisionist's theory-driven interpretation of the play. Shakespeare's use of notification demands from the audience a readiness to keep abreast of all the events offstage, since they will affect the attitudes and events that he is able to show us. Urkowitz lacks that readiness.

Kenneth Muir also refuted the revisionists' justification for the Folio's omission of 4.3. by drawing on practical theatrical experience. Taylor claimed that it is more satisfying to see and hear Cordelia than to be told about her, but Muir countered that this revisionist

> does not appreciate the serious disadvantage of omitting the account of Cordelia in this scene. She has been absent from the

> stage for 2,000 lines—the length of some of Shakespeare's entire plays—and she will have a difficult entrance in the next scene unless the audience has been reminded of her. She is presumably dressed as a soldier and some who have not read the play will wonder 'Who is she?' or even 'Who is he?' Cordelia's part, moreover, is the tiniest of any major Shakespearean character—just over 100 lines, and she often speaks in monosyllables. The account of her weeping, and Kent's comment on this, help to build up her importance in the scheme of the play.[56]

As for Urkowitz's complaints that the account of Lear's whereabouts in 4.4 contradicts 4.3, Muir dismissed them as "frivolous":

> It is made clear that it is only in his lucid moments (his 'better tune') that Lear remembers the situation, that his escape to the country in Act 4 Scene 4 is not inconsistent with the account in Act 4 Scene 3, that he is described as 'mad as the vexed sea', that he is clearly mad through Act 4 Scene 6, and that he recovers his senses in Act 4 Scene 7. His kneeling to Cordelia is the expression of his sovereign shame. Urkowitz seems to expect a madman to behave rationally and consistently. It is surely obvious that the motive of the cut is not to improve the play by subtle alterations, but simply to reduce its length.[57]

As we read these cogent objections to the Two Versions theory, it becomes ever more obvious that Shakespeare had no part in preparing the Folio. That conclusion is inescapable when we examine the cuts that the Folio made in 3.6. As we have seen, it omitted forty lines in the mock trial (3.6.17–56) and cut both Kent's speech "Oppressed nature sleepes" (97–101) and Edgar's closing soliloquy, "When we our betters see bearing our woes" (102–115). Steven Urkowitz notes that the scene, which occupies only sixty lines in the Folio, "is very quickly begun and finished." Approvingly, Urkowitz describes it as "a reasonable theatrical revision, designed to sustain the rapid sequence of actions in this part of the play, rather than allowing the pace to slow down as it does here in the Quarto version."[58]

This is a disturbingly vacuous comment. Quite apart from the lost substance of this scene, showing Lear's final, futile attempt to bring his evil daughters to justice, the abridged Folio version leaves two very obvious lacunae. It retains the compassionate comments of Edgar and Kent without having shown us anything in the king's behavior that would justify their feelings, together with Lear's otherwise inexplicable speech beginning "Then let them anatomize Regan . . ." To describe this as "a reasonable theatrical revision" is to have a low opinion of the theater.

At the end of this scene the Folio cuts Edgar's choric speech ("When we our betters see bearing our woes . . ."), which includes his comment explicitly linking the main and subplot: "He childed as I fathered." Urkowitz fails to see the significance of this link and dismisses Edgar's soliloquy as a series of "meditative cadences and rhymes," apparently lacking any other significance. This is to carry superficiality to new heights (or depths). Relying on the single criterion of speed, Urkowitz describes the speeches of Kent and Edgar in the Quarto as "noticeable pauses in the rushing action of this part of the play." Therefore, he imagines, the Folio "eliminates" them, thus achieving "several remarkably theatrical and different [*sic*] results." There is a vicious circularity in the Two Versions theory. Having hypothesized that Shakespeare made these cuts in order to speed up the action, the revisionists then congratulate him on his work. It is thanks to the Folio's cuts that "the end of 3.6 and the beginning of 3.7 are both unrelievedly urgent, compelling and threatening"—as if that sequence were not fuller and even more powerful and affecting in the Quarto. In upgrading the Folio, revisionists are patronizing toward the fundamental text. In Urkowitz's judgment, although "the Quarto text preserves a fuller literary record of obviously Shakespearean writing . . . the Folio offers a more vigorous rhythm of speeches and incidents."[59] But the Quarto is not a "literary record," to be studied in a library. It is a text for acting, the play as Shakespeare originally designed it, embodying a complex and compelling plot. The Folio's three cuts to the "trial scene" damage the play's moral and emotional development and its unity.

Other independent critics defended these scenes from the Folio cuts, so warmly endorsed by the revisionists. Ann Meyer described the mad trial scene as showing Lear's "refusal to tolerate the iniquity of his daughters and his earnest yet unavailing attempt to enforce justice."[60] The Quarto preserves Shakespeare's unique insight into the king's fluctuation between reason and madness. Lear orders the prisoners to appear before the court: "Ile see their trial first, bring in their euidence." Well aware that a trial should have more than one judge, he co-opts Poor Tom, "thou robed man of Iustice," inviting the Fool, "his yokefellow of equity," to "bench by his side." Evidently the Fool demurs, so Lear has to urge him to play his part: "you are ot'h commission, sit you too." The prosecutor can then address the accused:

> *Lear.* Arraigne her first tis *Gonoril*, I here take my oath
> before this honorable assembly kickt the poore king her father.
> *Foole.* Come hither mistrisse is your name *Gonorill.*
> *Lear.* She cannot deny it.
> *Fool.* Cry you mercy I tooke you for a ioynt stoole.
> (G4r6–8, 12–16; 3.6.46–56)

The Fool's line, "Cry you mercy, I tooke you for a ioynt stoole," as the *Riverside* edition notes, is "a jocular formula of apology for overlooking the presence of a person." This is a truly astonishing scene, in that it shows us a madman's interior vision. Shakespeare makes two of the bystanders comment. Edgar drops his disguise for a moment: "Looke where he stands and glares," while Kent expresses his unease at Lear's distracted behavior: "How doe you sir? Stand you not so amazd." From the Fool's joke Shakespeare allows us to infer that Lear's demented imagination has converted a joint-stool, the only piece of furniture in this hovel, into the shape of Goneril, just as he transformed Poor Tom's blanket, his sole piece of clothing, into the garb of a "robed man of justice." The whole trial takes place in Lear's mind and ends in confusion. As Meyer comments, it breaks up "with the King in an uproar, disgusted that his revelation of what is true and just will lead nowhere. Lear is frustrated by his inability to enforce justice" upon such people as Goneril and Regan who "have no humanity; they are inanimate objects," and is "outraged at those who stand by silently allowing corruption to pass unpunished."[61] If this scene draws on everything that has come before, it also looks forward to that amazing confrontation between mad Lear and blinded Gloucester, with its exposure of corruption summed up in that "great image of Authoritie, a Dogg's obey'd in Office" (4.6.158–159; TLN 2602–2603). Lear's mad trial of his ungrateful daughters links up with much that comes before and afterwards, in Shakespeare's complex design. The Folio's trimming of it was "the most unkindest cut" of all.

After Meyer's sensitive commentary on that scene it is shocking to read Gary Taylor's account of it as "the most dispensable" of the three mad scenes, because it "essentially gives us more of the same. The omitted passage—with Lear mad, poor Edgar playing Tom, the Fool fooling, and Kent trying to be reasonable—contains no new dramatic ingredients. All the new elements in the scene the Folio keeps, brings forward, or introduce."[62] This and other comments prove that exponents of the Two Versions theory are courtroom advocates rather than scholars, committed to promoting one interpretation and ignoring all evidence to the contrary. One of the advocate's tasks is to discredit the other side, acceptable tactics in a courtroom but almost unseemly when applied to the astonishing feat of Shakespeare's imagination as preserved in the Quarto text. As William Carroll observed, in approving the Folio's omission the revisionists' "denigration of the mock trial reaches to extraordinary lengths." Carroll summarized the whole litany of complaints that Taylor compiled about Lear's mad trial scene: it is "unfocused emotionally as well as politically" and fails "to communicate a vision of political reality," objections that many readers will find either puzzling—you can hardly expect a mad person to be "focused"—or irrelevant.[63] Taylor claimed that the Folio actually improved the scene by cutting it, thereby eliminating its "fuzziness of detail," a truly sophistic claim.[64] Taylor even complained that, because we cannot tell to whom Lear speaks when he asks, "False Justicer why hast thou let her scape?" his "question gains nothing by being addressed to" any of the characters onstage, and "actually loses significance as soon as we attempt to identify the specific 'False Justicer' to whom Lear speaks."[65] It seems as if Taylor is looking around to find faults in this amazing scene simply to justify the Folio's omission of it. But he diminishes the discipline of literary criticism by these pettifogging objections. Respecting his readers' patience, William Carroll declined to "work through the circularity and self-contradictions of Taylor's comment," but found time to document the *reductio ad absurdum* of Taylor's attempts to discredit the mad trial, his complaint

> about the 'joint-stool' used in the scene. Unlike other stage properties transformed 'into sharp foci of dramatic significance,' Taylor says, 'the joint-stool, for me, never suffers such a memorable "Sea-change | Into something rich, & strange'." Seeking some kind of dramatic correlative, Taylor concluded with this question: "how is Goneril like a joint-stool? I do not see how this property adequately typifies or symbolizes or encapsulates or even suggests Goneril's nature. What do the two have in common, besides hardness? And is hardness the essential, or even the most obvious, attribute of joint-stools?[66]

As Carroll put it, "It is difficult to imagine the answer which would satisfy this kind of question" (apart, perhaps, from "Cry you mercy, I took you for a literary critic").

The revisionists attempted to privilege a "theatrical" version of *Lear* over a "literary" one, as if the two were incompatible or mutually opposed, but attracted severe criticism for doing so. Robert Clare objected to a revisionist's justification for cutting the mad trial, "because it touches on issues that are better dealt with later in the play, in the 'Dover beach' scene with Gloucester (4.6)." As Kenneth Muir had done, Clare drew attention to the practical theatrical consequences if the Folio text were to be followed: "with the mock trial 'cut', Lear has only three lines before Edgar's aside, and there is not a sufficiently established context to make such a change of tone dynamically effective. There is no basis for meaningful transition and development. Lear has hardly entered when he speaks of Regan, and then he falls asleep. The scene is so brief that it is little more than a 'filler' that enables Gloucester to advance the plot." By comparison, Shakespeare's full text, as preserved in the Quarto, "prepares the way for the more developed reflections of Dover beach and helps the actor playing Lear to 'bridge' towards them." Clare concluded that "most Lears would argue that the journey to 4.6 is only made possible by playing the mock trial first."[67]

Certainly the evidence from the recent theatrical productions supports the Quarto, not the Folio text. Clare valuably charted the Folio / Quarto omissions as found in the promptbooks of seven major productions of the play between 1962 and 1993, six for the RSC and one for the National Theatre.[68] In Clare's chart comparing their respective treatments of seventeen passages that have been cut at one time or another, it is striking that all seven productions preserved the Quarto text of the mad trial, even though some of them were purportedly based on the Folio. As Clare records, Nicholas Hytner's 1990 production for the RSC set out to use the Folio throughout, but he was unable to "convince his actors that F's cuts in 3.6 are viable. John Wood (playing Lear) apparently objected before rehearsals even began, arguing that what is omitted is indeed essential to Lear's journey." Hytner accordingly "tested the variants of 3.6 in rehearsal, and agreed that the mock trial must be included since, without it, the scene lacked shape and rhythm, and didn't seem to be 'about' enough." The decision to include it proved fortunate, for "[t]he mock-trial turned out to be not only important but actually pivotal to Hytner's production, as his eventual staging of it made clear: the two joint-stools were placed in the same positions (relative to Lear) that Goneril and Regan had occupied in 1.1, and were to occupy again (in death) in the final scene."[69] A theater director can bring out unrecognized significances that a revisionist is unable to comprehend.[70]

The actors who prevailed on Nicholas Hytner to include the whole trial scene recognized that it was "actually pivotal" to that production, the stage grouping of the joint-stools providing a parody (in a serious sense) of the opening scene, where Lear gave away his power, love, sanity, and eventually life. The RSC's discovery of the scene's dramatic potential was echoed *in parvo* by a semi-professional production at the University of Rochester in the 1980s, based on the Quarto. David Richman's account of the production documents a number of unexpected difficulties caused by the cuts made by Nicholas Okes, for which the fuller Folio version had to be substituted.[71]

Conversely, the acting company judged that several of the Folio cuts—notably of Albany's denunciation of Goneril and the dialogue of the compassionate servants after Gloucester's blinding—weakened the play. Contrary to the revisionists' theory, "the scene whose loss would have taken most from our production was the mock trial." The company "did not find the scene problematic in rehearsal," and in production "the mock trial achieved stunning effects. It was indeed the epicentre."[72]

But the last word on the mock trial scene should be given to that erstwhile revisionist, Ernst Honigmann. In 1996 he reversed his previous belief that the passages found in the Folio *Lear* but not in the Quarto were added by Shakespeare: now he recognized them as having been cut from the Quarto. In affirming this position, Honigmann countered Nevil Coghill's judgment concerning another Shakespeare tragedy of which two versions survive, that "if *Othello* was shortened, if Q was a shortened version rather than the original version, the person responsible was guilty of 'stupid cutting' and 'destructive cutting.'" Honigmann replied, "True: yet we still have to ask whether stupid and destructive cutting should be ruled out an inconceivable in the Elizabethan theatre. After all, the most extraordinary things happen to Shakespeare's text even in our enlightened modern theatre," and there is no doubt that comparable destruction was wreaked "in Shakespeare's day, in his own company":

> At least one early production of *Henry V* omitted Chorus, arguably the second most important part in the play. And if *King Lear* was revised, some of the most powerful episodes were removed in the Folio, the 'revised' version—for instance, the mock-trial in 3.6, where Lear, Edgar and the Fool vie with each other in madness. 'The omission of the mad trial is, without question, the Folio's most surprising cut', said Gary Taylor, explaining that it was cut because it failed: 'uncertainty of focus is apparent in the scene's detail as well as its structure'. Others have also tried to justify this 'cut'—without, however, grappling with a related question. Isn't this episode indispensable, as the geometric centre of the whole play? And if it can succeed in the

> modern theatre, why should it have failed at the Globe? Is there any evidence that it failed?[73]

The answer to Honigmann's final question is that no evidence exists that the mock trial "failed" in production. The revisionists' claim that it must have done so was made simply to justify their claim that Shakespeare revised the play. The shortened Folio text, as Muir described it, left out something "indispensable, as the geometric centre of the whole play." Honigmann's metaphor uncannily echoes those used by two witnesses of the modern theatrical productions who described 3.6 as "pivotal," as an "epicentre." No person of judgment practicing "the disciplines of literary, theatrical, and textual criticism" would place this scene among the play's "disposable superfluities."

5. That Shakespeare Omitted Passages from the Quarto in Order to Change the Characterization of Edgar and Albany

It should now be apparent that the cuts in the Folio were opportunistic and clumsily managed, leaving gaps in action and motivation. The revisionists, however, adopted "an evolutionary, even a teleological argument," as William Carroll described it, which expressed "their own form of bardolatry. The Folio version is 'better' and its readings preferred, in effect, *because* it is later; they assume that Shakespearean genius *always* improves upon itself."[74] Ascribing a coherent design on Shakespeare's part to improve the play, they argued that he also wanted to change the relative balance between some characters. Obviously enough, when a play is shortened, for whatever reason, this will affect the length of individual roles. A study of the performance texts created by dominant actor-managers will show that their parts were only slightly cut, or even enlarged, by comparison with the rest of the cast. Setting aside this one-man focus, if a company finds that a chosen actor is not up to the role he has been given, the company may shorten it; if the personnel change within a season or from one season to another, some roles may need to be reduced. With the Folio cuts to *King Lear* none of those reasons seem to apply, other than a desire to shorten the performance time, a process that affected some roles more than others.

According to my computations, in which half-lines have been rounded up, characters' roles were reduced by approximately these amounts:

Kent	51 lines	(7 cuts)
Edgar / Poor Tom	41	(5)
Gentleman	40	(3)
Albany	28	(4)
Lear	21	(14)
Fool	20	(2)
Goneril	18	(7)
Edmund	12	(6)
Servants, Doctor, Captain	9	(12)
Gloucester	6	(3)
Cordelia	4	(2)
Regan	3	(2)

Scholars who accept that the Folio omissions were made by the King's Men to shorten the play in performance will observe that these cuts are fairly evenly distributed, the largest involving the omission of 4.3, which reduces the parts of Kent by 28 lines and the Gentleman by 27 lines. These two characters, whom Shakespeare used to notify the audience of events offstage or action to come, suffer other reductions in 3.1 (Kent: 12 lines; Gentleman: 9 lines) and at the end of 4.7 (Kent: 6 lines; Gentleman: 6 lines). Edgar is the next largest affected, with the cut of the "trial" scene (14 lines), the loss of his rhymed soliloquy (3.6.102–115), and the narrative of his reunion with Kent (5.3.205–222). The cuts in 4.2 deprive Albany of 23 and Goneril of 7 lines. Minor cuts elsewhere are as might be expected, the overall goal being to remove passages of reflection, description, and "notification."

For the revisionists, however, the effect of the cuts was not coincidental, as it would have been if the company had abbreviated the play, but deliberate. According to Michael Warren, Shakespeare made "a substantial and consistent recasting of certain aspects of the play," such that "Q and F embody two different artistic visions."[75]

Warren claimed that "in Q [Albany] closes the play a mature and victorious duke assuming responsibility for the Kingdom; in F he is a weaker character, avoiding responsibility."[76] This judgment is based solely on six cuts in Albany's role, amounting to thirty lines, of which twenty-three were deleted from his denunciation of Goneril and only seven from his public appearances. As I have shown, these cuts drastically reduce Albany's denunciation of Goneril and Regan for their ungrateful and inhuman treatment of Lear and certainly reduce the ethical significance of 4.2 in relation to the play as a whole. However, they do not eliminate Albany's role as the only articulate representative of human values in what remains of civic life. (At this point Kent, Edgar, and Gloucester are outside society, he knows not where.)

Kenneth Muir expressed a similar judgment when discussing Urkowitz's claim that, as a result of these cuts, "Albany 'seems to espouse no positively defined ethical standards'. This, he concludes, was the purpose of the alterations." In reply Muir again raised the key issue of whether this alteration was the consequence of the cuts, rather than their purpose:

> To this one must object that there seems to be no dramatic point in the alterations, and that the defence of the cuts is so feeble that it can hardly increase our confidence that they were Shakespeare's own. As two moral speeches are retained, it is absurd to pretend that Albany is deprived of defined ethical standards. Moreover, in the last scene of the play, Albany plainly expresses those standards. Presumably the cuts in Act 4 Scene 2 were made because the play was thought to be too long—possibly for a provincial tour—and they castrated Albany's part: it is surely probable that the mangling was not deliberate, but an unfortunate and inadvertent result of the cuts.[77]

Also reviewing Urkowitz, Philip Edwards expressed his serious "objection to the methods of this book: namely, the constant insistence that the fortuitous has been designed": "The usual view is that someone in the theatre has monkeyed about with Albany's part and ruined it by cutting almost all his longer expressions of doubt, anger, and dismay at the proceedings of his wife and her associates." Edwards rejected Urkowitz's claim that the changes "represent a deliberate and consistent re-characterization of Albany . . . In the first place, the re-characterization is pointless; and in the second, if Shakespeare *had* wished to refashion Albany's part it is certain that he would have *rewritten* at least one speech. He would not have worked entirely by excision. The new quality of Albany seems to me the fortuitous result of playhouse cutting."[78] Many Shakespearians will agree that if he had wanted to "refashion Albany's part" he would not have been satisfied with excision alone.

Eager to justify every change made in the Folio as Shakespeare's conscious choice, the Two Versions theorists failed to consider what effect those cuts have on Albany's role as experienced in performance. As I have obsreved, a play is an ecosystem: change it in one area and you create unexpected consequences in another. Robert Clare interviewed the actor who played Albany in Nicholas Hytner's 1990 RSC production, which was based on the Folio.

> When I asked him about the production, he said that he had been disappointed to lose what he felt were 'valuable lines', making Albany 'almost monosyllabic', and that he had difficulty negotiating the consequent 'leap' to his assumption of authority in the final Act; but he 'went for understatement', in the hope that 'disdain and loathing' could become the 'motor' that would drive along his performance. Other actors who saw the production were apparently sympathetic to his efforts (he singled out Sara Kestelman, who played Goneril in the RSC's 1982 *King Lear*, and so of consequence knew exactly what was missing), but the critics' response suggest that Albany simply dropped out of sight.

(Clare searched through more than forty reviews before he found a single mention of him, and that with the actor's and character's names confused: "'Paul Albany played Webster.'") Considering the damage that it suffers from these cuts, Clare's conclusion will be widely shared: "that [Shakespeare], who was himself an actor, 'planned' a positive adjustment to Albany's role, as the revisionists insist, is very hard to credit."[79]

The other changes to Albany's role occur in the final scene. The Folio cuts five lines in which he expresses his reasons for mobilizing his army: "*France* inuades our land" (K3r28; 5.1.25). The absence of these lines hardly shows Albany disclaiming responsibility, since he is still visibly leading that army. The revisionists' diagnoses of Shakespeare's "deliberate diminution" of Albany rest largely on the speech he makes immediately before Lear's death, which proposes what I would describe as an interim political settlement. He will return "absolute power" to Lear, and restore to Kent and Edgar their "rights," with the additional honors they have merited (5.3.299–303; TLN 3270–3274). According to the revisionists, Albany here "abdicates," an interpretation that Richard Knowles decisively rebutted:

> As for his supposed abdication from the position of victorious commander-in-chief and (since he is the sole survivor among Lear's heirs) presumptive successor to the kingship of all Britain, there is simply no evidence for it. He does say, when Lear appears in the last scene, that he will relinquish his 'absolute power' to the former king 'During the life of this old Majesty'—i.e., temporarily. But since Lear dies a moment later, Albany never does relinquish his power to him; the offer affirms Albany's nobility, but the gift does not occur. In his next speech he still assumes absolute authority, since he orders the removal of bodies and then urges Kent and Edgar, 'Rule in this Realme, and the gor'd state sustaine.' He says, clearly, rule *in* this realm, not rule this realm; yet several of the two-*Lear* critics insist that that is what he means—that he is in fact about to make himself subject to Edgar, a man of lower rank and of no experience whatsoever in leadership. No Jacobean could believe such a sudden and drastic twist of events.[80]

The Two Versions theorists claimed further evidence of revision in the fact that the Folio gives the play's closing lines not to Albany but to Edgar:

Edg. The waight of this sad time we must obey,
Speake what we feele, not what we ought to say:
The oldest hath borne most, we that are yong,
Shall neuer see so much, nor liue so long.
(5.3.324–327; TLN 3298–3301)

The apparent "reassignment" of these lines, however, is simply another instance of the Folio having access to a cleaner and more legible copy of Shakespeare's manuscript, which enabled it to correct one of many errors made by Nicholas Okes's compositors in their desperate attempts to compress the final scene to fit sheet L. The Quarto may give the last words to "*Duke*," but, as we have seen, the standard of printing in the final pages declined rapidly, and the Quarto contains many other erroneous speech prefixes. Ann Meyer cited several instances of variant speech headings in sheet L, "many of which have been judged by scholars as compositorial blunders. It is less surprising to find Albany, rather than Edgar, delivering the final speech in Q."[81] Ernst Honigmann cited three instances of misplaced speech prefixes in the final scene:

Q "*Gon.* That were the most, if hee should husband you." (L1r7)
[F: "*Alb.*" TLN 3012]
Q "*Bast.* Let the drum strike, and proue my title good" (L1r19)
[F: "*Reg.* Let the Drum strike, and proue my title thine" TLN 3026]
Q "*Lear.* Breake hart, I prethe breake." (L4r20)
[F: "Kent." TLN 3285]

However, since these three erroneous speech prefixes in the Quarto were all corrected by the Folio, which was most probably set from a scribal copy of the original 1606 promptbook, it is highly unlikely that the error in giving this speech to Albany should be an exception. As Honigmann questioned, "why should Shakespeare suddenly reshuffle speech prefixes so extensively in this scene and [not] at other points in the play?"[82]

This is a bibliographical problem, for which Meyer and Honigmann gave the appropriate bibliographical explanation. There were no authorial changes to the character. In both Quartos and the Folio Albany is still the dominant figure on stage, and in all three he delivers a decisive speech addressed to both Kent and Edgar:

> Beare them from hence, our present businesse
> Is general woe: Friends of my soule, you twaine,
> Rule in this Realme, and the gor'd State sustaine
> (5.3.319–321; TLN 3293–3295)

In reply, Kent, who only appeared onstage a hundred lines earlier, just after Edgar reported meeting him on the verge of collapse after all that he has endured—"His griefe grew puissant and the strings of life | Began to cracke" (L3r1–2; 5.3.217–218; not in F)—abjures any further duties in the state:

> I have a iourney Sir, shortly to go,
> My maister cals, and I must not say no.
> (5.3.322–323; TLN 3297–3298)

By the norms of Shakespearean dramaturgy we would expect Edgar to reply next, since in the preceding lines Shakespeare has made him and Kent speak alternately:

> *Edg.* He faints, my Lord, my Lord.
> *Kent.* Breake heart, I prythee breake.
> *Edg.* Looke vp my Lord.
> *Kent.* Vex not his ghost, O let him passe . . .
> *Edg.* He is gon indeed.
> *Kent.* The wonder is, he hath endur'd so long,
> He but vsurpt his life. (5.3.312–319; TLN 3284–3293)

The Folio's correction makes better sense dramatically, for Albany addresses both Kent and Edgar jointly ("Friends of my soule, you twaine"), while they reply separately. Albany offers them a share in the rule of England, a political settlement that Kent declines due to age and illness, complementing Albany's speech. Assigning the final speech to Edgar, the second most important surviving character, also has a theatrical function, giving him more presence onstage, since over the preceding seventy-three lines he has made only six short utterances, amounting to twenty-six words. Moreover the speech is one of general reflection, a choric commentary not inappropriate in the mouth of Edgar, for whom Shakespeare wrote several such speeches. His final words strike an emotional, not a political note, summing up the feelings of the survivors of this tragedy and memorializing Lear's stature and the extent of his suffering. The Quarto erred by giving two speeches to Albany but none to Edgar, while the Folio got it right, reproducing Shakespeare's intended symmetry. Nobody intended to weaken Albany's character; nobody took anything away from him.

Moreover, all the important administrative or political speeches in the closing stages of the play are still given to Albany. Dismissing the news of Edmund's death—"That's but a trifle heere"—Albany sets out to restore order:

> You Lords and Noble Friends, know our intent,
> What comfort to this great decay may come,
> Shall be appli'd. For vs we will resigne,
> During the life of this old Maiesty
> To him our absolute power, you to your rights,
> With boote, and such additions as your Honours
> Haue more then merited. All Friends shall
> Taste the wages of their vertue, and all Foes
> The cup of their deseruings: O see, see,
>
> (5.3.297–305; TLN 3269–3276)

At this point Albany breaks off at the sight of Lear (perhaps rising to his feet), but after the king's death he continues with the restoration of order and office, as he does in the Quarto. It must be obvious to everyone experiencing this play that Albany is in charge, so it was unjustified for Warren to claim that in the Folio "he is considerably effaced at the close" or to argue that in this version "Albany, a weaker man, abdicates his responsibilities."[83]

Warren linked his account of the supposed decline of Albany's status to the matching claim for Edgar's upgrading, a claim that also distorts the text. Warren failed to consider the theatrical problem Shakespeare faced with Edgar's disguise. If it was as thorough as the text implies—"my face Ile grime with filth, | Blanket my loynes, elfe all my haire with knots" (E3r22–23; 2.3.9–10)—there is a danger that the audience may forget that "Poor Tom" is still Edgar. One way that Shakespeare avoided that danger was to give Edgar five soliloquies: one in his own persona (2.3.1–21), two in his disguise as Poor Tom (3.6.101–115, 4.1.1–12), and two in his changed attire, *"dressed like a peasant,"* as the *Riverside* edition puts it. One of these concerns his father's frustrated suicide attempt (4.6.42–47); another—after he has killed the "seruiceable villaine" Oswald and discovered Goneril's love letter to Edmund—contains his reflections on the "indistinguish'd space of Womans will" (4.6.251–278; TLN 2704–2731). All of these speeches are in verse, his true medium, and in them we can hear Edgar's true voice, despite the disguise, as we can in the series of asides (again in his own person) that Shakespeare gave him in responding to Lear's madness—"Blesse thy fiue wits" (Q; 3.6.57) and "My teares begin to take his part so much, | They marre my counterfetting" (Q; 3.6.60–1). Edgar's compassion gives rise to his soliloquy (cut by F), beginning "When we our betters see bearing our woes," which, as we have seen, brings out the thematic parallel between the two main plots: "When that which makes me bend, makes the King bow. | He childed as I fathered" (3.6.109–110). When Edgar is confronted by his father's mutilated eyes Shakespeare gives him the same double reaction, first expressing the intensity of his compassion—"But who comes heere? My Father poorely led? | World, World, O world!" (4.1.9–10); and then making a general reflection: "O Gods! Who is't can say I am at the worst? | I am worse than ere I was" (4.1.25–26). On three occasions in this scene Shakespeare makes Edgar reveal the struggle he has to maintain his disguise:

—Bad is the Trade that must play Fool to sorrow,
Ang'ring it selfe, and others. Blesse thee Master.
—Poor Tom's a cold.—I cannot daub it further.
—And yet I must:
Blesse thy sweet eyes, they bleede.
(4.1.38–39, 52, 54; TLN 2224–2225, 2241, 2243)

The result of these instances of "asides" or direct address, far more numerous than those Shakespeare gave to any other character in the play, is to bring us into immediate contact with Edgar as he makes his extraordinary transformation from victim to hero, from a hunted outcast and "horrible object" to the compassionate helper and righter of wrongs, who administers to two "Foes | The cup of their deseruings" by killing both Oswald and Edmund.

To Michael Warren, however, the fact that Edgar speaks "much in aside and soliloquy" meant that he "is distanced theatrically from many of the events of the play." The word "distanced" may reflect a strange modern aesthetic, foreign to Shakespeare's theater of direct self-revelation; yet the fact is that for much of the later part of the play Edgar / Poor Tom is in the thick of things, playing a significant role in 3.4, 3.6, 4.1, 4.6, 5.1, 5.2, and 5.3. By my computation, these seven scenes total 1,011 lines; Edgar is onstage for 874 lines and speaks 374 lines himself. He is not "distanced theatrically" from any event in this part of the play, quite the contrary. Warren also felt that Edgar "appears at times to be distanced emotionally from the events around him," a view contradicted by the passages I have just quoted. Indeed, Warren expressed another disabling modern attitude, a distaste for the way Shakespeare uses choric voices (Lear's Fool, Edgar, Albany) for moral commentary. This distaste resulted in him making patronizing judgments on Edgar: "one may allow him his virtue while still seeing its weakness," Warren judged, before convicting him of a "frequently inadequate" response and "doubting the maturity of his judgments." Warren invoked other modern critics (William Empson, Nicholas Brooke, Stanley Cavell, and S. L. Goldberg) who share what I would describe as a contemporary distrust of Shakespearean characters who are presented as paragons or as morally admirable. He claimed that Edgar displays a "dangerous self-righteousness": by his irritating habit of summing up the moral lessons of the actions he does "unconscious psychic violence" to himself and others—a psychoanalyst's judgment.[84] The attendant assumption is that Shakespeare somehow judges Edgar critically, and that we are meant to share this criticism. Nowhere do these writers consider that Shakespeare is using the dramatist's power to present Edgar simultaneously as an actor in his own life story and as a commentator on it. Edgar, together with Kent and Albany, articulates the moral judgments that the dramatist wishes to enact through these characters. Certainly Edgar learns firsthand the limitations of putting one's trust in hope. Having uttered his belief that "The lowest, and most deiected thing of Fortune, | Stands still in esperance" (4.1.3–4; F) he is immediately confronted by his mutilated father and realizes that "the worst is not, | As long as we can say this is the worst" (4.1.27–28; Q). But this shock effect is part of Shakespeare's deliberate treatment of both Gloucester and Edgar in terms of the classical *consolatio*. As I have shown elsewhere, throughout his career as a dramatist Shakespeare juxtaposed facile attempts at consoling sufferers with the anguished response of those suffering, as if to say, "No one can offer consolation who hasn't experienced what I suffer."[85] By the time that Edgar takes charge of Gloucester he has earned the right to become a consoler, defining himself as

> A most poore man made lame by Fortunes blowes,
> Who by the Art of knowne and feeling sorrowes
> Am pregnant to good pitty
>
> (I4v35–37; 4.6.221–223; TLN 2668–2670)

Instead of recognizing this gradual transformation of Edgar under the weight of experience, Michael Warren argued that the Folio's omission of his narrated reunion with Kent was a good idea, in that it "diminishes the sense of Edgar as the immature, indulgent man displaying his heroic tale of woe"; the omission "reduces somewhat his callowness, his easy indulgence of his sensibility."[86] It is disappointing that Warren should impose an anachronistic modern dislike of explicit moral judgments onto his argument for Shakespeare's supposed revision of the Folio.

Several independent scholars took issue with Warren's claim that the alterations in the last two acts of the play were carefully designed (by Shakespeare himself) to reduce the importance of Albany and increase the importance of Edgar's role. Kenneth Muir raised the key objection to this teleological argument: "We may allow that this is the effect of the alterations, but it may be doubted whether they were so designed; and even if this was the purpose of the changes, they could be the result of a change in the cast. Most of the alterations are savage cuts, and cuts are usually motivated by the need to shorten a play, *King Lear* being one of the longest." Warren had argued that the Folio's omission of Edgar's rhymed soliloquy at the end of 3.6—"When we our betters see bearing our woes"—was a positive improvement, reducing the "quantity of sententiousness" in the play, so that "Edgar gains in prominence . . . by the loss of a speech." Muir rejected this sophism by defining one important theatrical function of this speech:

> During the whole of the act Edgar has been posing as Poor Tom, and he has been given only one brief aside in his own person. The soliloquy is therefore important to him as a character. He plays so many parts in the course of the play that we are liable to lose sight of the man behind the masks. The lines, moreover, make two vital dramatic points. They make the first verbal link between the two plots—'He childed as I fathered'—and they emphasize that the mental suffering of the king is harder to bear than the physical suffering of the Bedlam beggar, though he too has had more than his share of mental suffering in being rejected by the father he loves.[87]

William Carroll also took issue with those who endorsed the Folio's omission of Edgar's "highly dramatic fourteen-line soliloquy which ends one of the most traumatic and moving scenes in the play." Having quoted the mutually approving comments of Urkowitz, Taylor, and Roger Warren, Carroll complained that "none of these critics really looks at Edgar's speech" and "none of them considers what the play *loses* by its deletion."[88] Carroll filled in the elements of meaning that the revisionists simply ignored:

> Edgar's speech is not simply a piece of sententiousness, though it is partly that; it is also a full revelation of his state of mind after the agonies of the mock trial (we have only heard two somewhat cryptic asides from him earlier in the scene). His speech offers as well a comment on the Breughelesque spectacle we have just witnessed as Kent, Gloucester, and the Fool limp from the stage with the mad king. The speech also contains the

> powerful and ironic double grammar of Edgar's observation, 'He childed as I fathered'—a particularly rich moment which I, for one, do not care to lose.[89]

No independent scholar (apart from members of this group) has accepted the Two Versions theory that the Folio's omissions were intended to alter the relative status of Albany and Edgar.

6. That Shakespeare's Responsibility for the Folio Cuts Can Be Proved on Textual Grounds

In his preface to *The Division of the Kingdoms* Taylor described the contributors' aim "to produce a volume which, by drawing on the disciplines of literary, theatrical, and textual criticism, would demonstrate their necessary interdependence."[90] This was a laudable aim, but in practice the revisionists' a priori assumptions distorted all three disciplines and blurred fundamental differences between them. Andrew Gurr was the first critic to draw attention to the revisionists' departure from scholarly tradition in basing their evaluation of bibliographical issues on aesthetic rather than textual criteria. According to Gurr, Taylor launched this dangerous process in his one-volume edition of *Henry V*, where he used the "Bad Quarto" (1600), "a memorially recorded text of a cut-down provincial version," to alter the Folio text, which derived from Shakespeare's manuscript. For example, Taylor took it on himself to replace the Dauphin at the battle of Agincourt with the Duke of Bourbon, arguing that the inauthentic Quarto embodied Shakespeare's "deliberate decision, its aesthetic corollaries in other scenes duly worked out."[91] Gurr objected that Taylor had no textual authority for drawing on the Quarto of *Henry V*, exercising "an aesthetic judgement for which there is no mechanical basis"—that is, no marks left by print on paper. This justified objection recalls the distinction made by Fredson Bowers, that bibliography proper treats "textual problems from the mechanical point of view, using evidence which must deliberately avoid being colored by literary consideration." Bibliography is complemented by "non-bibliographical textual criticism [which] works with meanings and literary values" However, Bowers warned, "if these last are divorced from all connection with the evidence of the mechanical process that imprinted meaningful symbols on a sheet of paper, no check-rein of fact or probability can restrain the farthest reaches of idle speculation."[92] In Gurr's critique, the rupture that Bowers warned against had come to pass with Taylor's treatment of bibliographical matters from a literary-critical or aesthetic basis:

> The 'bad quarto' version [of *Henry V*] is judged to be Shakespeare's own revision, not an alteration by the Globe book-keeper or the provincial players' adapter, purely on the grounds of its literary merit. The arguments over the two versions of *King Lear* extend this exercise in subjective judgement to a point where they totally reverse the traditional priorities. Editors normally appeal to aesthetic choice only when the mechanical evidence is inconclusive. Now aesthetic arguments are being deployed as the primary evidence for two equally authoritative versions of *King Lear*, and the mechanical evidence is being reassessed to see if it supports that primary evidence.[93]

Having expressed his own and other scholars' misgivings at the revisionists' program to establish "the Folio text as Shakespeare's 'final version', while treating the Quarto as a 'separate aesthetic creation,'" Gurr ended his essay on this justifiably gloomy note: "It is worrying when aesthetic judgement finds small tinkerings having such drastic effects, and it makes our uncertainty whether the tinkerings are the product of a revising author or a theorising editor almost unbearable."[94] Other critics of the Two Versions theory objected that its advocates address textual issues "from a literary and theatrical standpoint only," mustering arguments that do not touch "on textual and bibliographical evidence."[95] The insuperable problem that they faced was the total lack of such evidence, their whole theory being based on passages omitted from the Folio.

The absence of bibliographical evidence, however, did not deter the revisionists from theorizing—indeed, it positively encouraged them to construct imaginary events to justify their belief that Shakespeare himself revised *Lear* by writing on a copy of Q1. The standard model for the transmission of *King Lear* would start from this simple basis, shown in Figure 1.

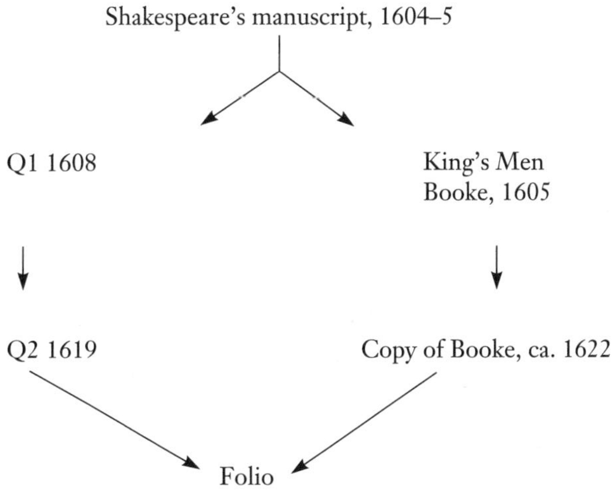

There are thus two lines of descent, one from a printed book derived from Shakespeare's original manuscript, the other from a copy of that manuscript, which an editor or compositor in Jaggard's employ supplemented by reference to a printed text. Okes's 1608 Quarto would have been the obvious choice, for although scholars have argued that Jaggard also referred to the 1619 Quarto, that suggestion has been disproved.[96] On the manuscript side we can assume with some degree of probability that the King's Men would have retained possession of their Booke, since it contained the valuable license to perform the play. Unless evidence to the contrary existed, we can also expect that the copy made for the Folio editors in about 1622 was the same play that had been the property of the King's Men throughout, but with a number of passages having been marked for omission at some point between 1606 and 1623.

This stemma of transmission has satisfied textual scholars as being based on the available evidence, but it did not satisfy the Two Versions theorists, since it left no space for Shakespeare's supposed revision. He cannot have intervened on the printed-book side of the stemma, since he died in 1616; in any case Q2 derived solely from Q1, with some editorial regularizing. Thus the revisionists had to devise a new narrative that would preempt the obvious explanation that in 1622 those involved in printing *King Lear* may have consulted the Quartos while setting the bulk of the play from a scribal copy of the theater manuscript. Their need to prove Shakespeare's revision meant that this process had to have taken place while he was alive and had to be given concrete manifestation as a physical object that could be inserted in the manuscript side of the stemma. Therefore, a series of events in the real world had to be postulated to account for an a priori literary theory, for which evidence was absent. In his 1980 monograph on the text of *King Lear* P. W. K. Stone had surmised that the King's Men's promptbook had been lost in the fire that destroyed the Globe in 1613 and that the company produced a new one by copying out Okes's Quarto.[97] Gary Taylor rejected "this reconstruction" since it "virtually presupposes that Shakespeare did not himself contribute to the Folio redaction; it also assumes, more objectionably, that the company would have felt that Q1 *needed* adapting, verbally and theatrically, before it could be used as a prompt-book."[98] Readers who wonder what provoked the phrase "more objectionably" must remember that the revisionists vehemently reject the "vulgar" notion that the theater company could have had any role in the Folio cuts. Having dismissed Stone's theory, Taylor then had to construct a narrative to explain how—always supposing that Shakespeare had changed his conception of the play—he could possibly have emended the Quarto in such a way as to affect the Folio text. Taylor solved that problem with some fertile invention:

> Alternatively, the redaction may be Shakespeare's, in which case we have no need to postulate the loss of the original prompt-book. Sometime after 1603 Shakespeare began to spend less time in London acting, and more time in Stratford with his family. If, at some point in or after 1608, he had decided to revise *Lear* during one of these sojourns in Stratford, he could hardly have taken the prompt-book with him: the company might need it in his absence, or he might lose it, and in any case he had no advance guarantee that the company would approve of his mutilating it. If he could not take the prompt-book, and could not take the foul papers (which had been sold), the only text of his play he could have taken with him was an exemplar of Q1—printed, he would have known, from his own foul pa-

> pers. He could annotate, revise, blot, and dirty a copy of Q1 as much as he wanted, without committing himself or the King's Men to anything; and if, when he had finished, the result seemed to him worth presenting to his fellow sharers as a new version of the play, then at some point he or someone else would have had to transcribe a new fair copy from Shakespeare's own heavily marked-up exemplar of Q1. This second reconstruction is, I believe, what actually happened.[99]

This concatenation of convenient suppositions is a classic example of free-floating speculation, sustained by the repetitions of "If . . . he had . . . he might . . . might . . . could not . . . could not . . . would have . . . could . . . if . . . would have had." These are all "counterfactuals," as linguists call them, referring to things that did not or cannot take place. Their proliferation exposes the fact that Taylor has no evidence for his belief that any of this "actually happened."

With that newly invented narrative Taylor achieved the revisionists' goal of inserting a material object representing Shakespeare's revisions, supposedly made during his lifetime, into the manuscript side of the stemma—but at what cost![100] Taylor had to hypothesize first that the King's Men had (conveniently for the revisionist thesis) lost their 1606 Booke, in order to break the direct line of transmission extending from it to its counterpart in the 1620s, which was either directly referred to by the Folio compositors or one from which a scribal copy was made. Second, Taylor hypothesized that Shakespeare revised his play in 1609–1611, making corrections and deletions in the margins of the 1608 Quarto, which was full of errors in typography, layout, and much else, and inserting 102 complete lines of "additions," together with an additional 143 isolated words and phrases in 64 separate locations, not to mention inaccurate speech prefixes and missing stage directions. Third, we are asked to believe that Shakespeare then persuaded the King's Men to convert this marked-up Quarto (Taylor having given Shakespeare permission to "mutilate . . . annotate, revise, blot, and dirty a copy of Q1 as much as he wanted") into the new, official promptbook—which would have had to incorporate, as his most trenchant critic put it, "some thousand changes of words and lineations."[101] As for the evidence that the

Folio may contain readings taken from the Second Quarto, printed seven years after Shakespeare's death, Taylor had to invent his final hypothesis—that in about 1622–1623 "these changes were all transferred *back* to the margins of a quarto, this time a copy of Q2 (1619) for use as Folio printer's copy."[102]

Many readers confronted by this theory for the first time may well wonder how anyone in Jaggard's printing house would have been able to collate the promptbook and the 1619 Quarto carefully enough to transfer thousands of verbal changes, and how they could possibly fit them into the margins of a small printed book. As I observed in an earlier chapter, this would have been extremely difficult, if not impossible. Richard Knowles pointed out that Taylor took up two positions regarding the "legibility of copy": "In one part of his essay Taylor argues vigorously that a quarto marked with more than a thousand alterations would be much too 'messy' to use as a promptbook, yet he is content to believe that it could serve as printer's copy. Perhaps; but illegible copy would result in needless error and stop-press correction."[103] Taylor put himself under so much pressure to design a scenario into which he could fit a putative Shakespearean rewrite that he was forced to invent a whole series of improbabilities. His flights of fancy are inimical to genuine textual criticism, a sober scholarly discipline concerned with establishing the process and results of textual transmission on the basis of material evidence. His speculations were created to support a theory imposed on, rather than derived from, the marks of print on paper.

The air of unreality that surrounds these speculations extended to the revisionists' exercises in textual criticism. Their theory allowed—indeed, compelled—them to treat any variant between the Quarto and Folio as a deliberate alteration. In his contribution MacDonald P. Jackson, otherwise a distinguished attribution scholar and editor, took up their banner by arguing that "the pattern of variation between the two texts . . . can, in fact, only be plausibly explained as the result of authorial revision."[104] Jackson was remarkably candid about the number of assumptions that would be needed to support a theory of revision by the dramatist himself:

> Let us assume that Q was set from Shakespeare's autograph and that 3.5 to 5.2 (roughly) of the manuscript was more finished

> than the rest of the play. Foul papers need not, after all, be uniformly 'foul', but can include relatively clean passages, either because of authorial transcription or because of greater ease in composition. Let us also suppose that Shakespeare, several years after the original composition of *Lear*, carried out revision by first annotating a copy of Q1. It would be natural enough for him to rework most thoroughly the beginning and end of the play, attending less fully to the middle section where revision was now mostly a matter of deletion.[105]

Readers should feel disinclined to "assume" or "suppose" any of those things, given the total lack of evidence. Why would Shakespeare want to revise *King Lear?* Even if he did, why would he choose to do so on an actual copy of the poorly printed 1608 Quarto, where the squeezing together of type, often not leaving space for commas, leaves little room for any marginal annotation, let alone the systematic correction that would be needed to reach the total of "over 850 variants" that Jackson computed. The evident improbability of the theory that Shakespeare made the Folio corrections on an actual copy of the 1608 Quarto is made more glaring by Jackson's confidence that he could intuit what a writer's "natural" procedure would be in carrying out revisions. As with Urkowitz's claim that 4.3 had been "interpolated" into the text, this group of critics must have had special access to past documents.

Having proposed a hypothesis loyally following Taylor's suppositions, Jackson extended his inquiry into the variants that occur between the uncorrected states of some sheets in the Quarto ("Qa") and the corrected ones ("Qb"), apparently assuming that Shakespeare realized that such things existed. (These differences were not noticed before the late nineteenth century, and only properly documented by Greg in 1940.) Jackson picked out the passage where Goneril offers herself to Edmund: "to thee a womans seruices are dew | A foole vsurps my bed," where the uncorrected sheet reads "My foote vsurps my body" (H3v23–24; 4.2.26). Jackson commented:

> In revising Q, Shakespeare would be anxious to correct downright errors throughout, but might overlook those not glaringly obvious, especially in passages where his chief concern was

> simply to add or delete. And to Qa's more or less indifferent variations from copy, as restored in Qb, he might often be indifferent himself. Thus, faced in 4.2 with Qa's 'My foote vsurps my body' he might realize that 'foote' ought to be 'foole', and yet be no less content with 'My' and 'body' than some modern editors have been, even though Qb's 'A' and 'bed' were the words he had once written.[106]

In piling one speculation on another, Jackson ascribed to Shakespeare the kind of open-minded acceptance of a printer's misreadings that Ezra Pound allegedly adopted in the *Cantos*.[107] So he suggested that, to Shakespeare, "Qa readings that were, strictly speaking, 'wrong' (in that they were compositorial misrepresentations of the Q manuscript copy) would not always have seemed so." We may wonder how Jackson can tell how things "would" or "would not" have seemed to Shakespeare or how he "would fairly consistently" have "corrected Q's misreadings"—always assuming that he possessed a copy of the 1608 Quarto containing those uncorrected sheets, and that he would read them with the eyes of a modern textual critic—or how "his other alterations to the Q text would *naturally* cluster within certain sections of the play." These are all instances of the revisionists' special pleading, designed to support a series of groundless suppositions. But like other advocates of the Two Versions theory, Jackson easily convinced himself of their truth, for a page later he declared that "much of the variation between Q and F can be proved due to revision."[108] It seems as if the need to find evidence of Shakespeare's invisible, intangible presence in the 1623 *Lear* has induced in the revisionist a kind of collective amnesia concerning accepted scholarly practices. As Fredson Bowers warned, when "textual criticism works with meanings and literary values" that are "divorced from all connection with the evidence of the mechanical process that imprinted meaningful symbols on a sheet of paper, no check-rein of fact or probability can restrain the farthest reaches of idle speculation."

It is unfortunate that Shakespeare's greatest play has suffered so much at the hands of printers and editors. Nicholas Okes, having just set up in business and printing a play for the first time, hired two inexperienced compositors, both perhaps apprentices, and gave them two difficult tasks: to make sense of Shakespeare's manuscript and to print it on an insufficient amount of paper. Isaac Jaggard and his employees were spared these difficulties when they printed *King Lear* in the Folio. But they used an officious editor, who corrected Shakespeare's grammar and regularized his prosody, while the apprentice compositor E was underqualified for this task. In addition to a low standard of printing and proof correcting, both the Quarto and Folio made cuts to the text, but fortunately the two abridgers made different choices, each preserving what the other had deleted. Also, each text derives from an authorial manuscript, and by restoring the missing passages we can restore the play to Shakespeare's original conception.

While neither of the early editions is a credit to the printer's trade, their faults can be corrected. The revisionist theory, embodied in the Oxford and Norton editions, however, has done far greater harm to the play. The two versions that they have created damage our understanding of Shakespeare by postulating, on mere supposition, that he became dissatisfied with his first, superbly constructed version; suffered a total lack of nerve and artistic judgment; and produced the butchered version found in the Folio. To form an accurate conception of the revisionists' effect on the play we must reverse the terms with which Stanley Wells recommended their project: "to split asunder the two texts of *King Lear* is a work of destruction, not of restoration."[109]

Conclusion: Toward a New Consensus

Readers who have followed my argument to this point may well be wondering how the revisionist theory, lacking any material evidence and based on a series of unsupported speculations, ever managed to become the new orthodoxy. How did it gather enough credibility to persuade two eminent academic publishers that Shakespeare's greatest play should be split in two? There would be several answers to this question, not all of which can be pursued here (such as the degree of exposure that the revisionists achieved through conference papers, networking, and media interventions), but the central issue has to be the notion of consensus.

The previous consensus of scholarly judgment on *King Lear* was that the two texts were interdependent, in that each contained passages omitted by the other, and that this complementarity meant that a combination of the two would restore their original unity. The Two Versions group attempted to overturn this consensus by arguing that the two texts were independent of each other. Their new theory was based on the passages omitted by the Folio; that is, on the *absence* of material evidence from which they conjured up the ghostly *presence* of Shakespeare. In the previous chapter I synthesized and extended critiques made by some of the leading scholars and editors of our time, who produced, between 1981 and 2008, extensive refutations of every element in their thesis. Evidently, in the eyes of these scholars at least, the revisionists had utterly failed to change the consensus.

Normally, in the humanities as in the sciences, new discoveries or interpretations may be gradually accepted by the scholarly community, but can also be modified or rejected. Some members of the revisionist group, however, did not wait for a larger community to endorse their claims, but in effect formed a mutually validating community of their own. Throughout *The Division of the Kingdoms* the contributors regularly endorsed each other's work in the most glowing terms, creating a cumulative effect of authority that must have influenced early readers and reviewers.[1] Stanley Wells set the tone for this product-endorsement process in his introduction, originally given in 1982 as a lecture at the Shakespeare Institute, Stratford, of which he was director.[2] Wells summarized Gary Taylor's supposition that the King's Men at some point, for no known reason, commissioned a new promptbook "of a revised text . . . influenced by the quarto" and endorsed this claim in these terms: "This argument, only recently advanced, has not yet been subjected to scholarly scrutiny. But its logic, though ingenious, seems undeniable." Two pages later Wells repeated the endorsement: "Taylor . . . persuasively argues that . . . the revision was made on a copy of the quarto that had been printed in 1608, and that it can be dated 1609–10." Finally, Wells praised Taylor's essay on "The War in *King Lear*" as "an excellent introduction" to the debate that "*demonstrates* that the two texts 'present coherent but distinct accounts' of the military actions of the fourth and fifth acts."[3] (As we saw in the previous chapter, when that essay was "subjected to scholarly scrutiny" the verdict was extremely unfavorable.) I have italicized the verb "demonstrates" since it characterizes the revisionists' tendency to hail a particular interpretation by one of their number as if it were definitive, awarding it an apodictic status—that is, "proved to be true by demonstration." In the essay originating the Two Versions thesis Michael Warren announced that he would "*demonstrate* the major alterations in the role" of Edgar.[4] According to Roger Warren, "several critics"—citing Taylor, Urkowitz, and Michael Warren—"have *demonstrated* that the whole trend of the Folio revisions is towards streamlining and simplification."[5] According to Taylor, not shy of tautology, his interpretation of a single press variant "*demonstrates conclusively* that the Folio text of *King Lear* represents a later version of the play."[6] Taylor accorded Kerrigan the same authoritative status as having "*demonstrated* that . . . the differences between Quarto and Folio *Lear clearly define* Folio *Lear* as an authorial redaction" and repeated the acclamation: "As John Kerrigan *demonstrates* . . ."[7] Kerrigan himself claimed certainty for his own interpretation: "That the Fool's role is better in F than Q, is, I think, *indisputable*," while Taylor praised his conclusion, reached "on what seem *indisputable* grounds."[8] William Carroll drew attention to this mutually endorsement process in a trenchant critique of the way in which the revisionists appealed to authority by citing each other's work, the end effect being that their collective volume turned into "a self-referential artefact."[9]

The apodictic status that the revisionists attributed to their claims gave the impression that the critical issues concerning *Lear* had been settled for all time. In one of many references to his own work Taylor rebuked both Madeleine Doran and W. W. Greg for not having "considered the possible structural or thematic implications of these Folio changes"—that is, the possibility that "thirteen lines of Kent's speech to the Gentleman [3.1.30–42] . . . might well have been consciously sacrificed to an altered dramatic vision of the last half of the play." Since neither Greg nor Doran shared the revisionists' belief that the Folio represents Shakespeare's considered alteration of the play, it is hardly surprising that they did not come up with this interpretation; fortunately, more enlightened critics have supplied the deficiency. In Taylor's modest formulation,

> the . . . implications of these Folio changes . . . have recently been defended—independently, and on purely artistic grounds—by both Steven Urkowitz (*Revision*, pp. 71–4, 93) and myself ('War'). As one of the proponents of this interpretation I can hardly pass an objective judgement on its merits; but a number of more disinterested readers have evidently found it persuasive. In any case, since censorship seems, on the historical evidence, extremely unlikely, conscious artistic alteration remains the only

> currently available explanation for this apparently interrelated set of variants.[10]

The reader who checks Taylor's footnote will find that the "number of more disinterested readers" who found the Urkowitz-Taylor interpretation "persuasive" was limited to one.[11] Despite the paucity of support, Taylor's assertion that they were in possession of "the only currently available explanation," namely that the Folio represents Shakespeare's "conscious artistic alteration," was typical of the Two Versions theorists' claims to exclusive and indisputable knowledge, a claim that challenges but also intimidates.

The most remarkable endorsement of the revisionist thesis came outside its pages, but from one of the contributors to their collective volume. A valuable feature of the annual *Shakespeare Survey* since its inception in 1948 has been its roundup of "The Year's Contribution to Shakespeare Study." In the volume for 1984, the section on "Editions and Textual Studies" was contributed by MacDonald P. Jackson, who included a review of *The Division of the Kingdoms*.[12] The editor of *Shakespeare Survey* at that time, Stanley Wells, evidently had no qualms about this arrangement, even though Jackson had been one of the authors represented in that collection and Wells himself had supplied its introduction. Jackson gave approving summaries of all the essays, praising Wells's introduction as "an elegant exposition of just what is at stake." He endorsed John Kerrigan's "fine critique," which "vindicates F: its Fool is 'dramatically superior' to Q's." Having modestly summarized his own contribution, Jackson reserved most approval for "Taylor's long and heavily documented final essay [which] draws together and supplements the various arguments." Jackson praised Taylor's "neat bibliographical argument" supporting his supposition that Shakespeare revised *Lear* "in 1610, beginning his revisions on an exemplar of Q," and informed readers that Taylor had surveyed "all important literary and dramatic differences between Q and F, so as 'to provide a comprehensive working model of the strategy of the Folio redaction.'" In conclusion, Jackson pronounced, "Cumulatively the case for revision in *King Lear* is overwhelming."

Many scholars will have been surprised that Wells, contrary to academic decorum, commissioned a review of this volume from one of its contributors. Whatever our judgment on that issue, Jackson's endorsement of the Two Versions thesis exemplified the degree to which its exponents praised each other's work, a mutual endorsement process by which they reassured each other of having succeeded, without having to wait for the scholarly community to form a consensus. When that consensus began to be visible, in reviews and journal articles written by "a number of more disinterested readers," as we have seen, their verdict was devastating. No part of the Two Versions theory survived.

I have described the revisionists as advocates, rather than scholars, since their main weapon was epideictic rhetoric, with its complementary techniques of *laudatio* and *vituperatio*. Just as they had lauded the Folio and disparaged the Quarto, so having praised each other they would damn their critics. Gary Taylor, their spokesman and driving force, published three essays between 1986 and 1994 in which he celebrated the revisionist victory. In the first of these, "Revising Shakespeare" (the punning title implying that Shakespeare was a revising dramatist) Taylor used the rhetorical tactic of trying to catch his opponents on the horns of a dilemma. In this ploy the debater offers two choices, as if they constitute the only possible positions to take. Taylor juxtaposed two groups of scholars, those who "contend that the play only makes sense, or makes better sense, if we combine and conflate material from both early documents"—"Stop here!" the experienced debater will say: "by using the terms 'combine and conflate' you have assumed that the Quarto and Folio are entirely separate texts, but all the evidence suggests that they were complementary." The other side of Taylor's dilemma, as is common in such ploys, favors the privileged position that we are meant to endorse: "as against those who argue that we should *not* conflate material from two different documents, but recognize instead that each document has its own artistic coherence, that each body has its own soul."[13] Taylor's pervasive question begging reaches its apex here: there are not only "two substantive editions" of *King Lear* but each also possesses a soul (a term that occurs for the first time in his writings). From this rhetorical height Taylor poured scorn on "those few critics who have tried to defend the entrenched conflationist orthodoxy against the new revisionist onslaught."[14] Taylor does not inform his readers who those unfortunate "few critics" were, but we can infer that they died in the trenches. He ended by dismissing "the unexamined belief that Shakespeare did *not* revise his work" in these terms: "It is like the pre-Copernican model of the universe: sustained only by the proliferation of improbable subsidiary complications."[15]

Taylor delivered this paper in 1985 to the Society of Textual Studies, New York, which had appointed as respondent G. Thomas Tanselle, a leading authority on textual criticism. Tanselle drew attention to Taylor's militarist rhetoric—"the revisionists have dramatized their cause as a challenge of entrenched dogma"—but denied them victory. The revisionists had failed to justify their main contention, that textual variants between a Quarto and a Folio text are proof that Shakespeare revised a play. As he put it,

> It is a significant step to move from authorial revision in general to the special class of revisions that produce separate works, and the link is not provided here. Revisionists must guard against letting their zeal cause them to see authorial revision everywhere, in nearly all variants that are not obviously erroneous, and in addition to find that these additions produce independent works. The tendency to overstatement that has repeatedly obscured the real contribution the revisionists have to make is not absent from this paper, for we are told here that the revisionist revelation is like the Copernican revolution. It is not, of course.[16]

Clearly, Taylor could not let Tanselle's rebuff stand, and in a later paper to that forum on "The Rhetoric of Textual Criticism," he accused his critic of having "shifted . . . discussion from the substance to the rhetoric of my paper."[17] That seems a serious complaint, and we might expect Taylor to then discuss the "substance" of his paper. Instead, with another rhetorical ploy he asserted that his analogy was mere rhetoric: "my literary allusion to the Copernican revolution was rhetorical, it carried an excess of extra-logical meaning." While admitting his own guilt, Taylor proceeded to indict everyone else in his profession with this rhetorical figure (its technical name is *anadiplosis*): "Textual criticism is about rhetoric, rhetoric is about persuasion, persuasion is about audiences."[18] This is a disturbing shift of argument, to use the traditional terms of rhetoric, from *res* (subject matter) to *verba* (language). It may be effective in the short term in disarming his critic, since they both supposedly made use of a "rhetorical ploy," but Taylor then generalized it ad absurdum: "The Copernican revolution was . . . a change in the rhetoric of science, which in turn permitted a change in the substance of science. The revisionist revolution in the editing of Shakespeare is, equally, a change in the rhetoric of textual criticism."[19] Historians and philosophers of science may be dismayed by that categorization of *De revolutionibus*, but textual critics will be equally dismayed to see their discipline described as being "about rhetoric," lacking any "substance." Worse still, according to Taylor, "[t]extual criticism, at the moment of decision, may be either *contra hominem* or *pro hominem*, but it is always *ad hominem*."[20] As we read Taylor's Hobbesian account of textual scholarship, it begins to seem that the qualities he ascribes to others are in fact a self-description: as he candidly admitted, "I . . . am characteristically disruptive, confrontational, paradoxical, and personal."[21] We may acknowledge his candor while wondering whether such attributes are appropriate for textual or indeed any other form of scholarship.

These qualities are certainly visible in the third of these papers, in which he presented the revisionists as constituting a "revolutionary" movement opposed, predictably enough, by "the rhetorics of reaction." This formulation cast Taylor in the sympathy-arousing role of defender, hardly borne out by the aggressive role he played in promoting the Two Versions theory between 1978 and 1983. (A history of this process would be valuable.) Taylor defined a "reactionary" as "someone who resists a real, or perceived, radical threat to prevailing cultural practices," the corollary being that "in our culture 'reactionary' is usually an insult, and 'revolutionary' usually a compliment."[22] Taylor thus complimented himself on belonging to "a group of scholars" opposed by "the 'reactionaries' . . . those scholars determined to resist this challenge to the fundamental structure of the prevailing editorial system."[23] It would have been interesting to see how Taylor might have acquitted himself in the arena of scholarly debate, where disagreements on matters of substance are fairly reported, open to discussion, with arguments on each side being subject to evaluation in terms of their internal coherence and their marshaling of evidence. But instead of engaging with his critics' arguments Taylor chose to devote forty pages to ridiculing his critics and justifying himself.[24] Taylor claimed that "[a]nyone who surveys the textual scholarship of the 1980s must be struck by the fact that most of the substantive new work was done by the so-called revolutionaries; the reactionary position was largely confined to reviews of those views. . . . Reactionaries do not need to create, because they are defending what has already been created; they claim to preserve what is."[25]

The self-regarding, self-promoting nature of this diatribe does not read well. Taylor thought to ridicule his critics simply by quoting their negative judgments on the "two-text revolutionaries" as if it were self-evident that, coming from "reactionaries," those judgments must be wrong. But the danger of citing unfavorable comments on this "revolutionary group" for their "hubris" or "arrogance" or for trying to "impose a moratorium on all save their own textual discussion" is that to readers who do not endorse their self-evaluation the comments may seem all too apt. Having quoted William Carroll's description of the "cross-referencing" by which contributors to *The Division of the Kingdoms* had praised each other's work, Taylor commented, in intended irony, that the ascribed behavior would put them on the same level as "the Mafia, or the Moonies, a closed, ingrown, self-supporting, conspiratorial sect."[26] That would be one way of putting it, no doubt extreme; yet Carroll's diagnosis cannot be dismissed so easily. The Earl of Chesterfield, quoting Shaftesbury, said that "ridicule is the best test of truth." Carroll's observation stands.

For all his vociferousness, Taylor chose to ignore the substantial critiques that had so far appeared by deflecting attention to other matters. He once again accused his critics of making "a characteristic reactionary diversion from substance to style," since some of them had drawn attention to the revisionists' modes of rhetorical emphasis. Taylor's response was a familiar debater's ploy, the *tu quoque* tactic, accusing the "reactionaries" of using rhetoric, "assertive magic," "incantatory repetition," the "trope of guilt-by-association," and so forth.[27] (In polemic it is only ever your enemies who use rhetoric or magic.) But in truth it was Taylor who made such a "diversion," ignoring the critiques made by the reputable scholars whom he labeled "reactionaries." This was a serious failure to observe the procedures of scholarship, in which differing interpretations of the evidence should be fairly summarized and then discussed in a rational manner, not presented in terms of a military campaign. Yet, without being too cynical, it can be effective to ignore the case made against you, for you may then persuade some observers that there is no case. Thus a recent historian of the Two Versions theory concluded that *The Division of the Kingdoms* and related works "were mostly well received by reviewers, and the revision hypothesis was broadly accepted."[28]

That is not true, but it must be admitted, with some unease, that the advocates of the "bi-textual" theory were undeniably successful in the marketplace. It is a strange irony, as Richard Knowles has noted, that their iconoclastic polemics against orthodoxy and authority resulted in their theory being accepted by one of the bastions of authority,

> the immensely prestigious and influential Oxford University Press and sanctioned by as highly respected a scholar as Stanley Wells. The rapid decision to print two *Lears* in the Oxford Shakespeare not only reified the revision theory but even seemed to institutionalize it overnight. Certainly high visibility also furthered acceptance, as a few enthusiasts busily promoted the revisionist views in several book, many essays, countless conference papers, and even media appearances. The idea of revision seemed suddenly everywhere and inescapable.[29]

Knowles wrote that "a few enthusiasts busily promoted the revisionist views," but from the bibliographical record it seems that Taylor was the only one who did so repeatedly. In his 1988 paper on "The Rhetoric of Textual Criticism" Taylor celebrated having successfully stormed this "bastion of authority":

> Politicians are not the only people to make use of bandwagons, *The Division of the Kingdoms*, a book published by Oxford Uni-

> versity Press in 1983, has been widely perceived as a turning point in discussion of the two texts of *King Lear.* The effect of the book depended, to a considerable though immeasurable extent, upon the fact that eleven different scholars, from America, Canada, England, and New Zealand, with a variety of different scholarly backgrounds, were all defending a single proposition: that the two texts of *King Lear* represent distinct versions. What had until that moment been an iconoclastic heresy, defended by a few isolated adherents who could easily be picked off one by one, now seemed to have become a mass movement, which could no longer be ignored.[30]

In this version the military analogy has changed from a collective "onslaught" to the workings of a sniper, who can "pick off one by one" the "few isolated adherents" of an antiquated textual theory.

Taylor presented the revisionist movement not as a Copernican revolution but one in the footsteps of Trotsky, who, as a standard reference work recorded, "order[ed] his Bolshevik forces to occupy crucial logistic and strategic points in Petrograd such as the telegraph and telephone offices . . . newspaper offices"[31]; more recent revolutionaries would seize the radio and TV stations. In line with such procedures, Taylor declared, "[A] successful revolution must also, at some point, seize the institutions of cultural power. That moment of seizure triggers an emotional crisis in the reactionary mind. The champions of authority find themselves deserted by their own authorities." In a rather unpleasant passage Taylor gloated over the revisionists' triumph because it discomfited their geriatric opponents: "In the case of Shakespeare, of course, the new textual revolutionaries, almost from the beginning, succeeded in hijacking the international resources and the cultural authority of Oxford University Press, not only the most respectable but commercially the most powerful of all academic publishers. This institutional reversal has provoked, predictably, enraged dismay among the reactionaries." Resisting Taylor's rhetoric, by which anyone who would react with dismay to this narrative would be defined as reactionary, I express regret that an author should see himself—perhaps in battle array, at the head of a select band of eleven revolutionaries—"hijacking" a publisher that had trusted him, at considerable expense, as a reliable scholar. At this point Taylor referred to his second commercial success in the Oxford Shakespeare, having persuaded the other editors to include his addition to Shakespeare's canon of the anonymous lyric, "Shall I die?" As Taylor put it, "Much of the outrage over 'Shall I die?' originated in a similar sense of betrayed impotence. Oxford University Press was going to force you all to swallow that dreadful poem."[32] Despite awarding himself the victor's crown, Taylor failed to record that his attribution of this lyric, which well-informed scholarship sees as a madrigal text dating from around 1611, has been universally rejected.[33] It *is* a dreadful poem, but nobody else swallowed it.

The common element in both these commercial victories was the method used to achieve them. Richard Knowles referred to the "few enthusiasts [who] busily promoted the revisionist views in several book, many essays, countless conference papers, and even media appearances," drawing attention to a new development in the academic world: the use of media hype to market a product. In the fiercely competitive world of textbook publishing it is advantageous to be able to claim that a new edition contains a new text. The first edition of the Oxford Shakespeare brought us "Shall I Die?," a divided *King Lear*, and an edition of *Pericles* padded out with verse created by Taylor and MacDonald Jackson from a novel by George Wilkins.[34] The publishers who allowed themselves to be persuaded by the revisionists' self-proclaimed consensus would be doing the world a service by recognizing that it was never supported by any textual or other evidence.

In attempting to chronicle the process by which the "Splitting of *King Lear*" was affected, we are faced with a strange phenomenon. The revisionist manifesto was published in 1983, and two of the prime movers, Gary Taylor and Stanley Wells, were able to give the theory material embodiment by publishing two separate editions in the Oxford Shakespeare (1986).[35] For many scholars that would already have been a satisfying demonstration of editorial power, the first time that a Shakespeare play had been divided against itself. But Taylor repeatedly returned to this victory in the seven years following *The Division of the Kingdoms*. Although we cannot know his motives they seem to have included a wish to mythologize "the revisionist onslaught" or provide it with a historical narrative. In 1990 he published a book with the ominous title *Reinventing Shakespeare*, in which he recalled the seminar held at the Shakespeare Association of America's (SAA) conference in in 1980. In it "four radical and as yet relatively unknown exponents of revision: Urkowitz, Randall McLeod, myself, and Michael Warren" are confronted in the seminar room by "three respected senior scholars."[36] Two of the three suddenly "announce their conversion to the revisionist cause," leaving the third—the respected scholar G. K. Hunter—as "champion of an orthodoxy that has lasted for centuries . . . suddenly surrounded and embattled": this may be the first time that a panel at the SAA, or anywhere else, has been described as a battlefield. The isolation of this single representative of the opposition, Taylor claims, has not only a military but also an aesthetic dimension, both signifying an imminent shift of power: "As in all the best plays, this peripeteia excites the audience; the revisionist position immediately acquires the intellectual glamour that David achieved by slaying Goliath." In this triumphalist narrative Taylor ascribes to the revisionists not only "intellectual glamor" but also a "sense of communal *potency*" as they "revise the accepted paradigms of editorial and critical practice. Their collective challenge to 250 years of Shakespeare texts does more than alter or displace hundreds of lines and stage directions in a dozen plays. Revisionism insists that texts are made; they become—they do not flash instantaneously into perfect and unalterable being."[37] Triumphalist complacency is followed by banality: we do not need revisionists to tell us that "texts are made"; everyone knows that, and nobody has ever thought that they "flash instantaneously" and so on. A straw man is erected and demolished, another debating society ploy.

Taylor juxtaposed his description of the 1980 seminar with an account of a parallel event in 1986, featuring Stephen Urkowitz debating the revisionist thesis with G. K. Hunter, one of the leading scholars of our times.[38] Their very appearance on the same platform, according to Taylor, demonstrates the reality of the revisionist cause: "The audience can see for itself that there are now at least two texts of *King Lear*: Hunter's and Urkowitz's." Once again Taylor writes off the opposition: "Hunter can offer his audience nothing new; in an intellectual economy based upon the constant production of novelty, he stands for an old text. But the revisionists, by doubling the number of texts of *King Lear* (or *Hamlet*, or *Othello*), more than double the potential for critical interpretation. *At a stroke*, all existing interpretations are rendered suspect; they must all be looked over again, in the light of this new theory. At the same time, critics are invited to examine two fresh new texts where before they had one stale old text."[39] As too often, Taylor the advocate cheapens the debate by dismissing Hunter, consigned to obsolescence as the "champion of an orthodoxy that has lasted for centuries," for having "nothing new to offer." He further trivializes the issue by reducing it to the choice between "two fresh new texts"—the Quarto and Folio texts of *King Lear* in the *Oxford Shakespeare*, two texts that Taylor and Wells had freshly conflated, each containing readings from the other—and "one stale old text," the composite version that respects the complementarity of the two original documents. (Taylor's language sounds uncomfortably like Edmund's scorn for the "dull, stale, tired" marriage bed.)

The general thrust of Taylor's self-justification was to discredit, disarm, and attempt to emasculate anyone who disagreed with the Two Versions theory. Compared to the revisionists' own proud "potency," he exemplified his belief that textual criticism must be *ad hominem* by diagnosing the independent critics as suffering from a common malady. He invoked the German sociologist Max Scheler, who, in Taylor's summary, had described the phenomenon of "*ressentiment*, a sense of *impotent* hatred, the anger of helplessness, which arises from the experience of reiterated humiliation. Such hatred will, by definition, only be redoubled—violently folded back upon itself again and again—by the succession of further proofs or victories for a revolutionary idea. Each new confirmation of the strength of the revolutionary position will aggravate and intensify the *ressentiment* of its opponents."[40] Taylor must have been pleased to find in Max Scheler's prophetic work a suitably pejorative term to denounce "reactionary" Shakespeare scholars. His hasty reading of this sociological classic, however, missed the point. Scheler described the phenomenon of *ressentiment* not as a "reiterated humiliation" effected by others but as "a self-poisoning of the mind . . . caused by the systematic repression of certain emotions and affects," notably "revenge, hatred, malice, envy, the impulse to detract, and spite."[41] Scheler argued that "*[r]essentiment* can only arise if these emotions are particularly powerful and yet must be suppressed because they are coupled with the feeling that one is unable to act them out—either because of weakness, physical or mental, or because of fear. Through its very origin, *ressentiment* is therefore chiefly confined to those who are *dominated* at the moment, who fruitlessly resent the sting of authority."[42] The feeling state that Scheler described is the internalized hatred that Shakespeare depicted in Iago, to whose anger at having been unfairly passed over by Othello is added the suspicion of having been cuckolded by him: "the thought whereof | Doth (like a poisonous mineral) gnaw my inwards."[43] As Scheler wrote, "the violent suppression of an impulse . . . subsequently revolts by 'embittering' and 'poisoning' the personality." Nothing in Scheler's psychological analysis fits the personalities or social positions of those who dared to criticize the revisionists, whether Richard Knowles, David Bevington, or the other scholars whom Taylor demonized as "reactionaries." Nor, indeed, do these critics necessarily belong to an older generation. A few minutes of research will show that some of the revisionists were as old as their critics.

Taylor cited approvingly Scheler's observation that "one 'situation generally exposed to *ressentiment* danger is the older generation's relation with the younger.'[44] The old see power being snatched away from them by the young, and know that in the long run there is nothing they can do about it."[45] But Taylor again misrepresented Scheler's argument by reducing it to a struggle between youth and age. Scheler placed this manifestation of *ressentiment* in a historical context, noting that in an earlier phase of western civilization respect for the old was common, but that in the modern era, "as the pace of 'progress' increases in all fields, and as the changes of *fashion* tend to affect even the higher domains (such as art and science), the old can no longer keep up with their juniors, and in such a competitive race, 'Novelty' becomes an ever greater value." This process is particularly strong, Scheler added, "when the generations compete with each other instead of cooperating for the creation of works which outlast them."[46] Curiously enough, Taylor's professed embrace of "an intellectual economy based upon the constant production of novelty" exactly fits Scheler's critical diagnosis of the lust for novelty and fashion in the modern world, but with none of the sociologist's regret for those changes. Taylor's bent is certainly for competition, not cooperation.

Taylor conceives the textual criticism and the editing of Shakespeare as a Darwinian or Oedipal struggle. As he sees it, "textual criticism is an apology for, or a prolegomenon to, the exercise of power: editors enact theories upon the bodies of texts. Editing exercises power, and it can only be understood by an analysis of power. Editors are always fighting each other, in a perpetual civil war designed to secure legitimacy for one faction or another."'[47] Those who do not share this philosophy may rather feel concern at "the bodies of texts" lying about the battlefield, as Taylor and others struggle for victory. In this worldview, "one of the greatest cultural expressions of this *ressentiment* against the revolutionary ingratitude of a new generation is, of course, ironically, *King Lear*. Revolutionaries are always the children of the culture they turn against, and overturn."[48] Unfortunately that argument backfires, since it would align the "Two-text revolutionaries" with Goneril, "Old fools are babes again" (1.3.20), and with Edmund: "The younger rises when the old doth fall" (3.3.77). Taylor's comments on older scholars, however, show that his conception of textual criticism as a Hobbesian struggle became a self-fulfilling prophecy. Having attempted to put down G. K. Hunter he attacked another target by complaining that, among those who had criticized him, "[t]he venerable Frank Kermode leads a chorus of gerontocrats in complaining that the Oxford editors . . . have ill-advisedly rushed into print."[49] Kermode's fault was to publish a critical review of the *Oxford Shakespeare*,[50] but history will remember him as an outstandingly perceptive scholar and critic, of whom Gary Taylor might have said "whose shoe's latchet I am not worthy to unloose."[51] It is a matter of some regret that, having had abundant opportunity to engage critics of the revisionist cause in a serious discussion, Taylor preferred to settle old scores. It recalls a passage in Dryden's 1697 Ode for St. Cecilia's Day, *Alexander's Feast;*

or the Power of Musique, in which Timotheus displays his skill with the lyre, rousing the king to a martial mood, in which he

> Fought all his battailes o'er again;
> And thrice He routed all his Foes; and thrice He slew the slain.[52]

In *Reinventing Shakespeare* (1990), recalling the SAA conference ten years earlier, Taylor endowed the revisionists' triumph with more dignity by presenting it not only in military but also in religious terms, as a conversion narrative. According to Taylor, three of the senior scholars (Stanley Wells, George Walton Williams, Thomas Clayton) suddenly "announce their conversion to the revisionist cause," an event that constitutes "a classic moment of theatrical recognition." Their "unexpected conversions . . . offer the participants and the audience a compelling model of anagnorisis; *suddenly, the scales fall from my eyes, and I can see the light.*"[53] Taylor's self-presentation as Paul on the road to Damascus is somewhat disingenuous, since he had been publicizing the Two Versions thesis for some years. But it conveys the sense that the revisionists did indeed behave, despite his disclaimer, as "a closed, ingrown, self-supporting" sect, sharing "a faith," as he put it elsewhere. The original group included Paul Werstine, who contributed to their volume the only independent scholarly essay of lasting value.[54] In an essay a decade later Taylor branded Werstine as an "apostate," having been "a—reluctant and uncomfortable—contributor" to the 1983 collection, "who has since built a reputation on conspicuously criticizing his erstwhile collaborators."[55] Apparently Werstine disagreed with Stanley Wells in two book reviews. ("Kent banish'd; his offence, honesty.")

However triumphalist Taylor may have sounded between 1983 and 1994, his declaration of victory was premature. The substance of my argument, together with the critiques made by a dozen independent scholars, shows that the revisionists failed to permanently change the scholarly consensus. By ignoring any contrary evidence, by ridiculing "hostile critics," and by a strenuous exercise of mutual praise, they succeeded for a while in creating the illusion of a revolution. What they lacked in "substance" they tried to make up for in "rhetoric," partly by constant repetition and partly by skating over the normal processes of scholarly argument. In their preface Taylor and Warren declared that the collective volume would discuss "the hypothesis that both texts represent independent Shakespearian versions of *King Lear*."[56] That seems a suitably tentative frame of mind when beginning a scholarly inquiry, suggesting that the question is open and that evidence and argument will be brought to bear before conclusions are drawn. Several of the independent scholars who evaluated the revisionists' work, however, observed that they constantly assumed what they were supposed to prove. In one of the earliest reviews of Urkowitz's 1980 monograph Richard Knowles found himself "constantly resisting exaggerated and forced interpretations, or the rhetorical tactic of hardening into certainty in one paragraph what was only hypothesis in the previous one."[57] In his review of that book Paul Werstine also noted the process by which the revisionists' initial assumptions hardened into certainties: "The middle of Urkowitz's book scarcely justifies the transformation of the moderate claims of his first chapter into the sweeping generalizations of his last. Indeed he assumes these generalizations throughout, sometimes relying on quite minor textual variants as indications of significant Shakespearean revisions in dramatic presentation."[58] One of the most acute analyses of the revisionists' methods of argument was provided by William Elton, who judged that "dual-*Lear* and Shakespeare-revision proponents evince easy slippage from hypothesis into fact. Questionable logic tends, moreover, to accompany a rhetoric of compulsion. What the proponents assert, *must* be true; what opponents' doubts are raised, *must* be false."[59] Reviewing *The Division of the Kingdoms*, Richard Knowles wrote that the essays as a whole were "weakened by persistent overstatement and special pleading. Several begin by openly assuming the thing to be proved, that only Shakespeare could have been the F reviser. Not surprisingly, given that premise, the F changes are generally found to be improvements over the Q original. Such conclusions are often arrived at by a kind of critical jujitsu that coverts apparent weakness into strength."[60] Clearly the group was so convinced of the rightness of its beliefs that its members felt justified in subordinating the normal procedures of scholarly argument to "a rhetoric of compulsion."

We have seen how the revisionists moved between the poles of praise for themselves and blame of their opponents, between praise of the Folio revision of *Lear* and diminution of the Quarto, exercising what Taylor defined as "the rhetoric of textual criticism." I have several times described them as advocates, in the sense that their scholarship was devoted to proving a case rather than pursuing the truth. In a recent essay on the adversarial legal system found in both the United States and Britain, the distinguished philosopher Susan Haack has illuminated the negative implications of the advocate's role: "an inquirer's business is to discover the true answer to his question, so his obligation is to seek out what evidence he can and assess it as fairly as possible. An advocate's business is to make the strongest possible case that this—our side's—answer is the true one; so he will be most effective if he selects and emphasizes whatever evidence favors the proposition in question, and ignores or plays down the rest."[61] That seems to me a fair description of the revisionists' method. As Haack underlined, "the concepts of inquiry and of evidence are intimately intertwined," reciprocally modifying each other: "if you are trying to find evidence to support a foregone conclusion rather than following the evidence where it leads, you aren't really inquiring."[62] This is precisely the objection that several independent scholars made to the Two Versions theorists. The process of inquiry, as Haack describes it, brings us back to the notion of consensus within a scholarly community:

> We describe disagreements among proponents of rival scientific theories or historical claims as "debates"; and participants in such controversies sometimes engage in something that looks a lot like advocacy. Moreover, eloquence and appeals to authority sometimes produce an artificial consensus, at least temporarily. But disagreements among real inquirers, unlike debates between rival advocates, cannot be decided by a vote on the basis of rival presentations: they will settle on a conclusion only if and when the evidence brings the community of inquirers to a genuine, unforced consensus.[63]

Haack's observation that "eloquence and appeals to authority sometimes produce an artificial consensus, at least temporarily" was partly true of the Two Versions theory. It enjoyed "an artificial consensus," having created a self-validating body and disregarding all independent criticism. Unchallenged, it has persisted far longer than it should and has misled a whole generation of readers.

I hope that this book may lead to a new consensus that will rescue *Lear* from the groundless disintegration it has suffered at the revisionists' hands. I have made two major claims. First, that the Quarto was damaged by a novice printer who had wrongly calculated the amount of paper that he would need, and was forced to compress the text by using a wide range of space-saving devices, but also to omit many lines and smaller phrases. As I have shown, both tactics were commonly used by printers in this period, but nowhere as extensively and as damagingly as in the 1608 Quarto. Secondly, far from the 1623 Folio representing Shakespeare's considered alteration of *King Lear* in about 1610, I have identified two stages of alteration by other hands. The book-keeper of the King's Men made several drastic and ill-judged cuts, pursuing an unknowable policy of abbreviating Shakespeare's most complex, most painful, yet most rewarding play. Taking over this abridged text, the editor employed by Jaggard then modernized Shakespeare's grammar, "regularized" his prosody, and made a great many changes expressing his personal linguistic preferences. (Such processes can be found in other Folio plays, but seldom as consistently as here.)

The new consensus I look for will be the recognition that by combining the deficiencies of the two abbreviated texts we can restore the play's original unity, indeed self-identity.[64] Having written *King Lear*, Shakespeare moved on to other projects: *Macbeth*, *Antony and Cleopatra*, *Coriolanus* . . . He had no reason to go back to his greatest pay. Nothing needed to be changed. It was, and it always had been, the one *King Lear*.

APPENDIX 1

APPENDIX 2

NOTES

INDEX

→ 1610s 20s James I reign

Appendix 1:
Illustrations and Commentary

Plate 1, D2r: corresponding to 1.4.244–295; TLN 753–811.

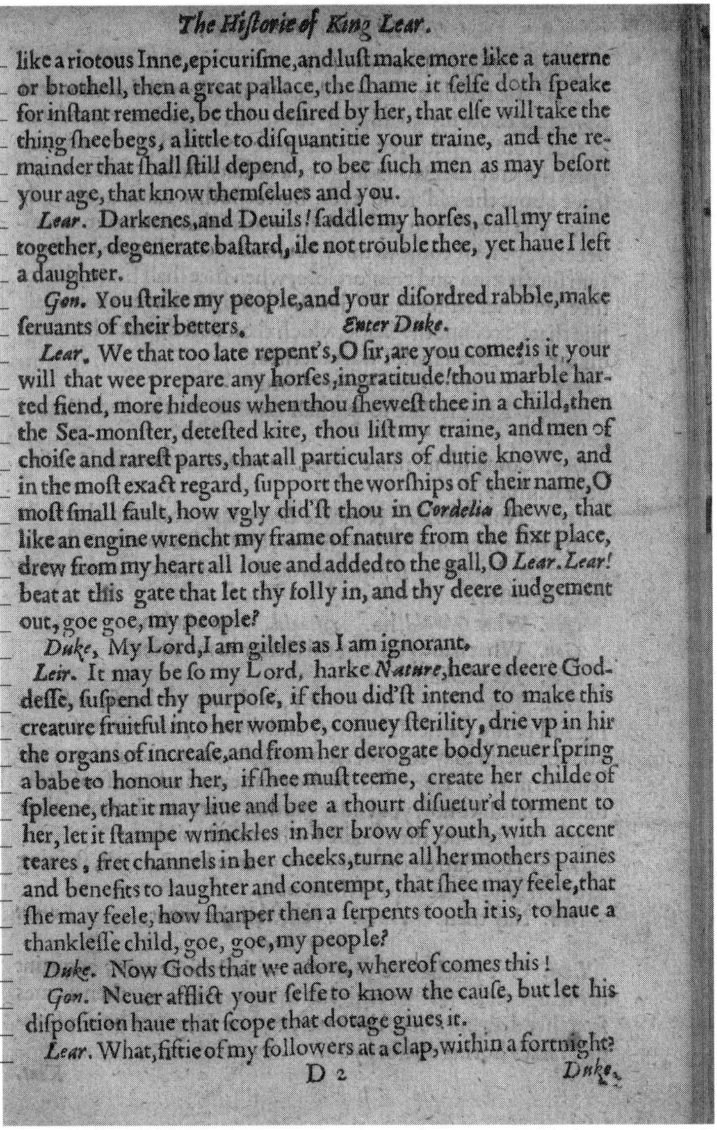

The Hiſtorie of King Lear.

like a riotous Inne,epicuriſme,and luſt make more like a tauerne
or brothell, then a great pallace, the ſhame it ſelfe doth ſpeake
for inſtant remedie, be thou deſired by her, that elſe will take the
thing ſhee begs, a little to diſquantitie your traine, and the re-
mainder that ſhall ſtill depend, to bee ſuch men as may beſort
your age, that know themſelues and you.

Lear. Darkenes,and Deuils! ſaddle my horſes, call my traine
together, degenerate baſtard, ile not trouble thee, yet haue I left
a daughter.

Gon. You ſtrike my people,and your diſordred rabble,make
ſeruants of their betters. *Enter Duke.*

Lear. We that too late repent's,O ſir,are you come? is it your
will that wee prepare any horſes,ingratitude! thou marble har-
ted fiend, more hideous when thou ſheweſt thee in a child,then
the Sea-monſter, deteſted kite, thou liſt my traine, and men of
choiſe and rareſt parts, that all particulars of dutie knowe, and
in the moſt exact regard, ſupport the worſhips of their name,O
moſt ſmall fault, how vgly did'ſt thou in *Cordelia* ſhewe, that
like an engine wrencht my frame of nature from the fixt place,
drew from my heart all loue and added to the gall,O *Lear*. *Lear*!
beat at this gate that let thy folly in, and thy deere iudgement
out, goe goe, my people?

Duke, My Lord,I am giltles as I am ignorant.

Leir. It may be ſo my Lord, harke *Nature*,heare deere God-
deſſe, ſuſpend thy purpoſe, if thou did'ſt intend to make this
creature fruitful into her wombe, conuey ſterility, drie vp in hir
the organs of increaſe,and from her derogate body neuer ſpring
a babe to honour her, if ſhee muſt teeme, create her childe of
ſpleene, that it may liue and bee a thourt diſuetur'd torment to
her, let it ſtampe wrinckles in her brow of youth, with accent
teares, fret channels in her cheeks,turne all her mothers paines
and benefits to laughter and contempt, that ſhee may feele,that
ſhe may feele, how ſharper then a ſerpents tooth it is, to haue a
thankleſſe child, goe, goe, my people?

Duke. Now Gods that we adore, whereof comes this!

Gon. Neuer afflict your ſelfe to know the cauſe, but let his
diſpoſition haue that ſcope that dotage giues it.

Lear. What,fiftie of my followers at a clap,within a fortnight?

D 2 *Duke*.

This page shows the effects of reducing verse to prose, compressing 52 lines to 38. At line 15, following "Sea-monster," Q omits Albany's interjection "Pray Sir be patient," as found in F1 (TLN 774). In line 11 an entrance has been set in the text. In approximately 15 instances, no space is left following a comma.

Plate 2, F4r: corresponding to 3.1.55, 3.2.1–42; TLN 1653–1694.

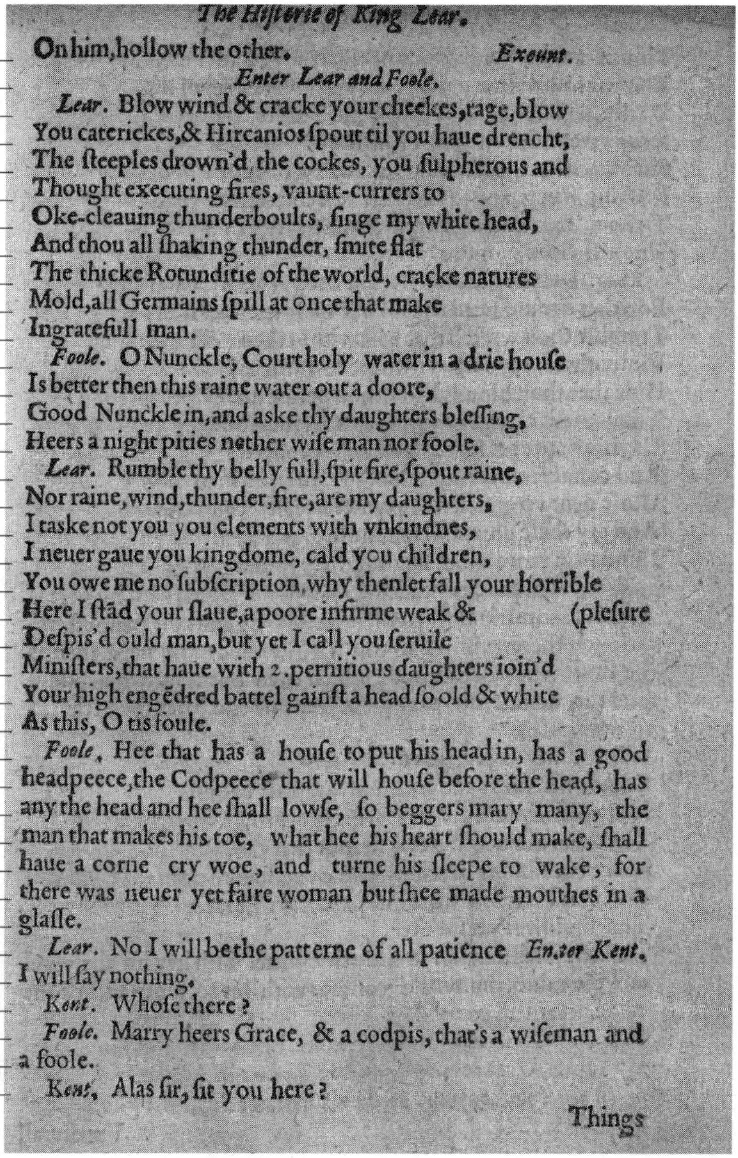

The Hiſtorie of King Lear.

On him,hollow the other. *Exeunt.*

Enter Lear and Foole.

Lear. Blow wind & cracke your cheekes,rage,blow
You caterickes,& Hircanios ſpout til you haue drencht,
The ſteeples drown'd, the cockes, you ſulpherous and
Thought executing fires, vaunt-currers to
Oke-cleauing thunderboults, ſinge my white head,
And thou all ſhaking thunder, ſmite flat
The thicke Rotunditie of the world, cracke natures
Mold,all Germains ſpill at once that make
Ingratefull man.

Foole. O Nunckle, Court holy water in a drie houſe
Is better then this raine water out a doore,
Good Nunckle in,and aske thy daughters bleſſing,
Heers a night pities nether wiſe man nor foole.

Lear. Rumble thy belly full,ſpit fire,ſpout raine,
Nor raine,wind,thunder,fire,are my daughters,
I taske not you you elements with vnkindnes,
I neuer gaue you kingdome, cald you children,
You owe me no ſubſcription,why then let fall your horrible
Here I ſtãd your ſlaue,a poore infirme weak & (pleſure
Deſpis'd ould man,but yet I call you ſeruile
Miniſters,that haue with 2.pernitious daughters ioin'd
Your high engẽdred battel gainſt a head ſo old & white
As this, O tis foule.

Foole, Hee that has a houſe to put his head in, has a good
headpeece,the Codpeece that will houſe before the head, has
any the head and hee ſhall lowſe, ſo beggers mary many, the
man that makes his toe, what hee his heart ſhould make, ſhall
haue a corne cry woe, and turne his ſleepe to wake, for
there was neuer yet faire woman but ſhee made mouthes in a
glaſſe.

Lear. No I will be the patterne of all patience *En.ter Kent.*
I will ſay nothing.

Kent. Whoſe there?

Foole. Marry heers Grace, & a codpis, that's a wiſeman and
a foole.

Kent, Alas ſir, ſit you here?

Things

From lines 1 to 19 the compositor has used the narrow measure, converting a prose speech by the Fool into four lines of verse. The measure switches to the wide setting at line 20, but still has to turn the line down. It seems to revert to narrow at lines 21–22, but returns to wide for the Fool's speech, of which lines 27–30 represent eight lines of rhymed verse. Oddly, the compositor set lines 26–30 wide, although he could easily have accommodated the Fool's last word ("glasse") and saved himself a line. He used space-saving devices on seven occasions: the ampersand (lines 3, 21, 36), the tilde (21, 24), and a numeral (23).

Plate 3, H4r: corresponding to 4.2.42–80; TLN 2304–2325.

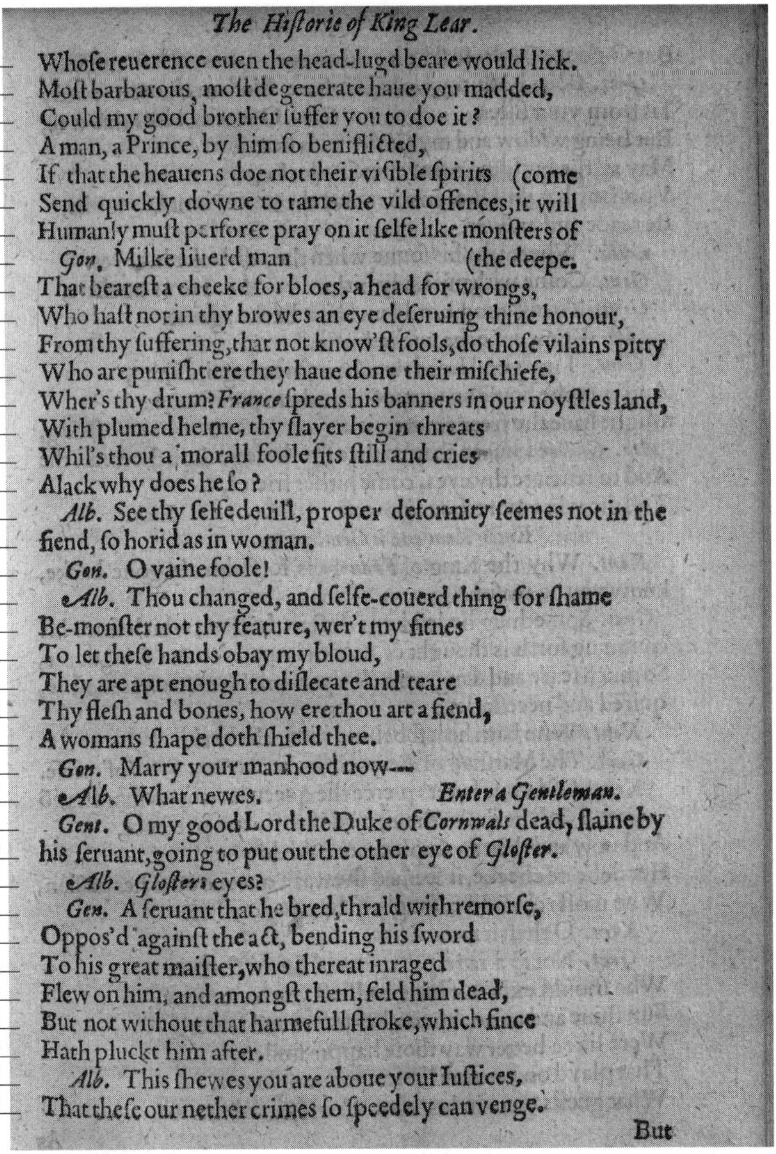

The Hiſtorie of King Lear.

Whoſe reuerence euen the head-lugd beare would lick.
Moſt barbarous, moſt degenerate haue you madded,
Could my good brother ſuffer you to doe it?
A man, a Prince, by him ſo beniflicted,
If that the heauens doe not their viſible ſpirits (come
Send quickly downe to tame the vild offences, it will
Humanly muſt perforce pray on it ſelfe like monſters of
Gon. Milke liuerd man (the deepe.
That beareſt a cheeke for bloes, a head for wrongs,
Who haſt not in thy browes an eye deſeruing thine honour,
From thy ſuffering, that not know'ſt fools, do thoſe vilains pitty
Who are puniſht ere they haue done their miſchiefe,
Wher's thy drum? *France* ſpreds his banners in our noyſtles land,
With plumed helme, thy ſlayer begin threats
Whil's thou a morall foole ſits ſtill and cries
Alack why does he ſo?
Alb. See thy ſelfe deuill, proper deformity ſeemes not in the
fiend, ſo horid as in woman.
Gon. O vaine foole!
Alb. Thou changed, and ſelfe-couerd thing for ſhame
Be-monſter not thy feature, wer't my fitnes
To let theſe hands obay my bloud,
They are apt enough to diſlecate and teare
Thy fleſh and bones, how ere thou art a fiend,
A womans ſhape doth ſhield thee.
Gon. Marry your manhood now---
Alb. What newes. *Enter a Gentleman.*
Gent. O my good Lord the Duke of *Cornwals* dead, ſlaine by
his ſeruant, going to put out the other eye of *Gloſter.*
Alb. *Gloſters* eyes?
Gen. A ſeruant that he bred, thrald with remorſe,
Oppos'd againſt the act, bending his ſword
To his great maiſter, who thereat inraged
Flew on him, and amongſt them, feld him dead,
But not without that harmefull ſtroke, which ſince
Hath pluckt him after.
Alb. This ſhewes you are aboue your Iuſtices,
That theſe our nether crimes ſo ſpeedely can venge.
But

This page begins in the narrow measure, compressing nine verse lines into eight, but having to use a turn-over and a turn-under. The compositor switched to the wide setting for Goneril's speech (9–16) and saved one verse line by extending the lineation at lines 10–13. For Albany's reply (17–18) he reduced three lines of verse to two of prose. At 27 an entrance is set in the text by switching to the wide measure, which is retained for lines 28–29, where three lines of verse are reduced to two of prose. On this page the Folio made three large cuts, amounting to twenty lines, only retaining 8–11 (up to "suffering"), 17–19, and 27–38.

Plate 4, K3r: corresponding to 4.7.96, 5.1.1–36; TLN 2845–2877.

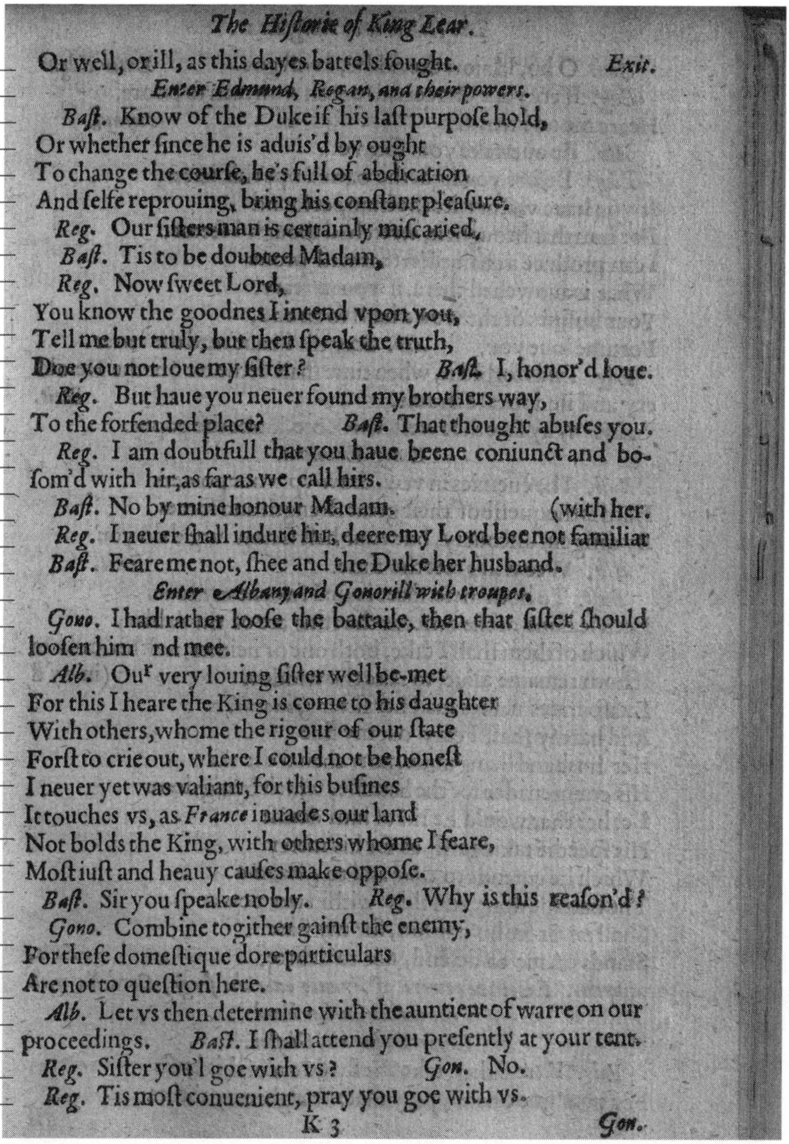

The Hiſtorie of King Lear.

Or well, or ill, as this dayes battels fought. *Exit.*

Enter Edmund, Regan, and their powers.

Baſt. Know of the Duke if his laſt purpoſe hold,
Or whether ſince he is aduis'd by ought
To change the courſe, he's full of abdication
And ſelfe reprouing, bring his conſtant pleaſure.
Reg. Our ſiſters man is certainly miſcaried.
Baſt. Tis to be doubted Madam,
Reg. Now ſweet Lord,
You know the goodnes I intend vpon you,
Tell me but truly, but then ſpeak the truth,
Doe you not loue my ſiſter? *Baſt.* I, honor'd loue.
Reg. But haue you neuer found my brothers way,
To the forfended place? *Baſt.* That thought abuſes you.
Reg. I am doubtfull that you haue beene coniunct and bo-
ſom'd with hir, as far as we call hirs.
Baſt. No by mine honour Madam. (with her.
Reg. I neuer ſhall indure hir, deere my Lord bee not familiar
Baſt. Feare me not, ſhee and the Duke her husband.

Enter Albany and Gonorill with troupes.

Gono. I had rather looſe the battaile, then that ſiſter ſhould
looſen him nd mee.
Alb. Our very louing ſiſter well be-met
For this I heare the King is come to his daughter
With others, whome the rigour of our ſtate
Forſt to crie out, where I could not be honeſt
I neuer yet was valiant, for this buſines
It touches vs, as *France* inuades our land
Not bolds the King, with others whome I feare,
Moſt iuſt and heauy cauſes make oppoſe.
Baſt. Sir you ſpeake nobly. *Reg.* Why is this reaſon'd?
Gono. Combine togither gainſt the enemy,
For theſe domeſtique dore particulars
Are not to queſtion here.
Alb. Let vs then determine with the auntient of warre on our
proceedings. *Baſt.* I ſhall attend you preſently at your tent.
Reg. Siſter you'l goe with vs? *Gon.* No.
Reg. Tis moſt conuenient, pray you goe with vs.

K 3 *Gon.*

The compositor set the first line wide in order to fit in the "Exit." He then switched to the narrow measure, but reverted to wide for lines 12 to 22, where he twice used "continuous printing" (setting speeches by two characters in one line); however, in setting the reply speech full right, he left large "pigeon-holes." Despite using the wide setting he had to turn up two words at 17–18. At 23 he reverted to the narrow measure, but at 31, 36, and 37 he used continuous printing again, with attendant pigeon-holes. He reduced four verse lines to prose (15–16, 18, 21–22, 35–36), but only saved two lines.

Plate 5, L2r: corresponding to 5.3.140–179; TLN 3095–3140.

The Historie of King Lear.

As bent to proue vpon thy heart whereto I ſpeake thou lieſt,
Baſt. In wiſdome I ſholud aske thy name,
But ſince thy outſide lookes ſo faire and warlike,
And that thy being ſome ſay of breeding breathes,
By right of knighthood, I diſdaine and ſpurne
Heere do I toſſe thoſe treaſons to thy head.
With the hell hatedly, oreturnd thy heart,
Which for they yet glance by and ſcarcely bruſe,
This ſword of mine ſhall giue them inſtant way
Where they ſhall reſt for euer, trumpets ſpeake.
Alb. Saue him, ſaue him,
Gon. This is meere practiſe *Gloſter* by the law of armes
Thou art not bound to anſwere an vnknowne oppoſite,
Thou art not vanquiſht, but couſned and beguild,
Alb. Stop your mouth dame, or with this paper ſhall I ſtople
it, thou worſe then any thing, reade thine owne euill, nay no
tearing Lady, I perceiue you know't, (me for't.
Gon. Say if I do, the lawes are mine not thine, who ſhal arraine
Alb. Moſt monſtrous know'ſt thou this paper?
Gon. Aske me not what I know. *Exit. Gonorill.*
Alb. Go after her, ſhee's deſperate, gouerne her.
Baſt. What you haue chargd me with, that haue I don
And more, much more, the time will bring it out.
Tis paſt, and ſo am I, but what art thou
That haſt this fortune on me? if thou bee'ſt noble
I do forgiue thee.
Edg. Let's exchange charity,
I am no leſſe in bloud then thou art *Edmond*,
If more, the more thou haſt wrongd me.
My name is *Edgar*, and thy fathers ſonne,
The Gods are iuſt, and of our pleaſant vertues.
Make inſtruments to ſcourge vs the darke and vitious
Place where thee he gotte, coſt him his eies.
Baſt. Thou haſt ſpoken truth, the wheele is come
full circled I am heere.
Alb. Me thought thy very gate did prophecie,
A royall nobleneſſe I muſt embrace thee.
Let ſorow ſplit my heart if I did euer hate thee or thy father.

L 2 *Edgar.*

Having run two lines together, the compositor set the opening line on the page wide. He switched to narrow for the next ten lines but reverted to wide for the speech of Goneril (12–14), compressing four lines of verse into three, and for that of Albany (15–17), reducing four lines of verse to three of prose. At line 18 he reduced Goneril's speech from two lines of verse to one, but had to turn up two words. He set Goneril's "*Exit.*" in the same line as her speech (20). Having reverted to the narrow measure for lines 19–37, he had to set the final line wide.

Plate 6, L4r: corresponding to 5.3.280–327; TLN 3254–3301.

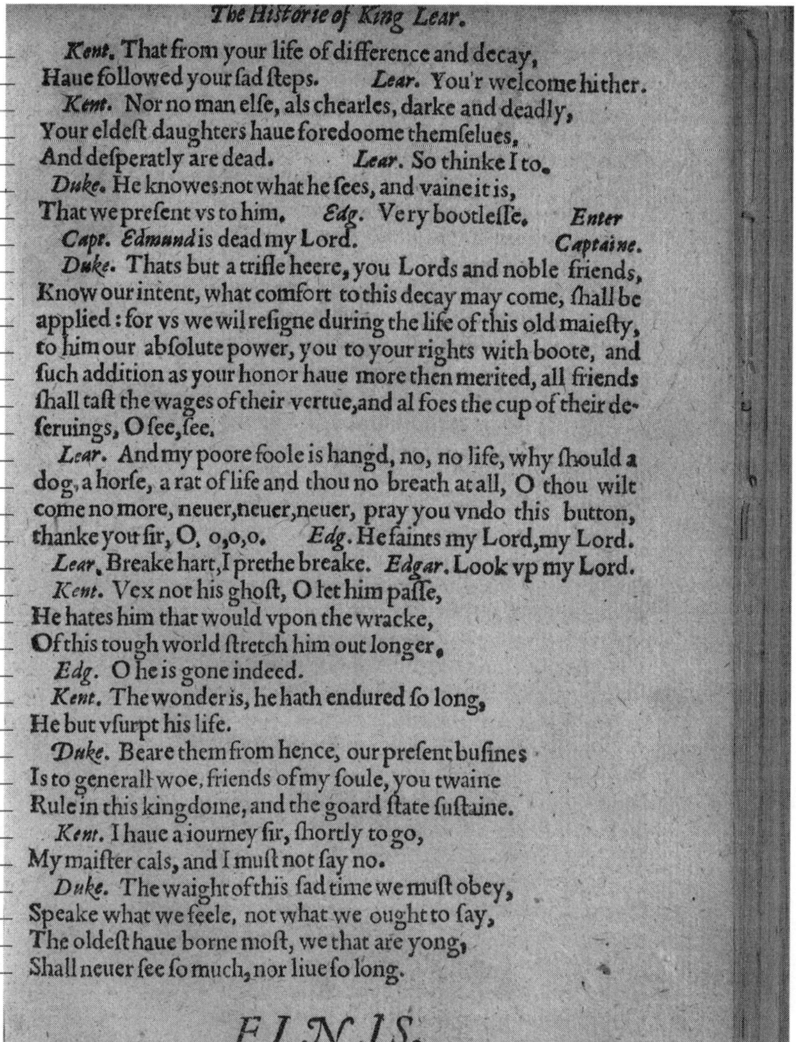

The Hiſtorie of King Lear.

Kent. That from your life of difference and decay,
Haue followed your ſad ſteps. *Lear.* You'r welcome hither.
Kent. Nor no man elſe, als chearles, darke and deadly,
Your eldeſt daughters haue foredoome themſelues,
And deſperatly are dead. *Lear.* So thinke I to.
Duke. He knowes not what he ſees, and vaine it is,
That we preſent vs to him. *Edg.* Very bootleſſe. *Enter*
Capt. *Edmund* is dead my Lord. *Captaine.*
Duke. Thats but a trifle heere, you Lords and noble friends,
Know our intent, what comfort to this decay may come, ſhall be applied: for vs we wil reſigne during the life of this old maieſty, to him our abſolute power, you to your rights with boote, and ſuch addition as your honor haue more then merited, all friends ſhall taſt the wages of their vertue, and al foes the cup of their deſeruings, O ſee, ſee.
Lear. And my poore foole is hangd, no, no life, why ſhould a dog, a horſe, a rat of life and thou no breath at all, O thou wilt come no more, neuer, neuer, neuer, pray you vndo this button, thanke you ſir, O, o,o,o. *Edg.* He faints my Lord, my Lord.
Lear. Breake hart, I prethe breake. *Edgar.* Look vp my Lord.
Kent. Vex not his ghoſt, O let him paſſe,
He hates him that would vpon the wracke,
Of this tough world ſtretch him out longer.
Edg. O he is gone indeed.
Kent. The wonder is, he hath endured ſo long,
He but vſurpt his life.
Duke. Beare them from hence, our preſent buſines
Is to generall woe, friends of my ſoule, you twaine
Rule in this kingdome, and the goard ſtate ſuſtaine.
Kent. I haue a iourney ſir, ſhortly to go,
My maiſter cals, and I muſt not ſay no.
Duke. The waight of this ſad time we muſt obey,
Speake what we feele, not what we ought to ſay,
The oldeſt haue borne moſt, we that are yong,
Shall neuer ſee ſo much, nor liue ſo long.

FINIS.

This final page contains three fewer lines than normal in order to accommodate the "*FINIS.*" It uses continuous printing on five occasions (2, 5, 7, 19, 20) and at line 7 even manages to squeeze in an entry at the right margin, albeit divided over two lines (7–8). The compositor reduced Albany's speech (9–15) from ten lines of verse to seven of prose, and that by Lear (16–19) from five to three-and-a-half verse lines. Compared to the Folio, this text omits the adjective "great" modifying "decay"(10), leaves out two repetitions of "neuer" (18), and substitutes "O, o,o,o." for the lines "Do you see this? Look on her? Look her lips' Look there, look there" (TLN 3282–3283). The Folio gives the speech "Breake hart,I prethe breake" (20) to Kent, and the final speech to Edgar (TLN 3298). It also includes the stage directions missing in the Quarto: "*He dies.*" (19), as well as the concluding direction: "*Exeunt with a dead March.*" (3302).

Appendix 2

Space Saving in Q1 *King Lear*

The table is divided into three sections:

I Text Arrangement

Column A identifies the inner (I) and outer (O) formes of each sheet.
Column B lists the individual pages, recto and verso.
Column C gives the amount of text carried on each page, keyed to J. L. Halio, *The First Quarto of King Lear.*
Column D gives the width of each page:
N: narrow (measure of ca. 80–81 mm), justified, turn-over lines within right margin
W: wide (93–4 mm), turned-over lines full out
N/W: narrow measure but with some prose lines set full
W/N: wide measure but with some verse lines justified
Column E gives the number of text lines (as in Halio) per Quarto page.
Column F lists the number of stage directions on each page.

II Typographical Adjustments

These are purely physical changes made by the printer to save space. In columns G–J an asterisk denotes the use of these devices in the wider measure.

Column G: use of the tilde
Column H: use of the ampersand (&)
Column I: use of numerals ("100")
Column J: lines of verse or prose turned up or down
Column K: medial commas, spaced
Column L: medial commas, unspaced

III Text Adjustments

These are changes made by the printer to the text itself to save space.

Column M: passages of verse set as prose
Column N: passages of verse relined, to occupy less room
Column O: more than one speech set on the same line
Column P: stage directions not fully displayed, in three categories:
omitted <SD>; placed in text line [SD]; in margin of text {SD}
Column Q: lines omitted
Column R: total number of lines saved

I: TEXT ARRANGEMENT						II: TYPOGRAPHICA		
Forme	Page	Text extent	Measure	No. of text lines	SDs	Tildes	&	Numera
O	B1r	1.1.1–19	W	19	2		1*	
I	B1v	1.1.20–55	N/W	36	3			
I	B2r	1.1.56–94	N/W	39			1	
O	B2v	1.1.95–130	N	34.5		1	2	
O	B3r	1.1.130–164	N/W	35.5				
I	B3v	1.1.165–200	N	35.5	1	2		
I	B4r	1.1.200–238	N	37.5		2		
O	B4v	1.1.239–273	N/W	34.5	1	2	1	
				271.5	7	7	5	0
O	C1r	1.1.273–285		43	2			1*
		1.2.1–31	W					
I	C1v	1.2.32–65	W	34		1*	1*	
I	C2r	1.2.66–100	W	35.5		1*	1*	
O	C2v	1.2.100–135	W	36		1*		
O	C3r	1.2.135–1.4.2	W/N	37	2		2*	
I	C3v	1.4.2–1.4.39	W	38.5	2			
I	C4r	1.4.40–1.4.74	W	35		2*	1*	
O	C4v	1.4.75–123	W	49				
				308	6	5	5	1
O	D1r	1.4.124–162	W	39	1		1*	
I	D1v	1.4.162–210	W	48			1*	1*
I	D2r	1.4.211–262	W	52.5				
O	D2v	1.4.262–1.5.4	W	46.5	1		2*	
O	D3r	1.5.5–41	W	37		1*		
I	D3v	2.1.1–39	W	39	1			
I	D4r	2.1.40–86	W	47	1			
O	D4v	2.1.87–126.5	W/N	40.5			1*	
				349.5	4	1	5	1
O	E1r	2.1.126.5–128		35.5	3			
		2.2.1–34	W					
I	E1v	2.2.35–71	W	38				
I	E2r	2.2.72–109.5	N/W	38.5			1*	
O	E2v	2.2.109.5–144	N/W	35.5		1	1	
		2.2.145–156						
O	E3r	2.3;2.4.1–3.5	N	35.5	2			
I	E3v	2.4.3.5–37	N/W	34.5			1	
I	E4r	2.4.38–74	N/W	37	1	1*		1*

ADJUSTMENTS | III: TEXT ADJUSTMENTS AND LINES SAVED

Turned lines	Medial commas		Verse→ Prose	Verse relined	Half-lines	SDs part	Lines omitted	Total saved
	Spaced	Unspaced						
	13	5						
1	9	13					8	8
1	14	12		3			4	7
1	9	8						
2	9	10		1			1	2
2	9	10		2				2
2	8	13		2				2
2	9	10		1				1
11	80	81	0	9	0	0	13	22
	21	12	8					8
	20	16						
	28	21					6	6
	23	17				{1}1	6	7
	17	15	1					1
	25	11	2		3			5
	25	11			2	<1>[1]		4
	32	4	6	4		[1]		11
0	150	107	17	4	5	4	12	42
	24	10	3					3
	33	17	8					8
	38	23	16			<1>[1]	2	20
	28	14	11		2	<1>	14	28
	12	15	1		3	{1}		4
	33	13	7		1	<1>		10
	34	24	12					12
	19	12	3	1	1			5
0	221	128	61	1	7	4	16	90
	32	12		1	4			5
1*	26	9		1				1
	13	9	1	2				3
1	14	9	1	1				2
1	22	3						
	10	12			3		2	5
1	15	11	3				9	12

I: TEXT ARRANGEMENT						II: TYPOGRAPHICA		
Forme	Page	Text extent	Measure	No. of text lines	SDs	Tildes	&	Numera
O	E4v	2.4.74–111	N/W	37	1	2	1	
				291.5	7	4	4	1
O	F1r	2.4.112–148	N	37		3	1	
I	F1v	2.4.149–180	N	32				
I	F2r	2.4.181–216	N/W	36		1*		
O	F2v	2.4.217–251	N	35				
O	F3r	2.4.252–278 3.1.1–10	N	37	2	1[S.D.]	1	1
I	F3v	3.1.11–46.5	N	36.5		1		
I	F4r	3.1.46.5 3.2.1–38	N/W	38.5	1	2	4;1*	1
O	F4v	3.2.38–3.3.1	N/W	38	1			
				290	3	8	7	2
O	G1r	3.3.1–20 3.4.1–14	N/W	34	1	4		
I	G1v	3.4.15–47	N/W	33				
I	G2r	3.4.48–84	W	37		1	1*	
O	G2v	3.4.84–124	W	40		1*	1*	
O	G3r	3.4.125–155 3.5.1–5	N/W	36	1			
I	G3v	3.5.6–20 3.6.1–23	W	38	1			
I	G4r	3.6.24–70.5	W	47.5		4*	2*	
O	G4v	3.6.70.5–104 3.7.1–5	W	39.5	1		2*	
				305	4	10	6	0
O	H1r	3.7.6–42	W	37	1	2*		
I	H1v	3.7.43–78	N/W	36		1		
I	H2r	3.7.79–105 4.1.1–10.5	W/N	36.5	2		2*	
O	H2v	4.1.10.5–44	N/W	34.5				
O	H3r	4.1.45–75 4.2.1–2	N	33	2		2	
I	H3v	4.2.3–39	N/W	37				
I	H4r	4.2.40–77.5	N/W	38.5				
O	H4v	4.2.77.5–95 4.3.1–20	W	38.5	1	1*		
				291	6	4	4	0
O	I1r	4.3.21–55 4.4.1–3	W	38	1			

ADJUSTMENTS			III: TEXT ADJUSTMENTS AND LINES SAVED					
	Medial commas							
Turned lines	Spaced	Unspaced	Verse→ Prose	Verse relined	Half-lines	SDs part	Lines omitted	Total saved
1	12	17		3			3	6
5	144	82	5	8	7	0	14	34
4	10	9		3			6	9
	13	7				[2]		2
	14	13						
	16	6						
2	9	13		1		{1}[1]	2	4
1	10	7		1			8	9
1	16	18	4	1		[1]		6
	25	10	3	1				4
8	88	73	4	6	0	4	16	34
2	20	11	1	1	1			3
1	22	11		2		<1>	5	8
	37	12						
	32	16	3			[1]		4
2	16	7	2	2				4
	22	7	1				3	4
2*	26	11	5					5
2*	9	17		3		[1]	1	5
9	184	92	12	8	1	3	9	33
3*	15	7	2	3	1	[1]		7
1	10	5		3	2	[1]		6
	21	11	3	1		[1]	3	8
1	12	8	1					1
3	15	9		1			1	2
2	18	12	2	2		<1>	1	6
2	13	7	2	2		[1]		5
3*	8	3		4	2			6
15	112	62	10	16	5	5	5	41
1*	11	3		2				2

I: TEXT ARRANGEMENT						II: TYPOGRAPHICA		
Forme	Page	Text extent	Measure	No. of text lines	SDs	Tildes	&	Numera
I	I1v	4.4.4–29 4.5.1–15.5	W	41.5	1			
I	I2r	4.5.15.5–42 4.6.1–6	N/W	33.5	1			
O	I2v	4.6.7–40	N	34				
O	I3r	4.6.41–76	N/W	36				
I	I3v	4.6.77–123.5	W/N	47.5	1	1;1*	1*	
I	I4r	4.6.123.4–169.5	W	47				
O	I4v	4.6.169.5–209.5	W/N	41	1		1*	
				318.5	5	2	2	0
O	K1r	4.6.209.5–249.5	N/W	41		1		
I	K1v	4.6.249.5–268 4.7.1–19	W/N	38.5	1			
I	K2r	4.7.20–55	W	36		1*		
O	K2v	4.7.56–93	W	41				
O	K3r	4.7.94 5.1.1–37	W	38	2			
I	K3v	5.1.38–71 5.2.1–2	W	35	4			
I	K4r	5.2.3–11 5.3.1–28	N/W	37	1	1		
O	K4v	5.3.29–64	N/W	36	1			
				302.5	9	3	0	0
O	L1r	5.3.65–99	N/W	35				
I	L1v	5.3.100–136	N/W	37	1			
I	L2r	5.3.136–174	W	38				
O	L2v	5.3.175–212	N	38				
O	L3r	5.3.213–247	N/W	34	1			
I	L3v	5.3.248–283	W	37	1			
I	L4r	5.3.284–322	W	39	3			
				258	6	0	0	0
	TOTALS			2985.5	55	44	38	5

ADJUSTMENTS			III: TEXT ADJUSTMENTS AND LINES SAVED					
	Medial commas							
urned lines	Spaced	Unspaced	Verse→ Prose	Verse relined	Half-lines	SDs part	Lines omitted	Total saved
1*	8	11	1	2		[1]		4
	6	10						
2	9	11		1				1
	15	11	3					3
1*	28	23	4	1	3			8
	28	23	3	4	2		6	15
	19	10	5		2			7
5	124	102	16	10	7	1	6	40
1	20	19	2	2		[1]		5
3*	7	1		4				4
	15	4		1		<1>		2
	11	10	4	0	2		1	7
1*	7	5	1	1	5			7
1*	16	3	1	1	1	[1]	1	5
2	3	22		2		<1>		3
1*	12	8		1				1
9	91	72	8	12	8	4	2	34
	11	14	3	0			3	6
2	12	8		3	2	<1>		6
1*	14	5	2	3			1	6
	17	4		1				1
1	15	6		2	3	[2]	2	10
	11	12			6		1	7
	19	16	4	1	5	[1]<1>	2	14
4	99	65	9	10	16	5	9	50
66	1293	864	145	84	56	30	102	418

Notes

Preface

1. *The Poems of John Keats*, ed. Miriam Allott (London: Longman, 1970), 295.

2. See the devastating review essay by David Bevington, "Determining the Indeterminate: The Oxford Shakespeare," *Shakespeare Quarterly*, 38 (1987): 501–519, at 509: "the reader may be instructed to learn that here are not in fact the pure Q1 *Lear* and F *Lear*; each is edited to some degree in the light of the other. (A colleague of mine who wanted to use the new Oxford as a teaching text to work on Q / F comparisons was crushed to learn of this.)." Bevington lists some of the editors' eclectic and inconsistent additions to each text of readings from the other (509–510). A full study of their editorial practice, including many textual emendations, is still needed.

3. For disparaging comments on the traditional practice of uniting the complementary Quarto and Folio texts as a "conflation [that] will bring us as close as we can hope to get to the lost archetype which each is supposed imperfectly to represent," see *The Division of the Kingdoms*, 6, 15, 20, 22, 75, 153, etc.

4. Madeleine Doran, *The Text of* King Lear (Stanford, CA: Stanford University Press, 1931).

5. Peter W. M. Blayney, *The Texts of* King Lear *and Their Origins*. Vol. I, *Nicholas Okes and the First Quarto* (Cambridge: Cambridge University Press, 1982). The second volume never appeared.

6. See Chapter 3.

1 King Lear *at the Printer*

1. I am indebted, in varying degrees, to the following studies: R. B. McKerrow, *An Introduction to Bibliography for Literary Students* (Oxford: Oxford University Press, 1928); Philip Gaskell, *A New Introduction to Bibliography* (Oxford: Oxford University Press, 1973; 2nd impression); George Walton Williams,

The Craft of Printing and the Publication of Shakespeare's Works (Washington, DC: Folger Shakespeare Library, 1985); William Proctor Williams, *An Introduction to Bibliographical and Textual Studies* (New York: Modern Language Association, 2009; 4th ed., with Craig S. Abbott); J. K. Moore, *Primary Materials Relating to Copy and Print in English Books of the Sixteenth and Seventeenth Centuries* (Oxford: Oxford Bibliographical Society, 1992); Peter W. M. Blayney, "The Publication of Playbooks," in eds. John D. Cox and David Scott Kastan, *A New History of Early English Drama* (New York: Columbia University Press, 1997), 383–422; Adrian Weiss, "Casting Compositors, Foul Cases, and Skeletons: Printing in Middleton's Age," in eds. Gary Taylor and John Lavagnino, *Thomas Middleton and Early Modern Textual Culture: A Companion to the Collected Works* (Oxford: Clarendon Press, 2007), 195–225.Weiss's essay gives an admirably concise and comprehensive coverage, with some valuable commented illustrations.

2. See William Proctor Williams, " 'vnder the handes of . . .' ": Zachariah Pasfield and the Licensing of Books," in ed. Marta Straznicky, *Shakespeare's Stationers: Studies in Cultural Bibliography* (Philadelphia: University of Pennsylvania Press, 2012), 63–94.

3. See, for instance, Lukas Erne, *Shakespeare as Literary Dramatist* (Cambridge: Cambridge University Press, 2003).

4. W. W. Greg, *A Bibliography of the English Printed Drama to the Restoration*, 4 vols. (London: Bibliographical Society, 1939, 1970), vol. 1, 398.

5. References to the First Folio are to *The Norton Facsimile;* here, sigA3r.

6. Four of these appeared in the Folio: *Titus Andronicus*, *Timon of Athens*, *Pericles*, and *Henry VIII; The Two Noble Kinsmen* appeared as a Quarto in 1634. See Brian Vickers, *Shakespeare, Co-Author: A Historical Study of Five Collaborative Plays* (Oxford: Oxford University Press, 2002).

7. See Alfred W. Pollard, *Shakespeare's Folios and Quartos* (London: Methuen, 1909) and *Shakespeare's Fight with the Pirates and the Problem of the Transmission of His Text* (London: Moring, 1917), 2nd ed., rev. (Cambridge: Cambridge University Press, 1920, 1967).

8. Alexander Schmidt, *Zur Textkritik des "King Lear"* (Königsberg, 1879), repr. in *Anglia*, 3 (1880) and in *Gesammelte Abhandlungen von Dr. Alexander Schmidt* (Berlin: Reimer, 1889), 222–252.

9. H. H. Furness, ed., *King Lear: A New Variorum Edition* (Philadelphia: Lippincott, 1880; New York, 1963), 370.

10. E. K. Chambers, *William Shakespeare: A Study of Facts and Problems*, 2 vols. (Oxford: Oxford University Press, 1930), vol. 1, 161–162, 465–466.

11. Greg, *The Shakespeare First Folio: Its Bibliographical and Textual History* (Oxford: Oxford University Press, 1955), 378–383.

12. See W. Matthews, "Shorthand and the Bad Shakespeare Quartos," *Modern Language Review*, 27 (1932): 243–262, and "Postscript," *Modern Language Review*, 28 (1933): 81–83; and G. I. Duthie, *Elizabethan Shorthand and the First Quarto of* King Lear (Oxford: Blackwell, 1949).

13. G. I. Duthie (ed.), *Shakespeare's* King Lear: *A Critical Edition* (Oxford: Blackwell, 1949); Alice Walker, *Textual Problems of the First Folio* (Cambridge: Cambridge University Press, 1953), 37–67; Greg, *First Folio*, 379–383.

14. Charlton Hinman, *Norton Facsimile*, xiv.

15. P. W. K. Stone, *The Textual History of* King Lear (London: Scolar, 1980).

16. Madeleine Doran, *The Text of* King Lear (Stanford, CA: Stanford University Press, 1931).
17. Ibid., 123.
18. Ibid., 126.
19. Ibid., 128.
20. Weiss, "Casting Compositors," 206.
21. See ibid., 208, and 210, for more details of paper costs.
22. Ibid., 207.
23. Ibid., 215.
24. See Peter W. M. Blayney, *The Texts of* King Lear *and Their Origins.* Vol. I, *Nicholas Okes and the First Quarto* (Cambridge: Cambridge University Press, 1982), 185–187. The second volume did not appear.
25. Joseph Moxon, *Mechanick Exercises on the Whole Art of Printing* (1683–1684), ed. Herbert Davis and Harry Carter, 2nd ed. (Oxford: Oxford University Press, 1962). I have not always reproduced Moxon's profuse use of italics.
26. Ibid., 29–39. From Moxon's illustration (32) the largest box was for the letter e, followed by c, d, m, n, u, t, i, o, a, and r.
27. Moxon provides an illustration of a composing stick (36, Plate 2E) and a full description (41–42), but note that earlier in the century the stick would not have had an adjustable slide.
28. Ibid. 204.
29. William Blades, *Shakspere and Typography* (London: Trübner, 1872), 72; cit. Doran, *The Text of* King Lear, 125.
30. Gaskell, *New Introduction to Bibliography*, 45.
31. See Weiss, "Casting Compositors," 216–217 and figure 11, showing various devices used to justify a passage in a Middleton Quarto.
32. Moxon, *Mechanick Exercises* 210–211.
33. McKerrow, *Introduction to Bibliography*, 14–18.
34. Ibid., 30–31.
35. See Weiss, "Casting Compositors," 215 and the authorities cited there.
36. Blayney, *The Texts of* King Lear *and Their Origins*, 218.
37. Moxon, *Mechanick Exercises*, 233–250. See also Gaskell, *New Introduction to Bibliography*, 110–116; Blayney, *The Texts of* King Lear *and Their Origins*, 188–218; and Percy Simpson, *Proof-Reading in the Sixteenth, Seventeenth, and Eighteenth Centuries* (Oxford: Oxford University Press, 1935).
38. See Weiss, "Casting Compositors," 215, and Blayney, *The Texts of* King Lear *and Their Origins*, 191.
39. Weiss, "Casting Compositors," 215.
40. Moxon, *Mechanick Exercises*, 234.
41. Ibid., 235–237.
42. Weiss, "Casting Compositors," 210–211, 216, and 220 note.
43. Blayney, *The Texts of* King Lear *and Their Origins*, 213.
44. Cit. David L. Gants, "The Printing, Proofing and Press-Correction of Ben Jonson's Folio *Workes*," in ed. Martin Butler, *Re-Presenting Ben Jonson. Text, History, Performance* (London: Macmillan, 1999): 39–58 (41).
45. Ibid., 44.
46. See Charlton Hinman, *The Printing and Proof-Reading of the First Folio of Shakespeare*, 2 vols. (Oxford: Oxford University Press, 1963).

47. Ibid., vol. 1, 333–4. See further the index entries, vol. 2, 548.

48. Blayney, *The Texts of* King Lear *and Their Origins*, 205.

49. Hinman, *Printing and Proof-Reading*, vol. 1, 332–333.

50. See ibid., vol. 2, Index 536, s.v. "Compositor E," and 544, s.v. "*King Lear.*"

51. See Gants, "Jonson's Folio," 40–45.

52. See Hinman, *Printing and Proof-Reading*, vol. 1, 7–8, 243–244.

53. Nikolas Delius, "On the Quarto and Folio of *King Lear*," *Transactions of the New Shakspere Society, 1875–1876*, 123–147; translated from the original essay, "Über den ursprünglichen Text des *King Lear*," *Shakespeare Jahrbuch* 10 (1875): 50–74, reprinted in Delius, *Abhandlungen zu Shakspere* (Elberfeld, 1878; [Charleston, SC] 2011), 359–370. Delius made significant contributions in several areas of Shakespeare scholarship. He produced the first critical edition of Shakespeare's works in Germany (7 vols., 1854–1861) and wrote several acute assessments of the canon.

54. P. A. Daniel, Introduction to *M. William Shak-spere's King Lear: The First Quarto 1608, a Facsimile by Charles Praetorius* (London: Praetorius, 1885); W. W. Greg, *The Variants in the First Quarto of 'King Lear': A Bibliographical and Critical Inquiry* (London: Bibliographical Society, 1940). Greg praises Daniel, who "established "the 'Pied Bull' as the true *editio princeps* of Shakespeare's play" and "who first pointed the way to a critical investigation of the subject by grouping the variants according to the sheets in which they occur" (2–3). Under the shelf-mark L.R.263a18 the British Library houses a collection of nine volumes (dated "1940") containing photostats of the 1608 Quarto of *Lear* taken from ten libraries in England and the United States. It looks very much like Greg's working copies for his *Variants.*

55. Greg, *Variants in the First Quarto of 'King Lear,'* 15, 151.

56. Ibid., 134, 136, 179 on the Folio as authoritative. For evidence that the Folio derives from an uncorrected Quarto sheet see 139–144, 147.

57. In quoting the Quarto and Folio texts I aim to reproduce their physical appearance as closely as possible. A vertical line represents the line division as found in the Folio.

58. Greg, *Variants in the First Quarto of 'King Lear,'* 141.

59. Ibid., 174–175.

60. Ibid., 155.

61. Ibid., 161–162. Greg found "a touch of irony" in Lear's moderation, but I think he is being sincere.

62. See Weiss, "Casting Compositors," 211, commenting on the word "iugling" in Middleton's early satire, *Micro-cynicon* (1594), which a modern editor emended to "juggling": the correct word is "ingling."

63. See Greg's list of "Misprints in the Original," *Variants in the First Quarto of 'King Lear,'* 66–79.

64. Delius, "On the Quarto and Folio of *King Lear*," 127. The *Ductus Literarum* is the shape of the handwritten letters.

65. Greg, *Variants in the First Quarto of 'King Lear,'* 47, 137.

66. Walker, *Textual Problems of the First Folio*, 41.

67. See Blayney, *The Texts of* King Lear *and Their Origins*, 10, 26–28, 30.

68. Ibid., 9–10.

69. Ibid., 184–185.

70. Weiss, "Casting Compositors," 199.

71. Gaskell, *Introduction to Bibliography*, 41; Blayney, "Publication of Playbooks," 406.

72. Blayney, *The Texts of* King Lear *and Their Origins*, 28–30.

73. Moxon, *Mechanick Exercises*, 239.

74. Ibid., 242.

75. Ibid., 243.

76. Ibid.

77. For illustrations of surviving manuscripts showing the marks made by a printer calculating page lengths, often recording the page number, see J. K. Moore, *Primary Materials Relating to Copy and Print in English Books of the Sixteenth and Seventeenth Centuries* (Oxford: Oxford Bibliographical Society, 1992), 11–12 and plates 7–49.

78. Charlton Hinman, "Cast-off Copy for the First Folio of Shakespeare," *Shakespeare Quarterly*, 6 (1955): 259–273 (261; author's emphases).

79. See Peter W. M. Blayney, *The First Folio of Shakespeare* (Washington DC: Folger Library, 1991), 12 (author's emphasis).

80. Hinman, "Cast-off Copy," 261.

81. Ibid., 262.

82. See, for instance, George Walton Williams, "Setting by Formes in Quarto Printing," *Studies in Bibliography*, 11 (1956): 39–53, who noted shortages of individual letters, including of the italic capital "M" in the 1595 Quarto of *Menechmi* (46) and of the italic capital "A" in the 1599 Quarto of *Alphonsus King of Aragon* (49), both due to the frequency of proper names beginning with those letters.

83. See Moxon, *Mechanick Exercises*, 170–172, on the size of quadrats: thick spaces measure four to the "em" (the body size of the type concerned), and thin measure seven to the em; and see 217–218 on their use for indenting verse.

84. As Blayney described his working method, he examined two copies of the Quarto "type by type under magnification. Every type that differed at all noticeably from the normal appearance of that character was noted by ringing the corresponding type on a photocopy of a facsimile. Over 7,000 types were thus marked," that total being whittled down to "nearly 6,000 potential clues" (*The Texts of* King Lear *and Their Origins*, 93). Blayney then studied the reappearance of distinctive types from one forme to another, enabling him to compile "a list of over 2,000 appearances made by 571 types, which are listed in Appendices IVA and IVB" (94). Two scholarly reviewers accepted Blayney's general conclusions, but regretted that he had only consulted two copies, rather than three. See the reviews by Anthony Hammond, *The Library*, 6th ser., 6 (1984): 89–93, and Paul Werstine, *Shakespeare Quarterly*, 36 (1985): 120–125.

85. Blayney, *The Texts of* King Lear *and Their Origins*, 184.

86. Ibid. Blayney promised to illustrate these consequences in the second volume, another reason to regret its nonappearance.

87. Ibid., 129. As Blayney established, "No play-quarto is known to have been set by Okes's predecessors since Judson established the business in 1598," and thus he inherited no experience of printing play texts.

88. Ibid., 142.

89. Ibid., 173–175.

90. See Weiss, "Casting Compositors," 213 note: "Current compositorial analysis as a method is quite primitive and unreliable in the context of a scientific statistical analysis of populations of alternate choices, given the extremely limited samples upon which such analyses are based."

91. Blayney, *The Texts of* King Lear *and Their Origins*, 144.

92. Greg, *Variants in the First Quarto of 'King Lear,'* Appendix II, "Misprints in the Original," 63–79.

93. Blayney, *The Texts of* King Lear *and Their Origins*, 103, 115, 139–141, 149–150.

94. Ibid., 159.

95. Ibid., 160.

96. Weiss, "Casting Compositors," 216.

97. See Blayney, *The Texts of* King Lear *and Their Origins*, 149.

98. Gaskell, *New Introduction to Bibliography*, 41. In some instances, however, such as the Quarto of *Richard II*, a play wholly in verse, printers could still get their counting wrong.

99. Blayney, "Publication of Playbooks," 406.

100. Moxon, *Mechanick Exercises*, 38, 350. I owe this observation to Professor David McKitterick.

101. Greg, *Variants in the First Quarto of 'King Lear,'* 28–29, 168.

102. Blayney, *The Texts of* King Lear *and Their Origins*, 104.

103. Theobald, 1733 edition, cit. Furness, *A New Variorum Edition of Shakespeare*, 158.

104. Scribes were just as prone to such errors as compositors and at times were unwilling to correct them. Paul Werstine has pointed out that, while transcribing Fletcher's *Bonduca*, Edward Knight interchanged lines 2 and 3 in copying this passage: "(1) and still to try these *Romanes*, whom I found (3) And be you witnesse, gods, and all my dangers) (2) (and if I lye, my wounds be henceforth backward, (4) As ready, and as full of that I brought . . ." Knight noticed his error, but "chose not to correct it and mar his beautiful page. Instead, he simply added it after the line he had skipped to, thus transposing lines." Werstine, *Early Modern Playhouse Manuscripts and the Editing of Shakespeare* (Cambridge: Cambridge University Press, 2013), 85.

105. Blayney, *The Texts of* King Lear *and Their Origins*, 215–216.

106. Ibid. 219–257, and Appendix VIA, "Press-Variants in Okes's Quartos, 1607–8," 559–600.

107. Ibid. 246.

108. Greg, *Variants in the First Quarto of 'King Lear,'* 159.

109. Blayney instanced "The generous, and grauest Citizens" (*Measure for Measure* 4.6.13) and "the best conditioned and vnwearied spirit" (*Merchant of Venice* 3.2.193). Blayney, *The Texts of* King Lear *and Their Origins*, 248.

110. Ibid.

2 *Adjusting Text Space to Print Space in the Shakespeare Folio and Quartos*

1. Gaskell, *New Introduction to Bibliography*, 42.

2. In Moxon's somewhat idealistic account, "A good *Compositor* is ambitious as well to make the meaning of his *Author* intelligent to the *Reader*, as to make his Work shew graceful to the Eye, and pleasant in Reading." Therefore "he reads his *Copy* with consideration; that so he may get himself into the meaning of the Author, and consequently considers how to order his Work the better," and thus "the better sympathize with the Authors Genius, and also with the capacity of the Reader." *Mechanick Exercises*, 211–212.

3. Ibid., 207–208.

4. Ibid., 235.

5. Ibid., 236–237.

6. Ibid., 237 n.

7. Hinman, "Cast-off Copy," 261.

8. Ibid.

9. Ibid., 264–266.

10. Ibid., 267.

11. *Tragedies*, 257; sig. Oo1r; *Hamlet*, 1.5.62–7. In quoting from early texts I attempt to reproduce the absence of spacing between words or after punctuation, that absence usually representing a printer's device to justify a line or to compress copy.

12. Hinman, "Cast-off Copy," 268.

13. *Tragedies*, 31; sig. ss3v. As Hinman noted, to insert this line in the proper place "would require some compression at the top of the column—where in the first page of a play, appearances were evidently considered especially important: every play in the book has a white line both above and below its initial entry-direction, however crowded the rest of the first page may be" ("Cast-off Copy," 269 n.). When setting "a Folio in sixes" page 1 of a quire was the last to be set, along with page 12, by which point the compositor had few choices available.

14. Hinman, "Cast-off Copy," 268–269.

15. Hinman, *Printing and Proof-Reading*, vol. 1, 5.

16. *Comedies*, 121; sig. L1[r].

17. Prosser, *Shakespeare's Anonymous Editors: Scribe and Compositor in the Folio Text of '2 Henry IV'* (Stanford, CA: Stanford University Press, 1981), 65, plate IV.

18. Ibid., 65.

19. See the facsimile, ed. J. L. Levenson and B. Gaines, *Romeo and Juliet 1597* (Oxford: Oxford University Press, 2000), 16–17, sigs C1v–C2r.

20. See the facsimile, ed. W. W. Greg, *Romeo and Juliet: Second Quarto, 1599* (Oxford: Oxford University Press, 1949), sig. C2r.

21. Q1 reads "atomi."

22. G. Blakemore Evans, ed., *Romeo and Juliet*, New Cambridge Shakespeare (Cambridge: Cambridge University Press, 1984), 209.

23. Ibid., 210.

24. John Dover Wilson, ed., *A Midsummer Night's Dream* (Cambridge: Cambridge University Press, 1924), 80. Cf. the facsimile edition by Thomas L. Berger, *A Midsummer Night's Dream 1600* (Oxford: Oxford University Press, 1995), 52–53, sig. G2v–G3r. The editor notes that sheet G contains uneven page lengths: "Most pages contain thirty-five lines of text," but "the first four pages of sheet G" vary from 34 lines (G1r, G1v, G2v) to 32 lines (G2r), suggesting that there were "some irregularities in the copy that produced the 'irregular' number of lines per page" (v). However, as Henry Woudhuysen has pointed out (personal communication, July 2015), "Berger missed the fact that G2r also contains 34 lines (including blank lines before SDs)—that is, the page depth is consistent with G1r-v and G2v."

25. Ibid., 81–82. In his Arden edition (London: Methuen, 1979) H. F. Brooks prints them separately as an appendix (163–164), as does Peter Holland, ed., *A Midsummer Night's Dream* (Oxford: Oxford University Press, 1994), Appendix: "Shakespeare's Revisions of Act 5," 257–268.

26. Wilson, *A Midsummer Night's Dream*, 83–85.

27. Greg, "Bibliography—an Apologia," *The Library*, 13 (1932): 113–143; repr. in J. C. Maxwell, ed., *The Collected Papers of Sir Walter W. Greg* (Oxford: Clarendon Press, 1966), 239–266, at 264–265. In his Arden edition of *A Midsummer's Night Dream*, Harold Brooks also praised "Dover Wilson's brilliant detection of marginal revisions" as "the result of the compositor's unsuccessful attempt to insert into the text as first written, coherent as that was in sense and versification, the equally coherent additions which had been crowded into the margin" (xi). But Brooks rejected Wilson's theory that the insertion showed Shakespeare's maturer style: "an inspired afterthought may come to an author after five minutes just as well as after four years" (ibid.).

28. Samuel Burdett Hemingway, (ed.), *A New Variorum Edition of Shakespeare: Henry the Fourth Part 1* (Philadelphia: Lippincott, 1936), 344.

29. All quotations are from the facsimile of *Henry the Fourth Part 1 1598*, ed. W. W. Greg, rev. Charlton Hinman (Oxford: Oxford University Press, 1966), which also reprints the fragment of Q0, following the main text.

30. See W. W. Greg, *A Bibliography of the English Printed Drama to the Restoration*, 4 vols. (London: Bibliographical Society, 1939–1959), vol. 3, 1639–1640, 4.clx.

31. Hemingway, *A New Variorum Edition of Shakespeare*, 345.

32. Folio; Q reads "smiles."

33. For ampersands in prose see also C4r, E1r, and G4r (twice).

34. The Folio compositor also used an ampersand to justify this line (TLN 450).

35. The Folio divided this line after "so" (TLN 1765–1766).

36. See C3v, C4r, D2r, D2v (twice), and E1v.

37. For instances of prose passages and stage directions being set on the same line see TLN 217, 738, 810, 815, 996, 998, 1038, 1050, 1238, and 1439. For instances of verse being set in the same line as stage directions see TLN 335, 451, 882, 1820, 2232, 2751, 2817, and 2825.

38. For unpleasantly cramped stage directions see TLN 342, 445, 2818, and 2826.

39. For entries squeezed in at a line ending see TLN 2825, 2865, and 2876.

40. See Hinman, *Printing and Proof-Reading*, vol. 2, 96–106; on the problems in setting 2 *Henry IV*, see 47–48.

41. For an overview of the Folio's makeup see ibid., vol. 1, 34–35.

42. This list of "The Actors Names" in fact lists those of the characters, prudently describing the rebels as "Opposites against King *Henrie* the Fourth."

43. Hinman, *Printing and Proof-Reading*, vol. 1, 38.

44. Ibid., vol. 2, 98.

45. Ibid., vol. 2, 100.

46. Prosser, *Shakespeare's Anonymous Editors*, 75.

47. Ibid., 90.

48. Ibid., 74.

49. On the omission of the rebels' scene see Alfred Hart, "Was the Second Part of *King Henry the Fourth* Censored?" in Hart, *Shakespeare and the Homilies* (Melbourne: Melbourne, 1934; New York: Octagon, 1977), 154–218, and René Weis, ed., *Henry IV, Part 2* (Oxford: Oxford University Press, 1998), 78–99.

50. Weis, *Henry IV, Part 2*, 92, commented that "Prosser's hypotheses offer a brilliant account of the problems F's compositors faced in this scenario of respective congestions and compensations of space, and she demonstrates how the solutions of Compositor B particularly can be made to bear on the textual authority, or lack of it, of F."

51. Ibid., 78.

52. Ibid., 78, 80.

53. Ibid., 80.

54. Ibid., 82.

55. See TLN 393, 436, 445, 450, 643, 651,688, 706, 707, 719, and 920.

56. Prosser, *Shakespeare's Anonymous Editors*, 85.

57. The passages within square brackets occur only in the Folio; the Quarto reads "the" for the first and lacks the second.

58. There is one further instance of "y[u]" (1701) and two ampersands (2251, 3074), despite space being available.

59. See his essay, "Of Ceremonies and Respect," in Brian Vickers, ed., *Francis Bacon: The Major English Works* (Oxford: Oxford University Press, 1996), 441.

60. Prosser, *Shakespeare's Anonymous Editors*, 80.

61. Ibid., 81.

62. Ibid., 84.

63. Ibid., 84.

64. Ibid., 87.

65. Hinman, "Cast-Off Copy," 269 n. 10.

66. In 1963 Hinman estimated the Folio's print run to have been "*about* 1200 copies"; *Printing and Proof-Reading*, vol. 1, 46. Peter Blayney, however, has suggested "a relatively small edition—probably 750 copies, and perhaps fewer": *The First Folio*, 2.

67. Prosser, *Shakespeare's Anonymous Editors*, 113.

68. Ibid., 85

69. Ibid., 51–121, 122–162.

70. Reviewing that year's textual studies, George Walton Williams praised Prosser for her "model analysis of the effects of casting-off on the contracting and expanding of the text, including even omission and substitution. . . . The very close analysis of Compositor B's squeezing is excellent and, in the main, unassailable": *Shakespeare Survey*, 35 (1982), 181. Yet very few textual scholars since then have even mentioned her work.

71. Prosser, *Shakespeare's Anonymous Editors*, 93–115.

72. See ibid., 103–113, and her summary of the passages added in the Folio (whether by compositor or editor) without any authority from the Quarto, and in the absence of any known authority: 120, 191–194. G. W. Williams judged that "though the distinction to be made between errors of the compositor and errors of the scribe is a nice one, Miss Prosser has made it ably and persuasively," and he even added a footnote to strengthen her case (*Shakespeare Survey*, 181 and note).

73. The Folio editor of 2 *Henry IV* evidently considered "yea" to be a vulgar expression, regularly emending it to "I" or "ay."

74. Prosser, *Shakespeare's Anonymous Editors*, 132.

75. Ibid., 143.

76. According to Moxon, writing in the 1670s, "by the Laws of *Printing*, a *Compositor* is strictly to follow his *Copy*, viz. to observe and do just so much and no more than his Copy will bear him out for; so that his Copy is to be his Rule and Authority": *Mechanick Exercises*, 192.

77. Prosser, *Shakespeare's Anonymous Editors*, 102.

78. Greg, "The First Edition of Ben Jonson's 'Every Man out of His Humour,'" *The Library*, 4th ser., 1 (1921): 153–160. See also Greg's edition for the Malone Society, *Every Man out of His Humour 1600* (Oxford: Oxford University Press, 1921).

79. Greg, "First Edition," 156.

80. Ibid., 156–157.

81. Compare Q1 K1r with Q2 I3v, for instance, and Q1 L3v with Q2 L1r. (I cite Q1 from Greg's facsimile and Q2 from a copy in the British Library.)

82. On L1r he used an ampersand, and on L3v he changed "than" to "thã."

83. Greg, "First Edition," 157–158.

84. David Bevington, Martin Butler, and Ian Donaldson, eds.,*The Cambridge Edition of the Works of Ben Jonson*, 7 vols. (Cambridge: Cambridge University Press, 2012). See my review essay, "At Feud with Sin," *Times Literary Supplement*, January 24, 2014, 3–5. For *The Cambridge Edition of the Works of Ben Jonson Online* see http://universitypublishingonline.org/cambridge/benjonson/.

85. Suzanne Gossett, "Textual Essay: *Eastward Ho!*" in *Cambridge Edition of the Works of Ben Jonson Online*, Essay 17.

86. Ibid.

87. Blayney, *The Texts of* King Lear *and Their Origins*, 160.

88. John Creaser, "Textual Essay: *Bartholomew Fair*," in *Cambridge Edition of the Works of Ben Jonson Online*, Essay 4. "The text of the play must at first have been set seriatim because the type is evenly spaced, and formes and gatherings frequently end in mid-phrase and even mid-word. See, for example, the end of gatherings B, C, and D: 'a head full / of Bees!'; 'a sleepy Watch- / man,'; 'this is old / *Ursla's* mansion'. It is probable, however, that—despite the difficulty

set by a manuscript in prose—there was some casting-off later in the text, for no forme later than gathering F ends mid-word, while three of the last five gatherings (H, I, and L) end with crowded text run into the direction line."

89. Tom Cain, "Textual Essay: *Sejanus*," in *Cambridge Edition of the Works of Ben Jonson Online*, Essay 50.

90. Ibid. For the text of Jonson's *Argument* see Cain's edition of *Sejanus*, *Works of Ben Jonson* vol. 2, 229–230. For another instance of a printer resorting to smaller type in an emergency, see Weiss, "Casting Compositors," 106, plate 3, showing Matthew Allde's edition of Middleton's *A Game at Chesse* (1624–25). Allde used black letter for section titles and roman for the text. However, when he reached the "Epilogue," in order "to avoid the expense of another half sheet of paper" he crammed it into the remaining space at the foot of the last page, but "had to switch from his Hamlin pica (82 mm) roman to his long primer (66 mm) roman," exactly the same solution that Eld had used for *Sejanus*.

91. Bland, *A Guide to Early Printed Books and Manuscripts* (Oxford: Wiley-Blackwell, 2010), 146–147.

3 Nicholas Okes Compresses the Play

1. Blayney, *The Texts of* King Lear *and Their Origins*, 99–100.
2. Ibid., 96.
3. Ibid., 49.
4. Ibid., 148.
5. Weiss, "Casting Compositors," 200; Blayney, "Publication of Play-books," 405.
6. Peter Blayney has commented, "Okes probably guessed (badly) that he could fit *Lear* into 10 ½ sheets—but it was Butter who supplied the paper and paid for the printing, and it would have been to Okes's advantage to confess that he'd miscalculated and ask to renegotiate. He'd earn more for printing twelve sheets." (Personal communication, April 11, 2014). I had suggested this quantity since Jaggard used twelve sheets when he reprinted *Lear* in 1619: see p. 120.
7. Williams, personal communication, June 2011. McKerrow noted that in the Elizabethan period "ordinary small books, pamphlets, and the like, a book of 10 or 12 sheets (80–96 pages in 4to, or 160 to 192 pages in 8vo) would normally be priced at a shilling . . . Quartos of plays, however, though they often ran to 10 or 11 sheets, seem to have generally cost only 6*d*." (*Introduction to Bibliography*, 134). It seems as if Okes had aimed for that low-earning market, not expecting to exceed ten sheets.
8. See Blayney, *The Texts of* King Lear *and Their Origins*, Index 710, s.v. "formats," referring to his Appendix II, "Checklist of Books, 1604–9" (334–431).
9. Ibid., 149.
10. As Blayney summed up his bibliographical analysis, "Pages C3v and C4r both belong to the inner forme, and so would constitute a single unit of text even in setting by formes. It is therefore reasonable to assume that the two pages were set consecutively. The order of the preceding pages is unknown, but if C4v was set after the distribution and C3r before it, setting was certainly not entirely by formes. In view of the fact that the subsequent sheets were set

seriatim, the same is almost certainly true of sheet C (and very possibly of sheet B also)." Ibid., 103.

11. See, e.g., R. A. Foakes (ed.), *King Lear*, Arden Shakespeare (London: Nelson, 1997), 122; Ann R. Meyer, "Shakespeare's Art and the Texts of *King Lear*," *Studies in Bibliography*, 47 (1994): 124–146 (143–144).

12. Halio, *The First Quarto of King Lear* (Cambridge: Cambridge University Press, 1994).

13. See the review by Eric Rasmussen, *Shakespeare Quarterly*, 50 (1999): 87–89, who estimated that there are "123 instances in Halio's edition . . . in which a Folio variant is chosen over the quarto alternative."

14. See Greg, *Variants in the First Quarto of 'King Lear,'* 18–35.

15. Prosser, *Shakespeare's Anonymous Editors*, 82, 86.

16. Hanmer's emendation (a "lym" is a bloodhound); Q has "him"; F reads "Hym."

17. Knowles, review of Adele Davidson, *Shakespeare in Shorthand: The Textual Mystery of "King Lear"* (2009), in *PBSA* 105 (2011): 247–52 (249).

18. Words enclosed within curly brackets { . . . } are variant readings. Here the Quarto reads 'flowes'."

19. Folio; Quarto misreads "reuenge."

20. Second Folio; Quarto misreads "festuant," and F1 reads "festiuate."

21. Folio; Quarto misreads "intelligence."

22. Greg, *Variants in the First Quarto of 'King Lear,'* 15.

23. Ibid., 66–79.

24. Ibid., 65.

25. Blayney, *The Texts of* King Lear *and Their Origins*, 179–181.

26. I estimate 1,360 instances of medial commas with spacing.

27. My totals for unspaced commas in the individual sheets are as follows: B 81, C 107, D 128, E 82, F 83, G 92, H 62, I 102, K 72, and L 65. Sheet D also has the highest number of verse lines set as prose: 61,which is nearly half the total (142). The next highest are I 23, G 17, and C 12.

28. Blayney, *The Texts of* King Lear *and Their Origins*, 144.

29. McKerrow, *Prolegomena for the Oxford Shakespeare: A Study in Editorial Method* (Oxford: Oxford University Press, 1939), 44, 46.

30. Greg, *Dramatic Documents from the Elizabethan Playhouses*, 2 vols. (Oxford: Oxford University Press, 1931), vol. 1, 206.

31. See Brian Vickers, *The Artistry of Shakespeare's Prose* (London: Methuen, 1968; Routledge, 2005), and "Shakespeare's Use of Prose," in ed. John F. Andrews, *William Shakespeare: His World, His Work, His Influence*, 3 vols. (New York: Scribner, 1985), vol. 2, 389–395.

32. *The Malcontent*, 1.4.43.1, ed. George K. Hunter (Manchester: Manchester University Press, 1999), p. 35.

33. Folio; the Quarto reads "then."

34. In Marlowe's *Tamburlaine* Bajazeth, the captive Turkish emperor, imprisoned in a cage, commits suicide: *"He brains himself against the cage."* When his wife Zabina discovers him, "His skul al ruin in twaine, his braines dasht out," she runs mad, her final speech being in prose, before killing herself as he has done (5.1.305–319). See also Traudl Eichhorn, "Prosa und Vers im

vorshakespearschen Drama," *Shakespeare Jahrbuch*, 84 (1950): 140–198. This subject needs more study.

35. Folio; Q omits this word.

36. See, e.g., Halio (ed.), *The First Quarto of King Lear*, who ascribed these changes to the compositors' "difficulty in following verse" (13).

37. See, e.g., Madeleine Doran, *The Text of* King Lear (Stanford, CA: Stanford University Press, 1931), 127.

38. See, e.g., W. W. Greg, "The Function of Bibliography in Literary Criticism: Illustrated in a Study of the Text of *King Lear*," *Neophilologus*, 18 (1932–1933): 241–262; repr. and cit. from J. C. Maxwell (ed.), *The Collected Papers of Sir Walter W. Greg* (Oxford: Oxford University Press, 1966), 267–297 (284).

39. Folio; Quarto misread as "you."

40. Chambers, *William Shakespeare: A Study of Facts and Problems*, 2 vols. (Oxford: Oxford University Press, 1930), vol. 1, 463.

41. Weiss, "Casting Compositors," 200 note.

42. Folio; Q misreads, successively, "The" (for "Thy"), "hested" and "the" (for "thee").

43. See B4 v: 1.1.283–285, F4 v–G1r: 3.3.1–20, H1r: 3.7.6–13, and H3r: 4.1.56–63.

44. W. W. Greg, *A Bibliography of the English Printed Drama to the Restoration*, 4 vols. (London: Bibliographical Society, 1939–1959), vol. 3, 1639–1640, 4.clx; *cit.* H. R. Woudhuysen, "Early Play Texts: Forms and Formes," in eds. Ann Thompson and Gordon McMullan, *In Arden: Editing Shakespeare. Essays in Honour of Richard Proudfoot* (London: Thomson, 2003), 48–61 (56).

45. Woudhuysen, *In Arden*, 57.

46. The Quarto gives this speech to Lear.

47. By reference to the Folio, the following necessary entrances were omitted by the 1608 Quarto: "*Enter Steward*" (C4r24; 1.4.62); "*Enter Foole*" (G1v19; 3.4.33), and "*Enter Edgar*" (G1v25; 3.4.37): the Folio ran these entrances together as "*Enter Edgar , and Foole.*" (TLN 1818); "*Enter Albany*" (H3v25; 4.2.27), "*Enter Edgar*" (K4r3; 5.2.4), and "*Enter Herald*" (L1v8; 5.3.101).

48. I have checked my count against that given in George Ian Duthie, *Shakespeare's KING LEAR: A Critical Edition* (Oxford: Blackwell, 1949), 109–115.

49. Appendix 2 records settings for each page, whether narrow ("N"), wide ("W"), or mixed ("M").

50. Moxon, *Mechanick Exercises*, 203–204, 240.

51. Greg, "*King Lear*—Mislineation and Stenography," *The Library*, ser. 4, 17 (1936): 172–183 (181).

52. Ibid., 182.

53. McKenzie, "'Indenting the Stick' in the First Quarto of *King Lear* (1608)," *PBSA*, 67 (1973): 125–130 (126–127). A similar, but less complete, explanation had just been given by John Feather, "Some Notes on the Setting of Quarto Plays," *The Library*, 5th series, 27 (1972): 237–244.

54. Citing Moxon, *Mechanick Exercises*, 171–172, 215, 217–218, 228–229. For further discussion of regular and "Quotation Quadrats" see ibid. 70, 349. Philip Gaskell, *A New Introduction to Bibliography*, 34, illustrates spaces and quads of varying widths.

55. An "em" is a phonetic representation of "the letters 'm' and 'M' [which] were cast on a square body" and thus provided a regular unit of measurement in typography, where the length of a line is given in ems; this is also the standard size of a "quad" or piece of spacing type. Peter Blayney calculated "the 'standard' prose measure" for the *Lear* Quarto as 22.76 ems (*The Texts of* King Lear *and Their Origins*, 530).

56. Weiss, "Casting Compositors," 212.

57. I owe these examples to the forthcoming New Variorum edition by Richard Knowles.

58. McKenzie, "'Indenting the Stick,'" 127–128.

59. Cf. Greg, *Variants in the First Quarto of 'King Lear,'* 33.

60. Ibid., 125, 128.

61. Blayney, *The Texts of* King Lear *and Their Origins*, 149; my italics.

62. For switches from prose to verse see, e.g., B1v (where, however, the compositor retained the wider measure for a few lines to accommodate a centered stage direction and a longer verse line), C3v, H3v, and I3r. For switches from verse to prose cf. C3v, G1r, G3r, H4r, and I4r. Note, however, that in both cases the "prose" was produced by the compositor having removed verse lineation.

63. For mixed measures on the same page, appropriate to the speaker (often with the Fool speaking prose) cf. E2r (Kent); E4r, E4v, F4r, G2r, and G4r (mad Lear); and K1r (Poor Tom's rustic dialect).

64. Appendix 2 shows the extent of Shakespeare's text contained on each Quarto page.

65. Folio; the Quarto compositor misread the manuscript word as "dialogue."

66. F; Q reads "tine."

67. Folio reading; the Quarto has "my," the last word in the line.

68. For the wider measure being used (in conjunction with setting verse as prose or running verse lines together) at the end of a page, see C3r, F2r, H2r, and L2r; at the beginning of a page, see H3v and I2r.

69. Folio; Quarto misread the manuscript as "dayes."

70. I use a double vertical line (||) to represent a turned-over line.

71. These are F1r, F1v, F2v, F3r, and F3v.

72. Blayney, *The Texts of* King Lear *and Their Origins*, 217.

73. Ibid., 126–139, 151–187.

74. See K3r, K3v, and L1r.

75. Personal communication, June 20, 2011.

76. Blayney noted in passing that, "since the question of measure proves to be of unexpected *textual* importance, I have reserved it for discussion in Volume II" (*The Texts of* King Lear *and Their Origins*, 164; author's emphases), which never appeared.

77. For this comparison I have used two texts in the "Shakespeare Quarto Facsimiles," ed. W. W. Greg: *Hamlet. Second Quarto 1604–5* (Oxford: Oxford University Press, 1940; repr. 1964, with new introduction by Charlton Hinman), and *Troilus and Cressida: First Quarto 1609* (Oxford: Oxford University Press, 1952). For *Lear* I have used the facsimile of the 1619 Quarto (falsely dated

1608), C.34.k.19, among the "Treasures of the British Library," http://www.bl.uk/treasures/shakespeare/homepage.html.

78. Doran, *The Text of 'King Lear,'* 37.

79. See Harold Jenkins, ed., *Hamlet* (London: Methuen, 1982), 36–43.

80. See, e.g., G3r, F3r, F4v, H3r, and H4r (Polonius).

81. See, e.g., G2v, G4r, H4r (twice in Hamlet's speech on the recorder), K1v, K2r, M1v, M2r, M3r, M3v, and N2v.

82. See C3v, F1v, G4r, Hr, K1v, K2r, and L2v.

83. Doran, *The Text of* King Lear, chapter II: "The Relation of Q2 to Q1" (19–38); Knowles, "The Printing of the Second Quarto (1619) of *King Lear,*" *Studies in Bibliography*, 35 (1982): 191–206. Knowles showed that the 1619 Quarto "was set from two type cases by two compositors working concurrently throughout sheets A to H, and thereafter from one of these type cases by a third compositor who by himself set the last three sheets, I to L" (191). Knowles refers to Jaggard "stretching" the text of Q1: I would rather call it "relaxing" or "decompressing."

84. Knowles, "The Printing of the Second Quarto," 192–193.

85. Doran, *The Text of* King Lear, 36–38; Knowles, "The Printing of the Second Quarto," 200–201.

86. Cf. A2r, C3r, C3v, and D2v. Apart from the first instance, which copies an ampersand in Q1, all three were introduced in Q2.

87. Knowles, "The Printing of the Second Quarto," 192.

88. See G1r, G2v (twice), H2v, H3v, H4r, H4v, I2v, and L2r.

89. See, e.g., F2r, H3r (twice), I4v, K1r, K2v, K3v, K4r, and K4v.

90. Knowles, "The Printing of the Second Quarto," 193.

91. Doran, *The Text of* King Lear, noted that "carelessness" in Q2 led to "the omissions of several necessary words" (37), but did not consider their cause.

92. As noted earlier, these figures are computed from my reference text, Halio's edition of the First Quarto.

4 *Nicholas Okes Abridges It*

1. In *The Shakespeare First Folio* (Oxford: Oxford University Press, 1955), W. W. Greg suggested that "the omissions in Q are probably accidental" (381).

2. Greg noted that "the recognized manner of indicating a cut—as can be seen in almost any dramatic manuscript—was by a bracket in the left margin, a line being drawn down opposite the lines to be omitted with horizontal arms marking the beginning and end": ibid., 332, note H.

3. W. P. Williams, personal communication, June 20, 2011.

4. Walker, *Textual Problems of the First Folio* (Cambridge: Cambridge University Press, 1953), 52.

5. Folio; Quarto reads "crauing."

6. See Brian Vickers, *In Defence of Rhetoric* (Oxford: Oxford University Press, 1988), 317–318, 328, 330–331, 335–337.

7. See G. K. Hunter, ed., *King Lear* (Harmondsworth: Penguin, 1972), 203. Hunter adds, "Edmund sings (I assume) the notes F, D, E, B natural (using

the names given to these notes in the first two hexachords of the musical system pertaining in Shakespeare's day). He thus moves across the interval of the augmented fourth, called *diabolus in musica* (the devil in music) in the current musical mnemonic: *Mi contra Fa est diabolus in musica.* The phrase reflects the enmity between the triton and the normal system of harmony. Shakespeare seems to be creating something like a musical emblem or 'motto theme' for the character of his discordant Bastard." The allusion was first recognized by the great historian of music, Charles Burney, in a note he submitted to Edmond Malone's 1790 edition of Shakespeare. See Brian Vickers, ed., *Shakespeare: The Critical Heritage*, Vol. 6, *1774–1801* (London: Routledge and Kegan Paul, 1981), 545.

8. As G. L. Kittredge observed, "Any word, if repeated over and over in a monotone, seems to lose its significance. Edmund plays this trick with *base* and *legitimate*, in order to prove that they are meaningless terms." Cf. Kittredge, ed., *Sixteen Plays of Shakespeare* (Boston: Ginn, 1946), 1162. Iago does a similar trick, contemptuously repeating a word and then juxtaposing it with a crude reduction, using the rhetorical figure *tapinosis*, as in "Virtue? a fig!" (1.3.319): see Vickers, *Artistry of Shakespeare's Prose*, 335–337.

9. Folio; the uncorrected Quarto reads "come and tends seruise"; the corrected reads "commands her seruice."

10. The Folio text; Q reads "*Historica.*"

11. Folio; Quarto misreads the manuscript as "shoot" and also reads "fell" instead of "felt."

12. See, for instance, 1.1.89–93, 1.2.23–26, 1.3.1–2, 1.3.22–6, 1.4.219–22, 1.4.311–12, and 2.1.38–40.

13. Folio reads "Heare Nature," so that Lear's imperious command occurs three times in this line. For other instances of Lear's repetitions, see the opening scene alone: "How nothing can come of nothing, speake againe" (90), "goe to, goe to, mend your speech a little" (94), "so yong and so untender" (106), "Heare me, on they allegeance heare me" (166–167), and "therefore be gone, | Without our grace, our love, our benison" (264–265).

14. Compared to other merciless cutting of verbal repetition, it may seem surprising that Okes allowed Lear's multiple "so, so . . ." to remain. But a glance at the Quarto will show that the compositor set these prose lines using the whole width of the page (G4v3–4) and still had room to place the stage direction within the text. This suggests in turn that, although the abridger must have marked passages for omission on the manuscript, in some cases it was left to the compositor to make cuts as he went along.

15. This is the F reading; Q misreads the manuscript as "dance."

16. From the corrected Quarto. The uncorrected version reads, "My foote vsurps my body"; the Folio reads, "My Foole vsurpes my body."

17. Chambers, *William Shakespeare: A Study of Facts and Problems*, 2 vols. (Oxford: Oxford University Press, 1930), vol. 1, 297.

18. Folio; Quarto misreads as "first."

19. There are two options to be considered: either Shakespeare wrote the complete speech, as printed here, at the same time as the rest of the text, or he added it later, in the putative revision that proponents of the Two Versions

theory ascribe to 1610–1611. I imagine that most readers would agree that the diction is all of a piece, completely homogeneous throughout the speech, both in the elevated tone and its insistent use of the royal plural, deployed fifteen times in nineteen lines, surely the most intense usage in Shakespeare.

20. Cf. 1.2.79–88, and Vickers, *Artistry of Shakespeare's Prose*, 354–358.

21. Folio; Q misread as "the."

22. Folio; Q misread as "We."

23. Folio; Quarto misread as "list."

24. Folio; Quarto misread as "and."

25. Folio; the uncorrected Quarto reads "deptouėd," corrected to "depriued."

26. Folio; Quarto has the probably phonetic spelling "one."

27. Folio reads "*Exit*," although both Kent and the Fool leave the stage; Quarto lacks a stage direction.

28. Folio; Quarto misreads as "experience."

29. Folio; Quarto reads "parti,eyd." But see R. J. C. Watt, "Neither Parti-Eyed nor Poorly Led: Edgar Meets the Blind Gloucester," *Review of English Studies*, 48 (1997): 51–56, for the convincing emendation "gory-eyed," based on common misreadings of secretary hand.

30. Folio; Quarto misreads as "tottered."

31. Theobald (1740 edn.); Folio reads "Place sinnes."

32. See Edward Hubler, "The Verse Lining of the First Quarto of *King Lear*," in ed. Hardin Craig, *Essays in Dramatic Literature: The Parrott Presentation Volume* (Princeton, NJ: Princeton University Press, 1935), 421–444. I came across Hubler's essay quite recently, in the late Trevor Howard-Hill's *Shakespearian Bibliography and Textual Criticism: A Bibliography*, 2nd ed., rev. and enlarged (Signal Mountain, TN: Summertown Texts, 2000), 181.

33. Hubler, "Verse Lining," 421–422, citing J. Q. Adams, "The Quarto of *King Lear* and Shorthand," *Modern Philology* 31 (1933): 135–163 (145). Madeleine Doran refuted this claim in "The Quarto of *King Lear* and Bright's Shorthand," *Modern Philology*, 33 (1935): 139–157.

34. See Appendix 2, "Space Saving in Q1 *Lear*."

35. Hubler, "Verse Lining," 426–427.

36. Doran, *The Text of* King Lear, 128, 133.

37. Hubler, "Verse Lining," 427.

38. Ibid., 430–431.

39. Ibid., 432. But this is a slightly misleading example, for the Folio compositor divided Cordelia's speech so as to make five lines, evidently to fill surplus space created by inaccurate casting off. This Folio page (ss1r) has an unusual amount of white space around stage directions and scene headings.

40. Ibid., 434.

41. Ibid., 430.

42. Ibid., 438. Hubler instanced two speeches by the Fool (1.4.117–127 and 3.2.74–77) and one by Poor Tom (3.4.120–124).

43. Ibid., 439.

44. Ibid., 440; my italics.

45. Ibid., 440–441.

46. Greg, "*King Lear*—Mislineation and Stenography," *The Library*, ser. 4, 17 (1936): 172–183. I hope to discuss Greg's dismissal of both Doran and Hubler's work elsewhere.

47. Evans, review of Blayney, *The Texts of* King Lear *and Their Origins*, *Modern Language Review*, 79 (1984): 901–904 (904; my italics).

48. Evans, review of the *Oxford Shakespeare* and *Textual Companion*, *Journal of English and Germanic Philology*, 88 (1989): 401–407 (404).

49. Ibid., 404.

50. *The Riverside Shakespeare*, 2nd ed. (Boston: Houghton Mifflin, 1997), 1343–1345 (double column). This note included an up-to-date bibliography (1344–1345), which listed eleven critiques of the Two Versions theory. When the second edition of the *Oxford Shakespeare* appeared in 2005 it took no notice of these and other critiques: see my review, *Times Literary Supplement*, August 11, 2006, 10–12.

51. *Riverside Shakespeare*, 1344; my italics.

5 One Play, One Manuscript, Two Printed Books

1. See Samuel Schoenbaum, *William Shakespeare: A Documentary Life* (Oxford: Clarendon Press, 1975); Peter Beal, *Index of English Literary Manuscripts.* Vol. 1, *1450–1625*, Part 2 (London: Mansell, 1980), 449–451; and the online revision *Catalogue of English Literary MSS 1450–1700* (http://www.celm-ms.org.uk/) *ShW 88.

2. See Simpson, "Are There Any Extant MSS. in Shakespeare's Handwriting?" *Notes and Queries*, 4th ser., 8 (1871): 1–3.

3. See W. W. Greg, ed., *The Book of Sir Thomas More*, MSR (Oxford: Malone Society, 1911), v–xix. This edition was reprinted in 1961, with a supplement to Greg's introduction by Harold Jenkins.

4. See Edward M. Thompson, *Shakespeare's Handwriting: A Study* (Oxford: Oxford University Press, 1916); Giles Dawson, "Shakespeare's Handwriting," *Shakespeare Survey* 42 (1990): 119–28; Beal, *Index of English Literary Manuscripts*, vol. 1, 449.

5. See J. Dover Wilson, "Bibliographical Links between the Three Pages and the Good Quartos," in ed. A. W. Pollard, *Shakespeare's Hand in the Play of Sir Thomas More* (Cambridge: Cambridge University Press, 1923), 113–141. These Quartos were either prepared by Shakespeare himself—*Venus and Adonis* (1593) and *The Rape of Lucrece* (1594)—or released for publication by his theater company: *Richard II* (1597), *Love's Labor's Lost* (1598), *1 Henry IV* (1598), *Romeo and Juliet* (1599), *2 Henry IV* (1600), *A Midsummer Night's Dream* (1600), *Merchant of Venice* (1600), *Othello* (1622), *Hamlet* (1604–1605), *King Lear* (1608), and *Troilus and Cressida* (1609). The one exception to these two classes of Quarto analyzed by Wilson is Shakespeare's *Sonnets* (1609), published by Thomas Thorpe. While the circumstances surrounding its publication are obscure, there is no doubt that the volume was set directly from manuscripts that reproduced Shakespeare's spelling.

6. See J. Dover Wilson, *The Manuscript of Shakespeare's* Hamlet *and the Problems of its Transmission*, 2 vols. (Cambridge: Cambridge University Press, 1934), vol. 1, 88–117, at 103–104.

7. Wilson, "Bibliographic Links," 117–118.

8. Ibid., 132–141; see also Wilson, *The Manuscript of Shakespeare's* Hamlet, vol. 1, 106–117. My quotations from the *Moore* manuscript, together with line references, come from the admirable edition by Thomas Clayton, *The "Shakespearean" Addition in the Booke of Sir Thomas Moore: Some Aids to Scholarly and Critical Shakespearean Studies* (Dubuque, IA: Brown, 1969). All Shakespeare references are to the *Riverside* edition.

9. Wilson, "Bibliographic Links," 126–131.

10. Ibid., 135.

11. The Folio *Lear* still spelled a few words in the old form: "basenes" (1.2.10; TLN 344), "roughnes" (2.2.97; TLN 1172), "busines" (1.2.70, 4.4.18: TLN 404, 2404) and "madnes" (3.4.94; TLN 1874), but some of these choices may have been influenced by the compositor's need to justify a line.

12. Doran, *The Text of* King Lear, 132. In place of her act, scene, and line numbers I have substituted references to Q by signature and line. Her concluding example, "And" for "One," occurs in the uncorrected Quarto (K4v1); however, the catchword preceding in the corrected Quarto remains "And" (K4r).

13. Ibid. Doran was evidently quoting from a copy of Q containing uncorrected sheets, shown by her citations "night more" and "deptoued," where the corrected text reads "night mare" and "deprived."

14. Ibid., 115–116, 124.

15. Ibid., 131.

16. Ibid.

17. See Dawson, "Shakespeare's Handwriting," 122.

18. Ibid., 125–127.

19. See Partridge, *Orthography in Shakespeare and Elizabethan Drama* (London: Arnold, 1964), 58–63, and *A Substantive Grammar of Shakespeare's Nondramatic Texts* (Charlottesville, VA: Bibliographical Society of the University of Virginia, 1976), 32–36, 59–63, 132–141.

20. See Halio (ed.), *The First Quarto of King Lear* (Cambridge: Cambridge University Press, 1994), 4.

21. Ibid., 10–12. For a recent discussion of common misreadings of secretary hand, with examples from *King Lear*, see Mark Bland, *A Guide to Early Printed Books and Manuscripts* (Oxford: Wiley-Blackwell, 2010), 89, 160–162.

22. Greg, *Variants in the First Quarto of 'King Lear,'* 133, 138, 146, 184, 187.

23. See Simon Palfrey and Tiffany Stern, *Shakespeare in Parts* (Oxford: Oxford University Press, 2007).

24. As W. K. C. Guthrie wrote in his book on Orphism, "I used to know more about Orpheus than I do today."

25. See Paul Werstine, *Early Modern Playhouse Manuscripts and the Editing of Shakespeare* (Cambridge: Cambridge University Press, 2013).The bibliography lists his own earlier studies (421) and those of Long (413).

26. See ibid., 1–11, and index, 425.

27. See ibid., 12–59 ("The Discovery of 'Foul Papers'") and 60–106 ("Redefining 'Foul Papers'").

28. Ibid., 98.

29. See Honigmann, *The Stability of Shakespeare's Text* (London: Arnold, 1965). 16–17 ("Note A: Foul Papers," and *The Texts of 'Othello' and Shakespearian Revision*, 150–151 (Appendix A: "Shakespeare's 'Foul Papers'").

30. Werstine, *Early Modern Playhouse Manuscripts*, 4.

31. See ibid., 107–148 ("Playhouse MSS: What Bookkeepers Did Not Do") and 148–199 ("Playhouse MSS: What Bookkeepers Did").

32. Ibid., 194.

33. Ibid., 358–391.

34. Ibid., 226–227.

35. Ibid., 228–229, citing A. W. Pollard, *Shakespeare's Fight with the Pirates and the Problem of the Transmission of His Text* (London: Moring, 1917). I quote from the second edition, revised and with an introduction (Cambridge: Cambridge University Press, 1920, 1967).

36. Ibid., 56–57.

37. Ibid., 71.

38. Madeleine Doran made a similar point, challenging the notion that "the printer of the folio" worked from a copy of Q1 collated with the theater manuscript: "First of all, the differences between the two texts are such that alteration of the one in accordance with the other would be a laborious and seemingly unnecessary task. We have seen how extensive in Q1 are both the errors and the good readings which differ from the folio, and how few of the latter, relatively, can be attributed to the printer of the folio. An editor who undertook to correct a copy of Q1 from the playhouse manuscript would have had to write in all the variant readings, both corrections of errors and good variants; he would have had to delete all the excrescent words which impaired the meter and which were not in his text; he would have had to supply lost parts, ranging from a single word to eighteen lines; he would have had to mark out all the lines which had been omitted from his text; and he would have had to indicate the line divisions of the great amount of verse that is either wrongly aligned or printed as prose. These alterations would have required a great deal of patching and interlining, and for the latter there is little room in the printed quarto. It is a question whether such copy would not have been very difficult for the printer to follow, and whether, if he had been using it, he would not have made more errors than he did": *The Text of* King Lear, 89–90.

39. "I am confident that I could correct any page of the Quarto so as to serve as copy for the Folio without making it in the least illegible or even difficult for the printer": Greg, "The Function of Bibliography," 294. He was undoubtedly taking issue with Doran: see note 38.

40. Craig, "The Composition of *King Lear*," *Renaissance Papers 1961* (1962): 57–61 (61).

41. Nosworthy, *Shakespeare's Occasional Plays: Their Origin and Transmission* (London: Arnold), 135.

42. Greg referred to Doran's work unfavorably in "The Function of Bibliography in Literary Criticism Illustrated in a Study of the Text of *King Lear*," *Neophilologus*, 18 (1933): 241–262; repr. in J. C. Maxwell (ed.), *W. W. Greg Collected Papers* (Oxford: Oxford University Press, 1966), 266–297. He repeated his criticisms in *The Editorial Problem in Shakespeare: A Survey of the Foundations of the Text* (Oxford: Oxford University Press, 1939; 3rd ed., 1954) and in *The Shakespeare First Folio: Its Bibliographical and Textual History* (Oxford: Oxford University Press, 1955). The Library of Trinity College, Cambridge, contains Greg's

copy of Doran's book, pungently annotated. I am grateful to the librarian, Professor David McKitterick, FBA, for alerting me to this copy and allowing me to inspect it.

43. Doran, *The Text of* King Lear, 21.

44. Ibid., 39–40.

45. As Doran showed, "in Samuel Harsnet, *A Declaration of Egregious Popish Impostures* (London, 1603), from which Shakespeare took the names of the fiends that are feigned to possess Edgar," one is called "Smolkin."

46. Ibid., 40.

47. Ibid., 41–42.

48. Ibid., 41.

49. Ibid., 42.

50. *OED*, "sophistication," 2a.

51. Doran, *The Text of* King Lear, 42.

52. Ibid., 91.

53. Ibid.

54. Ibid., 92.

55. Qb substituted "miscreant" for "ausrent."

56. Greg, "Principles of Emendation," 39.

57. Doran, *The Text of* King Lear, 93.

58. Ibid., 93–95.

59. Stone, *The Textual History of "King Lear"* (London: Scolar, 1980), 55, 101.

60. Ibid., 100–101, citing Doran, *The Text of* King Lear, 91–95.

61. Duthie, *Elizabethan Shorthand and the First Quarto of "King Lear"* (Oxford: Blackwell, 1949), 50–72.

62. Ibid., 52.

63. See Stanley Wells and Gary Taylor, *William Shakespeare: A Textual Companion* (Oxford: Clarendon Press, 1987), 529.

64. Kermode, "Disintegration Once More," *Proceedings of the British Academy*, (1994): 93–111 (99–102). Kermode's edition of *The Tempest* for the Arden series (London: Methuen, 1954; corr. ed. 1962) remains essential reading. Other notable studies include *Shakespeare's Language* (London: Allen Lane, 2000).

65. See Howard-Hill, "The Problem of Manuscript Copy for Folio *King Lear*," *The Library*, ser. 6, 4 (1982): 1–24 (13).

66. Ibid., 17.

67. Knowles, "The Evolution of the Texts of *Lear*," in ed. Jeffrey Kahan, *King Lear: New Critical Essays* (London: Routledge, 2008), 124–154 (144, 152 n. 15).

68. René Weis, ed., *King Lear: A Parallel Text Edition* (Harlow: Longman, 1993). In the second edition (Harlow, 2010), the publisher confused matters by failing to distinguish the original "Introduction" (1–35) from the important additional text, "The Integral *King Lear:* Its War and Variants of Convergence" (36–72). The relevant discussion here is "Q / F variants and palaeographic clues to an integral *Lear* text" (46–61).

69. Weis, *King Lear: Parallel Text*, 46.

70. Ibid., 46.

71. For illustrations of Shakespeare's various letter forms see E. Maunde Thompson, "The Handwriting of the Three Pages," in Pollard, ed., *Shakespeare's Hand in the Play of Sir Thomas More*, 57–112, plates V–VI, and R. B. McKerrow, *An Introduction to Bibliography*, 341–350 (Appendix 8, "A Note on Elizabethan Handwriting").

72. Weis, *King Lear: Parallel Text*, 50.

73. Ibid., 47.

74. Halio prints "warbling" in his 1994 edition of the Quarto (2.1.37), as does Stanley Wells in his "World's Classics" edition (Oxford: Oxford University Press, 2000), 147.

75. Weis, *King Lear: Parallel Text*, 50, 52.

76. Cf. Dawson, "Shakespeare's Handwriting," 125–127.

77. Weis, *King Lear: Parallel Text*, 53.

78. Ibid., 55–56.

79. Ibid., 60; author's emphasis.

80. Ibid., 68.

81. Ibid., 72.

6 *The Folio Editors Regularize Shakespeare*

1. Lesley Brown, ed., *The New Shorter Oxford English Dictionary on Historical Principles* (Oxford: Oxford University Press, 1993).

2. Chambers, *William Shakespeare: A Study of Facts and Problems*, 2 vols. (Oxford: Oxford University Press, 1930), vol. I, 164.

3. Ibid., 186, 188–189.

4. Ibid., 199.

5. Ibid., 465. An "indifferent" textual variant is one where, of two alternative readings, neither is clearly superior.

6. W. W. Greg, *The First Folio*, 244, 246, 281, 323, 373.

7. Ibid., 223.

8. Ibid., 77–78.

9. Ibid., 78.

10. See ibid., 256, 259, 269, 272, 326, 349, 365, 370.

11. Werstine, "Folio Editors, Folio Compositors, and the Folio Text of *King Lear*," in Gary Taylor and Michael Warren, eds., *The Division of the Kingdoms: Shakespeare's Two Versions of* King Lear (Oxford: Oxford University Press, 1983), 247–312 (252).

12. Greg, *The First Folio*, is still the most reliable guide to this topic.

13. Doran, *The Text of* King Lear, 44.

14. See Brian Vickers, "'Words' and 'Things'—or 'Words, Concepts, and Things'? Rhetorical and Linguistic Categories in the Renaissance," in eds. Eckhard Kessler and Ian Maclean, *Res et Verba in der Renaissance* (Wiesbaden: Harrassowitz, 2002), 287–335.

15. Doran, *The Text of* King Lear, 44.

16. See, e.g. Estelle W. Taylor, "Shakespeare's Use of *s* Endings of Verbs *to do* and *to have* in the First Folio," *CLA Journal* 16 (1972): 214–231, repr. in

V. Salmon and E. Burness, eds., *Reader in the Language of Shakespearean Drama* (Amsterdam: Benjamins, 1987), 371–388.

17. Stanley Wells, Introduction to *William Shakespeare: The Complete Works*, eds. Stanley Wells and Gary Taylor (Oxford: Oxford University Press, 1986), xxxv.

18. Howard-Hill, "Shakespeare's Earliest Editor, Ralph Crane," *Shakespeare Survey*, 44 (1992): 113–129.

19. Doran, *The Text of* King Lear, 50, citing E. A. Abbott, A *Shakespearian Grammar*, rev. ed. (London: Macmillan, 1870), paragraphs 459–473.

20. Ibid., 51, citing Folio, sig. ss 2r; p. 307 of the Tragedies.

21. Ibid., 45.

22. Ibid., 45.

23. Abbott, *A Shakespearian Grammar*, paragraphs 258–274 (pp. 175–187).

24. I take these examples from Jonathan Hope, *The Authorship of Shakespeare's Plays: A Socio-Linguistic Study* (Cambridge: Cambridge University Press, 1994), 27–28.

25. See, e.g., Brian Vickers, *'Counterfeiting' Shakespeare: Evidence, Authorship, and John Ford's* Funerall Elegye (Cambridge: Cambridge University Press, 2002), 121–138, for discussion of relevant studies in language change in the early seventeenth century by Charles Barber, A. C. Partridge, Mats Rydén, Olga Fischer, Matti Rissanen, Janet Bateley, Alfred Krüger, and Hans Peters.

26. Doran, *The Text of* King Lear, 47.

27. Hamlet asks the Ghost "why the Sepulcher | Hath op'd his ponderous and Marble jawes" (*Hamlet*, 1.4.50); the Duke reflects how "practice" or deception may "draw with ydle spiders strings | Most ponderous and substantiall things" (*Measure for Measure*, 3.2.276); Camillo asks Florizel whether "your most ponderous and setled project | May suffer alteration" (*The Winter's Tale*, 4.4.524). In all three cases "ponderous" is linked with another polysyllabic word ("and Marble," "and substantiall," "and settled"), appropriately so, given the decorum of speaker and subject matter. Cordelia's situation is hardly comparable.

28. Stone, *Textual History of "King Lear,"* 114.

29. Ibid., 127.

30. Ibid., 116.

31. Stone noted, "In the first scene of the play the reviser evidently thought it unreasonable that Lear, in banishing Kent, should allow him four days for preparation, and five for travel: in F the proportions are reversed (1.1.176 and 178). A similar fastidiousness causes the change from *British* to *English* at 4.6.256—Lear was not King of Scotland. Here and there the reviser was offended by rhetorical exaggerations, rephrasing them in more temperate terms (e.g. *houres* at 2.2.65 becomes *yeares; a 100* at 2.4.72 becomes *twenty*)": ibid. 116 n.

32. Ibid., 114.

33. I am grateful to Professor Knowles and to his publishers, the Modern Language Association of America, for permission to quote from the introduction to his New Variorum edition of *King Lear.*

34. See Hinman, *Printing and Proof-Reading*, index, vol. 2, 536.

35. See Werstine, "Folio Editors," in Taylor and Warren, *Division of the Kingdom*, 276.

36. Knowles, New Variorum.

37. Werstine, "Folio Editors," 279.

38. Knowles, New Variorum.

39. Ibid.; see also Honigmann citing Frederick O. Waller, "The Use of Linguistic Criteria in Determining the Copy and Dates for Shakespeare's Plays," in eds. Waldo F. McNeir and Thelma N. Greenfield, *Pacific Coast Studies in Shakespeare* (Eugene: University of Oregon Press, 1966), 1–19.

40. Cf. Waller, ibid., and Honigmann, *The Texts of "Othello" and Shakespearian Revision* 136–140.

41. See Richard Knowles, "The Evolution of the Texts of *Lear*," in ed. Jeffrey Kahan, *King Lear: New Critical Essays* (New York and London: 2009), 124–154 (141–144).

42. Werstine, *Playhouse Manuscripts*, 136.

43. Perrett, *The Story of King Lear*, 152.

44. Greg, *The Shakespeare First Folio*, 375. His parallel listing of the stage directions in Quarto and Folio *Lear* (375–377) is the most complete currently available.

7 *The King's Men Abridge a Tragedy*

1. See *The History of King Leir 1605*, ed. W. W. Greg (Oxford, 1907, 1956), v. For the ascription of this play to Kyd see Brian Vickers, "Thomas Kyd, Secret Sharer," *Times Literary Supplement*, April 18, 2008, 13–15.

2. See Wilfrid Perrett, *The Story of King Lear from Geoffrey of Monmouth to Shakespeare* (Berlin: Mayer & Müller, 1904), 143–289, and Geoffrey Bullough (ed.), *Narrative and Dramatic Sources of Shakespeare*, Vol. VII (London: Routledge and Kegan Paul, 1973), 267–420.

3. Bullough, *Narrative and Dramatic Sources*, 284.

4. See, e.g., Vladimir Propp, *Morphology of the Folk-Tale* [1928], tr. L. Scott (1958), 2nd ed. rev. L. A. Wagner, introduction by Alan Dundes (Austin: University of Texas Press, 1968), 71–73.

5. Other scholars give different figures. E. K. Chambers estimated that "[a]part from stray words and phrases, Q omits about 100 lines found in F, and F omits about 300 lines . . . found in Q" (*William Shakespeare*, vol. 1, 466). W. W. Greg repeated Chambers's computation in *The Shakespeare First Folio* (Oxford, 1955), 375, as did G. I. Duthie in the New Cambridge edition (Cambridge: Cambridge University Press, 1960), 24, and R. A. Foakes in the third Arden edition (1997), 113. Alfred Harbage estimated that the Quarto prints "about 283 lines" not found in the Folio: *The Pelican Shakespeare* (Baltimore: Penguin, 1969), 1104, while Gwynne B. Evans estimated that the Folio text "contains about 133 lines and part-lines" found in neither Quarto, while omitting "roughly 288 lines and part-lines" unique to Q1 and Q2: *The Riverside Shakespeare*, 2nd ed. (Boston: Houghton Mifflin, 1997), 1344.

6. Delius, "On the Quarto and Folio of *King Lear*," *Transactions of the New Shakspere Society, 1875–6*, 123–147; translated from "Über den ursprünglichen

Text des *King Lear*," *Shakespeare Jahrbuch* 10 (1875): 50–74, reprinted in Delius, *Abhandlungen zu Shakspere* (Elberfeld, 1878), 359–387.

7. Ibid., 133, 138.

8. Chambers, *William Shakespeare*, vol. 1, 467.

9. See, e.g., W. W. Greg, *The First Folio*, 375 ("it has been cut for representation").

10. Delius,"On the Quarto and Folio of *King Lear*," 125.

11. Rasmussen, "The Revision of Scripts," in eds. John D. Cox and David Scott Kastan, *A New History of Early English Drama* (New York: Columbia, 1997), 441–460 (444–445).

12. For cuts at the end of speeches see 1.2.144–152, 3.1.7–15, 3.1.30–42, 4.1.58–63, 4.2.31–50, 53–59, 62–68, and 5.1.23–28. For cuts at the end of scenes see 3.6.97–153, 3.7.99–105, and 4.7.84–96. The *Riverside Shakespeare* marks passages not included in the Folio with square brackets. In his 1997 Arden edition R. A. Foakes marks words and passages found only in the Quarto with a superscript ^{Q} and those only in Folio with a superscript ^{F}.

13. Rasmussen, "Revision of Scripts," 445–446.

14. Werstine, *Early Modern Playhouse Manuscripts and the Editing of Shakespeare* (Cambridge: Cambridge University Press, 2013), 163.

15. Ibid. 163–172.

16. Folio; Quarto reads "any."

17. Folio; Quarto reads "Arte."

18. Delius,"On the Quarto and Folio of *King Lear*," 142.

19. Knowles, "Revision Awry in Folio *Lear* 3.1," *Shakespeare Quarterly*, 16 (1955): 32–46 (34–36).

20. Weis, *King Lear: A Parallel Text Edition*, 38–39.

21. Delius,"On the Quarto and Folio of *King Lear*," 144. See also Weis, *King Lear: A Parallel Text Edition*, 38–39.

22. See Brian Vickers, "Lear's Fool and the Meaning of 'Snatching,' " *Notes and Queries* 258 (2013): 426–429. I should have noted that "snatch" was a colloquial term for rape: cf. *Titus Andronicus*, 2.1.95–96.

23. Quarto; Folio reads "high."

24. Delius,"On the Quarto and Folio of *King Lear*," 142.

25. Rasmussen, "Revision of Scripts," 446.

26. Philip Gossett, *Divas and Scholars: Performing Italian Opera* (Chicago: University of Chicago Press, 2006), 245.

27. Ibid., 245–246.

28. Delius,"On the Quarto and Folio of *King Lear*," 140.

29. See, for instance, R. B. Heilman's classic study, *This Great Stage. Inage and Structure in* King Lear (Baton Rouge LA: Louisiana State University Press, 1948).

30. Quarto; Folio reads "sticke."

31. Weis, *King Lear: A Parallel Text Edition*, 21.

32. See Brian Vickers, "*King Lear* and Renaissance Paradoxes," *Modern Language Review*, 63 (1968): 305–314.

33. See H. H. Furness (ed.) *King Lear*, New Variorum Edition (1880), 188. Delius seems to have been the first editor to propose this, and Edwin Booth adopted this practice.

34. I have introduced four accepted emendations: "trial" for "tral" (24), "robed" for "robbed" (36), "ioynt" for "ioyne" (52)—from Q2, and "on" for "an" (54).

35. Retrospectively Kent's concern for Lear's health is medically justified by the reactions of the doctor whom Cordelia has engaged to tend Lear. In answer to her wish to discover "What can mans wisedome | In the restoring his bereaved Sense," he knows a remedy: "Our foster Nurse of Nature, is repose, | The which he lackes" (4.4.8–13).

36. "It is a comfort to the wretched to have had companions in misery." Marlowe quotes it in *Dr. Faustus*, 2.1.40. The ultimate source seems to be Seneca's *De consolatione ad Polybium*, xii.2, but no author is known for the hexameter: see D. Bevington and E. Rasmussen, eds. *Marlowe, Dr Faustus* (Manchester: Manchester University Press, 1993), 140.

37. Delius,"On the Quarto and Folio of *King Lear*," 143.

38. Essay 23, "Of Wisdom for a Man's Self," in Brian Vickers, ed., *Francis Bacon* (Oxford: Oxford University Press, 1996), 386–387.

39. Quarto reads "ith."

40. Quarto reads "thes."

41. E. A. Abbott, *A Shakespearian Grammar* (London: Macmillan, 1886), para. 438, observed that Shakespeare used "[t]he prefix *be* . . . not merely with verbs of colouring, 'smear', 'splash', &c., to localize and sometimes to intensify action, but also with nouns and adjectives to convert the nouns into verbs." In addition to "Bemonster" he noted two further instances in *Lear:* "Bemadding" (3.1.38) and "Beweep" (1.4.324).

42. I have introduced three accepted emendations: "sir" for the Quarto's "say" (11); "stroke" for "streme" (16); and "seemd" for "seeme" (20).

43. See Brian Vickers, *The Artistry of Shakespeare's Prose* (London: Methuen, 1968; Routledge, 2005), 422–425.

44. Compare the description of Cordelia that Shakespeare gives to France: "A tardinesse in nature, | Which often leaves the history unspoke | That it intends to do" (1.1.234–236).

45. Peter de la Primaudaye, *The French Academie, wherein is discoursed the institution of manners, and whatsoever els concerneth the good and happie life of all estates and callings, by precepts of doctrine, and examples of the lives of ancient Sages and famous men*, tr. T. Bowes (London, 1577), 257.

46. Ibid., 257–258.

47. Delius noted that this passage "is cut out by the actors, but they have naïvely retained Regan's reply—'Why is this reason'd?'—which refers solely to Albany's word," adding, "In any case it is not Shakespeare's nature to destroy a feature so essential to the comprehension of Albany's character, and to the development of the plot." Delius,"On the Quarto and Folio of *King Lear*," 144.

48. Quarto reads "me."

49. See Donald A. Russell, ed., Quintilian, *The Orator's Education*, 5 vols. (Cambridge, MA: Harvard University Press, 2001), vol. 1, 19.

8 *The "Two Versions" Revisited*

1. Michael Warren, "Quarto and Folio *King Lear* and the Interpretation of Albany and Edgar," in eds. David Bevington and Jay L. Halio, *Shakespeare: Pattern of Excelling Nature* (Newark: University of Delaware Press, 1978): 95–107. Warren subsequently edited *The Complete King Lear 1608–1623*, (Berkeley: University of California Press, 1989), conveniently presenting parallel texts of Q1, Q2, and F in photographic facsimile.

2. Urkowitz, *Shakespeare's Revision of* King Lear (Princeton, NJ: Princeton University Press, 1980).

3. See Gary Taylor and Michael Warren, eds., *The Division of the Kingdoms: Shakespeare's Two Versions of* King Lear (Oxford: Oxford University Press, 1983; rev. with "Addenda," 1986). It contains essays by Stanley Wells, Steven Urkowitz, Roger Warren, Gary Taylor (two, amounting to 163 pages), Thomas Clayton, Beth Goldring, Randall McLeod, John Kerrigan, Paul Werstine, and Mac D. P. Jackson.

4. William C. Carroll, "New Plays vs. Old Readings: *The Division of the Kingdoms* and Folio Deletions in *King Lear*," *Studies in Philology*, 85 (1988): 225–244.

5. Robert Clare, "'Who is it that can tell me who I am?': The Theory of Authorial Revision between the Quarto and Folio Texts of *King Lear*," *The Library*, 6th ser., 17 (1995): 4–59. This essay was reprinted as "Quarto and Folio: A Case for Conflation," in James Ogden and Arthur H. Scouten, eds., Lear *from Study to Stage: Essays in Criticism* (Cranbury, NJ: Associated University Presses, 1997), 79–108.

6. Philip Edwards, review of Urkowitz, *Shakespeare's Revision*, and P. W. K. Stone, "The Textual History of KING LEAR," *Modern Language Review*, 77 (1982): 694–698.

7. William R. Elton, "*King Lear* Studies 1967–1987," in Elton, "*King Lear*" *and the Gods*, rev. ed. (Lexington: University Press of Kentucky, 1988), 339–345.

8. G. B. Evans, review of Blayney, *The Texts of* King Lear *and Their Origins*," *Modern Language Review*, 79 (1984): 901–904, and "Review of the Oxford Shakespeare *Complete Works* and *Textual Companion*," *Journal of English and Germanic Philology*, 88 (1989): 401–407.

9. Andrew Gurr, "The Once and Future *King Lears*," *Bulletin of the Society for Renaissance Studies*, 2 (1984): 7–19.

10. E. A. J. Honigmann, "Shakespeare's Revised Plays: *King Lear* and *Othello*," *The Library*, 4 (1982): 142–173; "The New *Lear*," review of *The Division of the Kingdoms*, *New York Review of Books*, February 2, 1984: 16–17; "Do-It-Yourself *Lear*," review of Michael Warren, ed., *The Complete King Lear, 1608–1623*, *New York Review of Books*, October 25, 1990: 58–60.

11. Frank Kermode, "Disintegration Once More," *Proceedings of the British Academy*, 84 (1996): 93–111.

12. Richard Knowles, review of Urkowitz, *Revision*, *Modern Philology*, 79 (1981): 197–200; review of *The Division of the Kingdoms*, *Shakespeare Quarterly*, 36 (1985): 115–125; "Revision Awry in Folio *Lear* 3.1," *Shakespeare Quarterly*, 46

(1995): 31–46; "Two *Lears?* By Shakespeare?" in Ogden and Scouten, Lear *from Study to Stage*, 57–78; "Merging the Kingdoms: *King Lear*," in eds. W. R. Elton and John M. Mucciolo, *The Shakespearean International Yearbook, 1* (Aldershot: Ashgate, 1999), 266–286; "Cordelia's Return," *Shakespeare Quarterly*, 50 (1999): 33–50; "The Evolution of the Texts of *Lear*," in ed. Jeffrey Kahan, *King Lear: New Critical Essays* (London: Routledge, 2008), 124–154.

13. Ann Meyer, "Shakespeare's Art and the Texts of *King Lear*," *Studies in Bibliography*, 47 (1994): 128–146.

14. Kenneth Muir, "The Texts of *King Lear:* An Interim Assessment of the Controversy," in Muir, *Shakespeare: Contrasts and Controversies* (Brighton: Harvester, 1985), 51–66. This text, originally given as a Folger lecture in November 1982, was first published in *The Aligarh Journal of English Studies*, 8 (1983): 99–113.

15. Sidney Thomas, "Shakespeare's Supposed Revision of *King Lear*," *Shakespeare Quarterly*, 35 (1984): 506–511.

16. Marion Trousdale, "A Trip through the Divided Kingdoms," *Shakespeare Quarterly*, 37 (1986): 218–223.

17. Brian Vickers, review of *Pattern of Excelling Nature*, *Shakespeare Quarterly*, 32 (1981): 402–407 (406 on Warren, "Interpretation of Albany and Edgar"); review of the Oxford Shakespeare *Complete Works* and *Textual Companion*, *Review of English Studies*, 40 (1989): 402–411; review of the Oxford Shakespeare *Complete Works*, 2nd ed., *Times Literary Supplement*, August 11, 2006, 10–12.

18. Paul Werstine, "Folio Editors, Folio Compositors, and the Folio Text of *King Lear*," in Taylor and Warren, *Division of the Kingdoms*, 247–312; review of Urkowitz, *Shakespeare Quarterly*, 36 (1985): 368–370.

19. Warren, "Interpretation of Albany and Edgar," 97.

20. Urkowitz, *Shakespeare's Revision*, 3.

21. Taylor and Warren, *Division of the Kingdoms*, v.

22. Wells, "Introduction: The Once and Future *King Lear*," in Taylor and Warren, *Division of the Kingdoms*, 1–22 (10–11). At this stage Wells's argument was hedged around with cautious counterfactuals: 'If . . . would have . . . would be . . . might be . . . should . . . would . . . should be'. Caution was soon abandoned.

23. Ibid. 15. Wells suggested this explanation, but only to ridicule it.

24. Jackson, "Fluctuating Variation: Author, Annotator, or Actor," in Taylor and Warren, *Division of the Kingdoms*, 313–45 (324).

25. Knowles, "Revision Awry" 32; see also Knowles, "Two *Lears?*" 63–64. Despite the admiration and gratitude I feel for Professor Knowles's scholarship, I must record my disagreement with the two passages where he suggests that the Folio contains "additions of a line or more to existing Q speeches, generally designed to expand or clarify motive or meaning" and "local additions of lines." My interpretation of the evidence is that these passages do not represent additions to the Folio but omissions from the Quarto.

26. Webster, dedication to *The White Devil* (London, 1612).

27. Knowles, review of Urkowitz, 197.

28. See, e.g., W. W. Greg, *The Shakespeare First Folio* (Oxford: Oxford University Press, 1955), 78–79.

29. Wells, "Introduction," in Taylor and Warren, *Division of the Kingdoms*, 18.

30. Ibid., 9.

31. Taylor, "The Date and Authorship of the Folio Version," in Taylor and Warren, *Division of the Kingdoms*, 351–451 (405).

32. Ibid., 415–422.

33. Knowles, "Two *Lears?*" 58–59.

34. Warren, "Interpretation of Albany and Edgar," 10.

35. Ibid.

36. Urkowitz, *Shakespeare's Revision*, 28–29.

37. Taylor, "The War in *King Lear*," *Shakespeare Survey* 33 (1980): 27–34 (28). But see Trousdale, "Divided Kingdoms," 220–221; Knowles, "Merging the Kingdoms," 270–277; and Honigmann, "Do-it-Yourself *Lear*," 59.

38. For an account of this genre see Brian Vickers, *In Defence of Rhetoric* (Oxford: Oxford University Press, 1988), 21–23, 52–62.

39. Taylor, "The War in *King Lear*," 28–29.

40. Ibid., 29–30.

41. Ibid., 30.

42. Urkowitz, *Shakespeare's Revision*, 51.

43. Ibid., 27.

44. Carroll, "New Plays vs. Old Readings," 231 (author's emphasis).

45. Kermode, introduction to *King Lear*, *The Riverside Shakespeare*, 1300 (author's emphasis).

46. Muir, "Interim Assessment," 56.

47. Ibid., 57. Kenneth Muir had directed a production of *King Lear* in the 1930s, "in collaboration with a professional actress," and took part "in the Leeds production in 1951 when Wilson Knight played Lear and I was Gloucester."

48. Urkowitz, *Shakespeare's Revision*, 3.

49. Ibid., 54.

50. Ibid., 55.

51. Having read English at Oxford, Clare trained to be an actor and was a member of the Royal Shakespeare Company for three years. Subsequently he worked as a staff director at the National Theatre on four productions, including David Hare's *Lear* (1986), before taking up a freelance career as an actor and director. His essay, which was published in *The Library* (1995) and awarded the Fredson Bowers prize for the best essay in bibliography, was written "from the perspective of the theatre practitioner."

52. Clare, "Authorial Revision" 40, citing Urkowitz, *Shakespeare's Revision*, 53.

53. Urkowitz, *Shakespeare's Revision*, 35.

54. Clare, "Authorial Revision," 41.

55. Ibid., 42.

56. Muir, "Interim Assessment," 61.

57. Ibid.

58. Urkowitz, *Shakespeare's Revision*, 17.

59. Ibid., 49–50.

60. Meyer, "Shakespeare's Art," 138.

61. Ibid., 139.

62. Taylor, "Monopolies, Show Trials, Disaster, and Invasion. *King Lear* and Censorship," in Taylor and Warren, *Division of the Kingdoms*, 75–119 (97).

63. Carroll, "New Plays vs. Old Readings," 232, 242–243.

64. Taylor and Warren, *Division of the Kingdoms*, 99.

65. Ibid., 93.

66. Ibid., 94.

67. Clare, "Authorial Revision," 49–50.

68. Ibid., 46–47

69. Ibid., 52.

70. Naturally enough, revisionists who saw Hytner's version could not see any improvement. Stanley Wells recorded his view on that production, "based on the edited Folio text but restoring a couple of passages from the Quarto, which to my mind convincingly demonstrates the superiority of the Folio version." See Wells, "Theatricalizing Shakespeare's Text," *New Theatre Quarterly*, 7 (1991): 184–6 (185). Note that Wells failed to mention that the "couple of passages" restored from the Quarto included the Folio deletions in the mad trial scene.

71. David Richman, "The *King Lear* Quarto In Rehearsal and Performance," *Shakespeare Quarterly*, 37 (1986): 374–82 (376–380).

72. Ibid., 381–382.

73. E. A. J. Honigmann, *The Texts of* Othello *and Shakespearian Revision* (London: Routledge, 1996), 10.

74. Carroll, "New Plays vs. Old Readings," 228.

75. Warren, "Interpretation of Albany and Edgar," 99, 104.

76. Ibid., 99.

77. Muir, "Interim Assessment," 55.

78. Edwards, review of Urkowitz and Stone, 697 (author's emphases).

79. Clare, "Authorial Revision," 47–48.

80. Knowles, "Two *Lears?*" 71–72 (author's emphasis).

81. Meyer, "Shakespeare's Art," 144 note. In Q the line "Hast thee for thy life" is assigned to "*Duke*" (L3v1), while in F it is given to *Edgar* (TLN 3210). In Q the "*Captain*" (L3v26; L4r8) is replaced once by "*Gentleman*" (TLN 3239) and secondly by "*Messenger*" (TLN 3276). There are eight occasions on which the Quarto changed "*Albany*" to "*Duke*" due to a shortage of the italic capital *A*, as Blayney observed (*The Texts of* King Lear *and Their Origins*, 141–142). Here the Folio continued to identify him by name not by rank (TLN 3192, 3199, 3205, 3215, 3226, 3262, 3267, and 3293).

82. Honigmann, "Do-it-Yourself *Lear*," 58. Honigmann cited textual evidence from the 'Booke' of *Sir Thomas More*, of which three pages are in Shakespeare's hand. Some of the speech prefixes in this scene "were added later. In the heat of composition, it seems, Shakespeare poured out the dialogue and did not bother to insert all the necessary speech prefixes and stage directions. . . .

Some of the 'revised' speech prefixes in *Lear*, then, might be explained as errors in Q1, owing to the fact that Shakespeare left blanks or abbreviated names" in the manuscript (59).

83. Warren, "Interpretation of Albany and Edgar," 101, 105.

84. Ibid., 102. But see Vickers, review of Warren, 406.

85. See Brian Vickers, "Shakespearian Consolations," *Proceedings of the British Academy*, 82 (1993): 219–284 (277–284).

86. Warren, "Interpretation of Albany and Edgar," 104.

87. Muir, "Interim Assessment," 53–54.

88. Carroll, "New Plays vs. Old Readings," 241 (author's emphasis).

89. Ibid. 242.

90. Taylor and Warren, *Division of the Kingdoms*, v.

91. Gurr, "The Once and Future *King Lears*," 13, citing G. Taylor, ed., *Henry V* (Oxford: Oxford University Press, 1982), 25.

92. Fredson Bowers, *On Editing Shakespeare and the Elizabethan Dramatists* (Philadelphia: University of Pennsylvania Library, 1955; Charlottesville, VA, 1966), 35.

93. Gurr, "Once and Future *King Lears*," 14.

94. Ibid., 16–17.

95. See Meyer, "Shakespeare's Art," 37; Clare, "Authorial Revision," 37.

96. The earlier studies by Doran, *Text of* King Lear, chapter II: "The Relation of Q2 to Q1" (19–38), and Knowles, "The Printing of the Second Quarto (1619) of *King Lear*," *Studies in Bibliography* 35 (1982): 191–206, were superseded by Knowles, "The Evolution of the Texts of *Lear*," in ed. Jeffrey Kahan, *King Lear: New Critical Essays* (London: Routledge, 2008), 124–154 (144, 152 n. 15). As noted in Chapter 5 (196), Knowles disproved the revisionists' claim "that a marked-up Q2, instead of or in addition to Q1, was printer's copy for F1."

97. Stone, *Textual History*, 97–99. Ernst Honigmann objected that "the assumption that prompt-books were lost in the 1613 fire must not go unquestioned. The F texts of so many plays are thought to be based on prompt-books that the 'disappearance' of the *Lear* prompt-book can hardly be seen as part of a general disaster": "Shakespeare's Revised Plays," 148 note.

98. Taylor, "Date and Authorship," in Taylor and Warren, *Division of the Kingdoms*, 365 (author's emphasis).

99. Ibid., 365–366.

100. For Taylor's "proposed stemma" involving several hypothetical stages of transmission, see Taylor and Warren, *Division of the Kingdoms*, 366.

101. Knowles, review of *Division of the Kingdoms*, 117–118.

102. Ibid., 118 (author's emphasis).

103. Ibid.

104. Jackson, "Fluctuating Variation," 315.

105. Ibid., 329.

106. Ibid., 328.

107. I owe this point to a conversation some years ago with Hugh Kenner.

108. Jackson, "Fluctuating Variation," 331.

109. Wells, "Introduction," in Taylor and Warren, *Division of the Kingdoms*, 20.

Conclusion

1. Michael Warren praised Gary Taylor's "precise study of many variants" in Act 1 of *Lear* in an "as yet unpublished book" (Taylor and Warren, *Division of the Kingdoms,* 72, n. 3), a book that MacDonald Jackson also hailed for its "brilliant critical analysis of QF differences in Lear's conduct of the love test" (344, n. 47). Taylor praised "Michael Warren's admirable account" of the Folio treatment of Edgar and Albany (425), and so on.

2. Ernst Honigmann, present in the audience, recorded his doubt at the time "whether 'the two versions of *Lear*' is a theory that has itself become fashionable only because the discussion itself has been largely restricted to a single play. 'Stanley has really swallowed it,' I heard one delegate mutter as the applause died down; new though it seems, the 'two versions' theory has already had a bandwagon effect, and that will stiffen the resistance"; "The New *Lear,*" review of *Division of the Kingdoms, New York Review of Books,* February 2, 1984, 16–18 (16).

3. Ibid. 17, referring to Taylor's essay in *Shakespeare Survey,* 33 (1980): 27–34; my italics.

4. Warren, "Interpretation of Albany and Edgar," 103.

5. Taylor and Warren, *Division of the Kingdoms,* 53; my italics.

6. Ibid., 359; my italics.

7. Ibid., 408, 418; my italics.

8. Ibid., 230, 403.

9. Carroll commented on the tactic by which Roger Warren concluded his defense of the Folio omission of the mock trial scene "by an appeal to 'authority'—always a non-argument—to none other than Taylor, Urkowitz, and Michael Warren . . . The circular reasoning reaches beyond the interior argument, then: Roger Warren quotes Taylor, Urkowitz, and Michael Warren; Gary Taylor quotes Michael Warren (425), Roger Warren (449), himself (95), himself (423), and himself again (449) on the various failings associated with the mock trial . . . The entire volume becomes a self-referential artefact." Carroll, "New Plays vs. Old Readings," 234, citing Taylor and Warren, *Division of the Kingdoms,* 53.

10. Taylor, "*King Lear* and Censorship," in Taylor and Warren, *Division of the Kingdoms,* 80–81.

11. Taylor cited the review by George Walton Williams, *Shakespeare Survey,* 34 (1981), 194.

12. *Shakespeare Survey,* 37 (1984): 208–210.

13. Gary Taylor, "Revising Shakespeare," *Text* 3 (1986): 285–304 (295); author's emphasis.

14. Ibid., 298, 302.

15. Ibid., 302–303; author's emphasis.

16. Quoted by permission, with thanks to Richard Knowles for having preserved this text.

17. Taylor, "The Rhetoric of Textual Criticism," *Text* 4 (1988): 39–57 (52–53).

18. Ibid., 47.
19. Ibid., 53.
20. Ibid., 51.
21. Ibid., 54.
22. Taylor, "The Rhetorics of Reaction," in Randall McLeod, ed., *Crisis in Editing: Texts of the English Renaissance* (New York: AMS, 1994), 19–60 (20).
23. Ibid., 21.
24. The critics who were attacked formed a larger group, since they included some of those who had criticized the Oxford Shakespeare, published by Wells and Taylor in 1986. Among them were David Bevington, William Carroll, Peter Davison, Philip Edwards, Ernst Honigmann, G. K. Hunter, Frank Kermode, Richard Knowles, Kenneth Muir, Sidney Thomas, René Weis, and William Proctor Williams.
25. Taylor, "Rhetorics of Reaction," 42.
26. Ibid., 35.
27. Ibid., 22–27.
28. See Gabriel Egan, *The Struggle for Shakespeare's Text. Twentieth-Century Editorial Theory and Practice* (Cambridge: Cambridge University Press, 2010), 141. Egan's account of "The Splitting of *King Lear*" (133–146) is wholly approving, apparently unaware of the many substantial critiques reviewed in Chapter 8.
29. Knowles, "Merging the Kingdoms," 268–269.
30. Taylor, "Rhetoric of Textual Criticism," 46.
31. See Jan Palmowski, *A Dictionary of Contemporary World History. From 1900 to the Present Day*, 3rd ed. (Oxford: Oxford University Press, 2008), 590.
32. Taylor, "Rhetorics of Reaction," 48–49.
33. See Brian Vickers, *'Counterfeiting' Shakespeare: Evidence, Authorship, and John Ford's* Funerall Elegye (Cambridge: Cambridge University Press, 2002), 1–53: "Prologue: Gary Taylor Finds a Poem."
34. See the review by David Bevington cited in the Preface, note 2.
35. The first edition placed them together in the putative overall chronology between *Timon of Athens* and *Macbeth*. In the second edition (2005) the Quarto text ("*The History of King Lear*") remains in that sequence, but the Folio text ("*The Tragedy of King Lear*") is made to follow *The Winter's Tale* and precede *Cymbeline*. The unwary reader is now led to believe that in 1610 Shakespeare went back to *Lear*, cut out 300 lines from the Quarto, added another 100 lines, and thereby created a new play. There is no evidence for this supposition, and I regard Wells and Taylor as guilty of misusing editorial power.
36. Taylor, *Reinventing Shakespeare: A Cultural History from the Restoration to the Present* (London: Hogarth, 1990), 358.
37. Ibid., 359; my italics.
38. Among other things, Hunter wrote a groundbreaking study, *John Lyly: The Humanist as Courtier* (London: Routledge and Kegan Paul, 1964); contributed an excellent edition of *King Lear* to the New Penguin Shakespeare (1972); produced a memorable volume in the Oxford History of English Literature, *English Drama 1586–1642: The Age of Shakespeare* (Oxford: Oxford University

Press, 1997); and published a stimulating collection of essays, *Dramatic Identities and Cultural Tradition: Studies in Shakespeare and his Contemporaries* (Liverpool: Liverpool University Press, 1978). Many scholars working today would envy his range of learning, mature judgment, and lucid prose style.

39. Taylor, *Reinventing Shakespeare*, 368; my italics.

40. Taylor, "Rhetorics of Reaction," 46; my italics.

41. See Max Scheler, *Das Ressentiment im Aufbau der Moralen* (1915); trans. W. W. Holdheim as *Ressentiment*, ed. L. A. Coser (New York: Schocken, 1961), 45–46.

42. Ibid., 48; author's italics.

43. *Othello*, 2.1.296–297.

44. Scheler, *Ressentiment*, 62.

45. Taylor, "Rhetorics of Reaction," 46.

46. Scheler, *Ressentiment*, 63; author's emphasis.

47. Taylor, "Rhetorics of Reaction," 19.

48. Scheler, *Ressentiment*, 47.

49. Taylor, "Rhetorics of Reaction," 48.

50. See Kermode, "How Do You Spell Shakespeare?" *London Review of Books*, 10 (May 21, 1987), 3–5, a review of the Oxford Shakespeare in both the modernized and old-spelling editions, reprinted in Kermode, *The Uses of Error* (Cambridge, MA: Harvard University Press, 1991). In fact, Taylor's accusation misrepresents what Kermode wrote, who reported a prediction by Fredson Bowers that "there was still so much to be done in the way of studying printing-house practices, compositors' vagaries" and other research topics that "an old-spelling edition of Shakespeare was a matter for the 21st century." Kermode praised the Oxford editors for their industry but criticized them for dressing up modern editorial emendations in "fake antique" English. Thus Warburton's brilliant emendation of Antony's "hearts | That panelled me at heeles" to "spanieled" is turned into "'spannell'd,' 'spanel,' or 'spannel' being an old form of 'spaniel' presumed, no doubt, to have been familiar to the compositor, though not current in Shakespeare's time so far as the OED is aware." Several reviewers deplored the Oxford editors' practice of "silent alteration" of Shakespeare's text, and their invention of spellings that never were.

51. John 1:26.

52. *The Poems and Fables of John Dryden*, ed. James Kinsley (Oxford: Oxford University Press, 1962), 507.

53. Taylor, *Reinventing Shakespeare*, 358; my italics.

54. Werstine, "Folio Editors, Folio Compositors, and the Folio Text of *King Lear*," in Taylor and Warren, *Division of the Kingdoms*, 247–312.

55. Taylor, "Rhetorics of Reaction," 40.

56. Taylor and Warren, preface to *Division of the Kingdoms*, v.

57. Knowles, review of Urkowitz, 200.

58. Werstine, review of Urkowitz, 369.

59. Elton, "*King Lear* Studies," 343–344; author's emphases.

60. Knowles, review of Taylor and Warren, *Division of the Kingdoms*, 116.

61. See Susan Haack, "Epistemology Legalized: Or, Truth, Justice, and the American Way," in Haack, *Evidence and Inquiry: A Pragmatic Reconstruction of*

Epistemology, 2nd expanded ed. (Amherst, NY: Prometheus Books, 2009), 361–381 (364).

62. Ibid.

63. Ibid., 366.

64. One endorsement of the Two Versions thesis even claimed that the existence of "many *Lears* instead of one" called in question "the fundamental status of the textual object before us," and that, as a result, "Shakespeare studies will never be the same because something long taken for granted has been cast into doubt: the self-identity of the work": Margareta de Grazia and Peter Stallybrass, "The Materiality of the Shakespearean Text," *Shakespeare Quarterly* 44 (1993): 255–283 (255). In a skeptical reply Martin Mueller pointed out that "the differences between the texts of *Lear* are not that great, as is shown above all by the easy conflatability of the versions of *Lear* into a composite text." Editors of a composite edition must make many choices between readings in the 2900 lines common to both texts, "but they face no serious problems of redundance or contradiction in extended passages. If the versions of *King Lear* were as different as they are now claimed to be, the business of constructing a composite version should require more thorough-going editing than it now does." Mueller, "Redrawing the Boundaries? Skeptical Thoughts about Literary Studies," *Centennial Review*, 38 (1994): 603–622 (614–615).

Index